FROM THE KITCHEN

of

THE COUNTRY COOKING OF GREECE

THE COUNTRY COOKING
of
GREECE

by DIANE KOCHILAS

photographs by VASSILIS STENOS

CHRONICLE BOOKS

SAN FRANCISCO

Library of Congress Cataloging-in-Publication Data available.
ISBN 978-0-8118-6453-4

Manufactured in China

Designed by Alice Chau
Prop styling by Cecilia Knutsson, Peter Poulos, Clare Amsel, Despina Velonia
Food styling by Cecilia Knutsson
Cover photograph by Joseph De Leo
Typesetting by Janis Reed

10 9 8 7 6 5 4 3 2 1

Chronicle Books LLC
680 Second Street
San Francisco, California 94107
www.chroniclebooks.com

ACKNOWLEDGMENTS

The soul of Greece lives in its country cooks. These are the people who tend the earth, keep animals, and maintain traditions. There are too many of them to thank here, but a few stand out: Marianthi Gerovasiliou, the mother of one of Greece's most renowned wine makers; Toula Foukou, who shared several traditional recipes with me; Avra Panasopoulou, who treated us to apples and cherries and opened the door to so many great people and flavors from her adopted neck of the woods, Agia, in Larissa. My neighbor in Ikaria, Titika Karimanli, has taught me many things about the country table. Christina Panteleimoniti, while not exactly a country cook, is the producer of many a country treat and made more than a few introductions in Lesvos.

A few Greek friends and colleagues opened the way for me to research and travel. Yiorgos Kalostos, director of the now defunct Business and Technical Development Office of the South Aegean, gave us an unprecedented opportunity to travel the islands on a research project, which gave me plenty of material for this book, too. Ditto for Panagiotis Yiorgiades, a wine-maker in northern Greece, who enabled me to delve into the cooking of some of the country's remotest places. I owe much to all my colleagues at *Ta Nea*, the paper I have been working for since I arrived in Greece one October day many years ago. Being a journalist has opened more doors than I ever imagined, and I am thankful for that. My work with the Hellenic Gourmet shop at the Athens International Airport brought me into contact with countless artisan producers and gave me more than a glimpse of the breadth of foods found all over Greece. As a longtime collaborator with the Hellenic Foreign Trade Board, I've also had the chance to meet cooks, producers, and other food artisans from all over the country and to share in the fun of promoting Greek foods abroad.

A few people in particular made this book a beautiful reality. First among them is my partner in more than writing books, Vassilis Stenos, whose photographs of Greece and of the food on the country table make this book so appealing. Many, many thanks to Cecilia Knutsson, who tested all the recipes, styled all the food, and always had an intelligent comment to share; and to Peter Poulos, whose idea of fun is to scour flea markets early on Sunday mornings for great tableware. He stood by as I mercilessly emptied his kitchen of props. Thanks, too, to Clare Amsel, for entrusting me with precious plates and for being an unwavering friend all these years. Evelina Foukou, office assistant par excellence, corrector of many mistakes, hawkeyed in matters of minutiae, helped in more ways than one on the manuscript.

I owe a special thanks to Christos Valtsoglou, the Parlamis family, and Louis Alexakis, owners, respectively, of Pylos and Boukies, Axia, and Avli restaurants, where I am consulting chef, for allowing me to experiment on the menus with many of the dishes in this book.

Without the trust of Bill Leblond, my editor, I wouldn't have been part of the venerable Country Cooking series. Sarah Billingsley showed inordinate patience and an eye for editorial detail that have made this manuscript all the better. To Alice Chau, I owe a debt of gratitude, for shaping the visual aspects of the book. Angela Miller, my agent, knows when to go to bat and always does, and I'm thankful for that.

But it's my family and closest friends I owe the most to. My kids, Kyveli and Yiorgo, are the most honest, lovable, and reliable critics. So are my friends, always willing dinner guests and even more eager judges of what's good and what's not. You know who you are. And, finally, to Koko, Trif, Athena, Paul, George, Tom, Kat, and Kris, even though I don't get to cook for them nearly as much as I'd like.

CONTENTS

INTRODUCTION

GOOD FOOD BEGINS IN THE FIELD. IF EVER THERE WAS A TRUISM THAT REFLECTS THE PHILOSOPHY AND FLAVORS OF THE GREEK COUNTRY KITCHEN, THAT WOULD BE IT.

My first experiences in the ways of Greek country cooks were in deep-country Greece, on a remote island called Ikaria. My father emigrated from Ikaria in the 1930s and my maternal grandfather emigrated at the turn of the nineteenth century, but they never severed their ties to the island. Instead, we grew up in its shadow, literally and figuratively. My father spoon-fed us stories about his village, Rahes, which I idealized in my mind's eye. A huge relief of the wing-shaped island (named after Icarus, the character from Greek mythology who fell from the sky) hung on our living room wall in New York.

I went to Ikaria for the first time as a twelve-year-old girl and felt immediately at home. It didn't matter that we had none of the amenities of an American life there. Electricity had just arrived. The only TV was in the pastry shop, which was the main gathering place. Back then, Irini, the owner, made ice cream and yogurt from her own goats' milk. In Ikaria, I ate my first real tomato; my first farm egg; my first knobby, rough-skinned summer apple. The island also gave me my first (reluctant) taste of a fresh Greek fig, a scary thing that looked alive but then wooed me like a siren with its compelling sweetness. I feasted on *vyssino*, a sour-cherry sweet in sugar syrup, all summer long. I saw my first goat, tied by its hind leg to a tree in my aunt's dusty garden, chomping on a bundle of branches she had cut for its dinner. A minute later, in her ancient kitchen, I tasted the day-old cheese its milk had provided.

That was in 1972. Ever since then, I have been lucky to spend at least two months a year in Ikaria. My husband's family roots are also on the island. Our kids have forged the same ties, with lifelong friendships and indelible memories of what it means to savor real food, fresh from the field, tree, garden, or sea.

I have lived in Greece since 1992 and have traveled all over the country. It didn't take long for me to realize that my ties to Ikaria are not unique. Every Greek feels a sense of homecoming in his ancestral village. Many go back to the family home, usually a simple house, sometimes shared with an extended network of relatives, which has been in the family for a few generations.

These ties to a village translate as ties to the land. Every Greek believes that the cornucopia of fruits, vegetables, cheeses, honey, olives, and olive oil that grow or are produced in his particular corner of the country is the best or the purest. Thousands of Greeks go back to their villages in summer and keep gardens or reap the rewards of a cousin's or neighbor's fields. Thousands have their own olive trees and produce their own supply of oil.

From time immemorial, regional loyalty has been a strong sentiment in Greece, reinforced by the country's polarized geography: mountains and islands. Steep gorges and lush valleys chisel their way through the mountains of the mainland, but also of Crete and other islands. A few wide alluvial plains soften the terrain. Mainland mountain villages that, until a few years ago, were accessible only by the crudest of roads, have retained, in their relative isolation, age-old food customs and farming practices. Islands, by their very nature, are self-contained and so is the local cooking.

Regionalism—*topiki kuizina* is the term for regional cuisine—is not a new concept in this ancient country. Greeks were, indeed, the first people to invent an appellation system for agricultural products. Stone tablets unearthed from Pylos in the Peloponnese, and from other sites, document the harvest, buying and selling, and transport of olive oil. The production and buying and selling of wine, which was transported all over the ancient world, was recorded in equal detail. Connoisseurs sought and wrote about dozens of place-specific delicacies: Pramnian, Thracian, or other wines; fish from Faliron Bay or the Efxinos Pontos (Black Sea) or elsewhere; honey from Attica; figs from Chios and Crete; almonds from Cyprus. The list goes on.

Modern Greeks share the same obsession about sourcing the best foods. When I first moved to Athens, I would traipse halfway across the city to buy a particular feta I liked. There is a great restaurant in Kifissia, a suburb north of Athens, called Gefseis me Onomasia Proelefsis—Appellation of Origin Flavors. Its owner, Panos Zoumboulis, is a master at obtaining the most unique regional Greek products. "As a boy," he said, "I used to take the bus with my father every Saturday to go to the Central Market, because he knew the places to find the best fish, the best meat. He developed my taste buds."

Topiki kuizina is much more than a dry list of regional products and recipes. It is the culture of food itself, forged by the wealth (or paucity) of natural resources in each region, by historical factors, and by each region's temperament. The Cretan table brims with dozens of fresh greens, herbs, snails, game, and ancient grains because the island is a wild foods paradise, but also because poverty and military conquests dictated that locals survive on what was available. The cooking of Macedonia is spicier and more aromatic than that of the rest of Greece because peppers have long been a traditional crop in the region, and because hundreds of thousands of Asia Minor refugees who landed here in 1922 brought little with them beyond the bare necessities and a trove of recipes for the perfumed cuisine of their beloved cosmopolitan cities, such as Constantinople and Smyrna. Epirus, in the mountainous northwestern part of Greece, is a land of savory pies, cheeses, and meat, all of which grew out of the shepherd's lifestyle. It's also a land of river fish and wild greens, because nature provides both. In the Peloponnese, where olive trees cover the terrain, olive oil drenches vegetables, beans, and even sweets. It's hard to make generalizations about the Aegean islands, but they do share a few common foods: goat's milk cheeses, goat meat and pork (the main source of animal protein), fish, of course, and, historically, whatever could be eked out of the meager land. The cuisine of the Ionian islands, on the western side of Greece, was shaped more than anything else by the Venetian influence on the island.

Ironically, though, until a few years ago most of Greece's regional bounty was unavailable in city shops or urban restaurants. Some foods, such as Kalamata olives or Dodoni feta, enjoyed both strong regional associations and large-scale production. They were easy to find at the local supermarket. But for the real country gems, you needed a network of family or friends willing to deliver a box of village goods to the porter at the ferry dock or bus stop. Then you needed the time to meet the boat or bus when it arrived in Piraeus or Athens. I have friends who still insist on procuring some of their most cherished foods this way. One heads repeatedly for his native Crete and carts back kilos of mountain goat meat and the creamiest *xinomyzithra*, a local cheese, to Athens. Another friend and chef who cooks at Alatsi, a Cretan restaurant in Athens, travels to the island once a week to secure his supply of greens, meats, honey, and other necessities from his favorite farmers and producers. My friend Tassos Kollias, who runs a well-known fish taverna in Piraeus, works with a complex network of Aegean fishermen, who send him fresh fish directly. During my last days in Ikaria, usually in early September, I rush to collect crates of fresh Muscat grapes and figs, oregano, almonds from the tree in our garden, and local honey, all to keep for the winter because, of course, for me, too, products from my village are the purest, tastiest, and most desirable. These are the things that comfort me, the *topiki kuizina* that revives my spirit and strengthens my personal ties to the land.

Some of the best local raw ingredients are in the farmers' markets, a barometer of the spirit of the day and the produce of the season. The provenance of almost everything is clearly marked: potatoes from Thebes or Naxos, where the damp earth has made the cultivation of the New World tuber easy; peaches from Naoussa; and apples from Tripoli. The farmers' markets are well organized and probably still the best place to find the freshest local seasonal fruits, vegetables, and fish. But they have never managed to step up to the task of bringing the most obscure regional farmers' products to city streets.

Until about a decade ago, there was neither a good enough transportation network to help make Greece's treasure trove of regional products accessible, nor a large enough market for them. The lack of demand was a social phenomenon. For one thing, most Greeks thought of country foods as the foods exclusively from their own place in the country, so buying the honey or olive oil from another area seemed almost traitorous.

Socially, Greece began to change dramatically during the 1990s. As I saw it from my urban perch in Athens, Greeks began to embrace everything but their own cuisine. A new generation of Greeks, many of whom had lived outside the country as students, returned with a more global perspective. They created a demand for international cuisine, and as a result, Japanese sushi, Spanish tapas, Thai, Italian, and even Indian restaurants sprouted all over Athens. At the same time, Greece's stock market high created a frenzy of high-end restaurants, which served everything but traditional Greek food. The corner taverna, a stronghold of Greece's traditional cuisine, became a boring remnant of the past. The country's entrance into the European Union opened the floodgates for thousands of foreign foods, which have since inundated the supermarket shelf. Even on tiny Ikaria, still an entrenched agrarian society, a huge Carrefour, the French supermarket giant, opened its doors.

But then, like all infatuations, the love affair with all things new and foreign started to fade. By the start of the new millennium, with the 2004 Olympics looming larger and larger in Greeks' collective mindset, and a growing international trend among serious cooks and environmentalists to seek out local food, chefs and retailers began to rediscover the wealth of regional Greek foods. High-end restaurants suddenly started serving obscure Cretan greens. Restaurant menus began to read like a map of Greece, explicitly listing the provenance of each and every ingredient. Most important, though, specialty retail shops carrying artisan cheeses, honey, olives, spoon sweets, and confections started popping up in cities. Now there's a specialty Cretan delicatessen in every urban neighborhood. Some shops specialize in the products of Greece's network of women's cooperatives, keepers of the flame of tradition and makers of things even most village cooks don't bother producing anymore: handmade pasta; *trahana*, a dairy-based, pebbly, pastalike product; and spoon sweets among them. I helped as an adviser to one such very visible shop, the Hellenic Gourmet store at Athens International Airport, where travelers can choose from a large range of regional specialty foods and wines for a final taste of rural Greece.

That experience led me to many of the artisans who have rediscovered the country foods of Greece and transformed their passion into profit. Small workshops now produce an impressive array of unusual, rediscovered, or reinterpreted regional fare. In rural outposts as far-flung as Lesvos and Kos, in a network of places connected by the Wine Roads of Northern Greece or by the agritourism lure, artisan producers are taking traditional products and marketing them in Greece and beyond. During the last decade, a new generation of savvy food exporters have founded companies that produce gourmet products based on traditional regional fare.

Today, hundreds of place-specific traditional Greek foods and wines enjoy the European Union's coveted Protected Designation of Origin (PDO), which indicates that they are of high quality and have been produced with traditional methods. These are the foods and wines that have grown out of Greece's formidable agricultural traditions.

Flying in the face of this return to the culinary roots of Greece, there is an official march to modernize (read that as "standardize") even the most sacred Greek products. Feta is a good example. The cheese won the EU's PDO a few years ago, but huge companies that hardly adhere to traditional methods of production benefited the most. The small producers were squeezed out because a maze of EU regulations made it too costly for them modernize. This is a constant phenomenon across Greece and Europe.

In this book I aim to celebrate not a rarefied museum piece called Country Greek Cooking, but rather the flexible, seasonal, ingredient-driven cuisine that is mainly, but not exclusively, regional; traditional, but not static. One of the greatest times I had in Greece during the last year was truffle hunting in a hazelnut forest south of Thessaloniki with Panagiotis Koukouvitis, who owns a renowned Greek gourmet shop in the city. Panagiotis shared his country truffle dish with me—grilled octopus with the aromatic tuber shaved over it. This is not exactly a dish his grandmother reared him on, but it's a good example of the meeting of tradition with the twenty-first century.

CHAPTER 1

SALADS

IN A COUNTRY LIKE GREECE, WHERE ABUNDANT SUN-SHINE AND A TEMPERATE CLIME WORK TO PRODUCE SOME OF THE MOST DELICIOUS RAW INGREDIENTS IN THE WORLD, IT STANDS TO REASON THAT THE IDEA OF A SALAD IS MORE THAN A MERE MÉLANGE OF GREENS.

It is one of the most important parts of a Greek meal. Greek children learn from a very young age to eat salad with dinner, even if dinner is a vegetarian dish. They also learn early on that while salad is a fixture on the dinner table, it is not a fixed concept, but rather something that changes seasonally, both in content and technique.

Summer is a time of juicy tomato salads, especially the classic Greek village one, with its timeless combination of great tomatoes, strong red onions, cucumbers, feta, oregano, olives, and olive oil. But it also is the season for plainer tomato-cucumber salads, or purslane, or boiled amaranth, the most widely available summer green, served cold. In the fall, salads change color with the addition of roasted red peppers and heartier vegetables, while in winter, cabbage salad and warm boiled

vegetable salads appear on the table. Lettuce salad, fragrant with refreshing snipped dill, spring onions, and lemon vinaigrette, is a springtime dish. Greeks enjoy bean salads year-round. Olive oil is the exclusive salve in all of these, poured over vegetables with abandon or whisked with acidic lemon juice or vinegar, depending on the dish. Greeks mostly prefer their raw vegetable salads with nothing but olive oil.

Then, as you will discover in the chapter on Greek meze, there is the whole array of "salads" that are not anything you can pierce with a fork or cut with a knife; these are the spreadable salads, like roasted eggplant "salad" (see page 53). A salad can mean many things; what's important, though, is that some plate of vegetables, raw or cooked, accompanies each meal.

ODE TO A GREEK SALAD

Some things are sacred, and Greek salad, a singularly simple dish that perfectly captures the robust, seasonal spirit of the Greek table, is one of them. I never get bored with the classic combination of great summer tomatoes, Greece's round-on-the-palate extra-virgin olive oil, sea salt, cucumbers, red onions, Kalamata olives, and feta cheese. During the last few years, this classic dish was fodder for some chefs' overeager imaginations. In Athens and elsewhere in Greece, the national salad morphed into a jumble of confusion: Nowadays a "Greek salad" might be a scoop of feta ice cream over tomato granita or candied olive macaroons, which add crunch to tomato-and-cucumber "air." For a while, the martini glass became the receptacle of choice for serving a Greek salad. I have eaten Greek salad as soup, gel, ice cream, and air.

Nothing, of course, beats the real thing, which is perfect so long as the raw ingredients are first-rate. In the United States, the best Greek salad is made either with Jersey beefsteak tomatoes in summer, or with Holland hydroponics. It goes without saying that the feta should be Greek; in my opinion a pungent, creamy feta works best. Of course, the olives should be true Kalamatas, and the olive oil Greek and extra-virgin. As for the cucumbers, go for texture and look for organic cukes. But the best part of a Greek salad is actually what's left after it's eaten. The juice—a creamy nectar of extra-virgin olive oil, Greek oregano, mashed bits of feta, pungent onion slices (preferably red), and soft tomato pulp—is an invitation to linger at table. Just make sure there is good crusty bread to dip into the bowl.

A WORD ON GREEK DRESSINGS

Greeks like their salads clean and simple, with as little seasoning as possible, the better to let the flavor of the country's excellent raw vegetables sparkle. The basic Greek dressing is *latholemono*—olive oil and lemon juice whisked together with a little salt in a tangy ratio of 2 parts olive oil for every 1 part lemon juice. This is the classic dressing for both raw and cooked greens, for boiled vegetables, and also for grilled fish, in which case the *latholemono* is served in a gravy boat for easy pouring. Olive oil and vinegar are also a classic combination, but they are typically reserved for boiled greens, especially bitter ones.

In the last few years, lots of other olive oil–based dressings have evolved in the home kitchen, including olive oil, lemon juice, herbs, and feta; olive oil, mustard, honey, orange juice, and herbs; and olive oil, vinegar, and *petimezi* (grape must syrup).

If I had to choose one dressing over all others, it would be the absolute simplest: raw extra-virgin olive oil—especially fresh, early-harvest oil, called *agourelaio;* or some of the exquisite regional Protected Designation of Origin (PDO) olive oils, such as the oils of Sitia and Kritsa in Crete and the Mani in the Peloponnese—with a sprinkling of coarse sea salt.

CLASSIC GREEK VILLAGE SALAD

HORIATIKI SALATA

SERVES 4

Although this is a classic recipe, I think some additions are perfectly acceptable, but others are not. Lettuce, for example, is an addition that wily diner owners began to make so that the dish, always a bargain on the menu, would look fuller. Nix it from the bowl; it detracts from the heart of the salad. Green peppers are another story. Seeded and cut into rings or strips, they go very well with the other ingredients. So do pickled peppers of varying degrees of heat. Pickled pepperoncini are the most common. If you have access to other Greek cheeses besides feta, you might want to try a soft, granular, pungent *xinomyzithra* cheese from Crete. Green olives instead of Kalamata are also acceptable.

3 medium firm, ripe Jersey beefsteak tomatoes or Holland hydroponics or 6 to 8 Campari tomatoes

1 medium red onion, halved and cut into ⅛-in/3-mm slices

1 large cucumber, peeled and cut into ⅛-in/3-mm-thick rounds

8 to 12 Kalamata olives in brine, rinsed and drained

Coarse salt or sea salt

⅓ cup/80 ml extra-virgin Greek olive oil

5 oz/140 g Greek feta, cut into 1 square piece

2 tsp fresh oregano leaves, or ½ tsp dried Greek oregano (see the box on page 24)

Cut the tomatoes in half and, using a sharp paring knife, remove the stem end. Cut each tomato half into 3 or 4 wedges, depending on its size. Put in a serving bowl.

Add the onion, cucumber, olives, salt to taste, and olive oil and gently toss. Place the feta on top and sprinkle the salad with oregano. To serve, break the feta up with a fork so everyone gets a little. The whole idea is for the feta to crumble into ever-smaller pieces as you consume the salad.

LETTUCE, ARUGULA, AND BORAGE SALAD

MAROULOSALATA ME ROKA KAI PORANTZI

SERVES 4 TO 6

Romaine lettuce, called cos lettuce in Greece and Europe, is the main spring salad vegetable, and is on the table from the start of Lent in March at least through Easter. There are many regional variations on the lettuce salad theme. Most of them pair lettuce with fresh dill, which is also in season in the spring. This version, made with borage leaves and flowers, is found in the Aegean islands. I first sampled it on the Easter table of a friend, Argyro Malahias, in our village in Ikaria. Borage, or starflower, is the herb of joy, thought to improve one's mood and fight off depression. It grows wild, even on the sidewalks in Greece, but fell out of use long ago, except among those who are well versed in the riches of Greece's wild flora. Its beautiful purplish-blue flowers can turn white vinegar wine-dark. The leaves taste uncannily like cucumber, and the flowers have a sweet, faint honey flavor. The variation, made with artichokes instead of borage, comes from Crete.

1 head romaine lettuce, trimmed and shredded

1 large bunch arugula, trimmed and shredded

3 scallions, trimmed and finely chopped

½ cup/30 g fresh mint leaves, cut into julienne strips

¼ cup/15 g fresh snipped dill

1 small bunch borage leaves, washed and trimmed

½ cup/30 g borage flowers

DRESSING

⅓ cup/80 ml extra-virgin Greek olive oil

2½ tbsp strained fresh lemon juice

Salt

Wash and spin-dry all the greens, scallions, and herbs. Toss all together in a large salad bowl. Add the borage flowers.

To make the dressing: Whisk together the olive oil, lemon juice, and salt to taste.

Pour the dressing over the salad. Toss and serve.

VARIATION: Replace the borage with 4 artichoke hearts (see page 153), quartered. Omit the mint and increase the amount of dill to ½ cup/30 g.

GREEK OREGANO

Oregano—mountain glory, as its name in Greek implies, from *oros*, the root for "mountain," and *ganos*, "joy" or "glory"—is the most enduring herb on the Greek country table. There are many varieties around the world. Three varieties account for most of the oregano grown in Greece: *Origanum vulgare*, which grows wild in mountainous regions all over the country; *O. onites*; and *O. dictamnus*, which is the *dictamo*, or "lover's herb," of Crete and is consumed as a tisane and infusion, not as a cooking herb. Hunters often carry a little oregano with them to place in the cavity of their kill as a way to stave off unpleasant smells.

Oregano likes water and tends to grow near rivulets or underground streams. Greeks collect it when its tiny white flowers blossom in the early summer. They take a bunch of sprigs, tie them together, and hang them upside down to dry all summer and sometimes into the fall. With a few exceptions, Greek cooks prefer dried oregano to fresh. Only in recent years has the fresh made its way to the Greek table. Although oregano is the quintessential wild mountain herb, in some parts of mainland Greece, namely Trikala and Karditsa, it is cultivated on a large scale for commercial purposes.

Dried Greek oregano is de rigueur in a traditional Greek salad, and it is often used in simple sauces and dressings. When combined with lemon juice, garlic, and olive oil, it lends a characteristic Greek flavor to countless other dishes, from fish and shellfish to pasta, meat, and more. Real Greek oregano tastes nothing like the flat, slightly bitter oregano from Mexico found in most American markets. Seek out the peppery wild Greek herb, which you can find in Greek shops.

THE KALAMATA OLIVE HARVEST

Pewter November skies, bone-chilling damp, a palette of browns and ochres and the silver-green of the trees themselves with branches hung with black fruit, these are the hallmarks of a typical olive harvest season. The occasional sparkle of a bursting pomegranate brightens up the scenery like a smile. Other than that, everything is heavy, and the dense oily smell of olive mass permeates the air so completely, it even seeps into the woolen or quilted vests workers wear to keep warm but unconfined as they teeter like acrobats in knobby trees, stretching in every direction to hand pluck the fruit from each branch. Wiry, black tarpaulin nets, discovered many years ago by one prescient olive man from Crete on a trip to Japan, now spread beneath all Greek olive trees to catch falling fruit.

The day is long and hard, starting at eight and ending at four, the only respite a short break outdoors called *kolatso*, or "snack," which is usually a container full of cooked beans and some bread and cheese, or halva, or something else to provide caloric, starchy sustenance for the energy needs of olive pickers. A generation ago, figs and fig bread were the midmorning snacks of most olive pickers, and the prefecture of Messinia, where the town of Kalamata is located, still has a thriving business in fig cultivation and packing. (In fact, figs and olives go to the same plants for processing.) The slow rhythms of a typical harvest day might be frustrated by fickle weather: If it rains, the picking stops; if it's dry and maybe even clear and sunny, workers are out on those three-legged ladders, with an array of unique comblike tools and poles to help with the job.

I saw all this in the heart of Kalamata olive country, in villages with names that would make David Lynch smile, such as Three Peaks (Trikorfo) and Good Hawk (Kalogeraki), about 1,300 ft/400 m up in the terraced mountains surrounding the great plain of Kalamata. That, too, is a blanket of olive trees, but they are different varieties—for oil, not for the table.

The Kalamata olive is almost exclusively a table olive and is arguably the world's most famous. It is the shiny mahogany-colored olive with the tight skin and pointy tips that graces Greek salads and a whole array of other dishes across the globe.

The best Kalamata table olives are cultivated in these hills, on sculpted terraces where no farm machine can plow or pull because the strips of land are too narrow and the terrain too rough. The manual work involved in planting and harvesting the olives is one of the reasons why Greek olives and olive oil are so fine. The plots of land are small and family-owned, and people tend to them with care, picking them by hand so as not to bruise the fruit.

In those mountain villages and others, the olives are *xerikes*, or "dry." That is, only rainfall nurtures them. They are not watered in order to plump them quickly. Putting up a struggle to survive makes the olives—like most fruit—more intensely flavored.

A day's worth of olives goes into large burlap sacks or red plastic barrels and then travels by pickup to one of the nearby processing plants, usually a maze of conveyor belts that move and sort olives by size, dropping them through corresponding slots. Kalamata olives need to be slit, which expedites the process of debittering them more efficiently. A machine does this in the plant. Then kilo upon kilo of the same-size olives are emptied into huge tanks of salt water and citric acid, where they spend anywhere from three weeks to two months. Watered olives need less time; the *xerikes* take months for their bitterness to leach out. Kalamata olives acquire their perky taste during the last phase, after debittering, when they cure in red wine vinegar.

Olive pickers and growers, of course, don't exactly rely on huge commercial processing plants to put up the few kilos of olives they consume at home. Families all over the region, indeed all over Greece, occupy themselves with the task of preserving their own olives when the wintry November harvest arrives. All that's needed is a good razor for slitting the olives (never down to their pits), a roaring fireplace for atmosphere and warmth, and some company. After that comes the lengthy saltwater bath and the curing: vinegar, of course, but also olive oil, lemon or orange slices, garlic, oregano, savory, or anything else with which one might want to season a jug of olives.

ENDIVE, CELERY ROOT, AND EEL SALAD

SALATA ME HELI, SELINORIZA KAI ANTIDIA

===== SERVES 6 =====

On moonless nights in November, eel fishermen ply their trade in the marshlands on the western coast of mainland Greece near Messolongi, farther north in the Amvrakikos Gulf, and in parts of the cove-laced coastline of Halkidiki. The eel, one of nature's most peripatetic creatures, is born and dies in salty ocean waters, but spends most of its life in fresh water. When its migrations bring it to Greece, the common Mediterranean *Anguilla anguilla*, which is the most prevalent species here, is a hermaphroditic creature. Its fatty flesh is loved by enthusiastic fans and hated by equally fanatic detractors. The richness of its flesh is one reason it is often smoked and paired with astringent or particularly refreshing salad greens. Smoked eel has become something of a gourmet delicacy in Greece during the last decade and a half, but Northern Italy imports most of the catch.

1 lemon, halved

1 medium celery root (about 1 lb/455 g), peeled, quartered lengthwise, and shredded or cut into julienne strips

1 large Granny Smith apple, peeled and grated

1 large Belgian endive, trimmed and cut into thin ribbons

1 large fennel bulb, trimmed, halved, and sliced thinly

8 to 10 oz/225 to 280 g smoked eel or trout fillets, cut into ⅛-in-/3-mm-wide strips

DRESSING

½ cup/120 ml extra-virgin Greek olive oil

¼ cup/60 ml strained fresh lemon juice

Pinch of saffron

Salt and pepper

Squeeze the lemon half over a bowl of ice water and add the shredded celery root. Let it stand for 10 to 15 minutes to curl and firm up a little. Squeeze the other lemon half over a small bowl of ice water, add the apple, and let sit to keep from discoloring until the celery root is ready.

Drain the celery root and apple and toss in a mixing bowl with the endive, fennel, and smoked eel.

To make the dressing: Whisk together the olive oil, lemon juice, saffron, and salt and pepper to taste.

Toss the vegetables and dressing together and serve.

PURSLANE-CUCUMBER SALAD WITH YOGURT AND HERBS

SALATA ME GLISTRIDA, AGGOURI KAI YIAOURTI

===== SERVES 4 TO 6 =====

Purslane—a weed of distinction and guardian against all ills, as Pliny the Elder noted—provides Greece's otherwise sun-parched summer terrain with a little respite. It is one of the few edible wild greens that flourish between June and September. It is also one of the most nutritious, a powerhouse of anti-oxidants and calcium whose small, succulent leaves have long been considered a therapeutic antidote for headaches, stomach pains, ulcers, and eye ailments.

Purslane is more common than most people think; it grows wild in backyard gardens in the Mediterranean, Western Europe, and the United States. You can also find it at many farmers' markets when it is in season.

3 cups/300 g purslane

6 small cucumbers, peeled, seeded, and shredded

2 tbsp chopped fresh mint

2 tbsp chopped fresh cilantro

2 tbsp chopped fresh flat-leaf parsley

1½ cups/360 ml strained Greek sheep's milk yogurt (or any thick Mediterranean-style yogurt)

¼ cup/60 ml extra-virgin Greek olive oil

3 garlic cloves, crushed with the flat side of a knife, and chopped

2 tsp ground coriander

Sea salt and pepper

Wash the purslane, spin dry, and trim away any tough stems. Transfer to a salad bowl. Wring the liquid out of the shredded cucumber by gathering it up with your hands, one small bunch at a time, and squeezing it between your palms. Transfer to the bowl and add the herbs.

Whisk together the yogurt, olive oil, garlic, and coriander and season with salt. Add the yogurt mixture to the vegetables and mix well. Season with pepper and additional salt if needed. Serve.

A SWEET EUPHEMISM FOR VINEGAR

I never thought, after nearly twenty years in Greece, that I'd see the day when winemakers bragged not about their vintages but about their vinegar. Traditionally it is almost taboo in most wineries to mention *xidi*, the Greek word for "vinegar" (from the Greek word *xino,* which means "sour"). You just might jinx the year's production. The superstition runs so deep that for centuries *xidi* was euphemistically called *glykadi,* which means "sweet."

Nevertheless, vinegar, as ancient as wine, is one of the most prized condiments in Greek cooking, so basic that without it many dishes can't be completed. Vinegar adds a balancing touch to so many of the olive oil–based stews and casseroles of Greece. It is also the basic preserving agent in pickled vegetables and even olives, the finishing touch in lentil soups and other bean dishes, the spritz that livens up some meat stews and offal dishes, and, of course, an essential ingredient of dressings, which flavor countless fresh and boiled seasonal salads.

For centuries in Greek country homes, cooks made their own vinegar. They carefully cultivated the *mana* ("mother," or starter), usually from local wine made from local grape varieties, which lent regional distinction to most country vinegars. The *mana,* which forms on the surface of vinegar as it ferments, is saved from year to year, and even from generation to generation. Vinegar was typically stored in oak or chestnut barrels to age.

With the advent of commercial vinegar, the home-grown art of making vinegar waned. Only in the last few years has it been resuscitated, mainly by boutique winemakers and a few small companies all over Greece. As

Epirus wine and vinegar producer Vassilis Vaimakis put it, "God made grapes with vinegar in mind; we humans stop it midcourse for wine."

Now there are vinegars made with single-grape varieties and vinegars made in the vein of balsamic. At least one type of traditional vinegar, though, is unlike any other, and that is *glykadi*. It is not just a winemaker's euphemism for "vinegar." *Glykadi* refers to an ancient combination of raisins and grape must that, thanks to its high alcohol content, was prone to oxidation. By the Middle Ages, Greece's famed Corinthian raisins were being used to make *glykadi*. The Peloponnese, where Corinth is located, became a major production center for this sweet-and-sour vinegar. *Glykadi* also goes by the name *kalogeristiko,* after *kalogeros,* the Greek word for "monk," because so much of it was made in monasteries.

Some of the most famous vinegars are still produced from Corinthian raisins in the Peloponnese. Other exceptional regional vinegars are made in the Aegean island of Santorini, from the Assyrtiko grape; in the island of Lefkada, where vinegar is imbued with the intoxicating scent of rose petals; and by some of the country's premier winemakers, among them Yiannis Boutaris, Vassilis Vaimakis, and Kostas Lazarides, all in the north. At least one company has resuscitated another ancient vinegar product, called *oxymelo,* which means "acid (as in vinegar) honey." It is a beguiling elixir that adds depth and roundness to even the most mundane boiled vegetables and works fabulously with grilled vegetables and other foods.

POPI'S PURSLANE
AND OLIVE SALAD

SALATA ME GLISTRIDA KAI ELIES

===== SERVES 6 =====

This recipe comes from a friend in Ikaria, where we spend our summers. Popi has a small taverna outside Evdilos, where she serves uncomplicated foods, most of which are harvested from her garden. Simple as this tangy salad is, I've never had another one like it anywhere in Greece. The secret is the red wine vinegar, which needs to be robust and sharp.

1 lb/455 g purslane

3 to 4 large garlic cloves

1 large seedless cucumber

1 cup/200 g small green olives, rinsed and drained

1 bunch fresh flat-leaf parsley

½ cup/120 ml extra-virgin Greek olive oil

3 tbsp red wine vinegar

Salt

Wash the purslane and spin-dry. Trim away any tough stems. Coarsely chop the purslane and transfer to a salad bowl.

Crush the garlic with the side of a large chef's knife and scrape, along with its juices, into the salad bowl. Peel and coarsely chop the cucumber. Remove the pits from the olives and quarter lengthwise. Finely chop the parsley. Put all the ingredients in the salad bowl. Pour in the olive oil, vinegar, and salt to taste. Toss and let sit at room temperature for at least 10 minutes before serving.

KOZANI RAW LEEK
AND OLIVE SALAD

SALATA ME PRASA KAI ELIES

===== SERVES 4 TO 6 =====

My friend Despina, a local cook in Ikaria, first introduced me to the seductive flavor of wild leeks and onions. In her kitchen in Perdiki, a small village perched high above the sea on the northern side of Ikaria, she prepared a salad of onion and leek greens, which she had blanched and then sautéed in some of her own olive oil. The greens were the stalks of onions and leeks that had been planted a few seasons earlier and never harvested, so they reappeared every year. I have come across similar salads, both raw and cooked, all over Greece, but mainly in the north. This version is adapted from a local recipe from the prefecture of Kozani, in western Macedonia.

3 leeks, white part only, washed well

1 very scant tsp salt

⅓ cup/80 ml extra-virgin Greek olive oil

1 to 2 tbsp red wine vinegar

4 Halkidiki green olives, drained, pitted, and halved

Cut the leeks into julienne strips as small as matchsticks. Put in a colander, sprinkle with the salt, and rub vigorously to soften. Do this for 5 to 6 minutes. Alternatively, blanch the julienned leeks in salteed water for 30 to 40 seconds, drain, and submerge in ice water for a minute or so before draining again.

Transfer to a shallow bowl and toss with the olive oil, vinegar, and olives. Let stand at room temperature, covered, for at least 1 hour, and serve.

POTATO SALAD WITH PURSLANE AND CRUMBLED FETA

PATATOSALATA ME GLISTRIDA KAI FETA

===== SERVES 4 TO 6 =====

Throughout the Aegean islands, purslane is a favorite in warm and cold salads. In Ikaria, where we live in the summer, it is almost always added to potato salad. Ikaria, with its rich soil and ample water, was one of the places in Greece that the New World potato took to very well. Other areas in Greece are more renowned for their potato crops and even enjoy the EU's Protected Designation of Origin status for their spuds.

6 medium potatoes (about 1½ lb/680 g total), cooked and peeled (and still warm; see Note)

2 cups/200 g coarsely chopped purslane

1 medium red onion, finely chopped

¼ cup/15 g finely chopped fresh flat-leaf parsley

DRESSING

½ cup/120 ml extra-virgin Greek olive oil

Juice of 1 lemon, about 4 tbsp, strained

½ cup/120 ml thick Greek yogurt

2 tsp coarse-grained mustard

Salt and pepper

½ cup/75 g crumbled Greek feta cheese

Dash of cayenne pepper

Cut the potatoes into thick slices or sixths. Combine with the purslane, onion, and parsley in a salad bowl.

To make the dressing: Whisk together the olive oil, lemon juice, yogurt, and mustard.

Season the salad with salt and pepper. Pour in the dressing and toss gently. Garnish with crumbled feta, sprinkle with cayenne, and serve immediately.

NOTE: To cook the potatoes, scrub the potato skins clean and wash well several times under cold running water. Put the potatoes in a large wide pot. Add enough water to cover by 2 in/5 cm. Bring to a boil, uncovered. Season generously with salt. Reduce the heat and simmer for about 20 to 25 minutes, or until the potatoes are fork-tender. Remove from the heat, drain the water, and gently transfer the potatoes to a colander. Rinse under cold water and when cool enough to handle, peel.

NAXOS SUMMER POTATO SALAD

PATATOSALATA NAXOU

===== SERVES 4 TO 6 =====

Greek potato salads are nothing like the mayo-laden potato salads most Americans know from deli counter cuisine. In Greece, hot potatoes are mixed with extra-virgin olive oil and various seasonal vegetables, usually fresh. In Ikaria, for example, potato salad is a summer dish, served warm with fresh cucumbers and tomatoes. This recipe comes from the island of Naxos, a paradise for Greek potato lovers. The New World tuber has flourished in the island's rocky soil since the mid-nineteenth century, and there is a research and cultivation center there that provides seedlings to farmers all over the country. The main varieties are Spunta, Liseta, Marfona, Vivaldi, and Alaska potatoes.

6 medium all-purpose or Yellow Finn potatoes (about 1½ lb/680 g), cooked and peeled (and still warm; see Note at left)

3 firm, ripe tomatoes, peeled and coarsely chopped

2 large red onions, halved and sliced ⅛ in/3 mm thick

1 medium cucumber, peeled, halved lengthwise, and sliced ¼ inch/6 mm thick

DRESSING

½ cup/120 ml extra-virgin Greek olive oil

2 to 3 tbsp red wine vinegar, or to taste

3 tsp fresh oregano leaves

Sea salt and pepper

4 to 6 salted sardine fillets, rinsed

Cut the potatoes into thick rounds or large chunks and transfer to a serving bowl. Add the tomatoes, onions, and cucumber.

To make the dressing: In a small bowl, whisk together the olive oil, vinegar, and oregano. Season with salt and pepper.

Pour about two-thirds of the dressing over the potatoes and vegetables and mix gently. Place the sardine fillets on top and drizzle with remaining dressing. Serve immediately.

CRETAN BEET SALAD WITH YOGURT AND WALNUTS

PATZAROSALATA KRITIS

 SERVES 4

There is nothing like the earthy flavor of fresh beets. Greek country cooks often toss beets with tangy yogurt, which offsets the natural sweetness of the vegetable.

2 lb/910 g beets, trimmed and scrubbed

Salt

1 cup/115 g coarsely chopped walnuts

DRESSING

½ cup/120 ml extra-virgin Greek olive oil

1 tbsp balsamic vinegar or Greek sweet vinegar (*glykadi*)

1 cup/240 ml thick Greek yogurt

2 to 3 small garlic cloves, crushed

Salt

2 to 3 tbsp water

Put the beets in a large pot of lightly salted water and bring to a boil over medium heat. Reduce the heat and simmer for 35 to 40 minutes, or until fork-tender. Remove from the heat, drain, and rinse. Peel the beets and cut into 1-in/2.5-cm cubes.

While the beets are boiling, toss the walnuts in a nonstick frying pan over medium heat until lightly toasted. Remove, set aside to cool slightly, and chop or pulverize in a food processor until coarsely ground.

To make the dressing: In a medium bowl, whisk together the olive oil, vinegar, yogurt, and garlic. Add a little salt to taste. Whisking all the while, dilute the dressing with the water. Mix in the walnuts.

Pour the dressing over the beets and add more salt if needed. Serve at room temperature or chilled.

BLACK-EYED PEA SALAD WITH DILL AND ONIONS

SALATA MAVROMATIKA ME ANITHO KAI KREMMYDI

SERVES 4 TO 6

There is nothing, really, to this simple salad, a popular taverna and home-kitchen dish on the islands and mainland alike. You might encounter it spiced up with some finely chopped hot peppers in northern Greece, or with finely chopped green peppers or even roasted red Florina peppers. This Greek island version calls for dill.

1 lb/455 g dried black-eyed peas

Salt

1 large red onion, coarsely chopped

1 garlic clove, minced

1½ cups/90 g finely chopped fresh dill fronds

½ cup/120 ml extra-virgin Greek olive oil, or more to taste

2 to 3 tbsp red wine vinegar

Pepper

Rinse the beans in a colander under cold running water. Bring to a boil in a large pot filled with water. Drain as soon as the water comes to a boil. Return to the pot and refill with water. Return the beans to a boil over high heat, reduce the heat to medium-low, and simmer the beans until tender, 35 to 45 minutes. About 10 minutes before they're done, add a generous amount of salt to the pot. When tender, drain the water and rinse the black-eyed peas under cold running water.

Put the peas in a serving bowl and toss with the onion, garlic, and dill. Pour in the olive oil and vinegar. Season with salt and pepper, toss again, and serve.

GREENS: WILD, EDIBLE, NUTRITIOUS

Spring is a time when the Greek countryside is blooming with many wild, delicious things. We are usually in Ikaria then, sometime between mid-April and early May, and during ten days or so, we prepare the garden for summer. But before we turn the soil or weed it to prepare for planting, the garden is an overgrown jungle of edible greens. I like to try an experiment at this time of year: we don't buy food for a week and try to live off the greens that grow in our own backyard.

One year, with the help of a friend who knows the greens lexicon a lot better than I do, I discovered about thirty edible wild plants within an 8-foot/2.4-meter radius of the kitchen door. These included wild carrots (you eat the tops), wild fennel (great in pies and fritters), two types of mint, oregano, marjoram, savory, sage, lemon balm (for pies and salads), mâche (eaten raw or cooked in salads), chicories of several shapes and pungencies (eaten boiled), aromatic tiny hartwort (for savory pie fillings and salads), dandelions (boiled for salads), spicy mustard greens, stinging nettles, salsify (the stuff of root beer), poetic prickly golden fleece, shepherd's purse, and shepherd's needles, to name a few. There were shoots of all sorts, too—best of all delicious vine shoots, with their slightly briny flavor.

It's no wonder that the variety of wild greens in Greece has spawned its own verb that means "to forage for greens," *vrouvologo*. This national pastime has also given rise to a special apron worn during the hours-long occupation of plucking wild greens from mostly rocky soil. It has very deep pockets, the better to stuff with all those healthful, natural leaves.

Greece is certainly not the only country in the Mediterranean where people love greens. However, it does boast the largest variety of wild, edible plants. The flora of Crete alone provides some 300 species of edible wild plants, including ancient delicacies such as asphodel and sow thistles.

The greens season is mainly from early winter through late spring. It rains then and the countryside is green and, literally, ripe for the picking. In summer the three main edible wild greens are amaranth, purslane, and black nightshade, which has to be picked before it flowers. (Black nightshade is the plant from which strychnine is produced.)

Most wild greens are boiled and eaten at room temperature. To cook them, clean and trim any tough leaves and stems. Then drop into a large pot of boiling salted water and boil until tender. Remove, drain, and serve with olive oil, salt, and either lemon juice or vinegar. Greeks consider vinegar better suited to bitter greens, lemon to sweeter greens like dandelion. A wide variety of greens are also eaten raw, especially sweet greens, such as wild chard.

Beyond the salad bowl, sweet greens go into bean, meat, and fish stews. There are countless savory pies made with sweet green fillings, some containing up to fifteen different varieties. There is also the whole range of buds and shoots enjoyed both raw and cooked: tender vine shoots, tomato and potato shoots, chickpea and fava bean shoots among them.

THE GREEK TOUCH

RUSKS

I DON'T THINK ANOTHER SNACK QUITE CAPTURES THE SPIRIT OF THE GREEK TABLE AS MUCH AS THE *PAXIMADI*, THE TWICE-BAKED HARDTACK, OR RUSK, THAT IS ONE OF THE MOST ANCIENT GREEK FOODS TO HAVE SURVIVED AND FLOURISHED THROUGH THE AGES.

Paximadia (the plural form) were possibly named for Paxamus, a prolific author and cook in Hellenistic Rome, who is thought to have imposed some gastronomic improvements on the twice-baked hardtacks that Greeks had been eating since at least the time of Aristotle and Hippocrates. The ancient Greek dried breads were called *dipyros*, Greek for "twice fired," which was translated into Latin as *biscoto* ("twice baked"). The word and the food itself eventually evolved to become the very English biscuit. Bread aficionados and armchair linguists might want to know that the Greek word *paximadi* spawned the Arabic *bashmat* or *basquimat*, the Turkish *beksemad*, the Serbo-Croatian *peksimet*, the Romanian *pesmet*, and the Venetian *pasimata*, as noted in the book *Siren Feasts* by English classicist Andrew Dalby.

Greek *paximadia* are thick, dense rounds or squares of unsweetened twice-baked bread. In country kitchens of yore, when wood was too scarce a fuel to burn every day in the backyard bread oven and refrigeration was unknown, *paximadia* were the Greeks' daily bread. They are still the stuff of fishing boat galleys, because they keep so well for so long and pair naturally with the fresh fish soups that fishermen simmer onboard, and they remain the midday snack of farmers and field hands, too.

Nowadays few home cooks make their own *paximadia*, dearth of wood not being an issue in this modern age of convection ovens and bakery chains, and lack of time and love of convenience having driven home bakers away from their backyard ovens, except on festive occasions now and then. Nevertheless, all the glories of Greece's food traditions are baked into the simple, rustic *paximadia*. Barley, an ancient Greek grain, is still the most popular for making *paximadia*, and hard wheat and rye are favored as well. In several places, most famously, Crete, chickpea starter and flour are the preferred raw ingredients. More than anything else, these ancient twice-fired breads are one of the Mediterranean's most healthful fast foods, able to provide the base for a salad or the filling sustenance in the bottom of a soup bowl.

There are regional distinctions. Cretan bakers are first among equals as the makers of so many different kinds of *paximadia* and champions at packing them well enough to travel far and wide. The largest manufacturers on the island are more often than not located in its remotest recesses, but they have managed to distribute this ancient food to Athens and beyond. (Bakers elsewhere, regardless of whether their region is known for a distinct *paximadi* style or flavor, have not shown the same business acumen.) Throughout the Greek islands, herbs and spices such as coriander seeds, cumin, fennel seeds, saffron, *mastiha* (mastic or tree resin crystals), cloves, and more season these ancient hardtacks. Luckily for modern Greeks, the proverbial corner bakery in any given city or town usually makes its own *paximadia*, and Greek shops and restaurants across the United States now carry and serve them too.

So, how to make this odd, ancient breadstuff? The technique is surprisingly simple and has remained unchanged over the centuries. The loaves of dough are baked more or less until the dough is set. Then they're removed from the oven, cut into thick slices, and laid out on large sheet pans. These are slipped back into the oven and slowly baked at a low temperature until all the moisture is cooked out of them. The best *paximadia* are made overnight in wood-burning ovens, which remain warm for hours. The resulting product is so brittle, nutty, and hard that it needs to be dipped in water, broth, or milk, or placed under some liquidy food, like a bed of grated or puréed fresh tomatoes, for a time in order to soften up enough to eat.

While *paximadi* is the generic Greek name for this ancient hardtack, some regions make special types, among them the square wedge called *dako* from Crete, and *mostra* from Mykonos. A donut-shaped *paximadi*, split horizontally to form a top and bottom, is known in Crete as *kouloura*. A caveat: Never serve the bottom half of a *kouloura* to a Cretan guest, because doing so implies that you want him to leave.

The traditional way to serve *paximadia*, presented in several of the following recipes, is to dampen them with a little liquid and top them with fresh tomatoes, good olive oil, herbs, and cheese. Contemporary cooks and chefs have been rethinking their uses in the kitchen, though, and have transformed them into conveyances for everything from smoked salmon to fruit salad. A few recipes in this chapter take their cues from these innovative approaches.

KALYMNOS-STYLE RUSK SALAD

MIRMIZELI KALYMNOU

SERVES 2

On Kalymnos, the sponge fisherman's island, this salad was always a staple at sea. The local rusk is typically made from the round barley bread, *Kouloura*, and is sometimes flavored with fennel seeds and/or cumin.

1 round whole-wheat rusk

2 medium tomatoes, seeded and finely chopped

1 onion, finely chopped

6 Kalamata or green olives, rinsed and drained

½ cup/75 g crumbled Greek feta cheese

2 salted sardine fillets, rinsed and finely chopped

1 tbsp capers

3 tbsp extra-virgin Greek olive oil

Salt

Fresh savory or marjoram leaves for garnish

Dampen the rusk under cold running water. Drain off all the water and break the rusk into chunks.

Combine the tomatoes, onion, rusk, olives, feta, sardine fillets, and capers in a mixing bowl. Transfer to a serving bowl and toss with the olive oil. Season with salt, garnish with the herbs, and serve.

BARLEY RUSK SALAD FROM CRETE

DAKOS

SERVES 2

Dako is the name of the round barley rusk of Crete. The name derives from *takos*, which is a short, stout support beam. In Rethymnon, the same barley rusk goes by a different name, *koukouvagia*, which means "owl," for reasons that are lost on this armchair linguist. *Dakos* can be dampened with water or left dry before spooning on the requisite grated or chopped tomatoes, crumbled feta or Cretan *myzithra* (a soft, mild whey cheese), salt, oregano, and olive oil. Nowadays *dakos* is also an urban dish, and is found dressed up on restaurant menus, despite its humble, practical beginnings as the midday snack of Cretan farmhands. For them, olive oil and cheese were either too luxurious to consume in quantities greater than what would fit over a rusk, or too difficult to carry separately to the fields. So the *dakos*, with its ability to absorb and hold oil, became popular.

½ cup/100 g fresh *myzithra* or drained ricotta cheese

½ cup/100 g Greek feta cheese, crumbled

2 large Cretan barley rusks

¼ cup/60 ml extra-virgin Greek olive oil

Sea salt

2 large, ripe tomatoes, peeled and grated or diced, with their juice

1 tsp fresh oregano

Mash the *myzithra* and feta together in a bowl. Run the rusks under cold running water and drain off all the water.

Put the rusks on a plate and drizzle with half the olive oil. Sprinkle with a little sea salt. Spoon the tomatoes on top, dividing them evenly between the rusks and letting them fall over the sides. Sprinkle the oregano and cheese mixture evenly over the rusks, drizzle with the remaining olive oil, and serve.

CRETAN RUSK, WILD ARTICHOKE, AND GRAVIERA SALAD

SALATA ME PAXIMADI, AGRIES ANGINARES KAI GRAVIERA

SERVES 4

Crete is probably the only place in Greece where artichokes are sometimes eaten raw. This salad is one of my favorite island dishes. It calls for *graviera* cheese, a mild, sweet, nutty cheese made from either sheep's or cow's milk. The best *graviera* is produced in Crete. You can find it in the United States and Europe, but you may also substitute Gruyère or Comté. The original recipe for this dish calls for olives, which are tiny green olives from Crete. They're impossible to find outside the island, and cracked green olives or any other Greek green olives are perfectly suitable.

2 Cretan barley rusks

¼ cup/60 ml plus 2 tbsp extra-virgin Greek olive oil

2 medium tomatoes, chopped

1 lemon

Salt and pepper

1 tbsp chopped fresh oregano leaves

1 scallion, trimmed and finely chopped

8 green Nafplion olives, or other Greek green olives, pitted and chopped

3 artichoke hearts from large globe artichokes (see page 153)

3 oz/85 g Greek *graviera* cheese, shaved into thin strips with a vegetable peeler

Place the rusks on the bottom of a serving bowl or platter. Drizzle each one with 1 tbsp of olive oil and spoon a quarter of the chopped tomatoes on top of each one. Let the rusks stand for 10 minutes to soften.

Juice the lemon and whisk together with the remaining ¼ cup/60 ml of olive oil, salt and pepper to taste, and the fresh oregano leaves.

Mix together the remaining chopped tomatoes, the scallion, and olives. Thinly slice the artichoke hearts and place over the tomato-covered rusks. Spoon the tomato-scallion-olive mixture on top. Pour over the dressing, top with the shaved *graviera*, and serve.

BREAD SALAD WITH WATERMELON, FETA, AND RED ONION

SALATA ME KARPOUZI, FETA KAI KREMMYDI

SERVES 4

Watermelon and feta, like cantaloupe and prosciutto, is one of the world's great flavor combinations, which appears in many Greek village kitchens in summer. This is a modern take on a favorite pairing.

1 Cretan barley rusk or 1 thick slice stale country-style bread

1 medium red onion, thinly sliced into rings

3 cups/500 g cold watermelon, cut into 1-in/2.5-cm cubes

1 cup/150 g cubed Greek feta (½-in/12-mm cubes)

1 tsp sherry or raspberry vinegar

Pepper

A few fresh mint sprigs for garnish

Dampen the rusk under cold running water. Drain off all the water and break the rusk into 1-in/2.5-cm chunks.

Place the chunks on the bottom of a serving bowl and scatter half the onion slices over them. Top with the watermelon and any accumulated juices, and then with the feta cubes. Drizzle with the vinegar and toss gently, being careful not to mash the watermelon. Season with pepper and garnish with the remaining onion slices and mint, and serve.

DAKOS SALAD WITH TANGERINE JUICE

DAKOS ME HYMO MANTARINIOU

SERVES 2

This salad is an adaptation of a classic Cretan meze. The tangerine juice is my addition. We serve this at Pylos Restaurant in New York, where I am consulting chef.

2 round Cretan barley rusks

½ cup/120 ml strained fresh tangerine juice

¼ cup/60 ml extra-virgin Greek olive oil

1 large firm, ripe tomato, seeded, and diced small

1 small cucumber, peeled and cut into ½-in/
12-mm cubes

1 small red onion, finely chopped

2 tbsp Greek capers, drained

10 green olives, drained, pitted, and chopped

2 to 3 tsp chopped fresh oregano leaves

Salt and pepper

3 oz/85 g Greek feta, cut into ½-in/12-mm cubes

Soak the rusks in the tangerine juice to soften.

Place each rusk at the bottom of a soup bowl or salad plate. Drizzle each one with 1 tbsp of the olive oil. Divide the remaining ingredients evenly between the rusks and build the salad, starting with the tomato, and then adding the cucumber, onion, capers, olives, oregano, salt and pepper to taste, and finally the feta cubes, letting them fall around the rusks. Drizzle with the remaining 2 tbsp of olive oil and serve.

FLAVORS OF THE AEGEAN

From my perch in Faro, a seaside village on Ikaria, I can spend hours staring out to sea at the Fournoi islands rising out of the water in the distance, baked purple in the evening sun and surrounded by the deepest blue sea I've ever seen. Islanders in the Aegean live with views like this everywhere, connected by this ancient mariner's sea, and yet cocooned in the customs and traditions of their own unique place. This paradox is apparent in the Aegean kitchen, too.

Each of the eighty-six inhabited Aegean islands has its own cuisine, shaped by the lay of the land, climate, geography, and history. While the local food customs on many of the islands share some common elements, the cuisines of others, like that of Ikaria, are worlds apart. Ikaria is one of the least developed islands. As a result, many of its food traditions are unspoiled. Others, like those of Santorini, Mykonos, Rhodes, and Crete, are a fusion of old and new. The affluence brought about by tourism has made people less dependent on old agrarian ways and less likely to take the trouble to maintain them. Nonetheless, even in the most developed islands, once the tourists go home, people revert to a simpler way of life, one that often revolves around the land and its bounty.

Traces of the past are still visible on island tables. Combinations of pulses and pasta, which we encounter in the Dodecanese, are one example of dishes that seem less Greek and more a legacy of the Italians, who occupied this group of islands for the first half of the nineteenth century. Dishes such as *raviolia* (a sweet in the Aegean), *kaltsounia* (vegetable- or cheese-filled dough packets),

cannellonia (stuffed crêpes), and *tziladia* (jellied fish or pork) may have borrowed something beyond their names from the Venetians and Genoese who once ruled parts of the Aegean. Yet the roots of many of these dishes are also ancient. On water-starved Santorini, the yellow split pea, an ancient pulse, is the most important local raw ingredient, transformed into dozens of dishes. Small game is also important here, but fish not so much, since the island's precipitous cliffs sent most denizens upland to build their villages. On Sifnos and Serifos the chickpea is favored, while in the Dodecanese, both lentils and chickpeas are more common than any other pulse or bean. Throughout the islands, vegetable fritters—easy, cheap food that required no wood for lighting ovens, and little more than what grew wild all around—are a leitmotif, reflecting the most available ingredients: tomato fritters in Santorini, wild fennel fritters in Ikaria and elsewhere, and chickpea fritters in Rhodes. Capers are the mineral-rich little gems that grow wild only on the driest Greek islands, among them Santorini, Mykonos, Sifnos, Naxos, Paros, and Serifos. Greek island meat is almost always goat and pork. The latter supplies protein throughout the year in a wealth of preserved products such as sausages, air-dried tenderloins, and more.

Sweets include a whole array of almond confections, especially in the Cyclades; *pasteli*, the sesame-honey confection, in more than a handful of places; and spoon sweets, which are localized specialties made with what is most abundant—lemon blossoms on Andros, tomatoes on Kos, walnuts on Ikaria, and raisins on Crete.

CHAPTER 2

MEZE

AS I WRITE THIS, MORE THAN A FEW GREEK CHEFS HAVE TAKEN TO CHRISTENING THE MEZE *TAPAS*. WHEN PROVENANCE GETS MIXED UP WITH POLITICS, ADAPTING A SPANISH CUSTOM SEEMS MORE ACCEPTABLE TO THE CURRENT NATIONAL PSYCHE THAN USING A TURKISH WORD.

As for the meze concept—eating, sharing, and washing down small plates of savory food with ample wine, ouzo, or *tsipouro* (similar to grappa), all the better for conversation to flow—that's uniquely Greek.

The idea of socializing around a table laden with all sorts of different foods is deeply rooted in the Mediterranean. I have always believed that the innate healthfulness of the Greek and Mediterranean diets extends beyond nutrition to something deeper, to a sense of well-being that derives from a positive experience at the table. Beyond mere sustenance, there is the human element, the indisputable notion that food and wine are meant to be shared with friends and relatives in a relaxed, unhurried, environment. It's a tradition that fosters what the Greeks call *kefi*—good spirits or mood. No other food tradition conveys this sense of conviviality better than *mezedes* (the plural form of *meze*).

The meze tradition can be traced back to the *propomata* of the ancient symposia, which was the custom of serving a selection of small delicacies to reclining, conversing symposiasts. For Greeks, implicit in a meze meal are distinct but subtle rituals. Mezedes are not antipasti, appetizers, or hors d'oeuvres. They are not part of an extended multi-course meal (a foreign concept in Greece, anyway), but rather an experience in their own right, enjoyed during the afternoon or evening with the goal of teasing rather than sating the palate. The whole point is the sharing and talking that goes hand in hand with a meze spread.

A proper meze spread has a little of everything, from smooth, cooling dips like *tzatziki* (see page 54) to spicy ones such as chile-spiked roasted eggplant spreads (see page 53); from crunchy fresh, salted cucumbers to tart olives; from crisp-fried fish or vegetable patties to succulent small meatballs. Sometimes a small plate of what otherwise would be served as a main course also is appropriate as a meze, such as baked or braised beans, meats, and vegetable stews. Pasta and rice dishes are generally not offered as mezedes, although savory pies and breads are.

Beyond the recipes for dips, spreads, and seafood and fish specialties that follow, mezedes are found throughout the book, in the chapters on eggs and cheese, meats, and vegetables.

HOW TO ASSEMBLE A MEZE SPREAD

It is easy to assemble a meze platter without ever going near the stove. An array of Greek cheeses, olives, and cured fish and meats; pickled or roasted peppers; and sun-dried tomatoes are examples of meze items available at good supermarkets and specialty Greek shops. Crunchy cucumbers marinated in Greek red wine vinegar, wedges of tomatoes sprinkled with coarse salt, *tzatziki* (see page 54), whipped feta and herbs, and bread would make satisfying choices for a vegetarian.

The range of cooked mezedes is vast. A seafood meze selection might include Batter-Fried Mussels (page 66); pickled or grilled octopus (see page 62); grilled or olive-oil-fried shrimp; cured Greek bonito, trout, salmon trout, or sardines; and *avgotaraho* (botargo), which is excellent with chilled *tsipouro*.

For meat lovers, you could offer *keftedes* (fried meatballs); one of the country's regional cured pork delicacies, such as *siglino* from Mani and Crete, chunks of orange-flavored pork in olive oil; sausages; Karpenissi prosciutto; and Lefkada salami.

Small pies make great mezedes, too, and so do many cooked bean dishes. The idea is to provide variety. Many of the dishes mentioned above are now produced by a growing number of artisan companies that use regional ingredients and traditional recipes. You'll find some of these products in the gourmet sections of large American supermarkets.

PAIRING WINES WITH MEZEDES

The type of mezedes offered usually dictates the most suitable quaff. Typically, anything that sprouts from or walks on land is a good match for wine, while anything that swims goes best with ouzo and *tsipouro*.

If one abides by the notion that local wines pair best with local food, then most Greek wines pair naturally with an array of robust mezedes. In the red wine category, the two main grape varietals are the Xinomavro from Naoussa in Macedonia and the Agiorgitiko from Nemea in the Peloponnese. Wines made with these grapes can be found in the United States and Western Europe.

A young Xinomavro pairs well with egg dishes, black olives, sun-dried tomatoes and tomato-based stews, and dishes that are spiced with cinnamon, cloves, and nutmeg. Kebabs, spicy meat dishes, and Greek cheese fritters all go very well with a more robust, older Xinomavro.

Soft Agiorgitiko wines pair up with a wealth of eggplant dishes, which often appear as meze offerings, especially those cooked in generous amounts of olive oil (see the chapter on *ladera*, page 135). Older Nemeas are a good match for wine-based meat stews, cinnamon-flavored meat casseroles, and even charcuterie, such as the fenugreek-rubbed cured beef, *pastourma*.

Greece's white wines tend to be acidic and citrusy. They make a great match for any of the wide range of Greek-style grilled fish and seafood. More aromatic whites made with the Moschofilero grape can stand up to richer seafood dishes flavored with garlic, olive oil, and lemon juice. Moschofilero also pairs well with mint, a popular herb in Greece, as well as with cooked cheeses like saganaki.

Try a crisp, dry Robolla from Cephalonia or an Assyrtiko from Santorini with sharp dips, feta, and strong fish like sardines. These go well with the classic spinach-cheese pie, *spanakopita*, too.

DIPS AND SPREADS

Greece is a country of bread lovers, so it makes sense that the meze table would be filled with offerings into which one can dip a chunk of bread. Dips and spreads qualify as salads according to Greeks and are often called so: *Taramosalata* is the spread made with fish roe, or tarama. *Melitzanosalata* is a smooth or chunky puree of roasted eggplants that is made in dozens of versions around the country. *Tyrosalata* is a spread made with cheese, called *tyri* in Greek.

Dips and spreads are served as part of the grazing landscape of a typical meze table. Greeks like to serve them together with fried fish, seafood, or with vegetables, either boiled or fried. The dips tend to be shamelessly robust, garlic-rich affairs that beg for a strong drink like ouzo or retsina, which can stand up to such forthright flavors.

RETSINA: GREECE'S OFFICIAL TRADITIONAL WINE

The best wine for the robust array of Greek mezedes may be the most traditional but also most problematic one: retsina, the resinated white wine that is a trademark of the Greek table. What exactly is it? Retsina is one of two officially designated traditional wines. It is produced in Attica, Viotia, and Evia, mainly from the region's local Savatiano and Roditis grape varietals. There is also a rosé retsina, called *kokineli*, made with either the Roditis grape or, more recently, with Xinomavro (indigenous to Naoussa) or Assyrtiko (native of Santorini).

Classic retsina is made just like any white wine, from pressing to fermentation in steel tanks. The only difference is that a small amount of pine resin, specifically from the Aleppo pine, is added at the start of fermentation. Aleppo pine (*Pinus halpensis*) flourishes all over the southern Mediterranean, but especially in Attica, Evia, Corinth, and the prefecture of Ilia in the western Peloponnese.

There are many theories on how the custom of adding pine to wine came to be. One thing is for sure: Greek winemakers have been making resinated wine since antiquity. Pine resin, which is notably thick, is both a natural sealant and an antiseptic. It is thought that the ancients used it to seal the clay amphorae in which wine was transported.

Unfortunately, the use of resin became a way to camouflage bad white wine, and retsina for a long time was a proverbial stain on the Greek wine industry, which, by the 1980s, was producing world-class wines. As Greeks themselves became more cosmopolitan, they snubbed rustic retsina in favor of the exciting new Greek vintages, expertly made by well-trained enologists.

However, retsina is now enjoying a renaissance of its own, thanks to the thoughtful approach of a few brave winemakers, who see in retsina a signature Greek wine that needs to be ushered into the twenty-first century. The new retsinas are crisp, light on the pine, yet based on the same traditional grape varieties. They have been taken out of the beer-cap bottle and poured into classier bottles with hip, modern labels, making Greece's best-known pour a fitting one for the international market. Certainly, no mention of mezedes would be complete without a toast to retsina.

BASIC ROASTED EGGPLANT SALAD AND VARIATIONS ON THE THEME

BASIKI MELITZANOSALATA KAI DIAFORES EKDOHES

SERVES 4 TO 6

Melitzanosalata, roasted eggplant spread, comes in too many versions to count. Regional variations from Macedonia are coarsely textured with ground walnuts and garlic, and spiced with hot peppers or tempered with sweet roasted red Florina peppers. In the Cyclades islands southeast of the mainland, *melitzanosalata* includes capers. Richer versions are made with milk, cream, or yogurt—specialties of the Greeks who came to the country as refugees from Turkey almost a century ago. There is something so inherently satisfying about the flavor and aroma of the flesh from a smoky, charred eggplant that many cooks are inspired to come up with their own riffs. Below is a very basic recipe (pictured on the facing page, top), to which you can add almost anything, and some variations.

3 lb/1.4 kg eggplants

Juice of 1 lemon

½ cup/120 ml extra-virgin Greek olive oil

Salt

Pinch of sugar

Place the eggplants on a low open flame, such as a gas burner or grill, and roast, turning with kitchen tongs, until the skin is charred and the very top of the eggplant, near the stem—which is the densest part of the flesh—is soft and spongy. Remove with tongs and transfer to a bowl. Cover with plastic wrap and set aside to cool.

Stir the lemon juice into a bowl of water. Transfer the eggplants to a cutting board and, using a sharp paring or chef's knife, cut them open lengthwise down the center. Cut around the contours of each eggplant and peel back its skin. With a spoon, remove the pulp and seeds in large chunks and drop into the lemon water. Let stand for 30 minutes, then drain well. Try to remove as many seeds as possible without wasting too much pulp.

Pour the olive oil into a nonreactive mixing bowl and transfer the eggplant pulp to the bowl. Stir and mash simultaneously with a fork until the eggplant has absorbed the olive oil but is still chunky. Season with salt and add the sugar. Serve immediately.

VARIATIONS: For a spicy-sweet rendition of Greek *melitzanosalata*, add to the mashed eggplants: 1 red bell pepper, roasted, peeled, and seeded (see Note on page 70); ½ to 1 tsp chopped fresh chile pepper; 3 oz/85 g of Greek feta cheese, crumbled; 2 tsp rinsed and drained capers; 1 medium garlic clove, peeled and crushed; 1 tbsp Greek sweet vinegar (*glykadi*) or balsamic vinegar; and 2 tsp grape must syrup (*petimezi*).

A version from the island of Tinos calls for adding to the mashed eggplants: 1 finely chopped medium red onion; 3 minced garlic cloves; 3 tbsp rinsed and drained capers; 1 large tomato, peeled, seeded, and diced; and 4 tbsp chopped fresh parsley.

For a completely different texture and rich flavor, transfer the mashed eggplants to a food processor and add 1 tbsp thick Greek yogurt, 3 minced garlic cloves, 1 tbsp red wine vinegar, and ½ cup/60 g walnuts. Pulse until the walnuts are ground and the *melitzanosalata* is a smooth purée.

STARCHLESS TARAMA SALAD

TARAMOSALATA XORIS AMYLO

SERVES 6

Traditional recipes blend the salty, grainy cod or carp roe, which is called *tarama*, with boiled potatoes, stale bread, and sometimes sweet nuts, such as almonds. Here I treat the *taramosalata* as mayonnaise, on the logic that roe is nothing more than eggs, so emulsifiable. The result is creamy (pictured on the facing page, center).

6 tbsp cold water

6 tbsp/100 g tarama, preferably white

Juice of 1 lemon, strained

⅔ cup/160 ml olive or canola oil

In the bowl of a food processor, whip together the water, tarama, and lemon juice. Drizzle the olive or canola oil (you can use a combination of both for lighter flavor) slowly into the mixture, working the motor all the while, until the *taramosalata* is as smooth and silky as mayonnaise.

VARIATION: Whip 2 to 3 tbsp of chopped smoked trout fillet into the mixture.

CLASSIC YOGURT, CUCUMBER, AND GARLIC DIP

KLASSIKO TZATZIKI

===== SERVES 6 =====

Yogurt is one of Greece's most beguiling traditional foods and one of its most popular exports, found nowadays in supermarkets all over the United States and Western Europe. Real Greek yogurt is creamy and thick and almost shockingly tart and sour. Traditional country Greek yogurt is made from sheep's or goat's milk and is often strained and very thick. Cow's milk yogurt was pretty rare in Greece until a generation ago. Now, major Greek yogurt producers and exporters make both strained and unstrained cow's milk yogurt.

No one knows for sure quite when this ancient food first made its appearance in the world but it was probably created in a warm climate, which facilitates the souring of milk, most likely by a nomadic group whose itinerant lifestyle forced them to live almost exclusively on whatever their animals provided. English classicist Andrew Dalby reports in his book *Siren Feasts* that the ancient Greeks consumed a product called *pyriati*, which Galen, the second century B.C. physician-philosopher refers to as *oxygala,* which means "sour milk." Today in the Greek countryside, the array of sour milk products, which modern Greeks categorize as cheese but which bear an uncanny resemblance to yogurt, abound.

Traditionally, yogurt was often the evening meal in Greece. It is also a component in or a side to countless cooked dishes, especially spicy meats, soups made with tomatoes, trahana, or bulgur, and greens pies with cornmeal crusts. It is also served as a dessert with honey or spoon sweets and used in cake batters for moistness and texture.

Tzatziki, one of the best-known Greek dips, is, of course, based on yogurt. It is a dish with roots in the distant past. Pierre Belon, the sixteenth-century French naturalist and traveler to Greece, reports in his book *Observations of Several Curiosities and Memorable Objects* that Greeks and Ottomans alike at Topkapi enjoyed a dish of pounded garlic mixed with *oxygala.*

1 large cucumber, peeled and seeded

2 cups/480 ml thick Greek yogurt, chilled

2 to 3 garlic cloves, minced

2 tbsp chopped fresh dill

3 tbsp extra-virgin Greek olive oil

1 tbsp red wine vinegar (optional)

Salt

Grate the cucumber on the coarse side of a box grater. Drain in a fine-mesh sieve for 10 minutes. Then, taking a handful at a time, squeeze out as much of the excess liquid as possible. Transfer to a medium mixing bowl.

Stir in the yogurt, garlic, dill, olive oil, vinegar, if using, and salt to taste. Mix well. Serve immediately. *Tzatziki* goes really well with toasted pita bread and with any of the fritters recipes (see pages 73 to 79). It should be served cold.

ARCADIAN WALNUT SKORDALIA

SKORDALIA ME KARYDIA APO TIN ARCADIA

===== SERVES 6 =====

Skordalia, a Greek garlic dip, belongs to the grand tradition of Mediterranean garlic pastes, in the same vein as aioli. It contains no eggs, however.

In Greece, skordalia almost always plays an accompanying role to fried fish and seafood—the classics being batter-fried salt cod (see page 246), batter-fried sand shark or skate, and Batter-Fried Mussels (page 66). It is also paired with some boiled vegetables, such as beets, zucchini, cauliflower, and sweet summer greens. Skordalia is delicious with fried vegetable slices, especially eggplant, pumpkin, and zucchini.

There are many regional versions of skordalia. Garlic, olive oil, and salt are the constants in all Greek skordalia recipes, but the base ingredients, the acid, and the dip's consistency vary from place to place. Dry bread, boiled potatoes, and nuts—especially almonds, pine nuts, or walnuts—may all be used as the base of this pungent specialty, either alone or together with stale bread or potatoes. Fresh lemon juice, fish stock or broth, and vinegar help balance the flavors. At least one version, a traditional recipe of the Asia Minor Greeks, calls for pistachios. The skordalia of the town of Neos Marmaras in the prefecture of Halkidiki is made with feta and mint. One delicious, obscure recipe popular in the traditional cooking of the Greeks who came to Greece from the Black Sea, is made with either walnuts and almonds, yogurt, and vinegar or lemon juice. The following recipe hails from Arcadia, in the Peloponnese.

½ loaf stale bread, crusts removed

3 to 7 garlic cloves (to taste), minced

Salt

1 cup/120 g coarsely ground walnuts

½ to ¾ cup/120 to 180 ml extra-virgin Greek olive oil

2 tbsp strained fresh lemon juice

2 tbsp red wine vinegar

Pepper

Break the bread into large chunks, dampen them under cold running water, and squeeze dry very well in the palms of your hands.

Combine the garlic and a little salt in a large mortar, and with the pestle, pound to a paste. Add the bread and walnuts. Pound all together with the pestle while slowly drizzling in the olive oil, lemon juice, and vinegar, alternating between them. Continue pounding until the mixture is uniform, but grainy. Season the skordalia with salt and pepper and stir. Serve at room temperature or chilled.

NOTE: The mortar and pestle remain the best tools for making skordalia because they give the cook more control of the speed with which he or she breaks down the starch in the potatoes or bread for the base. A food processor's blade is too swift and violent and usually results in a gummy skordalia. However, you may use a food processor to make skordalia with caution. Crush the garlic with the side of a knife, and put it in the bowl of the processor with a little salt and the bread. Pulse for a few seconds, until the bread becomes mealy. Add the nuts and pulse to a coarse meal. Add the liquids, alternating between them and pulsing after each addition, until the skordalia is uniform. Be careful not to process too much or it will become gummy. Serve immediately.

VARIATIONS: Replace the walnuts with almonds, omit the vinegar, and increase the amount of lemon juice to ¼ cup/60 ml. Pound as described above, adding 3 tbsp of thick Greek yogurt to the mixture.

You can also add tahini to the mix and toast the walnuts, in a variation from Mt. Pelion, in Thessaly. Toast the walnuts in a dry frying pan over medium heat. Omit the vinegar, and increase the amount of lemon juice to ¼ cup/60 ml, or to taste. Pound as described above, adding 2 tbsp of tahini and ½ to ⅔ cup/120 to 160 ml of water as you pound. Toss in some chopped fresh or dried mint. This skordalia is looser than most and makes a great sauce for boiled vegetables.

For a third variation, an old recipe from Arcadia, replace the walnuts with cooked ground chestnuts.

CRETAN MASHED FAVA BEAN SKORDALIA

SKORDALIA ME FRESKA KOUKIA APO TIN KRITI

===== SERVES 4 TO 6 =====

On Crete, there are dozens of island recipes for fresh and dried fava beans, even a few that call for grilling them like popcorn on a hot metal plate or potbellied stove. Mashed fava beans are typically served with salted fish, such as sardines and anchovies, and are a great meze for the island's local firewater, raki.

2 cups/900 g shelled fresh fava beans

¼ cup/60 ml strained fresh lemon juice

3 to 4 tbsp water

2 garlic cloves, minced

Salt and pepper

¼ to ½ cup/60 to 120 ml extra-virgin Greek olive oil

Using a sharp paring knife, remove the black "eye" from the fava beans. Blanch for 5 minutes in salted water and drain. Peel the outer skin off each bean and transfer to a blender.

Purée the beans with the lemon juice, water, garlic, and salt and pepper to taste until a thick mass is formed. With the blender running, gradually add the olive oil, blending until smooth and velvety. Taste for salt and pepper. Serve immediately or refrigerate to set slightly and serve cold.

CEPHALONIAN GARLIC-POTATO PURÉE

SKORDALIA, OR ALIADA

SERVES 8 TO 10

In the Ionian islands, skordalia is called *aliada*. Perhaps nowhere are the rituals of making skordalia older or more entrenched than among the elderly cooks of Cephalonia. Mortar and pestle are de rigueur as the cook pounds garlic cloves and salt to a smooth paste. In a separate bowl, tradi- tionally made of wood or fired clay, she mashes boiled pota- toes either with the pestle or with a fist-size smooth stone. A pot nearby contains salt cod that has been soaked and is now simmering to further desalt it. Its broth provides the gustatory undertones and depth of flavor in the final *aliada* and is added to the garlic and salt, to be followed by a few spoonfuls of partially mashed potatoes. Slowly, step by step and increment by increment, each of these ingredients is wedded to the final smooth and silky potato-based *aliada*, which is partnered with crispy fried salt cod or other small fried fish. Serve *aliada* with boiled vegetables or fried fish.

8 medium potatoes, peeled

8 to 10 garlic cloves, peeled and trimmed

½ to 1½ tsp salt

½ to 1 cup/120 to 240 ml hot cod or another fish broth

Extra-virgin Greek olive oil as needed

Juice of 2 lemons, strained

Put the potatoes in a large pot of salted water and bring to a boil. Reduce the heat and simmer until the potatoes are fork-tender.

Meanwhile, in a large mortar with a pestle, pound the garlic and salt to taste to make a thick paste. Add several tbsp of hot broth and pound until smooth.

Remove several potatoes from the pot and transfer to a large wide bowl. Mash with the pestle or a fork until chunky and add to the mortar, pounding the already mashed potatoes together with the garlic paste. Add olive oil, lemon juice, and additional fish broth as needed. Continue pounding and adding more potatoes, followed by oil, lemon juice, and broth until you've used up the potatoes and the mixture is smooth. Taste for salt and adjust the seasoning as needed before serving.

SYROS CHOPPED PARSLEY SALAD

MAINTANOSALATA SYROU

SERVES 8 TO 12

This recipe first appeared in my book *Aegean Cuisine*, published in Greece in 2008. It's a little like Italian pesto, and speaks volumes about the Venetian influence on the cooking of many Cycladic islands, where the doge ruled between the thirteenth and seventeenth centuries. This dish (pictured on page 52, bottom) is also one of countless ancient Mediterranean pastes made with stale bread and herbs. They are a vehicle for using up everything in the kitchen, turning even the humblest ingre- dients into something tasty. Try this on toasted bread, toss it with warm potatoes, or serve as a dip for everything from grilled meat to toasted pita.

2 cups/120 g chopped fresh flat-leaf parsley

1 large onion, finely chopped

2 garlic cloves, minced

2 tsp capers, rinsed, drained, and chopped

2 cups/100 g coarse dry bread crumbs (see Note)

½ to 1 cup/120 to 240 ml extra-virgin Greek olive oil

Juice of 1 lemon, strained

2 to 3 tbsp red wine vinegar

Salt and pepper

In the bowl of a food processor or in a large mortar with a pestle, pulse or pound the parsley, onion, garlic, and capers to a paste. Add the bread crumbs and toss or pulse to combine. Slowly add the olive oil, lemon juice, and vinegar in alternating streams, pulsing or pounding well after each addition. Continue mixing until the mix- ture is a smooth paste. Season with salt and pepper and serve.

NOTE: To make dry bread crumbs, take several slices of stale bread and arrange in a single layer on an ungreased cookie sheet. Bake in a preheated 300°F/150°C/gas 2 oven for 10 to 14 minutes, turning once. Remove from the oven, cool the bread, and shred. Transfer to the bowl of a food processor and pulse to grind.

GREEK SPIRITS: OUZO AND TSIPOURO

The two main spirits of Greece are ouzo and *tsipouro*. Ouzo, the anise-flavored national drink of Greece that turns milky white with the addition of water, is the liquor of conviviality. It's what one drinks—with company—before an array of colorful mezedes, a perfect choice, in fact, since it can stand up to the strongest flavors, from garlic to fried fish. As a rule, ouzo is the drink that accompanies seafood mezedes, while wine is best for meat-based small plates.

Ouzo's flavor reflects the spice mix each producer uses and the method of distillation. It is usually made from grain alcohol, but may also be distilled from grapes, or a combination of grapes and grain alcohol, or from potatoes. A handful of places, settled by Asia Minor Greeks in 1922 (who brought the art of making ouzo with them), have become synonymous with ouzo production: the island of Lesvos; Tyrnavo in the prefecture of Larissa, on the mainland; and Thessaloniki, on the northeastern coast. But ouzo is made all over Greece, and there are hundreds and hundreds of regional labels. The biggest ones have been bought out in recent years by large European beverage makers. Anise is the most recognizable spice in ouzo's flavor profile, but a whole range of other spices goes into the mix, from star anise to fennel seeds to herbs. Each producer has its own secret recipe.

The best ouzo is 100 percent distilled. Other ouzos are a combination of grain alcohol and distilled flavored spirit.

The water used to dilute the distilled spirit so that it reaches the desired alcohol content affects ouzo's flavor. Soft water produces light, smooth ouzos with soft mouthfeel; alkaline water produces a more angular final drink. Ouzo may be dry or sweet. Most connoisseurs prefer the drier kind; sweet ouzo has been enhanced with syrup or grape concentrate.

Ouzo is served in straight, relatively tall glasses, either straight up, on the rocks, or with both ice and cold water. It turns white thanks to a chemical compound called anethole, which is produced when the anise seeds macerate in the alcohol. When the drink is diluted to less than 38 percent alcohol by adding, say, water or ice, it causes the ouzo to cloud, giving it the characteristic milky hue.

While ouzo is definitely better known outside Greece than *tsipouro*, the latter is the spirit Greek food and drink enthusiasts like to imbibe most. *Tsipouro*, unlike ouzo, is a grape distillate and is usually—though not always—unflavored, allowing the grape's unique varietal character to shine. Produced in the fall, after the grapes have been pressed for wine, *tsipouro* is sipped as an aperitif, digestive, and all-around welcoming quaff, even in the unlikeliest locales. It is, for example, a typical offering in monasteries, many of which produce their own *tsipouro*. In small villages all over Crete, where it is something of a national drink, *tsipouro* is sometimes the morning brew that accompanies a steaming bowl of porridge.

The best *tsipouro* is distilled twice and is very smooth. Aromatic grape varietals such as Muscat make delicious distillations, while red varieties such as the northern Greek Xinomavro grape make a fuller-bodied drink. *Tsipouro* should be savored chilled.

LESVOS GREEN SPLIT PEA PURÉE

PRASINI FAVA LESVOU

===== SERVES 6 TO 8 =====

Fava in Greek refers to a legume purée that is made with yellow split peas but also, in some places, with dried fava beans. This recipe comes from Lesvos, from a small taverna about fifteen minutes outside Mytilene, its capital city. Green peas grow rampant on the island, especially near the fields of anise, which is cultivated to supply the island's thriving ouzo business.

Split pea *fava*, whether green or yellow, is a canvas for almost any topping, from grilled octopus to stewed vegetables. Try serving it garnished with baby arugula leaves and scallions, caramelized endives or leeks, grilled sliced sausages, or even truffle oil.

1 lb/455 g green or yellow split peas, rinsed

½ to 1 cup/120 to 240 ml extra-virgin Greek olive oil, plus more to drizzle

1 large onion, trimmed and quartered

2 bay leaves

Salt

Juice of 1 to 2 lemons, strained

1 medium red onion, chopped

Dried Greek oregano

Salted or brined sardine or anchovy fillets (optional, instead of the onion and oregano)

Rinse and drain the split peas.

Heat ⅓ cup/80 ml of the olive oil in a large, wide pot over low heat and sweat the onion until soft. Add the split peas, and stir to coat in the oil. Add the bay leaves and enough water to cover the split peas by 2 in/5 cm. Bring to a boil over medium heat, reduce the heat to low, and simmer until the mixture is thick and creamy and the peas have absorbed all the water, stirring occasionally to keep the peas from scorching on the bottom of the pot. Add a little more water if needed during cooking. Season with salt about 10 minutes before it's done. Remove from the heat and discard the bay leaves. Place a clean kitchen towel over the top of the pot, and let sit for about 20 minutes.

Using an immersion blender or food processor, purée the hot *fava*, adding lemon juice to taste and as much of the remaining olive oil as you need to create a smooth and creamy dish, alternating between the two liquids. Set aside, covered with the towel, until cooled and set. Spread the *fava* on a platter or spoon into a bowl, drizzle generously with additional olive oil, and garnish with the onions and oregano to taste, or with the sardine fillets. Serve.

VARIATION: You can try adding about ⅓ cup/80 ml milk to the hot *fava* as you purée it in the blender. This is a trick from my friend the Michelin-starred restaurateur Lefteris Lazarou. It gives the *fava* an extra smooth and creamy texture.

KASSOS TINY STUFFED GRAPE LEAVES

DOLMADAKIA KASSIOTIKA

===== SERVES 8 TO 10 =====

On several of the smaller Dodecanese islands, you can still see garlands of papery, sun-dried grape leaves hanging from the rafters of country grocers. Home cooks either pick their own grape leaves or buy them at the farmers' markets when they are in season in May and freeze them to use year-round. What distinguishes this recipe from others for stuffed grape leaves is their size and filling: It is common, especially in the islands, to make the smallest possible stuffed leaves, as though their diminutive size demonstrates the cook's skills. Kassos is known all over Greece for its tiny stuffed grape leaves, which, in the local dialect, are called *doumaes*. The filling always contains ground meat.

½ cup/120 ml extra-virgin Greek olive oil

4 large red onions, minced

⅔ cup/130 g medium-grain rice, such as Greek Carolina

1 lb/455 g ground beef

2 tbsp tomato paste diluted in 2 tbsp water

Salt and pepper

60 to 70 brined grape leaves

2 large, firm tomatoes, peeled, seeded, cored, and cut into ⅛-in-/3-mm-thick rounds, or juice of 1 lemon, strained

DOLMADES

I am not sure if there is a classic recipe for dolmades, or stuffed grape leaves. This well-known Greek dish is one of those polyethnic recipes, like baklava and pilaf, that people declare their own in regions far and wide, from Iraq to Bulgaria.

Being Greek American, however, I have always chauvinistically considered dolmades a dish that belongs solely to the culinary traditions of the land my father left behind. We ate them in the down-and-dirty Greek restaurants on Ninth Avenue in Manhattan, where we enjoyed many Sunday meals during the 1960s. We made them at home only on holidays because they are time-consuming to prepare. The whole kitchen would turn into a makeshift production line as my dad, the family cook, prepared the rice filling, blanched the commercially brined leaves (fresh leaves in New York City were impossible to come by then), laid them out, dotted them with filling, and rolled and rolled, a cigarette often dangling from his lip, in true old Greek cook fashion.

After doing some bedside culinary research, I have to admit that the Greek pedigree for dolmades is questionable. For one thing, the word *dolmades* comes from the Turkish, *yaprak dolmasi*, which means "stuffed vine leaf." And dolmades are stuffed with rice, a relative newcomer to the Greek kitchen, having made its way north and west from Persia into Turkey and then into Greece slowly over the course of the first millennium.

Today in Greece, dolmades are still made at home, mostly on holidays, but are pretty standard fare on taverna menus all over the country. The variety of Greek dolmades is mind-boggling. One meatless version is *dolmades yalantzi*, which are filled with rice, herbs, onions, and often raisins and pine nuts. *Yalantzi* dolmades are served during fasting periods but also are enoyed with a rich mound of thick Greek yogurt. Meatless dolmades are eaten cold or at room temperature and are served as a meze.

Then there are the meat-and-rice-filled dolmades, which are heartier, and always served warm. They are often considered a main course, and are usually served with avgolemono sauce, the traditional egg-and-lemon mixture, or béchamel. The meat can be either ground lamb or beef, or a combination of the two. There are some other, more obscure, regional dolmades recipes, such as the one filled with eggplant, or with pumpkin and rice, from the island of Kalymnos; with bulgur and cumin from Rhodes; bulgur and dried fava beans from the Asia Minor Greek immigrants; and with salt cod, rice, and herbs from the Peloponnese. One rule stands out when it comes to preparing dolmades: They must contain onions, which lend the requisite sweetness, regardless of the region from which the dolmades hail.

Heat ¼ cup/60 ml of the olive oil in a large, wide, deep frying pan or sauté pan over medium heat, and cook the onions, stirring, until very soft, about 12 minutes. Add the rice and stir to coat in the oil. Cook together for about 3 minutes and remove from the heat. Set aside to cool slightly and transfer to a large mixing bowl. Add the ground meat and diluted tomato paste. Season with salt and pepper and set aside, covered.

Bring a large pot of water to a rolling boil and blanch the leaves for 1 to 2 minutes, to soften. Remove with a slotted spoon, transfer immediately to a colander, and rinse under cold running water. Place the leaves vein-side up in rows on a clean work surface. Snip off the tough stems, and cut all but the smallest leaves in half lengthwise.

Place 1 tsp of filling in the center of each leaf, near the bottom. Fold in the sides and then roll the leaves up from the bottom toward the top to form small cylinders no larger than an average woman's pinkie.

Oil a large, wide pot and place a layer of ripped or otherwise unusable leaves on the bottom. Place half the rolled grape leaves seam-side down in the pot, packing them in together neatly and snugly in one layer. If using the tomatoes, layer half of the slices over the stuffed leaves. Place a second layer of rolled grape leaves on top, and cover those, too, with tomato rounds. Alternatively, pour in the lemon juice after placing the second layer of rolled grape leaves directly over the first.

Pour the remaining ¼ cup/60 ml olive oil into the pot and add enough water to come about two-thirds of the way up the rolled grape leaves. Cut a piece of wax or parchment paper to fit the circumference of the pot, and place over the leaves. Cover with a heat-proof plate, and then place the lid on the pot. Bring to a boil over medium-high heat, reduce the heat to low, and simmer for about 30 minutes, or until the rice and leaves are tender. Serve immediately.

GRILLED OCTOPUS

HTAPODI STIN SCHARA

===== SERVES 4 =====

Grilled octopus, like Greek salad, is an iconic dish, a postcard image of Greek cuisine in all its elemental glory. It's just as easy to do well at home in a backyard barbecue as it is to do in a restaurant. The trick is to understand what the final texture should be: not so soft from overboiling that the octopus is stringy and flaccid, not so tough from undercooking that you can't bite through it. Marinating for several hours or overnight helps. Great grilled octopus is like great steak in that you have to work at it a little, by chewing, to get at the real flavor.

1 medium octopus (about 4 lb/1.8 kg)

3 garlic cloves, crushed

1 bay leaf

2 to 3 fresh thyme sprigs

½ cup/120 ml dry red wine

½ cup/120 ml red wine vinegar

½ cup/120 ml extra-virgin Greek olive oil

2 to 3 dried Greek oregano sprigs, or 1 tsp dried oregano

1 tsp cracked black pepper

Coarse salt or sea salt (optional)

Using a large, sharp knife, cut off the octopus's sacklike hood just below the eyes and discard. Cut the octopus into 8 pieces along its tentacles. Place in a heavy saucepan with 1 garlic clove, the bay leaf, and thyme sprigs, and cover with the lid. Cook over low heat for 35 to 55 minutes (every octopus cooks up a little differently), or until the tentacles are tender. Do not overcook or the pink skin will become stringy. While cooking, the octopus will exude its own liquid—the sea, as the Greeks say. Remove from the heat and let cool slightly.

Measure out ½ cup/120 ml of the octopus's pan juices and discard the rest. Put the octopus in a container with a lid and add the reserved pan juices, the remaining 2 garlic cloves, the red wine, wine vinegar, olive oil, dried oregano, and pepper. If you like, taste for salt before adding. (Most octopus, especially if fished in the Mediterranean, is savory enough so that it does not need salt.) Marinate for at least 2 hours or overnight in the refrigerator. Bring to room temperature before grilling.

When ready to cook, light a hot fire in the grill or preheat a gas grill to medium. Remove the octopus tentacles from the marinade, pat dry, and grill for 8 to 10 minutes, or until lightly charred and tender. Serve hot.

VARIATION: Instead of marinating the octopus, before cooking it in the pot, add all the marinade ingredients to the pot. When the octopus is done, let cool in the pot, drain, and grill.

SEAFOOD MEZEDES

Nothing speaks of mezedes better than the bounty of the sea. The variety of seafood mezedes in Greece is enormous. Many dishes are regional specialties. Sea urchin, for example, is a delicacy found most commonly in the seaside tavernas of Crete. Grilled sardines belong to the entrenched meze culture of Thessaloniki but also, of course, to Lesvos, where sardines from the Bay of Kalloni (see page 240) are one of the country's most sought-after treats. Mountains of shrimp are boiled, fried, or grilled for classic mezedes; but the most cherished is the tiny fresh shrimp from Symi, a tiny island off the coast of Rhodes, and the southeastern Dodecanese islands. Regardless of the size, Greeks prefer to cook their shrimp with the shells on so the shrimp will retain its juices. Octopus is an all-time classic meze. There are dozens of ways to sample octopus all over Greece, but grilled octopus—charred, leathery, but toothsome—is the king of mezedes.

Fresh fish, preserved fish, and all sorts of fish croquettes—especially cod—make up a large part of the meze menu. Greeks prefer small fish over large ones as a meze, and like them mostly floured and fried. No self-respecting food lover squeezes lemon over fried fish because doing so results in a soggy rather than crunchy bite. Classics among the small species meant for the frying pan are bogue, whiting, and small fresh anchovies. Anchovies are also one of the great preserved fish. (Greeks leave them in salt and vinegar for a brief few hours and then preserve them in olive oil.)

Seafood mezedes are usually tangy, salty, and filled with the pleasant flavors of the sea, which includes faint hints of iodine and salt water. These are flavors that stand up well to some of Greece's crisp white wines, but the best thing to drink with seafood mezedes is ouzo.

VOLOS: MEZE MECCA

While mezedes and meze restaurants are part of the whole Greek culinary landscape, some places are singularly associated with the tradition. These tend to be places, such as Thessaloniki and Volos, where Greeks from Asia Minor settled in large numbers. Volos, a small city along the central coast of mainland Greece, developed a whole culture around mezedes, coupled with a thriving distilling industry, especially for *tsipouro* (similar to Italian grappa), in nearby Tyrnavos.

The restaurants that are devoted to serving *tsipouro* and mezedes are called *tsipouradika*, and they are an institution in Volos. The tradition began in 1922, with the arrival of Greek refugees from Turkey. Many were longshoremen who liked a shot or two of local Tyrnavos *tsipouro* straight up at any time of the day, typically out of small thimble-sized shot glasses. It was customary to stop by a *tsipouradika* for a shot on the way home, no sitting required. The *tsipouradika* were a man's world up through the late 1960s, but with the slow appearance of small food offerings such as grilled octopus, pickled cabbage, salted fish, and cheese, women began to venture in as customers, too, always accompanied by their spouses.

Volos's bustling docks welcomed local fishermen with their catch in an ad hoc market every morning— something that still exists in the city. These fishermen saw a small but growing market for delicacies such as shrimp and other shellfish, and small fish in the ever-more-popular *tsipouradika*. These small, rustic, working-class restaurants typically had no kitchen—just a makeshift grill for the seafood and maybe a potato or two. But a ritual evolved around the order of the food served, starting with a grilled octopus tentacle, then a bit of pickled cabbage or eggplant, then on to ever-more-salty preserved fish.

Local specialties began to make a dent on the menus, exotic things like batter-fried sea anemones, octopus ink pan-fried in butter, and pan-fried tails of small monkfish. No matter how intricate the menu, though, good-quality *tsipouro* and well-executed octopus were de rigueur. They remain the standard-bearers of *tsipouradika* to this day, even when there are forty or fifty offerings, which is sometimes the case. Each one is brought out in the traditional order, starting with delicacies subtle in flavor and moving on to more robust or spicy offerings with each round of *tsipouro*.

In Volos and its environs, especially in the villages of nearby Mt. Pelion, the meze and *tsipouro* tradition lives on. The idea of teasing the appetite is often forgotten these days as customers typically make a night of it, dining on more than a small array of mezedes and downing more than a quick thimbleful of *tsipouro*.

PORTRAIT OF A MUSSEL MAN

Morning in Katerini, a large seaside city just south of Thessaloniki in northern Greece, is a busy time, especially if you're in the taverna business and especially if your taverna is known all the way to Salonika and beyond for its excellent shellfish. For Nikos Hatzis, owner of Odos Ydras, one of the most famous tavernas, morning is doubly busy. Hatzis, a stout, robust, friendly man of about forty, owes much of his renown to two things: He knows how to run a shipshape eating establishment and he has an almost maniacal obsession with quality. The latter drove him, a few years ago, to join the legion of mussel farmers who cultivate this tasty, nutritious bivalve in the rich, sweet-salty waters of the Thermaikos Gulf.

Hatzis, like all mussel farmers, rents a plot of sea, typically around 20 to 30 *stremmata* (5 to 8 acres/2 to 3 hectares), from the local port authority. He goes out almost daily in his boat, a special flat-bottomed vessel outfitted with a crane. With the help of his partner and several crew members, he pulls up the vertical ropes, which are connected to a network of floating ropes and barrels. The mussels grow along the vertical ropes in colonies. When they reach a certain size, Hatzis is there, mechanically plucking them off. Then the mussels are scrubbed and packed on board his boat or at a packing plant near the dock. From there they are trucked or flown within twenty-four hours to Italy, a major market for Greek mussels, and also to France, Belgium, the Netherlands, and, even, ironically, Spain, the world's largest producer of farmed mussels. But a considerable part of Hatzis's daily catch goes to feeding his loyal clientele, who know time is of the essence when it comes to savoring shellfish. The fresher the better.

BATTER-FRIED MUSSELS

MYDIA TIGANITA

===== SERVES 4 TO 6 =====

Mussels are an ancient delicacy fished from the shallow, cove-laced waters off Greece's northern mainland. Most mussels are farmed today, and the total annual Greek catch is around 35,000 tons/31,752 metric tons. Mussel farming has become an important maritime industry, especially in the Thermaikos Gulf, which stretches from Salonika down the coast of Pieria south of Mt. Olympus, where about 350 producers farm. Conditions are ideal here for mussels, thanks to a handful of cold rivers that empty into the gulf, keeping the salinity levels below 15 percent and the water temperature a comfy 60°F/16°C. About two dozen other farms are located farther north, around Kavala, as well as in Halkidiki, which supplies most of Athens. Lesvos, Limnos, the Gulf of Corinth, just below Delphi, and the rich coastal waters off western Greece, between Igoumenitsa and Preveza, are also home to mussel farms. Throughout Greek waters the black mussel *Mytilus galloprovincialis* is the only species farmed. It is renowned for its plump flesh and high liquid content, which gives it a characteristic succulence. These are excellent accompanied by skordalia (see pages 54 to 57).

30 fresh mussels in the shell or frozen shucked mussels

BATTER

¾ cup/90 g all-purpose flour

¾ cup/90 g rice flour (*nisiste*) or cornstarch

2 tbsp ouzo

1 tbsp unseasoned white wine vinegar

1 tsp extra-virgin Greek olive oil

1 tsp sugar

1½ to 2 cups/360 to 480 ml water

Vegetable oil for frying

If using fresh mussels, scrub them very well and remove their little beards. Put in a steamer with 2 in/5 cm of water, cover, and steam for 5 to 7 minutes, or until the mussel shells open. Remove the mussels from the pot and drain. Discard any that have not opened. Remove the mussels from their shells and set aside. If using frozen shucked mussels, defrost and rinse them.

To make the batter: Combine all the ingredients except the water in a large bowl. Add 1½ cups/360 ml of the water and whisk until smooth and about as thick as pancake batter. Add more water if necessary. Let the batter sit at room temperature for 30 minutes to 1 hour.

In a large, deep frying pan, heat 3 in/7.5 cm of oil to 350°F/175°C. Mix the mussels into the batter. Remove a few at a time with a slotted spoon, allowing the excess batter to drip off, and drop them into the hot oil. Fry 7 or 8 mussels at a time. They will take just a few seconds to turn golden. Remove and drain on paper towels. Serve them hot.

PAN-FRIED SMALL SHRIMP

GARIDAKIA STO TIGANI

===== SERVES 4 TO 6 =====

Greeks fry shrimp in their shells, which helps retain their juiciness. These are floured, fried in hot oil, and served immediately. They are as crunchy as popcorn and go down just as easily.

1 lb/455 g small shrimp, with their shells on

Flour for dredging

Salt

Olive or another oil for frying

1 lemon, quartered

Rinse the shrimp under cold running water and set aside.

On a large plate, combine the flour and salt. Dredge the shrimp in the flour, turning once to coat both sides. Shake in the palm of your hand or in a colander to remove the excess flour and transfer to a clean plate.

While dredging the shrimp, heat about ¼ in/6 mm of oil in a large, heavy frying pan over high heat. (Do not let the oil smoke.) Put as many shrimp into the frying pan as will fit in one layer. Cook until the floury coating is light gold and the shells are bright red, turning once, about 1 to 2 minutes. Remove, drain on paper towels, and repeat with the remaining shrimp, replenishing the oil if necessary. Serve hot, garnished with lemon quarters.

ANCIENT ROE: BOTARGO

September is the season for harvesting *avgotaraho*, or botargo—Greece's answer to the finest caviars. Most comes from the lagoons that lace the country's western coast, from Igoumenitsa in the north to Kilini, in the Peloponnese. One man, more than anyone else, is the king of *avgotaraho*, an unassuming, extremely knowledgeable fifth-generation procurer and purveyor by the name of Zafiris Trikalinos, who learned the trade from his father. Trikalinos's product is available in American and European stores.

I followed Zafiris in early October on the last harvesting expedition of the year. For about a month from mid-September to mid-October, he sets out in his jeep from Athens two to three times a week, depending on the weather, to visit the still waters of the Amvrakikos Gulf near Messolongi, not too far from the chalk-white pyramids of freshly washed salt that tower along the coast.

Botargo, like caviar, is the roe of a particular fish. Greek botargo comes from the female grey mullet, which is plump and swollen with eggs from July until October. The fish is at its most desirable from early September through October, as it heads back out to sea to spawn. That's exactly when the mullet is caught.

Trikalinos buys raw botargo from a small group of fishermen who work together. Stooped over buckets of fresh grey mullets, the fishermen slice open the belly of each fish and remove its peach-colored swollen egg sac in one precise movement.

Trikalinos processes the roe himself in a state-of-the-art facility. The sacs are washed and salted for 2 to 3 hours, then rinsed so that their salt content does not exceed 1.5 percent. Then they are dried in special ovens, where he is able to control the moisture loss, which doesn't exceed 25 percent of the original raw roe. The next step is the most intriguing: The salted, dried roe sacs are dipped in beeswax, which preserves them and makes them look like little golden logs.

For Greeks, *avgotaraho* is the most precious delicacy there is, one known and revered by anyone with well-honed taste buds, including more than a few ancient Greek and Roman gourmands, and even the Pharaohs before them. From at least the seventeenth century there are records of the production and commerce of botargo. Besides being delicious, it's exceedingly nutritious, a great source of omega-3 fatty acids, vitamins A, B, C, and E, iron, and calcium.

The best way to enjoy this delectable treat is the simplest: Cut off the amount you want, peel away the beeswax and paper membrane around the roe sac, slice it paper-thin, and enjoy, either as is, or with a little lemon and cracked black pepper. It is delicious with fresh or dried figs or grated over pasta with early-harvest olive oil and pepper, and it is very compatible with lentils. But I still like botargo best by itself, with an iced glass of *tsipouro*.

MARINATED ANCHOVIES WITH ROASTED RED PEPPERS AND GARLIC

GAVROS MARINATOS ME PSITES PIPERIES KAI SKORDO

SERVES 6 TO 8

This dish is inspired by a tangy salad I had, with more ouzo than I care to think about, at Nissia, a well-known fish place in Thessaloniki.

8 oz/225 g fresh anchovies

Salt

¾ cup/180 ml white wine vinegar, or enough to cover the fish

¾ cup/180 ml extra-virgin Greek olive oil, or enough to cover the fish

2 red bell peppers, roasted, peeled, and seeded (see Note)

2 garlic cloves, peeled and cut into paper-thin slivers

¼ cup/15 g chopped fresh flat-leaf parsley

Pepper

With a small sharp paring knife, remove the heads and viscera from the anchovies. Hold a fish firmly by one of the tail fins, and tug gently on the other fin. Pull and remove the backbone, which comes off like a zipper sliding down.

Place a layer of anchovies on the bottom of a medium container with a lid. Sprinkle generously with salt. Add the remaining fish, one layer at a time, salting each layer. Pour in enough vinegar to cover the fish. Refrigerate for 6 to 8 hours. Remove and drain the fish. Pour in enough olive oil to cover the fish and store them this way, refrigerated. They will keep for about a week.

Cut the roasted peppers into small, thin strips and put in a salad bowl. Add the fish, garlic, and parsley and toss. Spoon onto a serving platter, sprinkle with pepper, and serve cold or at room temperature.

NOTE: To roast the bell peppers, preheat the broiler, place on a lightly oiled baking sheet, and roast about 6 in/15 cm from the heat, turning until charred on all sides. Remove from the oven and place in a bowl. Cover with plastic wrap and let cool.

YELLOW SPLIT PEA AND FENNEL PATTIES

FAVOKEFTEDES ME MARATHO

SERVES 6 TO 8

I first ran across this recipe in a small Greek cookbook on the foods of Sifnos and included it in a book I wrote for the Greek market, *Aegean Cuisine*.

It's difficult to choose one recipe among the many for yellow split peas throughout the Cyclades and Dodecanese islands. The small yellow legume is a local hero, the stuff of sustenance but also of imagination. Despite its humble nature it has become the main ingredient in countless local specialties. This particular dish marries the split pea with another local island trademark: wild fennel, which perfumes innumerable dishes from the Cyclades as well as the Dodecanese.

½ cup/120 ml extra-virgin Greek olive oil

1 large onion, finely chopped

1 cup/240 ml cooked puréed yellow split peas (*fava*; see Note)

½ to 1 cup/55 to 115 g all-purpose flour

1 small bunch wild fennel fronds, finely chopped, or 1 small bunch fresh dill plus 1 medium fennel bulb, finely chopped

Salt and pepper

Scant 1 tsp ground cinnamon

Olive oil for frying

Heat the ½ cup/120 ml oil in a large, heavy frying pan over medium heat and cook the onion until golden. Remove from the heat and transfer to a large mixing bowl. Add the cooked *fava*, ½ cup/55 g of the the flour, the fennel, salt and pepper to taste, and the cinnamon. Mix well until smooth and firm enough to make patties; add more flour if needed.

Take a heaping 1 tbsp of the mixture at a time and shape into small patties about 1½ in/4 cm in diameter. Dust with additional flour if desired. Heat a little less than 1 in/2.5 cm of olive oil in a heavy frying pan over medium heat. Pan-fry the patties, a few at a time, turning once. Remove when golden and crisp on the outside. Drain on paper towels. Serve hot or warm.

NOTE: To make the *fava*, use the recipe on page 60 and prepare it with yellow split peas.

FRITTERS

Fritters have a special place on the meze table and in the Greek kitchen. They are mostly, but not exclusively, made of vegetables, typically mashed, chopped, or puréed. Fritters are always seasonal: In winter, the meze table might include greens fritters with or without *tarama*, but in summer, tomato fritters and zucchini and cheese fritters are meze favorites.

These are poor man's food, which speak volumes about the inventiveness of country cooks. The crunch of fritters makes them attractive and mouthwatering, all the better to "open the appetite," as the Greeks say. Fritters are one reason to serve Greek dips, especially pungent ones such as *tzatziki*. They are also the way to make an accessible garden vegetable or wild green into something filling. Vegetable fritters are usually made more substantial with the addition of cheese, eggs, and some kind of starch binder, such as potatoes or dried bread. Traditionally, fritters were a cheap but delicious

way to feed an extended family or provide an inexpensive meze, sometimes on a moment's notice, when unexpected guests arrived.

There are a few tricks: For one, fritters should never be greasy or mushy, which is accomplished by making sure the oil is hot enough, but not so hot that the fritters cook on the outside but remain raw within. In addition, I can't stress how important it is to rely on good-quality, seasonal products. A winter tomato, whether it's from Santorini or California, usually has a higher water content (as do so many vegetables whose production is pushed to the limits), which surely affects the ultimate texture—and not for the best—of the tomato or whatever it is that's being fried.

Eat fritters sparingly! These are mezedes and are meant to be served with other things, too: salads, dips, spreads, cheese, and a shot or two of ouzo.

FRYING IN OLIVE OIL

Greeks fry in olive oil without a second thought. They do so because olive oil is the most widely used cooking fat in Greece, but also because Greek cooks usually pan-fry in a frying pan, for which olive oil is well suited (as opposed to frying in a deep fryer). Olive oil, contrary to common belief, has a high smoke point, 410°F/210°C.

The venerable *Joy of Cooking* recommends deep-fat frying at 365°F/185°C, which makes olive oil more than suitable. The good taste of olive oil also plays a role in the final flavor of most Greek fried foods. It gives Greek fried food its identity.

AEGEAN ISLAND WILD FENNEL FRITTERS

MARATHOKEFTEDES AIGAIPELAGITIKI

SERVES 6

Wild fennel (*Foeniculum vulgare*) has been known to and loved by the Greeks since Prometheus stole fire from the gods and secreted it away for mankind, wrapped in a bunch of aromatic fennel. The springtime perfume of Greece, fennel grows wild all over the country, but it is among the islands of the eastern Aegean and in Crete that we find the most recipes for it: in small pies and fritters; as a favorite addition to lamb, goat, or stuffed vegetables; and in fish and seafood, especially squid, cuttlefish, and octopus.

Wild fennel may be hard to find outside the Mediterranean, unless you pluck it from the streets and fields of Northern California, where I have seen it sprouting. You can't substitute the tough fronds of cultivated fennel bulbs for the long, feathery leaves of wild fennel. But for these small fritters and similar recipes that call for wild fennel, you can achieve a similar flavor by using fresh dill and chopped fennel bulb, and maybe some fennel seeds and a spritz or two of ouzo.

1 lb/455 g Swiss chard, trimmed, washed, spun dry, and chopped

1½ cups/90 g finely chopped wild fennel, or 1 cup/60 g finely chopped fresh dill and 1 large fennel bulb, trimmed and finely chopped

4 scallions, trimmed and finely chopped

Three 1-in-/2.5-cm-thick slices stale country-style bread, crusts removed

2 tbsp strained fresh lemon juice

1 large egg, lightly beaten

Salt and pepper

1 cup/115 g all-purpose flour

Olive oil for frying

Put the chard in a large bowl, and add the fennel and scallions.

Dampen the bread under cold running water and squeeze each slice very well between the palms of your hands. Crumble the bread into the greens mixture. Add the lemon juice, egg, and salt and pepper to taste and mix thoroughly with a spoon.

Taking a scant 1 tbsp of the mixture at a time, shape into patties about 2 in/5 cm in diameter and ½ in/12 mm thick.

Empty the flour onto a piece of wax paper or a large plate and dredge the patties, a few at a time. Meanwhile heat 2 in/5 cm of olive oil in a large, heavy frying pan until it reaches 325°F/165°C. Shake off the excess flour and fry the patties, a few at a time, flipping to brown on both sides. Remove with a slotted spoon when the patties are pale gold. They won't be too crisp on the outside. Drain on paper towels, cook the remaining patties, and serve.

CHEESE AND HERB FRITTERS FROM KYTHNOS

SFOUGGATO TIS KYTHNOU

SERVES 4

These cheese and herb fritters are something of a national dish on Kythnos, in the Cyclades. There is even an annual island food festival to celebrate them. This recipe is from my book *Aegean Cuisine*.

1 lb/455 g soft white cheese, such as *xinomyzithra*, or a combination of crumbled feta and soft *myzithra*, or well-drained ricotta

½ cup/30 g finely chopped fresh dill

½ cup/30 g finely chopped fresh parsley

½ to 1 cup/55 to 115 g all-purpose flour, as needed, plus extra for dredging fritters

½ cup/120 ml extra-virgin Greek olive oil

2 large eggs, lightly beaten

Salt and pepper

Olive or vegetable oil for frying

In a large bowl, combine all the ingredients except the oil for frying, using ½ cup/55 g of the flour at first and adding more as needed to make a dense mixture that holds its shape. Chill, covered, for 30 minutes to firm up further.

Using a tablespoon as a measure, shape the mixture into balls a little smaller than golf balls.

Heat 2 to 3 in/5 to 7.5 cm of oil in a large, deep frying pan over medium-high heat until it reaches 365°F/185°C. Put some flour on wax paper or a large plate and coat the cheese balls with the flour, shaking off the excess. Fry a few at a time in the hot oil until golden. Serve hot.

SANTORINI TOMATO FRITTERS

DOMATOKEFTEDES SANTORINIS

Tomato fritters are a uniquely Greek delicacy, an island specialty with many variations. The tomato fritters of Santorini, in the southern Cyclades, are the most famous, and are sometimes flavored with a pinch of cinnamon. On Syros, Tinos, and Kimolos, in the Cyclades, tomato fritters are sometimes made with sun-dried tomatoes and seasoned with wild fennel or parsley and a little garlic. Regardless of where they are from, tomato fritters sometimes go by the nickname *pseftokeftedes*, or "ersatz *keftes*" (meatballs). They are as filling as meatballs, but cheaper to make and so were more accessible to the farmers and villagers of yore, whose diet was once based solely on the limited range of local, seasonal ingredients.

1½ lb/680 g firm, ripe tomatoes, grated (see Note)

3 scallions, white and tender green parts, finely chopped

2 tbsp finely chopped fresh flat-leaf parsley

Salt and pepper

1¼ to 1½ cups/145 to 170 g all-purpose flour

½ tsp baking powder

Olive or vegetable oil for frying

In a large bowl, mix together the grated tomatoes, scallions, parsley, and salt and pepper to taste. Combine 1¼ cups/145 g of the flour and the baking powder in a small bowl and add it to the tomatoes, mixing well. Add more flour if necessary to give the mixture the consistency of a thick batter. Taste and adjust the seasoning with salt and pepper.

Heat about 1½ in/4 cm of oil in a large, heavy frying pan over medium-high heat. When the oil is very hot, drop the batter, a tbsp at a time, into the frying pan and fry the tomato fritters on both sides until golden. Remove with a slotted spoon and drain on paper towels. Serve hot.

NOTE: To grate the tomatoes, using a sharp knife, cut a piece the size of a quarter off the base of each tomato. With a box grater, grate the tomatoes until all that's left is a flattened-out piece of skin. Or grate the whole tomatoes, skins and all, using the grating attachment of a food processor.

IKARIAN ZUCCHINI FRITTERS WITH FRESH OREGANO AND MINT

KOLOKYTHOKEFTEDES IKARIOTIKOI ME FRESKIA RIGANI KAI DYOSMO

Ikaria, where my family originated, is a small island in the eastern Aegean whose cuisine exemplifies simple country cooking. Zucchini is in every garden in the summer, and local cooks make these delicious fritters.

2 lb/910 g zucchini, trimmed and grated

2 tsp salt

⅔ cup/100 g crumbled Greek feta cheese

2 large eggs, lightly beaten

5 scallions, whites and tender green parts, finely chopped

⅓ cup/20 g finely chopped fresh mint

¼ cup/15 g finely chopped fresh oregano

3 to 6 tbsp all-purpose flour, plus 1 cup/115 g for dredging

Pepper

Olive or vegetable oil for frying

Put the grated zucchini in a colander, sprinkle with the salt, and rub between your palms until wilted, wringing out as much liquid as possible from the vegetable.

Transfer the zucchini to a mixing bowl and add the feta, eggs, scallions, and herbs. Add flour, 1 to 2 tbsp at a time, until the mixture becomes a very thick batter. Season with salt, if needed, and add pepper to taste. Put the mixture in the refrigerator, covered, for 1 hour to firm up.

Put the remaining 1 cup/115 g of flour on wax paper or a plate. Using a tablespoon, shape the mixture into patties. Heat 2 to 3 in/5 to 7.5 cm of oil in a large, heavy frying pan over medium-high heat until it reaches 365°F/185°C. Dredge the patties lightly in flour, shaking off any excess. Fry a few at a time in the hot oil until golden, turning once carefully with a spatula. Remove with a slotted spoon and drain on paper towels. Serve hot.

NOTE: You can bake the fritters instead of frying them. Place a sheet of parchment or wax paper in a large, shallow baking pan and drop the fritter batter, 1 tbsp at a time, onto the baking sheet in neat rows. Bake in a preheated oven at 350°F/175°C/gas 4, flipping the fritters once to brown on both sides. Remove with a spatula and set aside to cool. Repeat with remaining batter until all the fritters are baked.

VARIATION: In the fall, substitute grated pumpkin or butternut squash for the zucchini. Omit the oregano, increase the mint to ⅔ cup/40 g, and proceed with the recipe.

SANTORINI TOMATOES

For all its ubiquity, the tomato is a relative newcomer to the cuisine of Greece. The seeds for the New World *Solanum lycopersicum* arrived in 1818 with a Capuchin monk in Athens, but the first mention of its cultivation was in the mid-nineteenth century travelogues of foreign visitors to Greece, who recorded seeing it in Santorini and Syros, in the Cyclades islands.

Santorini, with its inhospitable chalky, volcanic soil was an unlikely place for the tomato to first flourish, but flourish it did, most likely because in the nineteenth century, Santorini and Syros were under Venetian rule. By then the tomato had insinuated itself into Venetian cookery, which Venice effectively exported to its dominions.

To this day the Santorini tomato, which the Greeks dub *anydri*—"waterless"—is one of a handful of highly prized local Greek varieties. It is small and intensely sweet, with a dense, firm flesh; relatively thick skin; and deep, vertical grooves. Santorini's volcanic soil, which is rich in minerals, gives the tomato its extraordinary flavor. It's not easy to find the tomato off the island. Even on Santorini, its harvest is fleeting. In late June, most Santorini tomatoes are still green on the vine; by the end of July, the ripe tomatoes have been harvested and pretty much consumed.

Calling this small, flavorful tomato "waterless" is a bit of a misnomer. The island indeed is whipped by the brutal, summer *meltemi* winds and parched by Greece's merciless summer sun, but its porous soil and its atmosphere retain enough moisture to provide ideal, if unique, growing conditions for the local tomato as well as for local grapes. The latter has spawned a formidable wine industry, providing the second most important source of income after tourism.

Tomatoes once were an important local industry, too, and continue to be so to some extent today, thanks to the enduring efforts of the local cooperative, which cans a variety of products. For a long time, the most notable among the tomato products was the intensely flavored paste that local women used to make by drying their crop in the summer sun, as a way to preserve the fruit's pulp well into winter. In 1902, the first shipments of Santorini tomato paste went off to Turkey and Egypt. In 1920, the first tomato processing plant opened on the island. The business flourished, spawning a dozen or so similar operations. By 1949, the island was producing 7 million kilos (about 15 million pounds) of tomatoes, which twelve processors were either turning into paste or canning whole. The industry's death knell came in the devastating earthquake of 1956. From the 1960s on, farming of any kind took second place to developing this spectacular island for tourism.

Today the center of the Greek tomato farming and processing industry is the Peloponnese. As for that waterless tomato from Santorini, where it all started, it is a niche product, one of many now aimed at the growing gourmet market.

THE COUNTRY COOKING OF GREECE   75   MEZE

KOZANI SCALLION FRITTERS WITH PAPRIKA, OREGANO, AND MINT

KREMMYDOKEFTEDES ME KOKINI PIPERIA, RIGANI KAI DYOSMO KOZANIS

═══════ SERVES 4 TO 6 ═══════

I love these simple, rustic fritters from northern Greece because of the local palette of flavors—mainly paprika—which is used very sparingly, if at all, in other parts of Greece.

> 10 scallions
>
> 2 tsp salt
>
> 4 large eggs, lightly beaten
>
> Scant 1 tsp baking powder
>
> Scant 1 tsp paprika
>
> ½ tsp pepper
>
> 2 tsp dried Greek oregano
>
> 2 tsp dried mint
>
> 3 tbsp chopped fresh flat-leaf parsley
>
> 1½ to 2 cups/170 to 225 g all-purpose flour
>
> 1 cup/240 ml water
>
> Olive or vegetable oil for frying

Trim the root ends off the scallions and cut away about 1 in/2.5 cm or so from the tough dark green ends. Coarsely chop, using as much of the green part as possible. Put in a colander and rub vigorously with the salt, pressing the scallions against the sides of the colander until they wilt. This will take 6 to 8 minutes.

Transfer to a large bowl and add the eggs, baking powder, paprika, pepper, oregano, mint, and parsley. In a small bowl, mix 1½ cups/ 170 g of flour with the water, whisking to smooth out any clumps. Add this to the scallion mixture to form a thick batter, and add additional flour if necessary. Stir well.

In a large, wide pot or a deep, heavy frying pan, heat 3 in/7.5 cm of oil over medium-high heat to about 365°F/185°C. Deep-fry the fritters in batches until gold, taking a heaping 1 tbsp of the batter at a time and pushing it into the hot oil in the frying pan with another spoon. Remove with a slotted spoon and drain on paper towels. Serve hot.

VLACH WALNUT FRITTERS WITH YOGURT

VLACHIKOI KARYDOKEFTEDES ME YIAOURTI

═══════ SERVES 6 TO 8 ═══════

These northern Greek fritters are an old dish from the traditional cuisine of the Vlachs, who have lived as shepherds and merchants in the northern parts of Greece and the southern Balkans, possibly from the time of the ancient Romans. The fritters resemble many Greek dishes that approximate the satisfying texture of meat, without actually containing any. And they also grew out of the fasting tradition, which dictates that for almost half the year meat and dairy are omitted from the diet. The dish below is not a fasting dish, but it could easily become one, appealing to vegans, too, by simply omitting the milk. If you choose to do that, you won't need the bread either.

> 6 oz/170 g stale country bread, crusts removed, and cut into six 1-in/2.5-cm slices
>
> ½ cup/120 ml milk
>
> 1 medium potato, about 6 oz/170 g, peeled
>
> 1½ cups/170 g all-purpose flour
>
> 1 tbsp baking soda
>
> 2 cups/240 g coarsely ground walnuts
>
> 2 garlic cloves, minced
>
> 1 large red onion, finely chopped
>
> Scant 1 tsp cumin
>
> 4 tbsp finely chopped fresh mint
>
> Salt and pepper
>
> Olive or vegetable oil for frying
>
> Thick Greek yogurt for serving (optional)

Cut the bread into cubes or chunks and put in a bowl with the milk. Soak until the bread has absorbed all the milk, and then squeeze in batches between the palms of your hands, to wring out as much milk as possible. Transfer the bread to a large mixing bowl.

Grate or shred the potato with a hand grater or a food processor fitted with a grater disc. Squeeze the excess liquid out of the potato and add to the bread. Mix in ½ cup of the flour, baking soda, walnuts, garlic, onion, cumin, and mint. Season with salt and pepper. Knead the mixture until a mass forms that is firm enough to hold its shape when rolled into balls. Take 1 tbsp at a time and shape into balls. Pat down to form patties. Dredge lightly in the remaining flour. Set aside on a large platter or tray.

In a large, deep frying pan, heat 2 to 3 in/5 to 7.5 cm of oil over medium-high heat until it reaches about 365°F/185°C and pan-fry the fritters, in batches, until deep gold, flipping once to brown on both sides. Drain on paper towels and serve, accompanied by the yogurt.

TARAMA FRITTERS

TARAMOKEFTEDES

===== SERVES 8 TO 10 =====

Tarama is the roe of cod, grey mullet, or carp. There are two types: white tarama, which is considered better quality, and pink tarama, which is artificially colored and sometimes enriched with soy. Pink tarama is a commercial affectation, first concocted in the mid-twentieth century as a way to make the otherwise pallid beige cod roe, which is the most common tarama, more attractive.

Tarama Fritters are a savory meze usually enjoyed during Lent. There are also fennel and tarama pies from Chios. In fact, tarama has captured modern chefs' imaginations; I've seen it in various sauces, usually for fish, at high-end restaurants in Athens. Not all tarama fritters are fried. At least one recipe, from Macedonia, calls for baking them.

This recipe comes from the island of Kos. Most tarama fritters include greens or herbs to offset the saltiness of the roe.

3 oz/85 g white tarama

Water or milk, as needed

10 oz/280 g stale country bread, crusts removed and shredded

3 tbsp finely chopped fresh parsley

3 tbsp finely chopped fresh dill

3 scallions, trimmed and finely chopped

Pepper

2 tbsp extra-virgin Greek olive oil

3 tbsp all-purpose flour

Olive or vegetable oil for frying

Put the tarama in a small bowl and cover with water or milk by 2 in/5 cm. Let the tarama soak for 1 hour. Drain in a fine-mesh sieve.

While the tarama is soaking, put the bread in a bowl and cover with water to soften. Press between the palms of your hands to squeeze out the excess water.

Combine the bread and tarama in a mixing bowl. Add the herbs, scallions, and pepper. Mix the 2 tbsp of olive oil into the mixture. If it is too loose, add enough of the flour to firm it up, so that it holds its shape when formed into a ball. Put the mixture in the refrigerator for 30 minutes.

Heat 2 to 3 in/5 to 7.5 cm of oil in a large, deep frying pan or pot over medium-high until it reaches 365°F/185°C. Meanwhile, make a few tarama balls: Using a teaspoon, take a heaping mound of the mixture and shape into a small patty or ball. Dredge lightly in flour, shaking off the excess. Fry the tarama balls, a few at a time, until golden. Remove with a slotted spoon and drain on paper towels. Serve hot.

CHAPTER 3

CHEESE
AND
EGGS

CHEESE AND EGGS HAVE BEEN BASIC TO THE COUNTRY KITCHEN FOREVER.

The importance of cheesemaking in Greece is reflected in its mythology, ancient literature, and archeological finds. In Greek mythology, Aristaios, the son of Apollo, taught the art of cheesemaking to humans.

One of Homer's memorable stories in the Odyssey tells of Ulysses' entrance into the cave where Polyphemus, the one-eyed Cyclops, kept his treasured cheeses. From their descriptions, some are remarkably similar to the simplest island cheeses still made in Greece today. On Crete archeologists have found fired clay strainers that were probably used to drain the whey when people made cheese during the Neolithic and early Bronze ages (5000 to 3000 B.C.). At the Minoan Palace of Knossos, stone tablets depict men making cheese from both goat's and sheep's milk.

In both the islands and on the mainland, itinerant shepherds have roamed with their flocks, moving from the fertile valleys in winter to the cooler mountain highlands in summer, from prehistoric times to the present. Greece is a country with many microclimates, each with rich and varied regional flora, which provides the fodder for the country's sheep and goats, the two animals whose milk has always been most prized for the production of cheese.

Cheese was a source of income for many agrarian families and, until recently, was savored in measured doses, usually to provide a little protein to what was largely a plant-based diet. Today, Greeks consume more cheese than almost anyone else does, about 48 pounds/22 kilos per person per year.

Cheese is made almost everywhere in Greece. There are at least seventy different regional Greek cheeses. They fall into broad categories such as brined cheeses, the most famous of which is feta; soft, fermented (or naturally soured) cheeses; whey cheeses, both fresh and dried; yellow cheeses that range in texture from semisoft to hard; and cheeses that are part of the *pasta filata* family, with a squeaky, flexible texture that comes from reheating the curds in hot whey and kneading them.

Most Greek cheese is produced from sheep's milk or a combination of sheep's and goat's milk. There are a few notable cow's milk cheeses, too, and a few delicious oddities, among them the wine-aged cheeses of the Aegean. To make things even more complicated, Greek cheese producers, bowing to the demands of this cheese-loving nation, are continually developing new cheeses, most of which can be found in gourmet shops in Greece. Within each of these categories is an officially recognized group of cheeses with the EU's Protected Designation of Origin (PDO) status.

The number of dishes that call for cheese, from mezedes to sweets, and from breakfast to dinner, is proof enough of Greeks' love affair with it. Cheese is mashed into spreads, many of them spicy and pungent. It fills eggplant, tomatoes, peppers, and other vegetables, and finds its way into rustic stuffed meat dishes. Cheese is grated over pasta and shaved into gratinlike dishes, which Greek home cooks of a certain era called soufflés. Cheese is the main ingredient in countless pies, both sweet and savory, found in every corner of Greece and in Greek restaurants the world over. Fried cheese—the saganaki of meze fame—is a classic Greek snack and small plate, equally popular in the most remote Greek villages and in the Greek restaurants of New York City. The béchamel that tops classic moussaka and pastitsio like a soft pillow is often enriched with cheese. Need I say more?

EGGS

Eggs are endemic to the cuisine of Greece. They make the Christmas, New Year's, and Easter breads rise to fluffy heights. Dyed red eggs, symbolic of the blood of Christ and of Resurrection, adorn the paschal loaves, which are usually braided in a trinity of thick dough ropes. The egg is also the main ingredient in one of the country's most famous preparations, avgolemono, the egg and lemon combination that can be both a sauce and a soup.

Ironically, eggs are not a typical breakfast food in Greece. When served in the morning, usually to nourish a young child, they are either fried in olive oil sunny-side up, which is called *mati*, for "eye," or they are soft-boiled and served with *bastounia*—little"canes" or strips of bread. For breakfast in the country kitchen, where there are fresh farm eggs, a *ktipito avgo* is made for kids by vigourously stirring a raw egg yolk with sugar until it is thick and creamy.

For the most part, however, eggs are the stuff of a quick, filling afternoon or evening meal. Omelets, filled with vegetables, local sausages, or regional cheeses, are a classic fast meal in Greece. Sunny-side up eggs served over vegetables or yogurt are found in a number of regions. Scrambled eggs, to which tomato or cured pork might be added, are a country kitchen favorite.

MAKING CHEESE IN A GREEK ISLAND HOME

It's around eight on a hot summer morning on Ikaria and I hear Yiannis's old Yamaha grinding to a halt down the road. He wears a heavy *filaki*—a goat-hide bag—on his back and swings off the bike with a grace and economy of movement honed after years of negotiating the island's rough slopes twice a day with his goats. Yiannis, clad in bright red overalls and sporting the permanent tan of someone who spends many waking hours outdoors, is a local shepherd and friend. He is also the sole supplier of my organic goat's milk, which he delivers, still warm from the morning's milking, in sterilized liter-size water bottles three times a week to my front door.

For years now, in summer, my weekly routine involves the anticipation of that milk and the ensuing process of turning it into kathoura, the local cheese, a daylong process that captivated me from the first time I ever witnessed that transformation in the kitchen of a friend. Her only equipment was a pot, a pillbox-shaped packet of grainy rennin, a knife, cheesecloth, and, of course, fresh goat's milk.

I usually pour the warm milk straightaway into a large stainless-steel pot, to scald it over low heat. This is the home cheese maker's pasteurization process. Local cheese makers often don't go through this step, instead warming the milk to body temperature and then setting it with rennin. Heating it to the boiling point denatures the proteins, which results in more milk solids in the final cheese mass. It also changes the taste ever so slightly; pasteurized goat's milk cheese is definitely less complex than the same cheese made with raw milk. I do it for safety reasons, even though there is considerable debate around the issue. Once the milk returns to body temperature, I add a pinch of powdered rennet, mix it into the milk, and let it sit until the milk sets and resembles a gelatinous yogurt. That's the time to cut the curds, while gently heating the whole thing. The whey rises to the top, and what stays beneath the surface are the delicious, mild, warm curds, which I pour out into a cheesecloth-lined strainer, hang from my kitchen faucet, and let drip overnight until the cheese is solidified. This is the Ikarian kathoura, one of many simple Greek island goat's milk cheeses.

SPICY GREEK CHEESE SPREAD

TYROKAFTERI

SERVES 4 TO 6 AS A MEZE

Tyrokafteri translates literally as "spicy cheese." It is one of the classic meze dishes, which has dozens of variations. Feta is always included in the mix of cheeses, and more often than not is the only cheese in a *tyrokafteri*.

> 1 lb/455 g soft Greek feta, crumbled
>
> ½ cup/120 ml thick Greek yogurt or any of the soft, naturally fermented Greek mountain cheeses, such as *katiki* or *galotyri*
>
> ½ cup/120 ml extra-virgin Greek olive oil
>
> 1 tsp pepper
>
> 1 to 3 small chile peppers, seeded and finely chopped
>
> 2 to 3 tbsp strained fresh lemon juice
>
> Pita bread, country bread, or crackers for serving

Combine the feta, yogurt, olive oil, pepper, and chile peppers in the bowl of a food processor and process on high speed until smooth. Add lemon juice to taste.

Transfer to a bowl and refrigerate for at least 1 hour before serving. Serve with toasted pita bread, country bread, or crackers.

VARIATION: You can add 1 or 2 roasted red bell peppers (see Note on page 70) to this, as well as 1 garlic clove and fresh herbs. Thyme and oregano are best.

BAKED FETA WITH PEPPERS AND TOMATOES

BOUYIOURNTI

SERVES 6 AS A MEZE

Here is another classic meze and another variation on the feta-pepper theme that Greeks like so much, especially with a cool glass of chilled, milky ouzo.

> 2 large firm, ripe tomatoes, cored and cut into 4 to 6 round slices each
>
> Salt and pepper
>
> 2 tbsp extra-virgin Greek olive oil, plus extra for drizzling
>
> 11 oz/310 g Greek feta, crumbled
>
> 2 green bell peppers, seeded and cut into ⅛-in/ 3-mm rings
>
> ½ tsp dried Greek oregano
>
> Red pepper flakes, or 1 to 2 small fresh chile peppers, minced

Preheat the oven to 425°F/220°C/gas 7. Lightly oil a 6 x 9-in/ 15 x 23-cm ovenproof glass or ceramic baking dish or 6 individual shallow baking dishes with olive oil. Place the tomato slices evenly on the bottom of the baking dish (or dishes), and season very lightly with salt and pepper. Drizzle the 2 tbsp of olive oil over the tomatoes.

Sprinkle the feta evenly on top. Place the peppers over the feta, sprinkle with the oregano, and cover with aluminum foil. Bake for 30 to 35 minutes, or until the vegetables soften and the feta melts.

Remove the foil, sprinkle with red pepper flakes or chile pepper, and drizzle with additional olive oil. Serve immediately.

SHREDDED KATAIFI PASTRY STUFFED WITH CHEESE

KATAIFI ME TYRI

〰 SERVES 12 AS A MEZE 〰

Here's a rustic meze with a fresh twist. *Kataifi* is a shredded pastry that is usually stuffed with chopped nuts and sweetened with syrup. It is surprisingly versatile, however, and tavernas began making savory, cheese-stuffed versions several years ago, in part to catch up with the gourmet dining scene that exploded all over Athens, beginning in the late 1990s. The filling is seasoned with mastic, resinous spice crystals produced exclusively in twenty-two villages in southern Chios, an island in the northeastern Aegean. It is one of the most beguiling aromatics in the Greek kitchen.

1 lb/455 g fresh *anthotyro* or ricotta cheese

1 lb/455 g Greek feta cheese, crumbled

½ tsp saffron

2 large eggs, lightly beaten

6 tbsp/90 ml extra-virgin Greek olive oil

½ tsp *mastiha* (mastic) crystals

Salt and pepper

1 lb/455 g shredded *kataifi* pastry, defrosted and at room temperature

4 tbsp unsalted butter, melted

Preheat the oven to 325°F/165°C/gas 3. Combine the *anthotyro*, feta, saffron, eggs, and half the olive oil in a mixing bowl. Pound the *mastiha* crystals and ½ tsp salt in a mortar with a pestle and stir into the cheese mixture. Season with salt and pepper.

Untangle the *kataifi* pastry. Combine the butter with the remaining olive oil in a small dish. Take a piece of the pastry (about 4 oz/115 g), pull it open lengthwise. It should be about 2½ in/5 cm wide by 7 to 8 in/17.5 to 20 cm long. Brush with a little olive oil–butter mixture. Place a heaping 1 tsp of the cheese mixture on the inside and roll up into a plump cylinder, tucking the edges in so the cheese does not ooze out when heated. Place seam-side down on a buttered 9 x 13-inch/ 23 x 33-cm baking pan. Repeat with the remaining pastry and filling. Brush the *kataifi* generously with the remaining olive oil-butter mixture, melting more butter if necessary. Bake for 50 to 55 minutes, or until golden. Remove from the oven, cool slightly, and serve.

BUTTERY PHYLLO PASTRY WITH PASTOURMA, TOMATOES, AND KASSERI CHEESE

PITA KAISARIAS

〰 SERVES 12 AS A MEZE 〰

One of the great meze pies of the Greeks from Asia Minor, this spicy phyllo dish originated in Caesaria, in Anatolia. It relies on good kasseri cheese (see page 371), fresh tomatoes, and the fenugreek-flavored cured beef, *pastourma*.

7 sheets commercial phyllo, defrosted overnight in the refrigerator and brought to room temperature

½ cup/115 g unsalted butter, melted

2 cups/300 g grated kasseri cheese

2 medium firm tomatoes, very thinly sliced

Salt and pepper

12 thin slices *pastourma*, sticky spice rub removed

Preheat the oven to 350°F/175°C/gas 4. Lightly oil a 9 x 13 x 2-in/ 23 x 33 x 5-cm baking pan.

Layer 4 sheets of phyllo on the bottom of the pan, brushing each with 1 tablespoon of the butter.

Sprinkle one-third of the cheese over the surface of the phyllo, and spread half the tomato slices on top. Season with a little salt and pepper. Spread the *pastourma* slices over the tomatoes evenly. Cover with the remaining tomato slices and then sprinkle the rest of the cheese on top. Season with additional pepper.

Top the pie with the remaining 3 sheets of phyllo, brushing each with the remaining butter. Trim the edges with a sharp paring knife to make the rim neat. Score into serving pieces and bake for about 45 minutes, or until the phyllo is golden and the cheese is melted. Serve immediately.

SAGANAKI

Most people who have encountered saganaki in Greek restaurants outside of Greece know this dish as fried cheese. But in fact, *saganaki* refers to a wide range of dishes that take their names from the eponymous pan in which they are prepared. A saganaki pan is nothing more than a shallow, two-handled frying pan.

Saganaki, both the pan and the dishes made in it, came to Greece with the wave of Greek refugees fleeing political upheavals in Turkey in the 1920s. In their rush to get out, they usually took the bare essentials, among which was often a *sahanaki* pan, the vessel of choice for making the quickest, most delectable, and convivial dishes.

"There was a saganaki in every home," says Soula Bozi, a Greek from Turkey who has written several books (in Greek) on the cuisine of her displaced compatriots. "They were always made of tin, with two handles like ears. Mothers would use them to make filling breakfasts but they were the pan most used to make quick but full—and filling—meals. You got vegetables, protein, and starch, in the form of bread that everyone invariably used to soak up all those good pan juices," she adds.

The most common saganaki in the early part of the twentieth century were robust snacks like *pastourma* (a spiced cured beef) saganaki, with plenty of melted kasseri cheese; a breakfast saganaki made with eggs and kasseri or feta cheese and sometimes with *pastourma*, too; and a luscious dish made with the spicy beef sausage *soutzouki*, kasseri cheese, and tomatoes.

Thanks to the resourcefulness of Greek cooks in both simple restaurants and at home, saganaki evolved into a range of dishes that now include concoctions of seafood (especially shrimp or mussels), cheese, and wine; plain cheese cut into squares and seared to melting perfection; or a bubbling dish of seafood, tomatoes, feta cheese, and sweet and hot peppers, flambéed with a shot of brandy or ouzo just before serving. The two most famous versions of saganaki in the Greek kitchen are the shrimp and saganaki meze sometimes called shrimp Mikrolimano, and fried squares of plain cheese, dipped in flour and sautéed in butter or olive oil. The second dish has ancient roots. Fried cheese finished with hot broth was known to the Byzantine Greeks, according to the historian Phaedon Koukoules in his magnum opus, *Byzantinon Bios kai Politismos (Byzantine Life and Culture)*.

PORTRAIT OF A PASTOURMA MAKER

Fanis Arapian is my favorite *pastourma* merchant. Since his family arrived in Greece on the heels of the refugee crisis in Asia Minor in 1922, they have been producing this exceedingly pungent cured beef, covered with a layer of spices. Fanis's shop has a handful of different varieties, distinguished by cut and size.

Fanis starts with the proper cuts of beef, most of it from Drama, in northeastern Greece, where he has his workshop. He hangs the beef in a cooler for a couple of days, then scores and salts it. Most cuts take about two days before they absorb the salt. The next step is what gives *pastourma* its characteristic flat, square shape. "We have to press it," Fanis said, "to get the blood out. In the older days, we used marble slabs. Now, machines." After the blood has been pressed out, it is time for the spice rub, a mixture of rye or wheat flour (Fanis uses rye), fenugreek, cumin, garlic, pepper, and other seasonings.

Next, the spiced, flattened meat needs to cure in open air. The spiced beef takes about three to four months to mature and absorb the spices before it is ready to consume. Sometimes, if the spice rub is very thick, a producer will shave most of it off, leaving only a thin layer. Most people remove it before eating because it is very strong.

Pastourma is often paired with kasseri cheese and tomatoes, especially in buttery phyllo pies called Pita Kaisarias (page 88), named after Kaisaria, in Turkey. It is also chopped and baked into doughy boats called *peinirli*, added to soups, such as Chickpea Soup with Pastourma (page 111), and to beans, as in Giant Beans Baked with Roasted Peppers and Pastourma (page 168). But it's delicious served plain, a great meze for some of that ouzo Fanis insisted on pouring.

CLASSIC TAVERNA SAGANAKI

KLASSIKO TAVERNISIO SAGANAKI

SERVES 6 TO 8 AS A MEZE

This is by far one of the best-known Greek dishes. To some, it's a heart attack on a plate—just the idea of frying something as high in fat as cheese makes some folks cringe. But Greeks never eat a whole slice of this alone. One piece is often shared by four to six people, so that all you're really getting is about a 1-in-/2.5-cm-square forkful of it.

9 oz/255 g *kefalotyri* or *kefalograviera* cheese

1 cup/115 g all-purpose flour

Pepper

1 cup/240 ml water

4 tbsp unsalted butter

2 tbsp Greek brandy

1 lemon, cut into 4 wedges

Cut cheese into four 2- or 3-in/5- or 7.5-cm squares, about ½ to ¾ in/12 mm to 2 cm thick.

Put the flour in a shallow bowl and season with pepper. Pour the water into another shallow bowl and keep nearby. Pat both sides of the cheese in the flour, then dip in water, then pat it in the flour again.

Heat the butter in a large saganaki pan or nonstick frying pan over medium-high until it melts and bubbles. Put 2 pieces of cheese in the pan and fry, without moving the cheese, until the bottom crust is golden. Flip to cook on the other side, and then slide the pan away from the heat and pour in 1 tbsp of the brandy carefully, as the alcohol may flare up. Return to the heat, lowering it. As soon as the brandy burns off, transfer the cheese to a plate. Repeat with the remaining cheese and brandy. Serve the saganaki hot with the lemon on the side.

PISTACHIO-CRUSTED FETA SAGANAKI

FETA SAGANAKI ME KROUSTA APO FYSTIKIA

SERVES 4 AS A MEZE

A few years ago, chefs and home cooks in Greece began to experiment with the classic saganaki. Frying the cheese in all sorts of crusts was an interesting twist. Feta is delicious in a sesame crust, or pressed into nuts—such as almonds, pine nuts, and pistachios—before it's sautéed. The pistachios add great color and texture to this dish. It's a wonderful starter.

9 oz/255 g hard feta, preferably tinned not barrel-aged

1 large egg, lightly beaten

½ to ¾ cup/75 to 100 g finely ground unsalted pistachios

1 tsp crushed black peppercorns

¼ cup/60 ml extra-virgin Greek olive oil

Cut the feta into 2 slices, about ¾ in/2 cm thick. Pour the egg into a shallow bowl. Combine the ground pistachios and peppercorns and spread out on a large piece of wax paper.

Heat the oil in a large nonstick frying pan over medium heat. Meanwhile, dip both sides of a piece of feta in the egg and let the excess drain back into the bowl. Press one side of the cheese into the pistachio mixture and turn it to press on the other side. With your fingers, press the nuts into any bare spots.

Put the cheese in the frying pan and pan-fry over medium heat until it begins to soften, about 2 minutes. Turn to cook on the other side, another 2 minutes. Transfer to a serving dish and repeat with remaining cheese and nuts. Serve hot.

NOTE: You can coat and freeze the cheese before frying it, which helps the pistachios adhere. You can also coat the cheese with sesame seeds instead. Either way, this saganaki is also delicious with a drizzling of Greek honey.

SHRIMP AND FETA SAGANAKI

GARIDES SAGANAKI

Enjoyed from Adelaide to Athens, this dish is one of Greece's trademark recipes, a timeless salute to the versatility of Greek feta and its affinity for almost anything. It most likely originated in the meze restaurants of Thessaloniki, Greece's northern port city, when some anonymous but enterprising cook threw a handful of shrimp (which were readily available) into the pan, together with cheese and the usual assortment of vegetables. The dish also goes by the name *garides Mikrolimano*, after the quay in Piraeus where tavernas still serve it. A glass of ouzo or a crisp white wine goes well with this saganaki.

> 3 tbsp extra-virgin Greek olive oil
>
> 2 tbsp unsalted butter
>
> ½ cup chopped red onion
>
> 2 garlic cloves, chopped
>
> 16 large shrimp, heads and tails left on, deveined
>
> ½ cup/85 g good-quality chopped canned plum tomatoes
>
> 1 cup/150 g crumbled Greek feta cheese
>
> ½ cup/120 ml heavy cream
>
> ½ cup/120 ml ouzo
>
> Salt and pepper
>
> Chopped fresh flat-leaf parsley for garnish

Heat the oil and 1 tbsp of the butter in a sauté pan over medium heat. Sweat the onion and garlic, but do not brown. Add the shrimp and cook for 1 minute to color lightly.

Add the tomatoes and feta and stir gently. When the feta begins to soften, add the cream and ouzo. Simmer until you've cooked off the alcohol, 5 to 8 minutes. Season with salt and pepper.

Stir in the last 1 tbsp of butter. Remove from the heat, sprinkle with more pepper and a little chopped parsley, and serve.

ROASTED RED PEPPER SAGANAKI

SAGANAKI ME PIPERIES FLORINIS

Roasted red peppers are a natural match for all sorts of cheeses, but especially the sour, briny kind like feta, and the naturally fermented cheeses such as *galotyri* and *katiki*. This recipe calls for accessible and tasty Kasseri. The sweetness of the roasted peppers pairs beautifully with the tartness of these and so many other Greek cheeses. This dish comes from northern Greece, where Florina peppers are a regional signature. Long and horn-shaped, they are in season at the very end of summer and into early fall. Florina peppers are usually consumed roasted. You can find them commercially in brine or olive oil.

> 2 red bell peppers, roasted, with their juice (see Note on page 70); or 3 roasted red Florina peppers in brine or olive oil, drained and rinsed
>
> ¼ cup/60 ml extra-virgin Greek olive oil
>
> 1 large red onion, halved and sliced ⅛ in/3 mm thick
>
> Salt
>
> 1 tbsp Greek sweet vinegar (*glykadi*) or balsamic vinegar
>
> 4 oz/115 g kasseri cheese, cut into small cubes
>
> Pepper

Set aside the bell pepper juices that have collected during roasting. Peel and seed the bell peppers and cut into ½-in/12-mm strips.

Heat the olive oil in a nonstick frying pan. Add the onion, season with salt, and cook over medium heat for about 12 minutes, or until the onion begins to caramelize lightly. Add the roasted peppers and their juices, heat through, and stir in the vinegar. Continue cooking until the pan juices are reduced by half and almost syrupy.

Scatter the cheese over the onion–roasted pepper mixture, reduce the heat to low, cover the frying pan, and let the cheese and onion–roasted pepper mixture cook together for about 1 minute, or until the cheese is melted. Season with pepper and serve immediately.

AVGOLEMONO

Avgolemono is a whisked mixture of eggs and strained fresh lemon juice into which a slow drizzle of hot broth or pan juices is further whisked, forming an emulsified liquid that is added to soups as a thickener or served as a sauce.

Avgolemono flavors fish soup, which Greeks call *psarosoupa avgolemono*, and chicken soup, which they call *kotosoupa avgolemono*. Another popular dish is *yiouvarlakia*, meatballs cooked in broth and then thickened with the avgolemono emulsion.

As a sauce, avgolemono goes over various meat dishes, especially lamb, goat, and pork. It thickens and flavors a wide range of main courses and seasonal braised vegetables, especially artichokes. It is the defining sauce of Greek fricassee, which has nothing to do, beyond the name itself, with French fricassee.

Avgolemono is relatively easy to prepare. The trick is in the tempering: Once the egg-lemon mixture is whisked until smooth, add the hot broth or pan juices in the slowest and steadiest of streams, whisking all the while so that the eggs aren't shocked by the heat, which makes them curdle. Then, after slowly adding in about two ladles of hot broth, pour the avgolemono into the pot, tilting the pot to distribute it evenly. A caveat: Never cover the pot, or else your avgolemono will congeal into a solid omeletlike mass.

There are three basic techniques for making avgolemono: The first calls for using whole eggs and makes for a slightly thinner sauce or soup; the second calls for whisking just the yolks. The third calls for making a meringue with the whites, whisking the yolks separately, and then incorporating one into the other and tempering, as always, with the hot broth. This last method, used to make a sauce for a fish dish on page 232, results in the thickest, creamiest avgolemono. Some cooks cheat by whisking in a little cornstarch, which helps stabilize the eggs and thicken the sauce. There is a basic ratio of eggs and lemon to liquid when making avgolemono: 2 eggs and the juice of 1 medium lemon per quart or liter of hot liquid.

A WORD ON GREEK LEMONS

Greece is a country filled with lemon trees—big, generous trees that bear big, generous fruit with thick, oily, perfumed skin at least twice a year. The aroma of lemons—the fruit, the blossoms, even the leaves—fills the Greek kitchen and the national psyche. There is a famous passage in Nikos Kazantzakis's *Report to Greco*, where he describes the arrival of the mountain-dwelling grandfather, who brings a gift of roasted suckling pig wrapped in lemon leaves, the aroma of which pervades every corner of the living room.

Greeks squeeze lemons over nearly everything: over every piece of grilled, roasted, or fried meat; over fish, both grilled and baked (not over fried fish or seafood, though, lest they lose their crispiness); over fried potatoes and over boiled and sautéed vegetables; and in Crete, even over sunny-side-up eggs fried in local olive oil. Greek housewives rub fresh lemon juice on their hands as a soothing salve in winter, and they make the most refreshing lemonade syrup, to be diluted with cold water and ice in summer. The fragrant, delicate white blossoms, a symbol of purity, are woven into the headpieces of country brides. The blossoms also make for one of the country's most beguiling spoon sweets, a specialty of Andros, in the Cyclades (where orange blossoms are also put up in syrup). And finally, those leaves, exuding their intoxicating lemon scent, are the country serving plates for a delicious Cyclades sweet called *pasteli*, a sesame-honey brittle, which is served at weddings.

CLASSIC AVGOLEMONO SOUP

SOUPA AVGOLEMONO

===== SERVES 2 TO 4 =====

One of the measures of a good avgolemono soup has nothing to do with the emulsion and everything to do with the comfort level provided by the starch, which should be the short-grain, glazed sticky rice called *glasé* (gla-SEH), available in Greek markets across the United States and also in Europe. Carolina rice is also commonly used in soups. Both are glutinous varieties, which add creaminess to the avgolemono. So does orzo pasta, which also gives the final soup a satisfying texture. This recipe calls for either whole eggs or yolks in the avgolemono. The former will make for a slightly paler soup, while using just the yolks will give the soup a golden color. To make an avgolemono sauce for a stew or braised dish, you can adapt the technique, using the cooking or braising liquid instead of soup broth.

4 cups/960 ml fish or chicken broth

⅔ cup/140 g Greek *glasé* or another short-grain rice or short orzo

Salt and pepper

2 whole large eggs or egg yolks

Juice of 1 lemon, strained, or more to taste

Bring the broth to a boil in a soup pot and add the rice or orzo. Season with salt and pepper. Reduce the heat and simmer with the pot partially covered for about 15 minutes, or until the rice or orzo is tender.

While the soup is simmering, whisk the eggs or yolks in a non-reactive bowl until very frothy. Whisk in the lemon juice. Take a ladleful of the broth, skimming it off the top so as not to get any rice or orzo, and very slowly pour into the egg-lemon mixture, whisking vigorously as you do. Repeat with a second ladleful. Pour the avgolemono back into the pot, tilting the pot, as Greek cooks do traditionally, or stirring it to distribute the mixture evenly. Serve immediately.

VARIATION: One of my favorite variations is a relative newcomer to the Greek kitchen, saffron avgolemono. Add 6 to 8 strands of Greek saffron (Krokos Kozanis) to the egg-lemon mixture before pouring hot broth into it. Saffron avgolemono is excellent made with fish broth.

ZUCCHINI AND ZUCCHINI BLOSSOMS WITH EGG-LEMON SAUCE

KOLOKYTHIA KAI ANTHOI AVGOLEMONO

===== SERVES 6 TO 8 =====

This recipe is one of the many unusual dishes from Arcadia, in the central Peloponnese. It's a beautiful summer dish. Serve this with a simple grilled or sautéed fish and pour one of the region's aromatic Moschofilero wines.

1 lb/455 g young zucchini, about 1 in/2.5 cm in diameter and 3 to 4 in/7.5 to 10 cm long, with blossoms attached; or zucchini sliced into ½-inch rounds; plus 10 to 12 more blossoms (optional)

3 tbsp extra-virgin Greek olive oil

1 large red onion, finely chopped

2 garlic cloves, minced

1 cup/240 ml vegetable or chicken broth or water

Salt and pepper

½ cup/30 g finely chopped fresh flat-leaf parsley

½ cup/30 g finely chopped fresh dill

1 large egg

Juice of 1 lemon, strained

Remove the stem from the zucchini, but try to keep the flowers attached. Remove the stamens from inside the flowers. If a few flowers fall off, don't worry!

In a wide saucepan or deep frying pan, heat the olive oil over medium heat and cook the onion, stirring, until soft, about 10 minutes. Add the garlic and stir together a few times. Add the zucchini and additional blossoms (if using) and cook in the oil for a few minutes. Pour in enough broth or water to come about halfway up the contents of the pot. Season with salt and pepper and bring to a boil. Reduce the heat, cover, and simmer for 8 to 10 minutes, until the zucchini and blossoms are tender. Add the parsley and dill 3 to 4 minutes before removing from the heat.

Whisk together the egg and lemon juice vigorously. Take a ladleful of the pot broth and slowly drizzle into the egg-lemon mixture, whisking all the while. Continue ladling in broth until the mixture is warm, or tempered. Remove the zucchini from the heat and pour the egg-lemon mixture into the pot, tilting it so that the liquid is evenly distributed. Serve immediately.

GREEK OMELETS

When eggs are the main ingredient (as opposed to being exploited for their numerous other charms, such as leavening or binding), the real object of Greeks' affection is the omelet. A Greek omelet doesn't quite follow the dexterous rules of flipping and rolling that so characterize its French progenitor, and it is called by a dizzying number of regional names, such as *omeleta*, *sfoungato*, *froutalia*, and frittata. Most Greek omelets are whole-frying-pan affairs, cooked round, relatively thick, and a little drier than French omelets. They are served pie-shaped or cut into triangular pieces, and may be eaten warm or at room temperature. Typically, they contain either the best raw ingredients of the season or the specialties of particular regions.

In the Peloponnese and in Crete, for example, spring would not go by without at least one lunch or quick dinner of an *omeleta* filled with either young artichokes or the long strands of wild, tender asparagus. Summer in the islands and elsewhere is punctuated by casual meals of zucchini and herb omelets. In Andros and Tinos, two of the Cyclades islands, a quick, hearty meal is an omelet, called a *froutalia*, which might be filled with chunks of potatoes, local sausages, or fresh fava beans. In Mani and other parts of the Peloponnese, the region's cured pork, *siglino*, is a common addition. Omelets are also a showcase for the handful of different pork and beef sausages, flavored with orange, leeks, or strong garlic and fenugreek, that are made all over Greece. (The feta cheese omelet made famous by legions of Greek diners owes its provenance not to some country village in Greece but to the anonymous short-order cook who most likely invented it.)

ZUCCHINI-HERB OMELET WITH OLIVE OIL AND CHEESE

OMELETA ME KOLOKYTHAKIA, MYRODIKA KAI TYRI

SERVES 2

Regional versions of zucchini omelets abound in Crete and the other Aegean islands. For example, one, called *tiritim*, from the island of Syros, calls for scallions but no cheese. This recipe contains sheep's milk cheese, mint, and dill. It is a quick meal enjoyed all over Greece. Baby zucchini work best. Serve the omelet either hot or at room temperature.

5 oz/140 g baby zucchini

Salt

2 tbsp extra-virgin Greek olive oil

2 large eggs

Pepper

1 tbsp chopped fresh mint

3 tbsp snipped fresh dill

2 tbsp grated *ladotyri*, *kefalotyri*, or another hard, yellow sheep's milk cheese

Trim the zucchini and cut into ⅛-in-/3-mm-thick rounds. Put in an 8- or 10-in/20- to 25-cm dry, nonstick frying pan. Sprinkle with a little salt, and cook over medium-low heat until the zucchini exude most of their liquid, 4 to 5 minutes. Add the olive oil and cook the zucchini until they turn light gold.

Whisk the eggs, a pinch of salt, a pinch of pepper, the mint, and dill together in a bowl. Pour the eggs evenly over the zucchini, tilting the pan so that the eggs are evenly distributed. Cook until the eggs are set. Remove from the heat, flip onto a large plate, sprinkle with the grated cheese, and serve.

BAKED GROUND BEEF OMELET FROM LESVOS

SFOUNGATO APO TIN LESVO

SERVES 6

Sfoungato, a common Greek word for "omelet," probably derives, at least etymologically, from *ova sfongia*, a kind of pancake with eggs, milk, and flour made by ancient Romans.

⅓ cup/80 ml extra-virgin Greek olive oil

8 oz/225 g ground beef

3 scallions, white parts only, finely chopped

1 medium red onion, finely chopped

Salt and pepper

8 large eggs

½ cup/60 g grated *kefalotyri*, *ladotyri* from Mytilene, or another hard, yellow sheep's milk cheese

½ cup/30 g finely chopped fresh flat-leaf parsley

Preheat the oven to 350°F/175°C/gas 4.

Heat the olive oil in a 12-in/30-cm nonstick, ovenproof frying pan over medium heat and cook the meat, stirring, for about 8 minutes, or until it changes color from red to grayish-brown. Add the scallions and onion and cook, stirring, for about 5 minutes, until they have softened. Season lightly with salt and pepper.

Whisk the eggs vigorously in a bowl and season lightly with salt and pepper. Stir in the grated cheese and parsley. Pour the eggs over the ground meat mixture, tilting the pan so the eggs are evenly distributed. Place in the oven and bake until set, about 10 minutes. Remove from the oven, cool for a couple of minutes, cut into wedges, and serve.

CLASSIC OMELET WITH POTATOES AND SAUSAGE FROM ANDROS

FROUTALIA ME PATATES KAI LOUKANIKA

===== SERVES 4 TO 6 =====

Froutalia is a local specialty from the Cycladic islands of Andros and Tinos. It is usually made with sausages and potatoes, but it can also be found with broad beans and with local cheeses and eggs. It makes for an easy, quick, hearty meal.

2 tbsp unsalted butter

2 tbsp extra-virgin Greek olive oil

4 large waxy potatoes, peeled and cut into ¼-in-/6-mm-thick rounds

11 oz/310 g fennel-flavored pork sausage, cut into 2-in/5-cm pieces

Salt and pepper

4 large eggs

2 tbsp grated *kefalograviera* cheese

3 tbsp milk

Melt the butter with the olive oil in a heavy 12-in/30-cm frying pan over high heat. Add the potatoes and sausage and season with salt and pepper. Reduce the heat to medium and cover the pan. Let the potatoes and sausage cook slowly for 20 to 25 minutes, shaking the pan occasionally to keep them from sticking. The potatoes should be cooked through, crisp, and lightly browned.

In a small bowl, beat together the eggs, cheese, and milk. Season with a little pepper and salt if desired. Pour the eggs over the potatoes and sausage, tilting the frying pan so the eggs are evenly distributed. Cover and cook slowly over low heat, tilting the pan a few times until the eggs are set on the bottom, 4 to 5 minutes. Have a large plate ready. Remove the frying pan from the heat and place the plate over it (use an oven mitt). Flip the *froutalia* onto the plate and slide it back in the frying pan to cook until set on the other side, about 3 minutes. Slide onto a serving platter and serve hot.

VARIATION: Froutalia with Fresh Fava Beans. Replace the potatoes and sausages with 1½ lb/680 g of fresh young tender fava beans, unshelled, or 1 lb/455 g frozen shelled fava beans, defrosted. Blanch the favas in salted boiling water for 1 minute. Drain and pat dry. Sauté the favas and 2 tbsp of chopped fresh mint in the butter and olive oil for 5 minutes. Omit the cheese and milk and beat the eggs. Add them to the pan and proceed with the recipe.

WHITEBAIT OMELET

OMELETA ME ATHERINA

===== SERVES 2 =====

This unusual dish, from the cooking traditions of the Pontioi—the Greeks from around the Black Sea—is one of the pan-fried fish "cakes" that Greeks like to make with small fish. Similar dishes, with or without eggs, are enjoyed in the eastern Aegean islands.

3½-oz/100-g whole whitebait (*atherina*)

Flour for dredging

Salt and pepper

¼ cup/60 ml olive oil for frying

2 large eggs

2 tbsp water

Wash and drain the fish. Spread out two sheets of wax paper on a work surface. Put some flour on the wax paper and season with salt and pepper. Toss the fish in the flour, shaking off any excess.

Heat the olive oil in a 10-in/25-cm nonstick frying pan over high heat and place the floured fish in one even layer in the pan. Fry lightly, turning once to brown on the other side.

As the fish fries, whisk the eggs and water together and season with salt and pepper. When the fish is crispy, add the egg mixture, tilting the pan so the eggs are distributed evenly. Cook over low heat until set, about 5 minutes. Invert the omelet onto a plate and slide it back into the frying pan to cook on the other side for 4 to 6 minutes. Cut into wedges and serve warm.

SLOW-COOKED OMELET WITH CURED PORK

KAYIANAS

SERVES 4 TO 8

Kayianas is one of the most traditional Greek egg dishes; it's more like scrambled eggs with tomatoes and cured pork than like an omelet. It is a specialty of the Peloponnese, where it is served as a quick meal.

1 lb/455 g Greek cured pork (*pasto* or *siglino*), cut into 1-in/2.5-cm chunks, or any sweet sausage or cured pork, such as kielbasa, prosciutto, or Spanish jamón

⅔ cup/160 ml extra-virgin Greek olive oil

6 medium firm, ripe tomatoes (about 2 lb/910 g), grated (see Note on page 74)

8 large eggs, lightly beaten

Salt and pepper

Put the pork in a 10-in/25-cm nonstick frying pan and cook over medium heat until lightly browned and cooked through. Remove from the frying pan with a slotted spoon and discard the fat. Heat the olive oil in the same frying pan over medium heat. Add the tomatoes, lower the heat, and simmer until the tomatoes have lost most of their juices, about 25 minutes. Add the cooked sausage or cured pork and warm through, for about 5 minutes.

Pour the eggs over the tomatoes and sausage, tilting the frying pan so the eggs are evenly distributed. Cook over medium-low heat for 3 to 4 minutes. Then, using a wooden spoon or spatula, gently stir them in the frying pan until the eggs are set, but not too dry. Season with salt and pepper and serve.

EGGS COOKED ON A BED OF GREENS, FROM PELION

AVGA ME HORTA APO TO PELION

SERVES 4

Eggs are cooked with all kinds of seasonal vegetables in Greece. This dish, from Pelion—an area especially rich in wild greens—is great for brunch or lunch. Sunny-side-up eggs cook in small indentations made in the wilted greens. I suggest chard and spinach because these are easy to find, but any combination of sweet greens and herbs may be used here.

1 cup/240 ml extra-virgin Greek olive oil

3 red onions, finely chopped

5 garlic cloves, minced

2 lb/910 g greens, such as chard, spinach, or sweet dandelion greens, trimmed, washed, spun dry, and finely chopped

1 tbsp tomato paste

½ cup/120 ml hot water

1 cup/175 g chopped plum tomatoes (canned are fine)

Salt and pepper

4 large eggs

Heat the olive oil in a large, deep frying pan or wide, shallow pot (you will need a lid), over medium heat. Sauté the onions and garlic until the onions have softened. Add the greens and stir with a wooden spoon until wilted. (Add the greens in batches if they do not fit in all at once.) When the greens wilt and lose most of their volume, dilute the tomato paste in the hot water and add to the pan along with the tomatoes. Season with salt and pepper. Cover the pan partially, reduce heat to low, and cook for about 20 minutes, until the greens have lost all their water.

Make 4 wells in the surface of the mixture. Break the eggs carefully, one at a time, placing one in each well. Cover, reduce the heat to low, and cook until the eggs are done. Using a dull knife or metal spatula, divide the greens and eggs into quarters, which will make it easier to remove each egg with its bed of greens and transfer to an individual plate. Serve immediately.

GREEK EASTER AND EGGS

The egg is a universal symbol of life, and Easter in Greece would be unthinkable without baskets of ruby-colored eggs. There are many explanations for why people dye the eggs red for the holiday. Greeks have their own explanation, culled from a wealth of folk-tales. According to one story, when a woman carrying a basket of eggs heard the news that Christ was resurrected, all the eggs suddenly turned crimson.

There are other, more practical, reasons why we eat so many eggs at Easter, and why we dye them. First of all, March and April mark the season in which hens lay a profusion of eggs. Since traditionally, Christians did not eat eggs during Lent, by the time Easter arrived, eggs abounded in the barnyard. Boiling them was a way of preserving them. And dyeing them may have been a diversion.

In Greece, Easter eggs are always painted on Holy Thursday, sometimes called Red Thursday, which was the day Christ was crucified. At one time Greeks followed an almost ritualistic tradition. In many parts of the country, the number of eggs was limited to the number of family members, plus one extra in honor of the Virgin Mary. In some regions, eggs could be dyed only with a certain type of red wood, and the dye couldn't be discarded or removed from the premises. The first egg thrown into the dye, which was the egg of the Virgin Mary, was thought to keep children safe from the evil eye. Eggs that were sent to church to be blessed on Holy Thursday were also thought to possess protective virtues. Among the Pontioi, the Greeks from around the Black Sea, it was customary to take the eggs to church on Thursday, have them blessed, and keep them there until Easter.

CHAPTER 4

GREEK
COUNTRY
SOUPS

SUNNY, WARM GREECE IS NOT A COUNTRY WITH A GREAT
SOUP TRADITION, BUT THERE ARE PLENTY OF LOVELY,
RUSTIC SOUPS THAT BUBBLE ON STOVE TOPS IN COUNTRY
KITCHENS. BEANS ARE THE MAINSTAY OF GREEK SOUPS,
ESPECIALLY CHICKPEAS, LENTILS, AND NAVY BEANS.

They are usually simple, with few extraneous ingredients, like the Baked Chickpea Soup from Sifnos (page 111).

Trahana, a unique and very ancient pasta product (for lack of a better way of describing it) is another important ingredient in the Greek soup pot. Hearty vegetable and beef soups are winter food in Greece, while fish soups abound in every season. A number of regional oddities—northern Greek yogurt soups, Aegean island bulgur and tomato soups—round out the assortment.

More than a few sophisticated soups have evolved in restaurant kitchens as chefs experiment and push Greek food beyond the limits of tradition. One chef, Lefteris Lazarou of the restaurant Varoulko, in downtown Athens, seduces customers with his delicious concoctions. Many of these, like his onyx-colored squid-ink soup, have inspired other chefs to experiment with overlooked ingredients.

I am a great lover of soups, rustic and refined, and present a collection of both in the following recipes, which are organized by season.

ELEGANT TRAHANA SOUP

TRAHANOSOUPA EXEVGENISMENI

SERVES 6 TO 8

Pebble-shaped *trahana*, one of the most rustic and ancient Greek grain products, is the basis for this simple soup. It is a classic Greek country dish that is somewhat gentrified because the soup is puréed to a velvety cream and garnished elegantly.

¾ cup/180 ml extra-virgin Greek olive oil, plus extra as needed

1 large red onion, very finely chopped

2 cups/340 g sour *trahana*

8 to 10 cups/2 to 2.4 l hot chicken or vegetable broth

Salt and pepper

1 to 2 tsp red pepper flakes

2 cups/480 ml thick Greek yogurt for garnish

Heat ¼ cup/60 ml of the olive oil in a large soup pot over medium heat and add the onion. Cook, stirring occasionally, until the onion is soft, about 12 minutes. Add the *trahana* and stir to coat in the oil. Pour in 8 cups/2 liters of the broth. Raise the heat to high, bring to a boil, and reduce the heat to medium-low. Season with salt and pepper. Let the *trahana* soup simmer for about 15 to 20 minutes, until the grains of the *trahana* have almost completely disintegrated and the soup is thick, like porridge.

While the soup is still piping hot, transfer it, in batches if necessary, to a food processor. Pulse on and off, adding a little more olive oil and additional hot broth until the texture of the soup becomes creamy, like a velouté. Pour the soup back in the pot and heat before serving. Dilute it further if necessary, as the *trahana* will thicken as it cools.

Warm the remaining olive oil and red pepper flakes in a small frying pan over low heat. Serve the soup hot, drizzled with the pepper oil and a few spoonfuls of Greek yogurt.

VARIATIONS: You can also garnish the soup with raw julienned leeks or thin slices of botargo. You can also fry julienned leeks, first dredging lightly in flour, or sauté sliced button or other mushrooms and sliced leeks in a little olive oil. Remember to season lightly with salt.

CREAMY TRAHANA SOUP WITH PUMPKIN AND ONIONS FROM LACONIA

TRAHANA ME KOLOKYTHA APO TIN LACONIA

SERVES 6

This is a very simple country dish from one of the poorest parts of Greece, Laconia, in the southern Peloponnese. I took a few liberties with it in order to intensify the flavor and make it more appealing to American and Western European palates. In the Greek country kitchen, one wouldn't typically roast the pumpkin to get the most flavor out of it, as I've done here. Nor are the toasted seeds or broth part of the original recipe, which simply calls for cooking everything together in one pot.

2 lb/910 g pumpkin, cut into wedges, seeds removed and saved

Kosher salt or coarse sea salt and pepper

1 cup/240 ml extra-virgin Greek olive oil

1 large red onion, finely chopped

1 cup/170 g sour *trahana*

4 cups/960 ml water or chicken or vegetable broth

2 to 3 tsp strained fresh lemon juice

Preheat the oven to 400°F/200°C/gas 6. Season the pumpkin lightly with salt and pepper and put in a shallow baking pan. Roast until lightly charred, 35 to 40 minutes.

Meanwhile, wash the pumpkin seeds and pat dry with a paper towel. In a dry frying pan over low heat, toast the pumpkin seeds with a little salt and pepper. Remove from the heat and set aside.

About 15 minutes before removing the pumpkin from the oven, heat ¼ cup/60 ml of the olive oil in a large pot over medium heat and cook the onion, stirring, until wilted. Add the *trahana* and stir to coat in the oil. Add the water. Bring to a boil, lower the heat, and simmer the *trahana* until it is creamy and thick, about 20 minutes.

Remove the pumpkin from the oven. Cool slightly, scrape out the pulp, and add it to the *trahana*. Season with salt and pepper. Using an immersion blender, purée the soup, adding 3 to 4 tbsp of olive oil and water as needed, until very creamy. Stir in the lemon juice. Serve, drizzled with the remaining olive oil and the toasted pumpkin seeds sprinkled on top.

NOTE: You can strain the soup in a chinois or fine-mesh sieve to make it even more elegant and refined. Try serving it with a few drops of hot pepper oil or a dash of cayenne.

LENTIL SOUP WITH TINY PASTA BALLS

FAKES ME KOUSKOUSI

In Greek cooking, the marriage of lentils and pasta is unique to the Dodecanese, a custom that may have been adopted from the Italians, who ruled the Dodecanese between 1912 and 1943. This is a rustic soup, made in several versions throughout the Dodecanese. This particular recipe comes from Astypalea, where the soup is prepared with tiny homemade pasta granules. To make it easier, I suggest using Greek *kouskousi*, tiny dried pasta balls, which may be found in Greek markets throughout the United States and Western Europe. You can also make it with farro.

½ cup/120 ml extra-virgin Greek olive oil, plus extra for drizzling

2 large red onions, coarsely chopped

9 oz/255 g small green or brown lentils

6 cups/1.4 l water or vegetable broth

1 bay leaf

⅓ cup/100 g *kouskousi*

Salt and pepper

½ bunch fresh mint, leaves only, finely chopped

3 tbsp red wine vinegar

Warm the ½ cup/120 ml of olive oil in a large, wide pot over medium heat. Stir in the onions, cover, and lower the heat. Cook the onions until deeply caramelized, 25 to 30 minutes, checking and stirring occasionally so they don't burn.

Wash and drain the lentils. Add the lentils to the caramelized onions and stir. Pour in the water, add the bay leaf, and bring to a boil over medium heat. Immediately reduce the heat to low and simmer, partially covered, until the lentils are al dente.

Add the *kouskousi* and continue simmering, uncovered, until the mixture is thick and the pasta and lentils are tender, 10 to 12 minutes more. Remove the bay leaf and season with salt and pepper. Add the mint and vinegar and stir, drizzle with olive oil, and serve.

OUZO-SPIKED CHESTNUT SOUP

KASTANOSOUPA ME OUZO

Greece is blanketed with chestnut trees, many of them wild. In the savory kitchen, chestnuts most often appear in slow-braised meat dishes, especially pork, often in combination with dried fruits.

50 chestnuts in the shell or sous vide

4 leeks, white part only, washed well

4 tbsp unsalted butter

2 tbsp extra-virgin Greek olive oil, plus extra for drizzling

1 large fennel bulb, finely chopped

2 garlic cloves, minced

1 cup/240 ml ouzo

12 cups/2.8 l chicken broth

Salt and pepper

½ cup/120 ml heavy cream, plus more as needed

If using fresh chestnuts, score them with a sharp paring knife and put in a pot with enough water to cover by 2 in/5 cm. Bring to a boil over high heat, reduce the heat, and simmer until the chestnuts are soft, 35 to 40 minutes. Drain the chestnuts, let cool, and peel. If using sous vide chestnuts, put the bag in boiling water and cook according to the package directions. When the chestnuts have cooled, crumble them.

Chop 3 of the leeks finely and cut the fourth lengthwise into thin ribbons.

Heat 2 tbsp of the butter and the 2 tbsp olive oil over medium heat in a large soup pot and sauté the fennel, chopped leeks, and garlic until soft, 8 to 10 minutes. Add the chestnuts and stir. Pour in the ouzo. As soon as the ouzo produces steam and the alcohol has mostly evaporated, add the chicken broth. Bring to a boil, reduce the heat, and simmer for about 40 minutes.

Using an immersion blender, purée the soup in the pot. Alternatively, empty its contents in batches into the bowl of a food processor and process at high speed until smooth. Either way, strain the soup through a fine-mesh sieve and return to the soup pot. Taste and adjust the seasoning with salt and pepper.

Return the soup to a simmer, add the cream, and stir. Adjust the seasoning again if necessary. Right before serving, stir in the remaining 2 tbsp of butter. Serve in individual bowls with a drizzle of extra-virgin olive oil and the ribbons of leeks as garnishes.

BAKED CHICKPEA SOUP FROM SIFNOS

SIFNEIKI REVITHADA

===== SERVES 4 TO 6 =====

Chickpeas, an ancient legume in the Mediterranean, are a considered a national dish in Sifnos, in the Cyclades islands. This soup—prepared in tapered clay pots that narrow at the mouth, called *xespastaria* in the local dialect—is the de rigueur Sunday meal. Every family has its own such pot and brings it on Saturday night to the local baker, preferably one with a wood-burning oven. The soup bakes all night and is done just in time for families to pick it up on the way home from church the next day. Sometimes rice or dried corn is added to make the soup more filling. The clay pot is sealed with a strip of dough, which keeps the aromas and steam from escaping.

Salt

1 cup/115 g all-purpose flour

2/3 cup/160 ml water

One 1-lb/455-g bag dried chickpeas, picked over, rinsed, soaked overnight in water to cover, and drained

2 large red onions, coarsely chopped

1 cup/240 ml extra-virgin Greek olive oil

3 bay leaves

In a medium mixing bowl, combine 1 tsp salt, the flour, and water. Mix with a fork until a dough mass forms, then remove from the bowl and knead on a lightly floured surface until smooth and no longer sticky. Let the dough rest for 20 minutes, covered with plastic wrap, in a clean, lightly floured bowl.

Put the chickpeas in a large ovenproof clay or earthenware pot with a lid. Add the onions, olive oil, bay leaves, salt to taste, and enough water to cover by 3 in/7.5 cm. Place the lid on top. Roll out the dough into a thick rope and pat it around the rim of the clay pot, pressing with your fingers to seal.

Put the pot in a cold oven. Heat the oven to 260°F/125°C/gas ½. Bake the chickpeas for 8 hours. Remove from the oven, cool slightly, and break off the dough with a dull knife. Remove the bay leaves and serve.

VARIATION: Before you bake the chickpeas, add 2 peeled and finely chopped carrots and 2 finely chopped celery stalks. If you like, you can also add 2 to 4 tbsp of strained fresh lemon juice. Alternatively, add 2 fresh rosemary sprigs, 2 crushed garlic cloves, the strained juice of 1 navel or Seville orange, 2 tbsp honey, 1 tbsp balsamic vinegar, and 1 cup canned chopped tomatoes. Bake as directed.

CHICKPEA SOUP WITH PASTOURMA

REVITHADA ME PASTOURMA

===== SERVES 6 =====

We serve this on cold winter days at Pylos, in New York City. The recipe is inspired by many northern Greek bean and legume soups with a touch of spice. Try cooking the soup with 1 or 2 small dried chile peppers added to it. *Pastourma* is a spicy cured beef. You can find it in gourmet shops and Greek and Middle Eastern stores all over the United States and Western Europe.

1 small garlic bulb

8 sun-dried tomatoes

½ cup/120 ml warm water

½ cup/120 ml extra-virgin Greek olive oil, plus extra (optional) for drizzling

1 large onion, coarsely chopped

One 1-lb/455-g bag dried chickpeas, picked over, rinsed, soaked overnight in water to cover, and drained

6 cups/1.4 l chicken or vegetable broth or water, plus extra as needed

1 bay leaf

1 large red onion, chopped

Salt and pepper

Strained fresh lemon juice

3 slices (about a ½ oz/15 g) *pastourma* (spiced cured beef), trimmed and cut into small dice

Preheat the oven to 400°F/200°C/gas 6. Using a serrated knife, cut off the root end of the garlic bulb, leaving the cloves somewhat exposed. Wrap the bulb in aluminum foil and roast for about 45 minutes, until soft. Remove and cool slightly.

Soak the sun-dried tomatoes in the warm water for about 30 minutes, to soften. Drain, reserving the soaking liquid, and cut into thin ribbons or fine dice.

In a medium nonstick frying pan, heat 2 tbsp of the olive oil over low heat and add the coarsely chopped onion. Cook for about 40 minutes, stirring occasionally, until golden, soft, and caramelized.

Combine the chickpeas, broth, tomato soaking water, bay leaf, and red onion in a large pot and bring to a boil over medium-high heat. Reduce the heat to medium-low, cover, and simmer the chickpeas until very soft. The age of the chickpeas will affect their cooking time, which can range from 1 to 2½ hours. Remove the bay leaf.

Using a slotted spoon, remove about half the chickpeas from the pot and transfer to the bowl of a food processor. Squeeze the roasted garlic cloves into the bowl, too. Purée until smooth, and return to the pot. Return to a boil, season with salt and pepper, and add broth or water as needed to bring the soup to the desired consistency, which should be fairly thick and hearty. Add lemon juice to taste and stir in the remaining olive oil right before removing from the heat.

To serve the soup, ladle into individual bowls and place some of the tomato, *pastourma*, and caramelized onions in a small mound in the center of each bowl. Drizzle in a little more olive oil if desired.

PELOPONNESE BEAN SOUP WITH SARDINES AND FETA

FASOLADA ME SARDELES KAI FETA

SERVES 6

This hearty winter dish is a favorite midday meal during the harvest of Kalamata table olives, which takes place from November through January in Greece.

⅔ cup/160 ml extra-virgin Greek olive oil

3 large red onions, finely chopped

3 medium carrots, peeled and finely chopped

3 celery stalks, with leaves, finely chopped

1 lb/455 g dried medium white beans, such as cannellini, picked over, rinsed, soaked overnight in water to cover, and drained

8 cups/2 l water

Salt and pepper

6 to 12 salted sardine fillets, rinsed

8 oz/225 g Greek feta cheese, crumbled

Heat half the olive oil in a large pot over low heat and cook the onions, carrots, and celery together until softened, about 12 minutes. Add the beans and toss to coat in the oil. Pour in the water. Raise the heat and bring to a boil. Reduce the heat to low, cover, and let the beans simmer, skimming the foam from the top, for about 2 hours, or until the soup is thick and creamy and the beans and vegetables are very soft. About 10 minutes before removing from the heat, season with salt and pepper.

As soon as you remove the *fasolada* from the heat, pour in the remaining olive oil. Serve hot, with 1 or 2 sardines and a little feta sprinkled over each serving or on the side.

VARIATION: Toss a large strip of orange peel into the beans as they simmer, as cooks in Hania, western Crete, do.

LACONIC ASPARAGUS SOUP

SOUPA APO SPARAGGIA APO TI LACONIA

SERVES 6

This soup is from Laconia, in the deep Mani, the southernmost part of the Peloponnese. This rustic yet elegant soup is a Lenten special, traditionally eaten without cheese during Holy Week, which happens to be when wild asparagus and bryony, a local wild green that looks a little like asparagus, are in season. It is difficult to find either of them in the United States or northern Europe; I've suggested substituting cultivated asparagus. Just look for the tenderest, freshest stalks you can find.

2 bunches tender, green wild asparagus, or 1 lb/455 g cultivated asparagus

1 cup/240 ml extra-virgin Greek olive oil

2 garlic cloves, crushed and cut into thin slivers; or 3 garlic scapes, trimmed and chopped

6 scallions, trimmed and cut into 1½-in/4-cm lengths

8 cups/2 l water

Coarse sea salt and cracked black peppercorns

4 slices good country bread, 1 in/2.5 cm thick, preferably slightly stale

Juice of 2 lemons, strained

4 to 5 oz/110 to 140 g grated aged *graviera* or Parmesan cheese (optional)

Preheat the broiler.

Trim the asparagus, removing the coarse, fibrous bottom 1 in/2.5 cm or so of each stalk. Cut each stalk lengthwise down the middle and then cut each half in half again to get 4 lengths.

In a medium soup pot heat ¼ cup/60 ml of the olive oil over medium heat. Add the asparagus, garlic, and scallions. Reduce the heat to low, stir to coat the asparagus in the oil, and cook for 3 to 4 minutes. Pour in the water. Season with salt and cracked peppercorns and bring the water to a boil. Reduce the heat and simmer, uncovered, for about 20 minutes over low heat, until very tender.

Meanwhile, grill the bread under the broiler, charring it lightly on both sides.

Put each slice of bread on the bottom of a soup bowl. Whisk together the lemon juice and the remaining ¾ cup/180 ml olive oil. Remove the soup from the heat and pour in the olive oil–lemon mixture. Ladle the soup over the bread. Serve hot, sprinkled with grated cheese, if desired.

DODECANESE TOMATO-BULGUR SOUP

TSOURVA

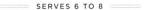

SERVES 6 TO 8

Bulgur, one of the most ancient wheat products in the Greek kitchen, is a constant in the cuisine of the southern Dodecanese and Crete. It is cooked into pilafs and stuffed into vegetables, Easter lamb, and goat. The custom of using it so copiously in these islands probably has to do more with economy than with anything else. Rice until just a few decades ago was an expensive, mostly imported grain. Bulgur, on the other hand, was always available, since wheat was a backyard crop in many Greek country homes. This soup, delicious in its simplicity, is a specialty of tiny Tilos, but similar recipes abound in other southern Aegean islands, too.

½ cup/120 ml extra-virgin Greek olive oil, plus extra for drizzling

2 large red onions, finely chopped

15 large, ripe tomatoes (about 4 pounds/1.8 kg)

1 cup/200 g coarse bulgur

10 cups/2.4 l water

Salt and pepper

1 to 2 tsp sugar (optional)

1 cup/150 g crumbled Greek feta cheese

Fresh mint leaves, chopped, for garnish

Heat the ½ cup/120 ml olive oil in a large soup pot over medium heat, and cook the onion until wilted, about 10 minutes. Add the tomatoes and bring to a simmer. Add the bulgur, stir, then pour in the water. Season with salt and pepper. Bring the soup to a boil over medium heat, reduce the heat, and simmer, partially covered, for about 45 minutes, or until the soup is thick and the bulgur is soft. Adjust the seasoning with additional salt, pepper, and sugar, if needed, to counter the acidity of the fresh tomatoes.

Serve in soup bowls, garnished with crumbled feta, chopped mint, and a drizzle of extra-virgin olive oil.

GRAPE LEAF VELOUTÉ SOUP

SOUPA ME AMBELOFYLLA

SERVES 8

In Ikaria, we're lucky to have lots of wild things growing all around us, including very old wild grapevines, which provide leaves and shoots for all sorts of dishes in the spring. One year around Easter, I decided to make this soup, inspired by one I had tasted at Aneton, a great little restaurant in the northern Athenian suburb of Maroussi. You will need to look for fresh grape leaves, which can be found in winemaking regions. Leaves in brine won't do. Serve the soup warm or chilled.

8 oz/225 g fresh grape leaves

4 tbsp unsalted butter, plus 2 tsp

2 tbsp extra-virgin Greek olive oil, plus extra for drizzling

2 large white onions, finely chopped

1 fennel bulb, finely chopped

2 leeks, washed well and finely chopped

2 garlic cloves, minced

½ cup/30 g fresh mint leaves, plus more (optional) for garnish

2 potatoes, peeled and cut into small dice

6 cups/ 1.4 l water or chicken broth

⅓ cup/80 ml heavy cream

Grated zest of 1 lemon

1 tbsp strained fresh lemon juice

Salt and pepper

Fried grape leaves (optional)

Rinse and finely chop the grape leaves.

Heat the 4 tbsp butter and the 2 tbsp olive oil in a large soup pot over medium heat and sweat the onions, fennel, leeks, and garlic for 10 to 12 minutes, until tender. Add the chopped grape leaves, mint, and potatoes. Stir to coat in the oil and butter and pour in the water. Bring to a boil, cover, reduce the heat, and simmer until the potatoes are very tender and the grape leaves are very soft.

Using an immersion blender, purée the soup in the pot. If desired, strain through a fine-mesh sieve and return to the pot. Add the cream and simmer to warm through. Just before removing from the heat, add the lemon zest and juice. Season with salt and pepper. Swirl in the remaining 2 tsp of butter. Remove from the heat and serve, garnished with fresh mint leaves or fried grape leaves and a drizzle of olive oil.

KAKAVIA

My story about *kakavia*, a classic fish soup, takes place on Ikaria, the small island in the eastern Aegean where I have family roots and a house, and where I spend as much time as two school-age children allow.

The waters around the island are deep and cold and the fishing is good, especially for large fish like bass, grouper, and rockfish, the kind that people love in soups. The best *kakavia* I've ever had was at our fisherman friend Niko's little shack on the rocky western coast, in a tiny village called Nanoura. After a day of spearfishing, he emerged with mesh sacks filled with lots of good fish for soup. The variety is important for a proper *kakavia*, but so is another ingredient, more easily obtained: seawater. Niko dutifully filled an old bucket and poured the seawater into the pot. The whole thing was cooked outside over a wood fire. The accompaniments were bread, ripe tomatoes, and rustic country wine.

Kakavia is named for the pot in which it is cooked, a *kakavi*, which is a cauldronlike vessel that is slightly narrower at the top. *Kakavia* is the traditional soup of Greek fishermen, made on board the boat or, like that day in Nanoura, in some small coastal stopover. Fishermen usually make *kakavia* from fish that they deem commercially unsuitable—maybe a little torn up, for example—but always fresh. The real thing requires a variety of fish, a hot fire, copious amounts of olive oil, and fresh lemon juice. The best fish for *kakavia* are the deepwater kind, fish that like depths of 20 to 200 meters (65 to 650 feet), a category that includes scorpion fish and perch. Other fish, especially sea bass, with its gelatinous flesh, are perfectly suited, too, the better to thicken the soup.

Density and texture are important. A great *kakavia* is filling and hearty, so cooks often add potatoes, which break down and help thicken the broth. Celery, carrots, and tomatoes are also added sometimes.

Typically, the vegetables are cooked in a lot of olive oil over very low heat before the fish enter the pot. Then, just enough water, more olive oil, and lemon juice follow. The fish is served either separately or in the broth, usually with a *paximadi* (rusk) at the bottom of the bowl.

There are a number of regional variations. In the Cyclades, vinegar and onions are de rigueur. In the Dodecanese, local cooks consider a *kakavia* incomplete without sea bream, crabs, or shrimp. The version on page 118 is something of a local specialty in the southeastern islands of Symi, Rhodes, and Kastelorizo.

CLASSIC GREEK FISHERMAN'S SOUP

KAKAVIA

===== SERVES 8 =====

This classic fish soup is traditionally made with seawater, and cooked onboard the fishermen's boats.

2 cups/480 ml extra-virgin Greek olive oil, plus more for serving (optional)

4 large red onions, finely chopped

2½ lb/1.2 kg whole firm-fleshed fish with big bones, such as grouper, any of the bream, scorpion fish, sea bass, or porgies, scaled and gutted

Coarse salt and pepper

¼ to ½ cup/60 to 120 ml strained fresh lemon juice

8 barley rusks

***Latholemono* for serving, if using**

Heat 1 cup/240 ml of the olive oil in a large soup pot over medium heat. Add the onions, reduce the heat to very low, and sweat the onions in the oil until very soft, 15 to 20 minutes.

Place the largest whole fish on the bottom of the pot and layer them by size so that the smallest are on top. Add enough water to cover the fish by about 2 in/5 cm. Season generously with salt and pepper. Cover and bring to a boil over high heat. Reduce the heat to low and simmer for 20 to 25 minutes, until the fish is very tender and the broth is flavorful.

Using a slotted spoon, carefully remove the fish from the pot. Add the remaining 1 cup/240 ml olive oil and lemon juice to taste and stir briskly. Put a barley rusk in each soup bowl and ladle the soup over the rusks. Clean the bones from the fish and serve the flesh in the broth or separately, dressed with olive oil or *latholemono* (see page 21). Serve immediately.

NOTE: You can wrap the fish in cheesecloth before putting it in the pot to prevent any bones from breaking off into the soup.

VARIATION: Add 2 garlic cloves, 1 to 2 diced celery stalks, and 1 diced carrot to the pot and sweat with the onions. When the vegetables are soft, add 1½ cups/140 g diced zucchini, and 3 to 4 chopped fresh peeled plum tomatoes. Add the fish and water. For added flavor, put a few sprigs of fresh oregano or thyme in the water before cooking the fish, and proceed with the recipe.

EASTER LAMB SOUP

MAGEIRITSA

===== SERVES 8 TO 10 =====

Every Greek, save for a few timid souls, waits all year for Holy Saturday to arrive so he or she might indulge in a plate of *mageiritsa*, the Easter soup made unapologetically of every manner of offal. The soup, named after the Greek word for "cook," *mageirevo*, is one in a long array of offal and viscera specialties, but its name implies a certain embrace on the part of the cook of almost anything that a lamb or goat has to offer and that a cook can make good use of.

There are regional versions of the soup all over Greece. The following recipe is common almost everywhere. In addition to the innards, it includes romaine lettuce, a lot of dill, and a tempering dose of avgolemono. For all its wealth of offal and viscera, *mageiritsa* is actually meant to calm the stomach after the arduous forty-day Easter fast and prepare for the roasted, carnivorous delights of Easter Sunday.

In some places, local custom dictates that cooks wash the intestines and braid them before adding them to the soup; others boil the lamb's or goat's head or hooves in the broth. Regional variations include the mint-flavored *mageiritsa* of Thessaly, in central Greece, which is more like a stew; the tomato-based version from the Peloponnese; and a garlicky one from Corfu.

Intestines, heart, lungs, liver, and other organ meats of 1 lamb

Lemon juice

8 cups/2 l water

Salt

¼ cup/60 ml extra-virgin Greek olive oil

1 lb/455 g boneless lamb, finely chopped (optional)

8 scallions, white and tender green parts, finely chopped

2 cups shredded romaine lettuce

1 cup/60 g chopped fresh dill

Pepper

½ cup/120 g Greek *glasé* or another short-grain rice

AVGOLEMONO

5 large eggs

Juice of 2 large lemons, strained, or more to taste

Cut the intestines into 12-in/30.5-cm lengths. Attach the pieces to the water faucet, one at a time, and run warm water through them until they are very clean, squeezing them between thumb and fore-finger, if necessary, to force out any impurities. Make sure to do this thoroughly. Set aside in a bowl and squeeze a little lemon juice over the intestines. Next, wash all the remaining viscera very well under cold water. Chop into small pieces.

Bring the water to a rolling boil, salt generously, and drop in the intes-tines. Blanch for 2 to 3 minutes and remove with a slotted spoon. Let cool, then chop into small pieces, about ½ in/12 mm long. Leave the cooking liquid in the pot.

Heat the olive oil in a large, heavy frying pan over medium heat and sauté the liver and other viscera until lightly browned. Remove with a slotted spoon. Sauté the lamb bits (if using) in the same frying pan until lightly browned and remove. Sauté the scallions until wilted.

Return the intestines and sautéed meats to the pot. Bring the water to a boil and add the scallions, lettuce, and dill. Return to a boil, season with salt and pepper, reduce the heat, and simmer for about 1 hour. Add the rice and continue simmering until the rice is soft, about 20 minutes.

To make the avgolemono: In a medium bowl, whisk together the eggs and lemon juice until frothy. Very slowly whisk in one ladleful of the soup in a slow, steady stream, then repeat with the second one, beating vigorously with a whisk to keep the egg from curdling.

Pour the avgolemono into the pot and stir well with a wooden spoon. Adjust the seasoning with additional salt, pepper, and lemon juice to taste, if desired, and serve immediately.

VARIATION: Lamb Shank *Mageiritsa*: Skip the innards and bone-less lamb and make the soup with lamb bones and shanks. Begin by sautéing the bones and shanks, and then proceed with the recipe.

CHAPTER 5

PLENTY OF VEGETABLES

GREECE, WITH ITS SUNNY CLIME AND AGRICULTURAL ECON-
OMY, IS VERY MUCH A VEGETABLE LOVER'S PARADISE. THE
PREPARATION OF VEGETABLES ON THE COUNTRY TABLE GOES
BEYOND THE GOAL OF MERE NOURISHMENT; THE SOCIAL,
RELIGIOUS, AND PRACTICAL ARE ALL INTERTWINED IN THIS
COUNTRY'S TREMENDOUS RANGE OF VEGETABLE DISHES.

The social is evident in Greeks' ties to the land, which is typically near their ancestral villages. Many urban Greeks still spend vacation time or even retire to their native villages, often to the family house, which might be a few generations old. It is in these village settings that they reconnect with nature. Many people keep gardens, even city folks like me, when they return to their village in summer. The garden provides nourishment for the family but also basketfuls of gifts—zucchini, tomatoes, summer greens, and more—that people exchange all summer long.

The social also comes into play at the open-air farmers' markets that come to every city neighborhood once a week, where Greeks shop for their vegetables. Here women mostly do the perusing, filling their shopping carts as they chat with each other and with the vendors. A shopper might ask how to make something with an unusual green, or complain about the price of things, or test the veracity of a hawker's claim to quality by trying a slice or two of some fresh vegetable or fruit. There's a lot of shouting back and forth, most of it good-natured.

The markets are a lesson in seasonality. With the exception of a few vegetables, mainly hothouse tomatoes and cucumbers, virtually everything else arrives when nature intended it to. To this day, seasonality is one of the basic tenets of the Greek vegetable table.

Vegetable cookery has some ties to the religious practices of the country, too: During periods of fasting, which account for roughly half the year

for those who follow the rules strictly, fish and animal products are off the table. Vegetables and legumes, cooked mainly in copious amounts of delicious extra-virgin Greek olive oil, are on. (See The Greek Touch: Ladera on page 135.)

Vegetable cookery is also practical. It is extremely flexible, for example. Many vegetable-based dishes may be served hot, warm, or even at room temperature. Quite a few can be served as either a main course or an accompaniment. There are plenty of nights in my house when *spanakorizo*—spinach rice pilaf—is the main meal, served with a little feta and some bread. But it's also a dish that can be transformed into an elegant, simple base for, say, a piece of grilled salmon. That's just one example of dozens, if not hundreds, of such foods.

Greeks have been accidental vegetarians long before the term came into vogue in the United States. While today the population boasts the dubious honor of being among Europe's greatest carnivores, vegetable cookery is still vibrant. Greek vegetable dishes, mostly seasonal, are a good thing for sustainable agriculture. These dishes are simple, and include a wealth of one-pot dishes, stews, and casseroles, and many braised bean and vegetable recipes. But there is also a range of humble, inexpensive dishes that make for some of the Mediterranean's most delicious foods.

MASHED POTATOES WITH FETA AND GREEK YOGURT

POURES ME FETA KAI YIAOURTI

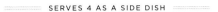 SERVES 4 AS A SIDE DISH

This rustic version of olive oil mashed potatoes makes a great accompaniment to grilled meats and all kinds of ground meat dishes. Try it with the Smyrna-Style Small Meat "Sausages" (page 299).

- 4 medium boiling potatoes, skins left on, washed well
- 1 garlic clove, minced
- ¼ cup plus 2 tbsp/90 ml extra-virgin Greek olive oil
- ¼ cup/60 ml Greek yogurt
- 3 tbsp milk
- 8 oz/225 g Greek feta cheese, crumbled
- 2 tbsp finely chopped fresh parsley
- Salt and pepper

Put the potatoes in a pot of cold salted water to cover. Bring the water to a boil and cook the potatoes until the skins burst and the potatoes are fork-tender. Drain, remove from the pot, cool slightly, and peel.

Put the potatoes in a medium nonreactive bowl and mash with a potato masher, gradually adding the garlic, olive oil, yogurt, milk, and feta and continue mashing until smooth and well blended. Add the parsley and season with salt and pepper. Serve hot.

POTATOES COOKED IN OLIVE OIL WITH OREGANO AND PAPRIKA

PATATES SYVRASI

SERVES 6 TO 8 AS A SIDE DISH

Paprika is the telltale sign that this dish comes from northern Greece, which is pepper country. It's an old recipe from Kozani.

- 2 lb/910 g potatoes
- 2 to 3 tbsp all-purpose flour
- ½ tsp paprika
- Salt and pepper
- 1 cup/240 ml extra-virgin Greek olive oil
- 2 medium firm, ripe tomatoes, grated (see Note on page 74)
- 2 tsp dried Greek oregano

Peel the potatoes, cut into rounds ½ in/12 mm thick, and pat dry. Combine the flour and paprika in a medium bowl. Season with salt and pepper. Toss the potatoes in the flour, shaking off the excess.

Heat the oil in a large, heavy frying pan over medium-high heat, and add the potatoes. Cook, turning gently, until lightly browned and crisp, 7 to 9 minutes. Pour in the grated tomatoes and continue cooking until the potatoes are tender and the tomato sauce has thickened, 25 to 30 minutes. Adjust the seasoning with a little more salt and pepper. Season with the dried oregano and serve.

GREEK GRANDMOTHER'S ROASTED POTATOES

YIAYIOUDISTIKES PSITES PATATES

SERVES 6 AS A SIDE DISH

These roasted potatoes are a delicious accompaniment to meats and fish.

2 lb/910 g large roasting potatoes

Coarse salt and pepper

2 tbsp dried oregano

3 garlic cloves, chopped

⅔ cup/160 ml extra-virgin Greek olive oil

Juice of 1 large lemon, strained

Preheat the oven to 350°F/175°C/gas 4. Peel the potatoes. Cut them lengthwise into quarters, or if they are extra large, into eighths. Spread out the potatoes in a baking pan large enough to hold them in one layer. Toss with salt and pepper, and the oregano, garlic, olive oil, and lemon juice. Bake for about 1 to 1½ hours, tossing occasionally, until the potatoes are tender and lightly browned. Serve hot.

VARIATION: In the name of lightness, many Greek home cooks now blanch their potatoes before baking them. Here's one of my favorite foolproof recipes: Heat the oven to 450°F/230°C/gas 8. Place the potatoes in a large pot of salted water and turn the heat to high. As soon as the water begins to boil, cook for 8 minutes. Remove, drain, peel, and quarter the potatoes. Whisk or shake together 1 cup/240 ml dry white wine, ½ cup/120 ml extra-virgin Greek olive oil, ½ cup/120 ml fresh, strained lemon juice, 3 tbsp dried oregano, 4 garlic cloves (chopped), 1 tbsp/30 ml Dijon mustard, salt, and pepper. Place the potatoes in a single layer in a baking dish and pour in the wine mixture. Bake for 10 minutes, uncovered, then lower the heat to 375°F/190°C/gas 5 and continue baking for 20 to 25 minutes, until fork tender. Remove and serve.

GREEK FRIES

PATATES TIGANITES

SERVES 4 AS A SIDE DISH

If I had to guess how often people in the Greek countryside eat potatoes fried in olive oil, I'd say, based on my own experiences in a Greek village, at least a once a week. The potatoes pair well with fried eggs for a quick meal or with more elaborate meat stews for a Sunday lunch.

6 Yukon gold or White Rose potatoes

Olive oil for frying

Coarse salt

1 tbsp dried oregano

¼ cup/30 g grated *kefalotyri* cheese

Scrub and rinse, but do not peel, the potatoes. Cut into rounds. Put the potatoes in a bowl of ice water in the refrigerator and let soak for 1 hour. Remove, drain, and blot the pieces dry with a lint-free kitchen towel.

Heat about 1 in/2.5 cm of olive oil in a large, heavy frying pan or nonstick wok and carefully drop as many potatoes into the pan as will fit in one layer. Let the potatoes cook in the oil until lightly browned on both sides, turning once. Remove with a slotted spoon and transfer to a bowl lined with a few paper towels. Repeat with remaining potatoes. Remove the paper towels and toss the fries with salt, the oregano, and grated cheese. Serve immediately.

AT THE FARMERS' MARKET

Almost everyone in Greece is lucky enough to have a bustling weekly farmers' market right in the neighborhood. As a cook, one of my greatest pleasures is to shop for fruits and vegetables at my local outdoor market. I like to get there early, especially in winter, when the vendors are just setting up. At around 5:30 in the morning they pull up to their spot with vans, or pickups, or larger trailer trucks and begin unfolding their long wooden tables on both sides of the road. For a good hour, they move back and forth between truck and table, piling up mounds of fresh seasonal fruits or vegetables from the stacks of blue, red, and green crates that spill out of their trucks. Every few steps, someone lights a small fire inside a tall wooden drum; this will keep the vendor warm during the seven or eight hours the market is open on a cold day.

These markets are a testimony to the importance of seasonality in the Greek kitchen. The colors of the market change with the season. The comforting brown, beige, ochre, and deep green of winter squashes, cabbages, and *horta* (wild greens) segue into a symphony of vibrant shades of green when spring arrives, bringing with it several varieties of artichokes, wild fennel, sprightly peas, fava beans, young carrots with their greens intact, and more. Then, as summer arrives, the market blooms with every shade of red, yellow, orange, and purple: strawberries, apricots, cherries, medlars, peaches, and nectarines. Watermelons, cut open and proffered to passersby as proof of their sweet pedigree, share a stall with tomatoes in every size and eggplants in every shape.

Some vendors sell dried foods: handpicked oregano, mountain tea, and lavender; sacks of regional beans and varieties of Greek rice. Others sell household goods, from inexpensive table napkins to socks and pajamas. On the outskirts of every market, gypsies set up shop, selling everything from rugs to potatoes from their pickups.

Everywhere, shoppers with carriages and carts in tow navigate a crowded passage, surveying the wares with a keen interest in finding the best for the least money. Wooing them becomes a shouting match between vendors who roar out claims like "Honey, sugar, aroma like the best perfume," to describe their selection of Marathon melons, Naoussa peaches, and Tripoli apples. These often rough-and-tumble vendors will take offense loudly should some economy-minded shopper mention that she saw the same mushrooms for half the price down the road. The sellers also exchange their frank opinions on the politics of the day, holding forth over their customers' heads in this most public and democratic of arenas. In fact, these traveling markets are actually called "people's markets," *laiki agora* in Greek.

Some hawkers are just vendors, making a 3:00 A.M. stop at the huge commercial vegetable market in an industrial section of Athens before setting up. The best, though, are real farmers, whose fields are usually within a two-hour drive of the market. A few are artisan agrarians who grow heirloom vegetables, unique herbs, and unusual greens. More and more are turning to organic farming, too.

For city dwellers like me, the local *laiki* is a place to feel closer to nature when nature seems too far away. It is also the place that reminds me of why Greeks probably eat about twice as many fresh fruits and vegetables as Americans. Greek fruits and vegetables, ripened under months of relentless sunshine, are delectable.

OUZO-BRAISED CABBAGE
WITH PORK SAUSAGE

LAHANO STO TETZERI ME LOUKANIKO KAI OUZO

===== SERVES 4 TO 6 AS A SIDE DISH =====

Interpretations of this dish can be found in the country kitchens of several Cyclades islands, especially those with a strong charcuterie tradition, among them Syros, Tinos, and Mykonos.

6 oz/170 g pork sausage, preferably seasoned with fennel seeds, removed from its casing

½ cup/120 ml extra-virgin Greek olive oil

1 medium cabbage, trimmed and coarsely shredded

1 large fennel bulb, cut into julienne strips

1 garlic clove, minced

½ cup/120 ml ouzo

Salt and pepper

Grated zest and strained juice of 2 lemons

1 tbsp all-purpose flour

1 tbsp chopped fresh wild fennel or dill

In a medium, heavy frying pan over low heat, cook the sausage meat until lightly browned. Remove and set aside.

Heat the olive oil over medium heat in a large, wide pot and sauté the cabbage, fennel, and garlic, stirring occasionally, for 5 to 6 minutes, or until the cabbage wilts and reduces to half its original volume. Add the ouzo and season with salt and pepper. Cover the pot, reduce the heat to low, and simmer the cabbage for about 15 minutes. Add the lightly browned sausage meat to the cabbage mixture.

Whisk together the lemon zest, juice, and flour. Stir this mixture into the pot and simmer for another 7 minutes. Add the chopped fennel and serve immediately.

SAUTÉED SPINACH
WITH ORANGE AND GARLIC

**SPANAKI SOTARISMENO ME PORTOKALI
KAI SKORDO**

===== SERVES 4 TO 6 AS A SIDE DISH =====

In the Mani—the southern part of the Peloponnese, and one of the agriculturally poorest parts of the country—little flourishes besides citrus and olive trees. I sampled this humble dish in the home of a local cook many years ago and have made it countless times since. Oranges and olive oil and a generous dose of garlic provide the flavor palette, which enhances the spinach. I haven't seen this combination of flavors anywhere else in Greece.

1 large navel orange

⅔ cup/160 ml extra-virgin Greek olive oil

1½ lb/680 g spinach, trimmed, washed, and spun dry

2 garlic cloves, thinly sliced

Salt

Using a sharp knife, remove the rind of the orange and cut into 1-in/2.5-cm strips, including some of the pith and fruit as you go.

Heat the olive oil in a large, deep frying pan over medium heat. Add the spinach. As soon as the spinach wilts, add the garlic, season with salt, and add the orange rind. Cover the frying pan, lower the heat to medium-low, and cook the spinach for about 20 minutes, or until dark and completely soft. Serve warm in a deep dish or bowl, together with the cooking juices, garlic, and orange rind.

PUMPKIN-SWEET POTATO MOUSSAKA

MOUSSAKAS ME KOLOKYTHA KAI GLYKOPATATES

===== SERVES 8 =====

Greeks are obsessed with moussaka. It's their culinary flag, a patriotic symbol of all that's Greek. This obsession with moussaka is expressed by modern cooks in endless searches for ways not so much to better the original as to change it. This dish is one of my contributions to the moussaka archives, a recipe I first developed for Pylos restaurant in New York City (where I have a small stake and a lot of freedom to experiment), and then adapted for use in my own home kitchen. It has become a favorite in late fall, when pumpkins and sweet potatoes are easy to find. Sweet potatoes have been available in Greece for a few hundred years, and are cooked in myriad ways throughout the Ionian islands. Pumpkins have been around for about as long, and Greeks love to use them in the fall in both savory and sweet dishes.

CHEESY BÉCHAMEL

4 tbsp unsalted butter

¼ cup/30 g all-purpose flour

4 cups/960 ml milk, at room temperature

2 large eggs, lightly beaten

1 cup/150 g grated or crumbled Greek feta cheese

½ cup/60 g grated Parmesan or *kefalotyri* cheese

Salt and pepper

½ tsp grated nutmeg

VEGETABLES

2 tbsp olive oil for sautéing, plus extra

4 large red onions, coarsely chopped

Flour for dusting

1½ lb/680 g pumpkin, peeled, seeded, and cut into ¼-in/6-mm slices

1½ lb/680 g yellow squash, trimmed but not peeled, and cut lengthwise into ¼-in/6-mm slices

1½ lb/680 g sweet potatoes or yams, peeled and cut lengthwise into ¼-in/6-mm slices

Salt and pepper

1 cup/60 g chopped fresh mint

½ cup/30 g chopped fresh flat-leaf parsley

To make the béchamel: Melt the butter in a large pot over medium heat and when the butter stops bubbling, add the flour. Cook, stirring with a whisk, until lightly colored. Pour in the milk slowly, whisking constantly, and continue whisking until the sauce thickens, 10 to 12 minutes total. Remove from the heat and pour in the eggs, whisking vigorously. Stir in the cheeses. Season with salt and pepper and stir in the nutmeg. Set aside.

To prepare the vegetables: Heat the 2 tbsp olive oil in a large, nonstick frying pan over medium heat. Add the onions and cook slowly until soft and lightly caramelized, 15 to 20 minutes. Remove from the heat.

While the onions are cooking, put the flour in a shallow bowl, and heat about ¼ in/6 mm of olive oil in a second large frying pan. Dust the pumpkin slices very lightly with flour, shaking off the excess. Sauté until lightly browned, turning once, and drain on paper towels. Repeat, dredging and sautéing the yellow squash. Pour off the oil and wipe the frying pan clean. Add a little more oil and sauté the sweet potatoes, turning, until lightly colored around the edges. Remove and drain on paper towels.

Preheat the oven to 350°F/175°C/gas 4. Lightly oil a 12 x 8 x 2-in/ 30.5 x 20 x 5-cm baking pan. Layer the sweet potatoes in the bottom of the pan. Season with salt and pepper and sprinkle with one-third of the mint and a little parsley. Spread a scant layer of caramelized onions on top. Pour about one-third of the béchamel over the onions, spreading it evenly with a spatula. Repeat with a layer of pumpkin, salt and pepper, herbs, onions, and a little béchamel. Repeat once more with the yellow squash, topping that, too, with salt and pepper, herbs, onions, and the final coating of béchamel. Bake for 35 to 40 minutes, until the béchamel is puffed and golden and the vegetables are tender. Remove from the oven and let rest for about 10 minutes before serving.

PUMPKIN ROASTED WITH FETA, TOMATOES, AND MINT

KOLOKYTHA PSITI ME FETA, DOMATA KAI DYOSMO

===== SERVES 6 TO 8 =====

Surprisingly to most non-Greeks, the cuisine is filled with dozens of unusual pumpkin recipes, both savory and sweet. Several, like this recipe, fall into the category of rich, oozing-with-cheese, layered casseroles. You can reinvent this as individual terrines, too.

2 lb/910 g pumpkin, peeled, seeded, and cut into ⅛-in/3-mm slices or thinner

Salt

4 tbsp extra-virgin Greek olive oil

2 large red onions, finely chopped

3 large tomatoes, peeled, seeded, and diced

Flour for dusting

Pepper

¾ cup/45 g finely chopped fresh mint leaves

2 cups/300 g crumbled Greek feta cheese

Place the pumpkin slices in layers in a large colander in the sink, salting each layer lightly.

While the pumpkin is draining, heat 2 tbsp of the olive oil in a large frying pan over medium heat and sauté the onions for 7 to 8 minutes, until soft. Add the tomatoes and continue cooking until most of their liquid is gone, about 10 minutes more.

Preheat the oven to 350°F/175°C/gas 4. Lightly oil an 8 x 8 x 3-in/ 20 x 20 x 7.5-cm baking pan. Pat the pumpkin dry. Put some flour in a shallow dish and toss the pumpkin lightly in the flour, shaking off any excess.

Put a layer of pumpkin slices in the bottom of the pan. Season with a little pepper. Spread some of the tomato-onion mixture on top, and season lightly with salt. Sprinkle a little mint and feta over the tomato-onion mixture. Repeat until all the ingredients are used up, pressing down lightly with a spatula as you go and ending with a layer of the tomato-onion mixture, sprinkled with cheese. Drizzle the remaining 2 tbsp olive oil over the pan, cover with aluminum foil, and bake for about 50 minutes, until the pumpkin is tender. About 10 minutes before removing from the oven, remove the aluminum foil to so that the top layer browns lightly.

VARIATION: In Chios, an island in the northeastern Aegean, a similar dish is made in the frying pan and is a little reminiscent of potatoes Anna, but with pumpkin. Use all the same ingredients as here, omitting the tomatoes. Do not sauté the onions. Dredge the pumpkin slices and, in a large, heavy, oiled skillet, make alternating layers of pumpkin, salt, pepper, onions, feta, and mint, ending with a layer of pumpkin. Cover the skillet and cook the pumpkin over very low heat until the bottom slices have browned, about 25 minutes. Slide onto a plate and flip back into the skillet carefully, to cook on the other side, for about another 15 minutes, covered. This dish is a dinner party showstopper.

CHEESE, POTATO, AND ZUCCHINI PIE FROM HANIA

BOUREKI HANIOTIKO

SERVES 8 TO 10

Boureki is the name of a delicious layered summer pie from Hania, in western Crete. It typically calls for a local cheese, *xinomyzithra*, which is difficult to find in the United States and Western Europe. You can use a combination of *anthotyro* or ricotta, and feta, as I suggest below.

2 lb/910 g zucchini, cut into ¼-in-/6-mm-thick rounds

Salt

8 oz/225 g fresh *anthotyro* or ricotta cheese

8 oz/225 g Greek feta cheese, crumbled

5 large potatoes

5 tablespoons extra-virgin Greek olive oil

Flour for dusting

Pepper

Heaping 1 tbsp dried mint

Layer the zucchini in a colander in the sink and salt each layer lightly. Press the zucchini down in the colander with the cover of a pot and let it drain for 30 minutes. Rinse and pat dry with a lint-free towel. In a large bowl, mix together the *anthotyro* and feta.

Peel the potatoes and cut into ¼-in-/6-mm-thick rounds. Oil a 15-in/38-cm round baking pan, or a 12 x 15 x 2-in/30.5 x 38 x 5-cm rectangular pan with 1 tbsp of the olive oil. Preheat the oven to 375°F/190°C/gas 5.

Put the flour in a large, shallow dish and mix with a little salt. Toss a handful of the zucchini in it to dredge, shaking off any excess.

Cover the bottom of the baking pan with a single layer of potatoes and season lightly with salt and pepper. Spread a layer of zucchini on top. Dot generously with a layer of the cheese mixture, season with pepper, and sprinkle with some mint. Repeat the layers until all ingredients are used up. Drizzle the remaining olive oil over the top and bake until golden, about 50 minutes. Remove from the oven and let cool for at least 15 minutes before serving.

WARM WHOLE ZUCCHINI WITH LEMON, OLIVE OIL, FETA, AND HERBS

KOLOKYTHAKIA ME LATHOLEMONO KAI FETA

SERVES 6 AS A SIDE DISH

This simple dish is a take on the more-pedestrain boiled zucchini salad found in tavernas all over Greece.

1 tbsp pine nuts

¼ cup/60 ml extra-virgin Greek olive oil

2 lb/910 g small zucchini, trimmed and left whole

2 tbsp strained fresh lemon juice

1 garlic clove, minced

2 tsp chopped fresh basil

2 tsp chopped fresh parsley

2 tsp chopped fresh mint

Salt and pepper

2 tbsp crumbled Greek feta cheese

In a small, heavy, dry frying pan, lightly toast the pine nuts over low heat until pale gold. Remove from the pan and set aside.

Heat half of the olive oil in a large frying pan over medium heat and sauté the zucchini until lightly colored. Reduce the heat to low, cover, and cook for 6 to 8 minutes.

Whisk together the remaining olive oil, lemon juice, garlic, and herbs. Season with salt and pepper. Plate the zucchini, drizzle with the dressing, and sprinkle with the pine nuts and feta. Serve immediately.

VARIATION: You can omit the pine nuts and whisk the feta right into the vinaigrette instead.

THE GREEK TOUCH

LADERA

IF IT EXISTS, THE GREEKS HAVE A WORD FOR IT. AND WHEN IT COMES TO THE ENORMOUS RANGE OF BEAN AND VEGETABLE DISHES BATHED IN COPIOUS AMOUNTS OF GOLDEN-GREEN GREEK OLIVE OIL, THAT WORD IS *LADERA*.

To prepare *ladera,* olive oil is used as the cooking fat, to soften onions, garlic, and every vegetable and bean imaginable. Then more olive oil is poured into the pot as it comes off the heat.

And still more is splashed over the food when it is plated. *Ladera* are mainly, but not exclusively, the dishes on which Greeks sustain themselves during periods of fasting. In winter and early spring, dried beans, artichokes, fresh fava beans, peas, young carrots, and greens are the stuff of *ladera*. But *ladera* are also the dishes of the long Greek summer: tender green beans, okra, eggplants, squash, summer greens, and bell peppers are all cooked in olive oil, often with tomatoes.

Ladera take their name from the Greek word for oil, *ladi*, which almost always refers to olive oil. When I was first learning to cook, my husband's grandmother gave me the soundest advice regarding these dishes: they are done when the only liquid left in the pot is the vegetables' olive oil. A unifying process takes place during cooking, a marriage of flavors that melds everything together most agreeably. Indeed, that's exactly what happens when vegetables and beans are cooked in very little liquid with a bold amount of olive oil, sometimes as much as 1 cup/240 ml for 2 pounds/1 kilo of vegetables.

Ladera are for the most part stove-top dishes. Nothing is al dente in a Greek olive oil–based dish. Vegetables cook for one hour, even two in some

cases, morphing into soft, comforting, almost caramelized flavors, made even more soothing by the pleasing unctuousness of the oil.

The olive oil does more than add flavor and provide a medium for cooking. According to scientists, it actually makes vegetables and beans more palatable, reducing them to a pillowy softness and smoothing the way so they are easily digested. This may be one reason why Greeks consume about 1 pound/½ kilo of vegetables a day, which is twice as much as Americans eat. Vegetables and beans aren't drained in a *ladera* dish, so by soaking up the velvety pot juices, you are also soaking up vitamins and minerals. Most important, according to food scientist Harold McGee, many nutrients, especially beta-carotene, an important antioxidant, are fat soluble, not water soluble, so we don't absorb them simply by chewing and swallowing. Cooking them in olive oil allows us to extract and absorb these nutrients more efficiently.

The sweet taste and texture of *ladera* vegetables and beans are balanced by acidic foods. Lemon juice and vinegar are almost always added to the pot. In addition, cheese—mainly feta—and sharp Greek yogurt are served with many *ladera*. *Ladera* are usually served at room temperature. Greek gourmands say that they are even better the next day.

A FEW GREEK OLIVE OIL FACTS

Olive trees grow in fifty out of fifty-four prefectures in Greece, and their cultivation and harvest occupy a considerable amount of time and energy for many a country cook, mainly because most groves are small, family-owned plots of land, requiring the efforts of an extended network of family members to tend. That also means that the olives are harvested with care, which has an immediate effect on the quality of the oil produced. Greece is the world's third-largest producer of olive oil, and the first-largest in the production of extra-virgin; some 80 percent of all the olive oil produced in the country is extra-virgin. Greece is also the leader in consumption, about 19 quarts/18 liters per person annually.

There are ten major oil olive varieties. The most important is the Coroneiki, grown mainly in the Peloponnese and Crete. An increasing percentage of Greek olive oil is organic.

LEEK AND CHESTNUT STEW WITH GREEN OLIVES

PRASA KAI KASTANA ME PRASINES ELIES

SERVES 2 TO 4 AS A VEGETARIAN MAIN
COURSE OR 6 AS A SIDE DISH

The idea of stewing leeks is unique to northern Greece, where leeks are a local favorite. I love this dish because its ingredients reflect the importance of seasonality in the Greek kitchen. This is a winter dish. It's great as a main dish with some rice, or as an accompaniment to grilled or roasted meats and pan-seared fish.

12 large chestnuts in the shell, sous vide, or canned (not in syrup)

4 leeks, white part only, cut into 1½-in/4-cm cylinders

2 celery stalks

¾ cup/180 ml extra-virgin Greek olive oil

1 carrot, peeled and halved crosswise

2 tsp all-purpose flour

1 cup/240 ml red wine

1 tbsp red wine vinegar

Salt and pepper

10 large green olives, pitted

If using fresh chestnuts, score them with a sharp paring knife and place in a pot with enough water to cover by 2 in/5 cm. Bring to a boil over high heat, reduce the heat, and simmer until the chestnuts are soft, 35 to 40 minutes. Drain the chestnuts, let cool, and peel. If using sous vide chestnuts, put the bag in boiling water and cook according to the package directions.

Put the leek cylinders in a bowl of cold water and swish around with your fingers, changing the water several times if necessary to rid the leeks of dirt and sand. Rinse thoroughly and set aside. Cut the celery into 1-in/2.5-cm pieces.

In a large, wide pot or deep frying pan, heat half the olive oil over medium heat. Add the leeks, celery, and carrot. Cook, covered, stirring occasionally, until the leeks begin to brown very lightly, about 12 to 15 minutes.

Sprinkle the vegetables with flour, stir for a minute or so, and pour in the wine. When the wine steams up, add enough water to come about halfway up the vegetables. Add the chestnuts, vinegar, and salt and pepper to taste. Cover and simmer until the sauce is thick and the leeks are tender, 20 to 25 minutes. About 5 minutes before the leeks are done, stir in the olives. Adjust the seasoning and remove from the heat. Discard the carrot halves. Pour in the remaining olive oil, stir, and serve.

LEEKS COOKED IN OLIVE OIL WITH TOMATOES AND PRUNES

PRASA LADERA ME DOMATES KAI DAMASKINA

SERVES 4 AS A VEGETARIAN MAIN
COURSE OR 6 TO 8 AS A SIDE DISH

Greeks enjoy leeks raw in salads; roasted; with chestnuts and various meats and fish; in vegetable soups, such as a leek and celery soup with avgolemono, from Andros; and slowly cooked with rice, potatoes, or beans. There is an endless number of leek pies found in every region of Greece, but primarily on the mainland, from Thessaly to Macedonia and Thrace to Epirus. In northern Greece, even octopus is cooked with leeks (see page 261).

The recipe below comes from Kozani, in Macedonia, where cooks add prunes—both sour and sweet—to meat dishes and to a few vegetable dishes. This is an old Lenten specialty, which I love and cook often, either as a side dish to accompany meat or as a simple main course, served with rice. Some versions are baked and others, like this, are cooked on the stove top.

2 lb/910 g leeks, cut into 2-in/5-cm cylinders

⅓ cup/80 ml extra-virgin Greek olive oil

1 large red onion, finely chopped or grated

1 tbsp all-purpose flour

1 cup/175 g peeled, seeded, and coarsely chopped plum tomatoes (canned are fine)

½ cup/120 ml white wine

2 to 3 fresh oregano sprigs

10 pitted dried prunes

Salt and pepper

Paprika for garnish

Put the leek cylinders in a bowl of cold water and swish around with your fingers, changing the water several times if necessary to rid the leeks of dirt and sand.

In a large wide pot or Dutch oven, heat the olive oil over medium heat. Add the onion, stir, and reduce the heat to low. Cover and cook until the onion is very soft but not browned, about 10 minutes. Add the leeks and cook, covered, until tender but al dente, about 12 minutes. Sprinkle in the flour and stir for a few minutes. Add the tomatoes to the pot and pour in the wine. Add the oregano sprigs and prunes. Season with salt and pepper. Cook, partially covered, until the leeks are tender and the sauce is thick, about 20 minutes. If necessary, add a little water to the pot during cooking. Transfer to a platter or shallow bowl, sprinkle with paprika, and serve.

NORTHERN GREEK-STYLE BRAISED LEEKS AND CELERY ROOT WITH PAPRIKA AND LEMON

PRASOSELINO KOZANIS

===== SERVES 4 =====

Celery root is one of the most traditional winter vegetables in Greece. At markets it is often sold with its thin green stalks and leaves still attached. Braised leeks and celery root is a dish made all over Greece. What gives it a northern accent is the addition of hot paprika. It is often served with either egg-lemon sauce (avgolemono) or egg and flour (called *alevrolemono*).

2 leeks, white part only, washed well and cut into 1-in/2.5-cm cylinders

1 cup/240 ml extra-virgin Greek olive oil

1 medium onion, finely chopped

1 celery root, about 4 to 5 in/10 to 12 cm in diameter, peeled and cut into 1½-in/4-cm cubes

2 celery stalks with leaves, coarsely chopped

2 medium carrots, cut into ½-in-/12-mm-thick rounds

Salt and pepper

1 tbsp all-purpose flour

Juice of 1 lemon, strained

Hot paprika (or sweet, if you prefer)

Put the leek cylinders in a bowl of cold water and swish around with your fingers, changing the water several times if necessary to rid the leeks of dirt and sand. Rinse thoroughly and set aside.

Bring a pot of lightly salted water to a boil. In the meantime, heat ½ cup/120 ml of the olive oil in a large, wide pot over medium heat and cook the onion, stirring, until wilted, 5 to 6 minutes. Add the celery root, celery stalks and leaves, and carrots and toss to coat with the oil. Cover, lower the heat, and sweat the vegetables in the oil until the celery root begins to color slightly around the edges, 5 to 6 minutes.

While the celery and carrots are cooking, blanch the leeks in the boiling, salted water for 2 minutes. Drain and add to the pot with the vegetables. Season with salt and pepper and add enough water to come about halfway up the contents of the pot. Cover and simmer the vegetables over low heat for 30 to 35 minutes.

Whisk together the flour and lemon juice. Pour into the pot about 5 minutes before removing the vegetables from the heat. When the pot juices thicken, remove from the heat, adjust the seasoning with salt and pepper, and sprinkle with a little paprika. Pour in the remaining ½ cup/120 ml of olive oil. Tilt the pot back and forth to distribute the oil evenly. Serve hot or warm.

QUINCE COOKED IN OLIVE OIL FROM KOZANI

KYDONIA LADERA APO TIN KOZANI

===== SERVES 4 TO 6 AS A SIDE DISH =====

Quince is not a vegetable, of course, but Greek cooks like to use it in savory dishes. Quince stews made with lamb, beef, and pork abound. This unusual dish, from Kozani in northern Greece, makes a great winter side dish to accompany meat and game dishes. It's perfect fare for a cold day.

Juice of 1 lemon, strained

2 cups/480 ml water

2 lb/910 g quinces

¼ cup/60 ml extra-virgin Greek olive oil

1 medium red onion, chopped

⅓ cup/65 g sugar

Salt

Pinch of paprika

Mix the lemon juice with the water in a medium bowl and set aside.

Rub the quinces with a kitchen towel, to remove the fuzz on their skins. Do not peel. Cut in half, and then cut each half into 3 or 4 wedges. Using a sharp paring knife, remove the seeds from each wedge. Submerge the quince in the acidulated water to keep from oxidizing.

Heat the olive oil in a large, heavy frying pan over medium heat. Add the onion, reduce the heat to low, and cook until golden brown, 15 to 20 minutes. Remove the quince slices from the acidulated water, pat dry, and add to the frying pan. Cook together with the onion, stirring gently, until the quince pieces begin to brown. Sprinkle in the sugar and season with salt and paprika. Cook until the quince is tender, about 20 minutes. Serve immediately.

EGGPLANT, QUINCE, AND SWEET POTATO STEW

LADERES MELITZANES ME KYDONIA KAI GLYKOPATATES

==== SERVES 4 TO 6 ====

I came across a version of this unusual vegetable stew in a book called *Lefkaditika Mageiremata* (Lefkada Cooking) by a Greek colleague, Evi Voutsina, who is one of the most experienced and respected culinary researchers in the country.

> **Juice of 1 lemon, strained**
>
> **2 cups/480 ml water**
>
> **2 large quinces**
>
> **⅔ cup/160 ml extra-virgin Greek olive oil**
>
> **4 long, thin Japanese eggplants, cut into 2-in/5-cm cubes**
>
> **Salt and pepper**
>
> **3 medium sweet potatoes, peeled and cut into 1-in/2.5-cm cubes**
>
> **1 large red onion, finely chopped**
>
> **3 garlic cloves, minced**
>
> **1½ cups/260 g peeled, seeded, and chopped plum tomatoes (canned are fine)**

Mix the lemon juice with the water in a medium bowl and set aside.

Rub the quinces with a kitchen towel to remove the fuzz on their skins. Do not peel. Cut in half, seed, and then cut into 1½-in/4-cm cubes. Submerge the quinces in the acidulated water to keep them from oxidizing.

Heat ⅓ cup/80 ml of the olive oil in a large, deep frying pan over medium-high heat, and sear the eggplant cubes until golden brown, about 4 minutes, stirring gently. Season lightly with salt and pepper. Remove with a slotted spoon and set aside. Drain the quince and pat dry. Add quinces and sweet potatoes to the frying pan. Sear, stirring, until golden brown, about 5 minutes. Season lightly with salt and pepper, remove from the pan, and set aside.

Heat the remaining ⅓ cup/80 ml of olive oil in the frying pan, add the onion, and cook over low heat until soft and lightly colored, about 12 minutes. Stir in the garlic. Return the vegetables and quince to the frying pan and stir gently for 1 minute. Season to taste.

Add the tomatoes, cover, and bring to a boil. Reduce the heat and simmer until the vegetables are tender and the sauce is thick, 20 to 25 minutes. Don't overcook; the vegetables and quince should retain their shape. Serve immediately.

SMOTHERED SUMMER VEGETABLES FROM IKARIA

IKARIAN SOUFICO

==== SERVES 4 TO 6 ====

Soufico is one of my favorite summer dishes, and it comes from my family's native island, Ikaria. To make it the traditional way requires patience. You salt each of the vegetables individually and let it drain. Then you sauté each vegetable separately in olive oil, before layering them all together in a large stew pot, Dutch oven, or another heavy pot. People cheat by cooking everything together or by using a deep fryer, but the results pale in comparison to the real thing, a dish of layered, caramelized summer veggies melded together with a copious amount of olive oil. When we owned a restaurant on the island, this was our best seller. The word *soufico* may have originated from the Italian *sofocare*, "to smother," as in smothered in all that olive oil! The *soufico* goes exceptionally well with a slice of feta on the side.

> **Salt**
>
> **4 medium zucchini, cut into ¼-in-/6-mm-thick rounds**
>
> **2 medium eggplants, cut into ¼-in-/6-mm-thick rounds**
>
> **2 large green bell peppers, seeded and cut into 1-in/2.5-cm strips**
>
> **½ cup/60 ml extra-virgin Greek olive oil, plus more for frying**
>
> **3 large onions, finely chopped**
>
> **3 garlic cloves, finely chopped**
>
> **2 large potatoes, peeled and sliced into ¼-in-/6-mm-thick rounds**
>
> **Pepper**
>
> **3 large, firm ripe tomatoes, grated (see Note on page 74)**

In separate colanders, lightly salt the zucchini, eggplant, and bell peppers. Drain for 1 hour. Wipe dry without rinsing.

In a large frying pan, heat about ¼ in/6 mm of olive oil over medium heat. Lightly fry the onions and garlic until wilted, 6 to 7 minutes. Remove with a slotted spoon and set aside. Replenish the oil in the frying pan if necessary. Add the potato slices and fry lightly until their edges begin to color.

In the meantime, pour the ½ cup olive oil into a large, wide pot or Dutch oven. Remove the potatoes from the frying pan with a slotted spoon and place in the pot, in one or, at most, two layers. Season with a little salt and pepper and strew some of the onion-garlic mixture over them.

Lightly fry the zucchini in the frying pan, adding more olive oil if necessary. When lightly colored, remove with a slotted spoon and place over the potatoes, again in one or, at most, two layers. Strew with some of the onion-garlic mixture. Fry the eggplant, place over the zucchini, and sprinkle with a little of the onion-garlic mixture. Next, fry the bell peppers ever so lightly, just to soften. Layer over the eggplant slices and season with a little pepper. Pour in the grated tomato. Cover and simmer for 20 to 30 minutes, or until the vegetables are very tender and have almost melded together into a kind of napoleon.

Serve warm or at room temperature. Using a metal spatula, cut each serving out of the pot so that it contains a bit of each layer of the *soufico*.

VLACH SUMMER STEW WITH FRIED CHEESE

MANTZA

SERVES 4 TO 6

Mantza (or *mantzia*) is the word for "stew" in the local Vlach dialects of central Macedonia and the regions a little farther north and west, toward Prespes. The Vlachs were itinerant shepherds and then merchants who settled in various parts of northern Greece and are thought to be descendants of ancient Roman guards. There are many versions of this simple, hearty dish. Some are purely vegetable stews; others combine vegetables, especially the local red pepper, with river fish like carp. This recipe includes red bell peppers and *batzos*, a regional cheese.

> 2 large eggplants, trimmed and cut into 1-in/2.5-cm cubes
>
> Salt
>
> 2 to 3 medium zucchini, trimmed and cut into 1-in/ 2.5-cm cubes
>
> ½ cup/120 ml extra-virgin Greek olive oil
>
> 1 large onion, finely chopped
>
> 3 red bell peppers, seeded and cut into 1-in/ 2.5-cm chunks
>
> 2 large firm, ripe tomatoes, grated (see Note on page 74)
>
> 1 cup/240 ml water
>
> 8 oz/225 g *batzos*, *kefalotyri*, or pecorino, cut into 1-in/ 2.5-cm cubes
>
> 2 to 3 tbsp all-purpose flour
>
> ¾ tsp sweet paprika
>
> ¼ tsp cayenne pepper
>
> 3 to 4 tbsp finely chopped fresh flat-leaf parsley for garnish

Put the eggplant cubes in a colander and toss lightly with salt. Put a plate over the eggplant and a weight on top, such as a large can of tomatoes, and let the eggplants drain for 1 hour. Set aside. Do the same for the zucchini cubes in a separate colander. Do not rinse. Pat dry.

Heat 2 tbsp of the olive oil in a large, deep frying pan or wide pot over high heat and sauté the onion and bell peppers for a few minutes to soften. Push the onion-pepper mixture to one side, or remove it with a slotted spoon from the frying pan.

Add 4 tbsp olive oil to the frying pan and sauté the eggplant and zucchini over high heat until the vegetables are lightly browned and crisp around the edges. Return the onion-pepper mixture to the frying pan. Pour in the tomatoes and water. Lower the heat to medium and cook, uncovered, until the mixure is thick.

While the vegetables are cooking, heat the remaining 2 tbsp olive oil in a nonstick frying pan over high heat. Toss the cheese cubes lightly in the flour, shaking off the excess, and sauté in the oil until golden and crisped around the edges. Just before removing the vegetables from the heat, toss the cheese cubes into the pot. Adjust the seasoning with salt and add the paprika and cayenne. Remove from the heat and serve on a platter or on individual plates, garnished with a little fresh parsley.

AMARANTH, PURSLANE, AND ZUCCHINI STEW

VLITA, GLISTRIDA KAI KOLOKYTHAKIA YIAHNI

SERVES 6

Two of the three main ingredients in this dish, amaranth and purslane, are garden weeds that grow rampant all summer long. They also happen to be extremely nutritious. This is a classic Greek island dish, which we basically live on all summer long in Ikaria.

> ½ cup/120 ml extra-virgin Greek olive oil
>
> 3 large red onions, finely chopped
>
> 5 garlic cloves, minced
>
> 2 lb/910 g amaranth, trimmed, washed, and dried
>
> 1½ lb/680 g purslane, trimmed, washed, and dried
>
> 3 large firm, ripe tomatoes, grated (see Note on page 74) or peeled and chopped
>
> 1 cup/240 ml water
>
> 6 small zucchini, about 1 in/2.5 cm in diameter and 4 to 5 in/10 to 12.5 cm long
>
> Juice of 2 lemons, strained
>
> Salt and pepper

Heat the olive oil in a large, deep pot or Dutch oven over medium heat and add the onions and garlic. Reduce the heat to medium-low and sweat the onions and garlic until tender, about 12 minutes.

Add the amaranth and purslane, cover, and cook, stirring occasionally, for 8 minutes, or until wilted. Add the tomatoes and water. Simmer, partially covered, until most of the liquid has evaporated, about 12 minutes, over medium heat.

Add the whole, trimmed zucchini and the lemon juice and season with salt and pepper. Simmer for another 6 to 8 minutes, or until the zucchini is tender. Serve warm or at room temperature.

SPINACH, POTATO, AND HERB STEW
BONAMATSI

SERVES 4 TO 6

This recipe, from Halkidiki, in northern Greece, is a classic village dish, homey and healthy. In the traditional version, there is typically no nutmeg and no lemon garnish, but they add depth and balance to the final dish. *Bonamatsi* is a type of stewed greens dish that is found all over Greece. In Crete, a similar dish, made with a variety of greens, is called *tsigarista horta*; while in Corfu, stewed greens are called *tsigarelli*.

²⁄₃ cup/160 ml extra-virgin Greek olive oil, plus extra for drizzling

1 large red onion, finely chopped

2 garlic cloves, minced

8 to 10 small potatoes, preferably new potatoes, peeled and left whole

3 large firm, ripe tomatoes, grated (see Note on page 74) or finely chopped, with their juice

Salt and pepper

2 fresh bay leaves, or 1 dried

1 lb/455 g young spinach, trimmed, washed, spun dry, and coarsely chopped

½ cup/30 g snipped fresh dill

½ cup/30 g snipped wild fennel, or 1 star anise

Pinch of freshly grated nutmeg

1 lemon, cut into wedges (optional)

Heat ⅓ cup/80 ml of the olive oil in a medium saucepan over medium heat and sauté the onion until tender, 7 to 8 minutes. Add the garlic and stir. Add the potatoes and stir to coat in the oil. Pour in the grated tomatoes, season with salt and pepper, and add the bay leaves. Cover and simmer over low heat until the tomato mixture is thick, about 20 minutes.

Add the spinach to the tomato sauce, in batches, and cook, covered, until the spinach has lost most of its volume and is wilted. Add the dill and fresh fennel or star anise. Toss gently to combine, being careful not to break up the potatoes. Adjust the seasoning with additional salt and pepper and sprinkle in a little nutmeg. Cook, covered, until the contents of the pot are thick, and the potatoes tender, about 10 minutes. Remove from the heat and remove the bay leaves. Pour in the remaining ⅓ cup/80 ml of olive oil, and serve with the lemon wedges, if desired.

SUMMER VEGETABLE STEW FROM IKARIA
MAGEIRIO OR PAMPEION

SERVES 6 TO 8

Mageiro is one of a handful of traditional summer vegetable dishes from the Blue-Zone island of Ikaria, where longevity rates are off-the-charts high thanks, in part, to a diet of these kinds of dishes. The word derives from the Greek word for cooking. Locals on the south side of Ikaria call it *Pampeion*.

½ cup/120 ml extra-virgin Greek olive oil, plus extra (optional) for drizzling

3 lb/1.4 kg green beans, trimmed and halved crosswise

2 medium red onions, coarsely chopped

3 ears corn, shucked and halved

4 medium waxy potatoes, peeled and cubed

3 large firm, ripe tomatoes, grated (see Note on page 74)

2 large zucchini, trimmed and cubed

Salt and pepper

Heat the olive oil in a large pot over medium-high heat and add the green beans and onions. Reduce the heat to medium-low, stir to coat the vegetables, and cook for about 5 minutes. Add the corn and potatoes and stir to coat with the oil. Add enough water to barely cover the vegetables. Cover, increase the heat to medium, and bring to a boil. Reduce the heat to low and simmer for 25 minutes.

Add the tomatoes and zucchini and season with salt and pepper. Stir gently to combine, cover, and simmer over low heat until all the vegetables are tender, another 25 minutes or so. Serve warm or at room temperature, drizzled, if desired, with additional olive oil.

MUSHROOMS À LA GRECQUE

Greeks have always considered mushrooms one of nature's most valuable and delicious wild foods. Low in calories, mushrooms are rich in vitamins B, C, and D, as well as iron, zinc, potassium, and niacin. Wild mushrooms' ephemeral nature and potential deadliness, if one picks the wrong one, have given them a mysterious quality.

The vast array of wild mushrooms in northern Greece includes some of the most treasured in the world, among them chanterelles, morels, porcini, trumpets, and *Amanita caesarea*, or "Caesar's Egg." This last mushroom is among the rarest. Its large orange cap has been a gourmet prize from remotest antiquity to the present. In 1979 an Italian businessman, recognizing the commercial possibilities of northern Greece's mycological riches, established the first facility for processing wild mushrooms. Today there are several.

In the country kitchen, mushrooms are typically either grilled, fried in olive oil, sautéed for omelets, or preserved in olive oil and vinegar. Morels go especially well in braised lamb dishes. Trumpets, which grow wild all over Macedonia and Thrace, have a delicious smoky flavor and pair especially well with game. Chanterelles, with their fruity taste and golden yellow color, are best with white sauces and with fish and chicken, although they are also delicious with lamb. A wild mushroom that has been cultivated with much commercial success in northern Greece is the porcini, or cèpe, with its nutty, fleshy, earthy taste. It is a favorite for the grill.

MUSHROOMS WITH GARLIC SAUCE

VASILOMANITARA SKORDATA

Greeks call porcini mushrooms *vasilomanitara*—"the king of mushrooms." The best *vasilomanitara* in Greece come from Grevena, a rugged, mountainous area in western Macedonia, not too far from the boundary with Epirus. This local recipe calls for cooking them in a hearty garlicky sauce, which appears in various forms throughout the region. These sauces, based on a roux, sometimes contain eggs (in which case they are called *avgalevria*), and sometimes ground walnuts instead of flour. In this dish, vinegar is added to counter the deep, earthy flavors of the mushrooms.

1 lb/455 g fresh porcini or other wild mushrooms

¼ cup/60 ml plus 2 tbsp extra-virgin Greek olive oil

2 large garlic cloves, minced

1 tbsp all-purpose flour

1½ cups/360 ml chicken broth or water

½ cup/120 ml dry white wine

2 to 3 tbsp red wine vinegar, plus more to taste

Salt

2 tsp finely ground walnuts

Cayenne pepper or paprika for garnish

1 to 2 tbsp minced fresh flat-leaf parsley for garnish

Rinse the mushrooms briefly and pat dry. Heat 2 tbsp of the olive oil in a large frying pan and cook the garlic for 1 minute over low to medium heat. Add the mushrooms, raise the heat slightly, and sauté until they lose some volume and exude their liquid. Remove from the heat. Drain the mushrooms, reserving their liquid, remove from the pan, and set aside.

Wipe out the frying pan, and heat the remaining ¼ cup/60 ml olive oil over low heat. Stir in the flour and whisk, stirring constantly, until it begins to turn light gold. Pour in the broth or water, the wine, and reserved mushroom liquid. Bring to a simmer. Reduce the heat to low and cook, stirring, until the sauce is as thick as a cream sauce, 6 to 7 minutes. Add the vinegar in tbsp increments to achieve the desired acidity. Season with salt.

Put the mushrooms in the sauce and cook for a few minutes to warm them up. Transfer the mushrooms and sauce to a shallow, wide bowl or platter. Sprinkle with the ground walnuts and a little cayenne pepper, and garnish with chopped parsley before serving.

MUSHROOMS BRAISED WITH GREEN TOMATOES

MANITARIA ME PRASINES DOMATES

This is an old dish from Arcadia, in the central highlands of the Peloponnese. It is made with green tomatoes, which speaks volumes about the economical habits of village cooks. Because of the country's temperate climate, you see many tomato plants heavy with firm, green fruit in November, but they don't ripen because the weather isn't warm enough. They don't go to waste, however. Green tomatoes are usually dredged and fried and served forth as an unusual meze throughout Greece. This recipe marries them with one of the great treasures of the season—the year's first mushrooms, which pop out of the earth right after the first fall rains, if temperatures are warm enough.

2 lb/910 g mixed porcini, button mushrooms, portobellos, and oyster mushrooms, in any combination

⅔ cup/160 ml extra-virgin Greek olive oil

2 large boiling potatoes, peeled and cut into 1-in/2.5-cm cubes

1 large onion, finely chopped

2 garlic cloves, minced

½ cup/120 ml white wine

1 tbsp tomato paste diluted in 2 tbsp water (optional)

2 to 3 fresh thyme sprigs

6 green tomatoes, cut into wedges

Salt and pepper

Pinch of sugar (optional)

Wash the mushrooms briefly, pat dry, and trim. Cut into strips about 3 x 1½ in/7.5 x 4 cm.

Heat the olive oil in a large, wide pot over medium heat. Cook the potatoes for 8 to 10 minutes, stirring. Add the mushrooms and stir for 1 or 2 minutes. Add the onion and garlic, stir to combine, and cook all together, stirring frequently, until the onions are tender, about 6 minutes.

Add the wine and as soon as it steams up, add enough water to come about halfway up the contents of the pot. Bring to a boil, add the diluted tomato paste (if using) and the thyme. Reduce the heat and simmer, covered, for about 15 minutes, checking occasionally to make sure there is enough liquid and adding a bit more water if the stew seems dry. Add the green tomatoes and cook for another 10 minutes or so, until soft. Season with salt and pepper. If the stew is a little too acidic, add the sugar. Cook for a few more minutes. Remove from the heat, cool slightly, and serve.

THE GREEK TOUCH

ARTICHOKES

ARTICHOKES ARE THE TELLTALE SIGN IN GREECE THAT SPRING IS ON THE WAY. LEFT TO GROW WILD, THEY SPLASH COLOR ON THE BROWNS OF A GREEK SUMMER, EACH FLOWER ALL GREEN AND LAYERED, WITH A CROWN OF MAGENTA PETALS THAT LOOK LIKE A THISTLE, WHICH IS IN FACT WHAT AN ARTICHOKE IS.

In the United States, people associate artichokes with California, but not with Greece. *Cynara* to the ancients, artichokes were noted by Theophrastus, the fourth-century B.C. recorder of Greek flora. They were savored by his contemporaries, and twenty-five hundred years later, by his heirs.

Artichokes are cultivated mainly in the Peloponnese and Crete. They reign supreme on the Easter table in both places as well as among the Greeks from Asia Minor, who make a famous old dish, artichokes *a la polita*, on Easter Sunday (and throughout the season).

There are dozens of regional recipes for this hard-to-trim vegetable, including stews, which incorporate other seasonal vegetables like fresh fava beans, wild fennel, peas, young carrots, and potatoes. There are also lots of variations on the artichoke and lamb theme, a popular combination on Easter tables in the Peloponnese. These can be either braised dishes or tangy, drier roasted specialties.

Three main varieties of artichoke arrive at Greek markets in spring. The globe artichoke is the most common, followed by a purple-hued species called the Iodine of Attica. The third is the small, thorny Cretan "wild" artichoke, which is about the size of a kiwi. It is the only artichoke savored raw, in salads with other Cretan goodies like *graviera* cheese and barley rusks (see page 43).

Greek country cooks will tell you that artichokes need two things: lemons to keep them from oxidizing before they go into the cooking pot, and a little sugar to counter their acidic bite. Their acidity makes artichokes a difficult vegetable to pair with wine.

HOW TO CLEAN ARTICHOKES THE GREEK WAY

Squeeze the halves of 1 lemon into a bowl with 4 cups/960 ml of cold water and set aside. This is the acidulated water needed to keep the artichoke hearts from oxidizing.

Remove the artichoke heart from each artichoke: First remove the coarse outer leaves. Next take a serrated knife and cut the artichoke top off, leaving a base of about 1¼ in/4 cm. Lay the artichoke on its side and, using the serrated knife, remove any remaining leaves. Take a teaspoon and scrape out the inedible purple fuzzy choke. Trim the stem, removing the tough outer part and a bit around the top so that about 2 in/5 cm of stem are left. The final cleaned artichoke should look like an inverted champagne glass. Rub immediately with a cut lemon half and drop in the acidulated water.

ARTICHOKE FLAN
FROM TINOS

ANGINAROPITA TIS TINOU

SERVES 6 TO 8 AS A SIDE DISH

In the mineral-rich soils of the eastern side of Tinos, the Aegean island's tiny, firm, complex-flavored artichoke flourishes. Local authorities concerned about developing a more sustainable local economy have taken this artichoke to heart, organizing festivities around its cultivation and promoting it throughout Greece. Artisans have taken up the cause, putting the small vegetable up in brine or steeping it in excellent olive oil and selling it at a premium. Taverna cooks have been inspired, too. One began making a kind of flan with the artichoke and bread, called it a *pita*—the Greek work for "pie"—and started a local trend. This dish is now found in most of the tavernas on the island. My version of it follows.

One 1-lb/455-g loaf semolina or another type of bread, with crust on, cut into 1-in/2.5-cm cubes

2 tbsp unsalted butter

2 tbsp extra-virgin Greek olive oil

2 large or 3 medium leeks, halved lengthwise, washed well, and cut into ½-in/12-mm pieces

12 whole artichoke hearts from globe artichokes (see page 153), or 2 lb/910 g frozen artichoke hearts, defrosted

3 large eggs, lightly beaten

1½ cups/360 ml heavy or light cream

1½ cups/360 ml whole milk

Generous pinch of grated nutmeg

Salt and pepper

¼ cup/15 g snipped fresh dill

1½ cups/150 g grated *graviera* cheese

Preheat the oven to 300°F/150°C/gas 2. Spread out the bread cubes on a baking sheet and bake for 12 to 15 minutes, turning once, until dried out and pale gold. Remove from the oven and let cool.

Raise the oven temperature to 350°F/175°C/gas 4. Lightly butter a 9 x 13 x 2-in/23 x 33 x 5-cm baking pan.

In a large, heavy frying pan over medium-high heat, melt 1 tbsp of the butter with 1 tbsp of the olive oil. Add the leeks and cook, stirring, until lightly colored, 10 to 12 minutes. Set aside.

In a separate frying pan, melt the remaining 1 tbsp of butter with the remaining 1 tbsp olive oil over medium-high heat and sauté the artichoke hearts for about 8 minutes, or until they begin to turn brown along the edges.

Beat the eggs lightly in a medium mixing bowl. Add the cream, milk, and nutmeg, season with salt and pepper, and whisk until frothy and well combined. In a large mixing bowl, toss together the bread cubes, vegetables, egg mixture, and dill. Season with salt and pepper. Mix in one-third of the *graviera* cheese.

Spread out half the mixture in the baking pan and sprinkle a third of the cheese over the top. Spread remaining mixture and sprinkle with the remaining cheese. Using the back of a large spoon or a spatula, press down slightly and let the whole thing sit in the pan for 15 minutes while the bread cubes absorb the liquid.

Bake for about 50 minutes, or until crusty on the surface. Remove from the oven, cool slightly, and cut into serving pieces. Serve hot.

CRETAN ARTICHOKE AND FAVA BEAN STEW WITH LEMON SAUCE

ANGINAROKOUKIA TIS KRITIS

===== SERVES 4 TO 6 =====

Artichokes and fava beans are both in season in the early spring in Greece and they pair naturally well together. This dish is a specialty of Crete, where the artichoke and the fava bean are local specialties. Crete grows considerable quantities of both. It's also the only place in Greece where these two harbingers of spring are savored raw, as in the salad noted in the variation.

⅔ cup/160 ml extra-virgin Greek olive oil

2 scallions, white and tender green parts, chopped

1 garlic clove, minced

2 lb/910 g fresh fava beans, shelled

6 to 8 whole artichoke hearts from globe artichokes (see page 153)

Salt

Scant 1 tbsp all-purpose flour

Juice of 2 lemons, strained

Heat the olive oil in a large, wide pot over medium heat and add the scallions and garlic. Toss to coat in the oil, reduce the heat to low, and simmer, covered, for 5 minutes. Add the fava beans, toss to coat, and add enough water to cover by 1 in/2.5 cm. Cover, bring to a boil, reduce the heat to medium-low, and simmer for 10 minutes. Place the artichoke hearts, top side down, in the pot. Season with salt. Add enough water to come about halfway up the artichokes. Cover and simmer over low heat until the artichokes are very tender, 30 to 35 minutes.

Whisk the flour and lemon juice together in a small bowl. Add a ladleful of the pan juices to the flour and lemon mixture in a slow, steady stream, whisking all the while. Pour this mixture into the pot, tilting the pot back and forth so the mixture spreads evenly throughout. Simmer until the sauce thickens, 3 to 4 minutes. Remove from the heat and serve.

VARIATION: Baby Fava Bean and Raw Artichoke Salad: Serve this dish as a salad. Combine 1 lb fava beans, shelled; 4 artichoke hearts; 2 scallions, thinly sliced; and 1 small bunch of fresh dill, chopped, in a bowl. Whisk together ½ cup/120 ml extra-virgin Greek olive oil, the strained juice of 1 large lemon, and salt and pepper to taste. Dress the salad and serve immediately. This is a classic Cretan springtime salad.

ARTICHOKE MOUSSAKA WITH CARAMELIZED ONIONS AND FETA

ANGINARES MOUSSAKA

===== SERVES 8 TO 10 =====

Artichoke moussaka is one of several variations on the moussaka theme in the Greek country kitchen. This is a delicious meatless version, made sweet by the copious amount of caramelized onions that are layered in the pan. We serve this classic Greek dish at Pylos, a restaurant in New York, and it's an all-time favorite.

2 tbsp unsalted butter

1 tbsp extra-virgin Greek olive oil

8 onions, coarsely chopped

14 whole artichoke hearts from globe artichokes (see page 153)

3 to 6 tbsp olive or other oil for frying

3 medium potatoes, peeled and sliced lengthwise ⅛ in/3 mm thick

BÉCHAMEL

6 tbsp unsalted butter

¼ cup plus 2 tbsp/45 g all-purpose flour

5 cups/1.2 l milk

1 cup/240 ml heavy cream

2 large eggs, lightly beaten

⅓ cup/50 g crumbled Greek feta cheese

¼ cup/35 g grated Greek *kefalotyri* or Parmesan cheese

½ cup/110 g Greek fresh *anthotyro* or ricotta cheese

Salt and pepper

1 tbsp chopped fresh thyme

1 tbsp chopped fresh basil

1 tbsp chopped fresh flat-leaf parsley

1 tbsp chopped fresh oregano

1 cup/50 g plain bread crumbs

Salt and pepper

1½ cups/225 g crumbled Greek feta cheese

In a large, wide pot or deep frying pan, melt the 2 tbsp butter with the 1 tbsp olive oil over medium heat until the butter begins to bubble softly. Add the onions, reduce the heat to low, and cook for about 40 minutes, stirring occasionally until the onions acquire a deep amber hue.

While the onions are cooking, bring a large pot of salted water to a rolling boil. Fill a large bowl with ice water. Blanch the artichoke hearts for 1 minute. Drop immediately into the ice water.

In a large frying pan, heat the 3 tbsp olive oil and sauté the potato slices for a few minutes, turning once, just until softened.

To make the béchamel: In a medium pot over medium heat, melt the 6 tbsp butter. When it stops bubbling, add the flour and cook, whisking constantly, for about 5 minutes, until the flour is golden. Pour in the milk and cream and cook, whisking constantly, until thick, 10 to 12 minutes. Remove from the heat and add the eggs, whisking vigorously. Mix in the three cheeses, and season with salt and pepper. Set aside.

Toss the herbs together in a small bowl. Preheat the oven to 350°F/175°C/gas 4. Oil a large roasting pan and assemble the moussaka. Sprinkle a handful of bread crumbs over the bottom of the pan. Layer a third of the potatoes in one layer. Season with salt and pepper. Sprinkle with a handful of bread crumbs. Add about a third of the onions and a third of the herb mixture. Layer a third of the artichoke hearts evenly over the herbs and onions. Season with salt and pepper and sprinkle with another handful of bread crumbs. Sprinkle with ½ cup/75 g of the feta. Repeat the layers in the same order two more times.

Pour the béchamel over the moussaka. Bake, uncovered, until pale gold, about 55 minutes to 1 hour. Remove from the oven and cool slightly. Cut into squares and serve.

ROASTED ARTICHOKE HEARTS WITH POTATOES AND OLIVE OIL

ANGINARES PSITES ME PATATES

===== SERVES 4 TO 6 AS A SIDE DISH =====

This is a springtime country dish from the island of Milos in the Cyclades islands.

> 12 artichoke hearts from globe artichokes, halved (see page 153)
>
> 5 to 6 medium potatoes, peeled and quartered
>
> 1 cup/240 ml extra-virgin Greek olive oil
>
> 3 garlic cloves, minced
>
> Juice of 1 large lemon, strained
>
> Sea salt and pepper

Preheat the oven to 350°F/175°C/gas 4. Arrange an oven rack so that it's about 8 in/20 cm from the heat source of the broiler (which you will use later).

Toss the artichoke hearts and potatoes with the oil, garlic, lemon juice, and a little sea salt and pepper. Spread out the mixture evenly in a baking pan large enough to hold the vegetables in one layer. Bake for about 1 hour, just until the artichoke hearts and potatoes are tender. Turn off the oven and turn on the broiler. Broil the vegetables so that the artichokes and potatoes become crusty and brown. Remove from the oven and serve immediately.

CRETE IS FOR FOOD LOVERS

Good food is to be found nearly everywhere on Crete. Indeed, the more obscure the venue—a *cafeneion* (a traditional Greek café) on some forgotten dirt road in a remote mountain village, for example—the more promising the meal is likely to be. It was in places just like that, run by home cooks, that I learned the most about this island's formidable cuisine.

Cretan cooking has a certain integrity. The food is simple, but hardly poor. Here, more than anywhere else in Greece, cooks have learned to make the most out of vegetables and wild greens, marrying them with grains, rice, and every imaginable protein to make the nutritious, memorable dishes that are the backbone of the Cretan diet.

I have eaten greens on Crete that I haven't eaten anywhere else in Greece, including ancient cardoons like a nest of thorns, plucked fearlessly from a wet slope on a cold, windy November day. I've slurped briny urchin "salads"—basically their squirmy coral flesh afloat in a simple plate—at seaside tavernas all over the island. I've failed at self-restraint more times than I can remember when confronted with a plate of *sfakiani pita*, a buttery phyllo pastry filled with soft, sour cheese and sweetened with thyme honey. I've walked into mountain villages during the *kazania*—the distillation of *raki*, the island's firewater—on ominous winter evenings when a storm had knocked out the electricity and the only source of light was the flame underneath the local still. Inside, a table of accompaniments for that firewater was loaded with things like roasted whole potatoes and green olive oil; stewed fennel-flavored goat; Cretan sausages, with their distinct, vinegary flavor; and cheeses, nutty, sweet, and sharp, all to wash down with liquid fire. Thanks to buttery festive pilafs, I've managed to keep my head at Cretan weddings, where one custom is *koupes* ("cups")—accepting the challenge from a fellow guest to swallow in one gulp the high-octane contents of a glassful of *raki*. Once someone does it, Crete's social rules dictate that all must follow. Hot, soothing rice cooked in a mixed meat broth helps keep in check whatever might come of such antics.

Olive oil, virtual rivers of it, fill the cooking pots all over the island, for Crete is one of Greece's major producers of extremely fine oils. Greens, honey, barley, coarse-grain products like bulgur and *trahana* (called *xinohondros* on Crete), snails, and rabbits are some of the ancient foods that are still important there today. Crete, the fifth-largest island in the Mediterranean and home to almost 10 percent of the Greek population, is a true cradle of local traditions. The simple, varied cooking of the Aegean islands comes together there.

CHAPTER 6

BEAN CUISINE

BEANS, NUTRITIOUS BEANS, HAVE SUSTAINED GREEKS FOREVER. THE ANCIENTS BELIEVED IN A GOD OF BEANS, CYAMITES, WHO PRESIDED OVER THE CULTIVATION OF FAVA BEANS AND WAS WORSHIPPED AT A SMALL TEMPLE EN ROUTE FROM ATHENS TO ELEUSIS, WHERE HE WAS A HERO OF THE MYSTERIES.

Ancient Greek literature is filled with references to beans and pulses, and remnants of these seminal foods have been found at many archaeological sites, some dating to the early Bronze Age.

The oldest beans and pulses in the Greek diet are fava beans, lupines (a medium-size, flat, pale yellow pulse), lentils, peas, chickpeas, and vetches, all of which are used in the country kitchen in one way or another. Without beans and pulses, Greeks would not have made it through wars, famine, or the Nazi occupation. They'd have had much less protein over the course of their history, especially during periods of fasting, which amount to almost half the year.

One of the most unique aspects of Greek bean cookery is that beans and pulses are eaten both dried and fresh. Chickpea shoots are savored in the spring. Black-eyed peas are eaten both fresh and dried. Fava beans are savored at the peak of green tenderness in March and April, while the dried beans are used in aromatic stews.

Bean dishes abound in every region of Greece, but especially in areas where they are cultivated. Lentils are best from Englouvi in the highlands of Lefkada, one of the Ionian islands. The best fava beans come from the Lasithi plateau in Crete. The chalky, volcanic soil of Santorini is famous for its yellow split peas. In Nyssiros, the black-eyed pea is the signature legume, but in Rhodes and Sifnos, chickpeas are cooked more than any other pulse. All the white beans, such as kidneys, elephants, and *gigantes* ("giant beans"), are best when they come from the fertile, damp terrain of northern Greece.

I could probably write a whole book on Greek bean cookery; there are so many regional recipes and endless combinations. Beans are married with greens, pork, *pastourma*, beef, lamb, and chicken in the stew pot. Greeks also enjoy them with fish, rice, bulgur, and pasta. Beans and pulses cooked with vegetables form the backbone of the simple cooking of the Aegean islands. Beans are mashed, puréed, boiled into soups, braised, baked, fried whole, made into fritters, and even grilled. One old Cretan treat is grilled fava beans, which are served with *raki*, the local firewater.

Many Greek bean dishes may be served either warm or at room temperature. The few that are in this chapter may be served either as main courses or as mezedes. There are many other recipes for beans and pulses throughout the book—in soups, salads, mezedes, and more.

GIANT BEANS BAKED WITH SPINACH AND FETA

GIGANTES STON FOURNO ME SPANAKI KAI FETA

===== SERVES 4 TO 6 =====

Row after row of tepee-shaped bean stalks line the great inland plateau of north-central Greece, around Kastoria. With its ample rainfall, moderate climate, and calcium-rich soil, the region is, among other things, bean country. So good, in fact, are the beans—especially the giant beans (*gigantes*) and small and medium-size white kidney beans—that many now enjoy the EU's Protected Designation of Origin (PDO) status. These beans are available in Greek and gourmet shops across the United States and Western Europe.

Below is one of my favorite bean dishes, a traditional recipe from Epirus, in the country's northwestern corner.

8 oz/225 g dried Greek giant or elephant beans, picked over, rinsed, soaked overnight in water to cover, and drained

2 lb/910 g spinach, trimmed, chopped, washed well, and spun dry

½ cup/30 g snipped fresh dill

½ cup/30 g chopped fresh flat-leaf parsley

1 medium leek, white and tender green parts, coarsely chopped and washed well

Salt

½ cup/120 ml plus 2 tbsp extra-virgin Greek olive oil

2 large onions, coarsely chopped, or 5 scallions, white and tender green parts, chopped

1½ cups/225 g crumbled hard Greek feta cheese, preferably goat's milk

2 cups/350 g peeled and seeded plum tomatoes (canned are fine)

Pepper

⅓ cup/15 g coarse dry bread crumbs (see Note on page 57)

Put the drained beans in a large pot with enough water to cover by 3 in/7.5 cm and bring to a boil. Reduce the heat to medium-low and simmer the beans until al dente, about 1 hour.

Meanwhile put the spinach, herbs, and leek in a colander and sprinkle lightly with salt. With the palm of one hand, rub the mixture against the holes of the colander, almost in a kneading motion, so that the greens exude liquid. Do this for 10 minutes, and then put a plate over the greens and a weight on top of the plate (such as a large can of tomatoes) and leave to drain for 1 hour.

Heat the 2 tbsp olive oil in a medium frying pan over medium heat and cook the onions, stirring, until wilted, about 5 minutes. Preheat the oven to 350°F/175°C/gas 4.

Combine the drained greens with the cooked onions and 1 cup/150 g of the feta in a large bowl. Drain the beans, reserving 4 cups/960 ml of the cooking liquid and add to the bowl. Add 1 cup/175 g of the tomatoes and toss to combine. Taste and add salt, if desired, and some pepper.

Put the beans-and-greens mixture in a large casserole or baking dish and mix in ¼ cup/60 ml olive oil and 2 cups/480 ml of the bean cooking liquid. Spread the remaining 1 cup/175 g tomatoes over the beans and sprinkle the remaining ½ cup/75g feta and the bread crumbs on top. Drizzle the remaining ¼ cup/60 ml olive oil over the surface and bake, covered with aluminum foil, until the beans are very creamy and soft, but not disintegrating. Depending on the age and condition of the dried beans, this could take anywhere from 1 to 2½ hours. Add more liquid to the pan during cooking if necessary to keep the beans from drying out. Serve hot or at room temperature.

NOTE: Salting the greens and letting them drain in a colander is the old-fashioned, traditional Greek way to soften them without losing nutrients.

AROMAS FROM MACEDONIA AND THRACE

The cuisine of Macedonia and Thrace remain largely undiscovered by outsiders.

The largest single influence on the local cuisine came with the million or so Greek refugees from the shores of Asia Minor and from the Black Sea (present-day Turkey), who arrived in 1922 as a result of the political upheavals. They brought with them a wealth of new, sophisticated, spiced dishes and culinary traditions, including moussaka, stuffed vine leaves, unusual cheeses, pasta, and the whole meze tradition. The region's ability to absorb and co-opt these diverse influences continues to this day. The dissolution of the Soviet Union in the 1980s returned thousands of Greeks who had been living in former Soviet territories in the Caucasus and around the Black Sea, back to their homeland. With them arrived another layer of foods and customs to be woven seamlessly into the tapestry of Greece's north.

NORTHERN GREECE'S UNIQUE PRODUCTS

History set a part of the Macedonian table, but the region's own geography has probably played the strongest role in how the cuisine developed. All over Macedonia and Thrace, the natural bounty is generous. Greece's highest mountains, Olympus and the Pindus range, divide Macedonia from Epirus. They surround vast plains that supply the country with wheat, corn, and other crops. On their slopes, the country's most delicious apples, pears, peaches, apricots, cherries, and vines flourish. Macedonia's coldest mountain enclaves are where the best Greek elephant beans—the baked, buttery *gigantes* of so many taverna menus—are grown, especially around Prespes, the lake region that borders Albania.

Macedonia is also where the best nuts, everything from almonds to walnuts to hazelnuts, grow. They find their way into local cooking in some distinctly regional ways. Walnuts, for example, provide the stuffing for the myriad syrupy phyllo sweets that are among the pastry specialties of Thessaloniki, Greece's second-largest city and Macedonia's capital. They also go into sauces, dips, and savory pies. Macedonian roasted eggplant spread (*melitzanosalata*) as well as skordalia (the garlicky dip made with fried cod) typically contain ground walnuts.

The region's traditional dishes and palette of flavors offer the most insight into the real wealth of the Macedonian and Thracian table. In Thessaloniki on any day of the week, for example, the marketplace bustles with dozens of tiny meze restaurants serving up the food that defines this region better than anything else. A single long, green hot pepper grilled to charred perfection might be one meze offering; a plate of butterflied sardines, grilled, dressed in olive oil from Halkidiki (the region's temperate peninsula to the east), and garnished with paper-thin raw onion rings might be another. The beloved eggplant sometimes makes its appearance as crunchy, stuffed pickled baby eggplants wrapped with thin strands of Greek celery, garlic, and parsley.

The region's bountiful seafood from its lattice-work of coves and bays shows up in many a meze dish. Foremost among them are the small, thin local mussels cultivated off the coasts of Halkidiki and Pieria. In local tavernas they come batter-fried, stuffed with rice and onions, cooked with a tiny local pasta called *kouskousi*, or lightly braised in either wine or tomato sauce in one of the myriad versions of saganaki. Those same mussel-spawning coves also provide mackerels, tunny fish, and sardines that are stuffed, grilled, and cured, making for more of the endless mezedes that fill the small convivial plates of Thessaloniki and beyond. In Thrace, the cured fish tradition thrives. Local specialties include some of the rarest in Greece, including *likourinos*, which is either brine-cured or smoked grey mullet, and smoked trout.

Robust is a word that describes well how Macedonians and Thracians like their food, and they find the perfect vehicle in the region's rainbow selection of peppers. Perhaps no other raw ingredient so defines the cooking of Macedonia and Thrace as the pepper: sweet or hot, fresh or dried, flaked or powdered. Peppers appear in massive quantities from midsummer to midfall all over the region and they insinuate themselves into everything from aromatic stews to one of the most popular Greek regional dishes around, *htipiti*, a fiery spread of creamy feta, olive oil, lemon juice, and peppers in various stages of heat.

GIANT BEANS BAKED WITH SORREL

GIGANTES ME LAPATHO

===== SERVES 4 TO 6 =====

Sorrel, with its lightly sour flavor, is a popular green in Epirus, in the northwestern corner of Greece, where this recipe is from.

8 oz/225 g dried Greek giant or elephant beans, picked over, rinsed, soaked overnight in water to cover, and drained

2 lb/910 g sorrel, stems trimmed, finely chopped, washed well, and drained

Salt

1 cup/240 ml extra-virgin Greek olive oil

2 cups finely chopped red onions

3 garlic cloves, minced

Dash of cayenne pepper

Pepper

1 cup/175 g peeled, seeded, and chopped plum tomatoes (canned are fine)

Juice of 1 lemon, strained

Put the drained beans in a pot with enough water to cover by 3 in/ 7.5 cm and bring to a boil. Reduce the heat to medium-low and simmer the beans until al dente, about 1 hour.

While the beans are simmering, put the sorrel in a large colander and sprinkle lightly with salt. With the palm of one hand, rub the mixture against the holes of the colander, almost in a kneading motion, so that the greens exude liquid. Do this for 10 minutes, then put a plate over the greens and a weight over the plate (such as a large can of tomatoes) and leave to drain for 1 hour. Or, chop and sauté the sorrel in 1 tbsp of olive oil to soften. Add to the beans in the last step.

Heat 2 to 3 tbsp of the olive oil in a large frying pan over medium heat and cook the onions and garlic, stirring, until soft. Season with salt. Remove from the heat and set aside. Preheat the oven to 350°F/175°C/gas 4.

Drain the beans and reserve their cooking liquid. Combine the beans, drained sorrel, and onion-garlic mixture in a large casserole. Season with salt, cayenne, and pepper. Add the tomatoes and remaining olive oil and toss. Pour enough of the reserved bean cooking liquid into the casserole to cover the beans by about ¾ in/2 cm. Cover the casserole with aluminum foil and bake for about 1½ hours, tossing occasionally and adding more liquid as necessary to keep the beans moist as they bake. The beans are ready when they are extremely creamy and soft in consistency, but are not disintegrating. Depending on the age and condition of the dried beans, this could take anywhere from 1 to 2½ hours. About 5 minutes before removing from the oven, stir in the lemon juice. Serve immediately.

VARIATION: Giant Beans Baked with Leeks: Follow the recipe, omitting the sorrel. Cut 3 leeks, white and tender green parts, into ½-in-/12-mm-thick rounds and cook with the garlic and onions.

GIANT BEANS BAKED WITH ROASTED PEPPERS AND PASTOURMA

GIGANTES ME PIPERIES FLORINIS KAI PASTOURMA

===== SERVES 4 TO 6 =====

This is a favorite dish in Macedonian tavernas, especially on cold winter days.

5 oz/140 g dried Greek giant or elephant beans, picked over, rinsed, soaked overnight in water to cover, and drained

Salt

½ cup/120 ml plus 1 tbsp extra-virgin Greek olive oil

1 large red onion, finely chopped

1 large garlic clove, minced

4 large red Florina peppers or 2 large red bell peppers, roasted, peeled, and seeded (see Note on page 70)

2 bay leaves

Pepper

4 to 6 slices *pastourma* (spiced cured beef), trimmed of the spice rub along the edges

3 tbsp red wine vinegar

1 to 2 tbsp grape must syrup (*petimezi*)

Put the beans in a large pot of water and bring to a boil. Lower heat and simmer, partially covered, for about 1 hour, or until the beans are al dente, about halfway cooked. Season with salt about 5 minutes before removing from the heat. Drain the beans and reserve their cooking liquid.

While the beans are simmering, heat 3 tbsp of the olive oil in a large frying pan over medium heat and cook the onion and garlic, stirring, until soft, about 10 minutes. Finely chop the roasted peppers and add to the pan. Cook, stirring, for 2 minutes. Remove from the heat.

Preheat the oven to 375°F/190°C/gas 5. Combine the beans and the onion-pepper mixture in a large baking dish. Pour in enough of the cooking liquid from the beans to come about halfway up the contents of the baking dish. Add the bay leaves and season with salt and pepper. Cover with aluminum foil and bake for 1 hour, or until the beans are soft and buttery, but still intact, and have absorbed almost all the pan liquids. Add the *pastourma*, vinegar, and *petimezi* about 10 minutes before removing from the oven, stirring gently to combine. Remove the beans from the oven when ready, gently mix in the remaining olive oil, and let stand for at least 15 minutes. Remove the bay leaves and serve either hot, warm, or at room temperature. The beans are also great the next day, at room temperature.

SPICY DRIED FAVA BEANS
BAKED WITH RED PEPPERS

KOUKIA XERA ME KOKINES PIPERIES

SERVES 4 TO 6

Dried fava beans, rather ominous looking with their greenish-brown leathery skin and pitch-black "eye," are a main ingredient in a few stews. The stews are usually fragrant with herbs—this one contains oregano—and sweet with lots of onions. Mashed dried fava beans are another island specialty.

1 lb/455 g dried fava beans, picked over, rinsed, soaked overnight in water to cover, and drained

½ cup/120 ml extra-virgin Greek olive oil, plus extra for drizzling

3 large red onions, finely chopped

1 dried red chile pepper

Salt and pepper

1 bay leaf

3 red bell peppers, roasted, peeled, seeded, and chopped (see Note on page 70)

2 cups/350 g peeled, seeded, and chopped plum tomatoes (canned are fine)

Pinch of sugar

2 tsp dried Greek oregano

Using a sharp paring knife, cut away the black "eye" of the fava beans.

Preheat the oven to 375°F/190°C/gas 5. In a Dutch oven or another ovenproof pot, heat ¼ cup/60 ml of olive oil over medium heat and cook the onions until soft and golden, about 12 minutes. Add the fava beans, chile pepper, salt and pepper to taste, and enough water to cover the beans by 2 in/5 cm. Add the bay leaf. Bring to a boil over medium heat, reduce the heat, cover, and simmer for about 50 minutes, or until the fava beans are about three-quarters of the way cooked. Add more water if necessary during cooking.

Gently stir in the bell peppers, tomatoes, and sugar. Transfer the fava beans to the oven and bake until tender and the sauce is thick. Mix in the oregano a few minutes before removing from the oven. Stir in the remaining ¼ cup/60 ml of olive oil. Remove the bay leaf and serve hot or warm.

FRESH FAVA BEANS
WITH YOGURT

KOUKIA ME YIAOURTI

SERVES 4 TO 6

Although country cooks all over Greece prepare fava beans, Cretan country cooks seem to use them most, and in myriad ways. There is even a local fava bean festival on the island.

Several different varieties are cultivated in Greece: a long, shapely bean known as Sevilli (from the Spanish); early-harvest fava beans, which grow in Chios; and two from Crete, the *misiriotika*, which are like the Egyptian *ful*, and the common, large fava bean.

The fresh beans are enjoyed in braised dishes and one-pot stews with the whole range of other spring vegetables, including peas, artichokes, young leeks, carrots, fennel, and garlic scapes. In Crete they are eaten raw as a salad. This is a lovely springtime dish found not only in Crete but all over the Aegean islands.

2 lb/910 g fresh small fava beans

½ cup/120 ml extra-virgin Greek olive oil

3 medium red onions, finely chopped

3 large firm, ripe tomatoes, peeled, seeded, and finely chopped

1 tsp salt

½ tsp pepper

Scant 1 tbsp sugar

3 tbsp finely chopped fresh mint

¼ cup/15 g finely chopped fresh flat-leaf parsley

1½ cups/360 ml thick Greek yogurt for serving

Using a sharp paring knife, remove the eye of each fava bean and cut away the stringlike fiber along the seam of each pod. Wash and drain in a colander.

Heat ¼ cup/60 ml of the olive oil over medium heat in a large, wide pot. Add the onions, lower the heat, cover, and sweat for 7 to 8 minutes, until soft. Stir occasionally to keep from burning. Add the tomatoes and fava beans, and pour in enough water to come about two-thirds of the way up the contents of the pot. Season with salt and pepper and add the sugar.

Bring the mixture to a boil over medium heat. Reduce heat to low and simmer the fava beans until tender, about 20 minutes. Add the herbs about 5 minutes before removing from the heat. Pour in the remaining ¼ cup/60 ml of olive oil as soon as the fava beans come off the stove. Stir gently. Serve hot or at room temperature, accompanied by the yogurt.

FAVA BEANS STEWED WITH FENNEL

KOUKIA ME MARATHO

===== SERVES 4 =====

Fava beans, *koukia* to the Greeks, are among the ancient pulses, a food that has been enjoyed for thousands of years. For most Greeks, fava beans are the telltale sign of spring, a verdant segue from the ash gray of the Mediterranean winter to the bright blossoms of sunshine and warm weather. The best are the youngest because they are tender and can be eaten whole in the pod. Aegean islanders like them the most and eat them raw in salad or floured and fried in olive oil.

This classic springtime stew is another specialty of the Aegean, where wild fennel perfumes so many savory dishes.

4 lb/1.8 kg fresh fava beans, preferably young, shelled

¼ cup/60 ml extra-virgin Greek olive oil, plus extra for drizzling

1 large red onion, finely chopped

1 cup/60 g finely chopped wild fennel (see Note)

2 garlic scapes, trimmed and coarsely chopped; or 1 garlic clove, minced

1 tbsp all-purpose flour

½ cup/30 g chopped fresh dill

3 oz/85 g smoked ham, finely chopped (optional)

2 tbsp strained fresh lemon juice

Pinch of sugar

Salt and pepper

Using a paring knife, remove the "eye" of each fava bean. Bring a pot of salted water to a rolling boil and blanch the beans for a few minutes. Remove, drain, and rinse under cold water. Peel the outer skin off each bean and set the beans aside.

In a wide pot or deep frying pan, heat the olive oil over medium heat. Add the onion and fennel and cook, stirring, for 7 to 8 minutes, or until soft. Add the garlic scapes and stir for 1 minute.

Add the fava beans to the pot. Stir to coat in the oil. Sprinkle in the flour and stir all together for a minute or so. Add the dill. Pour in enough water to just about cover the beans. Cover and cook for 20 to 25 minutes, until the beans are tender. Five minutes before removing from the heat, add the chopped smoked ham (if using). Add the lemon juice and sugar, stir, and season with salt and pepper. Drizzle in additional olive oil just before serving.

NOTE: If you can't find wild fennel, cook 1 finely chopped fennel bulb together with the onion until soft. As soon as you add the water to the pot, add 1 star anise. Double the quantity of dill.

BORLOTTI BEANS WITH CARAMELIZED WHOLE ONIONS AND CUMIN

HANDRES STIFADO

SERVES 4

Handres means "beads" in Greek, and it's also the word for borlotti beans. *Stifado* is a type of stew that is often sweet and sour and is made with small whole onions. While many *stifados* are made with meat, this is a meatless dish, which is Lenten fare par excellence. It's from the island of Lefkada.

½ tsp cumin seeds

½ tsp dried rosemary

½ tsp pink peppercorns

⅔ cup/160 ml extra-virgin Greek olive oil

1 medium red onion, minced

4 garlic cloves, minced

2 cups/455 g dried borlotti beans, picked over, rinsed, soaked overnight in water to cover, and drained

1 cup/175 g peeled, seeded, and chopped plum tomatoes (canned are fine), with their juice; grated tomato (see Note on page 74); or cherry tomatoes

2 cups/480 ml water or a light vegetable broth, plus more as needed

1 large bay leaf

1 tbsp red wine vinegar

1½ tsp grape must syrup (*petimezi*)

10 small onions, about 1½ in/4 cm in diameter, peeled and left whole

Salt and pepper

2 to 3 tbsp chopped fresh flat-leaf parsley

Using a small mortar and pestle, grind the cumin seeds, rosemary, and pink peppercorns together and set aside.

Heat ⅓ cup/80 ml of the olive oil in a medium pot over medium heat and cook the chopped red onion, stirring, until wilted, about 7 minutes. Add the garlic and stir once or twice. Add the beans and stir to coat in the oil. Add the ground spices and stir to bring out their flavor. Pour in the tomatoes and the water or broth. Add the bay leaf, vinegar, and syrup. Cover the pot and simmer the beans over low heat for about 1½ hours, or until very tender. The cooking time may vary, depending on the age of the beans.

While the beans cook, heat the remaining ⅓ cup/80 ml of olive oil in a medium nonstick frying pan, preferably well-seasoned cast iron. Put the small whole onions in the frying pan, season with salt, and cook over low heat for 20 to 25 minutes, until deep gold and caramelized. Add them to the beans and continue cooking until the beans are done. Check the level of the liquid every now and then and add water or broth if necessary. The beans should be stewlike and thick, but not too soupy. Season with salt and pepper and adjust the flavor with additional spices, if necessary. Right before removing from the heat, add the parsley. Remove the bay leaf and serve.

BRAISED BLACK-EYED PEAS
WITH CHARD

MAVROMATIKA ME SESKOULA

========= SERVES 4 TO 6 =========

There are countless variations on the bean and greens theme all around Greece. This is peasant food at its best: easy, extremely nutritious, and delicious.

1½ cups/360 ml extra-virgin Greek olive oil

8 spring onions or scallions, trimmed and finely chopped

2 garlic cloves, minced

2 lb/910 g Swiss chard, trimmed and coarsely chopped

1 small bunch sorrel, washed well, drained, trimmed and finely chopped

1 small bunch wild fennel, finely chopped; or 1 medium fennel bulb, trimmed and coarsely chopped

1 lb/455 g black-eyed peas, rinsed and drained

Salt and pepper

In a large, wide pot heat ¾ cup/180 ml of the olive oil over medium heat and add the spring onions. (If using a fennel bulb, cook together with the spring onions.) Cook, stirring, until soft, about 5 minutes. Stir in the garlic and cook for another minute or so, until soft.

Add the Swiss chard, sorrel, and wild fennel to the pot and cover. As soon as the greens lose about half their volume, stir in the black-eyed peas. Add enough water just to cover and replace the lid. Bring the water to a boil over medium heat, reduce heat to low, and simmer the peas until cooked and all the liquid in the pot has been absorbed, about 45 minutes to 1 hour. Season toward the end of the cook time with salt and pepper. Pour in the remaining ¾ cup/180 ml of olive oil and serve.

VARIATION: Add 1 cup/175 g chopped canned plum tomatoes to the pot, stirring them in just before you add the water.

CHAPTER 7

PASTA
AND
RICE

GREECE IS A NATION OF BREAD LOVERS, BUT PASTA AND RICE FIGURE PROMINENTLY IN COUNTRY COOKING, OFTEN AS A MAIN COURSE. PASTA IS AN ANCIENT FOOD IN GREECE, HAVING EVOLVED FROM THE EVERYDAY GRUEL THAT SIZZLED ON HOT STONE IN ANCIENT HOUSEHOLDS.

It was called *laganum* and might have been a precursor to the flat, wide noodles used for lasagna today. Rice, on the other hand, was a relatively rare and expensive imported luxury food until fairly recently. Bulgur wheat, *trahana* (a small, pebbly wheat product), and dried corn were used in everyday dishes like pilafs, soups, and stuffings.

PASTA IN THE GREEK COUNTRY KITCHEN

Greece has surprisingly diverse pasta traditions. Some well-known classics, such as pastitsio, are from the beginning of the nineteenth century, when Greek homemakers embraced French culinary techniques (such as the béchamel poured over a pastitsio) to demonstrate their sophistication. But most Greek pasta dishes are rustic, hearty, and simple, geared to the daily needs of a country cook with country chores to deal with.

In Greece there are dozens of different pasta shapes, which fall into several broad categories: Greek noodles, called *hilopites*, are generally made with eggs and often with milk, and are shaped into long, flat ribbons. The other two categories are shorter, slightly curled ribbons; and tiny squares. There are dozens of short, twisted, and ear- or cup-shaped varieties. The smallest pastas include the granular *kouskousi* (nothing like the North African couscous) and various rice-shaped pastas, called *kritharaki* in Greek. Most homemade pasta is not necessarily consumed fresh. Often it's dried and stored, typically in muslin bags.

Greeks eat pasta as a main course, and they like it soft, well beyond al dente. There are combinations that show up repeatedly in the Greek country kitchen, like variations on a theme. One is the pasta-cheese-fat trinity: pasta, often egg noodles, is boiled until comfortingly soft, and served with grated cheese and hot oil or browned sheep's milk butter.

Another great pasta combination is the rooster-noodle duo. Roosters are traditionally a festive meat, savored for a special Sunday meal or for holidays. Many Greek country recipes call for boiling the pasta in the broth from a long-simmered rooster or hen and serving it topped with grated cheese. These are rustic dishes, delicious in their simplicity and utterly dependent on the very best, freshest raw ingredients from a real country home to be authentic.

Pasta is served with red meat, especially braised beef and veal, in various country dishes. Ground meat sauce is another classic on the country table, the Greek answer to Bolognese sauce, seasoned aromatically with cinnamon and allspice. Greek country cooks still serve these dishes during long Sunday family lunches or other festive occasions. Most of the time they eat simpler pasta dishes, such as chicken with *kritharaki* (orzo), and *makaronia me kima* (ground meat sauce). There are a few simple regional bean and pasta dishes, too.

RICE IN THE COUNTRY KITCHEN

Greeks learned about rice, like so many of the foods of the East, when the armies of Alexander the Great returned in the fourth century B.C. The men had seen this precious grain in the foothills of the Himalayas, as they marched their way from Persia onto India. Theophrastus, the ancient world's most famous chronicler of plants, wrote of rice, but probably without firsthand knowledge of the grain that feeds half the planet today. Acquiring that knowledge would take approximately 2,000 years. Rice most likely entered the Greek kitchen from the East in the tenth century A.D. The Byzantines had access to it by then, but it was too rare to be a food for the masses. The Ottomans, who loved rice and embraced the prophet Mohammed's favorite food—pilaf—disseminated rice throughout their empire.

It took many centuries more for rice to become a common food in Greek kitchens. That really didn't happen until after World War II and the Greek Civil War in 1949. As part of the post-war relief effort, the American government sent an agronomist named Walter Packard to Greece. To the amazement of many villagers, he helped turn the dry salt plain around the Spercheios River delta in northern Greece into a sea of green rice shoots. By doing so he opened the way for villagers to increase their incomes beyond what anyone could possibly have imagined in war-torn Greece.

Before 1949, rice was a rare, expensive import. Its place as a luxury food made it the de rigueur starch on Christmas and New Year's tables, especially in elaborate stuffings studded with nuts and dried fruits. Rice was and still is wedding food and, in fact, almost every village in Greece has its version of *gamopilafo*, "wedding rice," which is typically cooked in rich meat broth and enriched with butter. Because of its place of honor in the kitchen, rice remains the thing to serve to the ill, notably in the form of chicken and rice soup; plain, tender rice with a little lemon juice and olive oil (called *lappas*); and rice pudding.

In the Greek country kitchen, rice goes into stuffed vegetables and rolled leaves such as grape leaf dolmades. It is a filler for soup and savory pies. Rice is still the centerpiece of the Sunday table in buttery pilafs that accompany roasted meats or baked fish. One of the most delicious is *mydopilafo*, mussel pilaf studded with pine nuts and raisins and sweetened with onions, a traditional dish of Asia Minor Greeks.

One of the most unique aspects of rice cookery in Greece is its place as a main course in dishes like *spanakorizo*, a soft, comforting, long-simmered rice and spinach dish, which is a classic of the Lenten table but also a favorite year-round. There are many such vegetable-rice main courses, which often include tomatoes, cabbage, leeks, or lentils.

GREEK RICE VARIETIES

There are several rice varieties cultivated in Greece, each with a preferred use in the country kitchen. The soup and pudding rice of choice is *glasé*, a polished white, round, somewhat glutinous variety. *Glasé* grows mainly in the Spercheios delta, the Acheloos delta, and near Thessaloniki. Stuffed vegetable recipes usually call for a medium-grain rice, which in Greece would be either the chalk-white Carolina, which, confusingly, is sometimes referred to as a long-grain rice. It grows mainly in Serres in central Macedonia, and around the Strymon River delta. Carolina is the rice in *yiouvarlakia*—meat-and-rice balls cooked in broth and finished with egg and lemon sauce and in dolmades. *Nihaki*, "little fingernail," is the long-grain variety most Greek home cooks make pilaf with because its grains stay nicely separated when cooked. Like Carolina, it is also a popular rice in stuffed vegetable dishes.

SEAFOOD ORZO

KRITHAROTO

Kritharoto is a new name in the Greek culinary lexicon, a hybrid borrowed from Italian *risotto* and Greek *kritharaki*, the name for orzo. This dish essentially is a variation on the great northern Greek classic mussel pilaf.

- 4 medium squid, preferably fresh
- 2 lb/910 g mussels
- ½ cup/120 ml white wine
- 1 whole garlic clove, peeled, plus 2 garlic cloves, minced
- ⅓ cup/80 ml extra-virgin Greek olive oil
- 1 large red onion, finely chopped
- 4½ oz/130 g orzo
- 3 cups/720 ml hot fish broth or water
- ½ tsp saffron threads dissolved in 2 tbsp warm water
- Salt and pepper
- 2 medium zucchini, cut into ½-in/12-mm dice
- 1 tbsp unsalted butter
- 3 to 4 tbsp grated *kefalotyri* or another hard, yellow sheep's milk cheese

If you're using fresh squid and they have not been cleaned, wash and clean them. Hold a squid in one hand and with the other, pull out the head and viscera. Using your index finger or a long teaspoon, remove and discard the gelatinous viscera inside the squid's cavity, on the bottom. Rinse well inside and out and set aside. Cut the head of the squid just below the eye to remove the tentacles. Do not include the eyes, which can be bitter. Pull the quill out of the body. Chop the tentacles. Cut the body crosswise into ¼-in/6-mm rings. Set aside. Repeat with the remaining 3 squid.

Wash the mussels very well, trimming off their beards and scrubbing their shells to get rid of any grit. Rinse well under cold water.

In a large, wide pot, combine the wine, mussels, and whole garlic clove. Cover and bring to a boil. Steam the mussels over high heat until their shells open. Remove from the heat and drain, reserving the mussel broth. Strain the broth through a fine-mesh sieve lined with cheesecloth and set aside. Discard any mussels that have not opened. Set the rest aside, covered.

In a clean large, wide pot, heat 3 tbsp of the olive oil over medium heat. Cook the onion, stirring, for 10 to 12 minutes, until soft. Add the chopped garlic and stir. Add the orzo and stir to coat with the oil and brown very slightly. Pour in the mussel broth. Add the fish broth and bring to a boil. Add the saffron and season with salt and pepper. Reduce the heat and simmer while the orzo cooks for 15 minutes.

Five minutes before the orzo is ready, heat the remaining 2 tbsp olive oil in a medium frying pan over high heat and sauté the zucchini for a few minutes, until al dente. Add the squid and continue cooking for another 2 minutes. Season with salt and pepper.

Transfer the zucchini and squid mixture to the pot with the orzo. Toss gently and cook for 3 to 4 minutes to blend the flavors. Just before removing from heat, stir in the butter and grated cheese. Serve topped with the warm mussels.

GREEK ISLAND LOBSTER PASTA

ASTAKOMAKARONADA

Lobster as the Greeks know it generally is the spiny lobster, which is more like a giant shrimp, rather than the two-clawed Atlantic kind. The latter exists, too, a gift to Greece by the U.S. government under the auspices of the Marshall Plan. The only place it survived in Greek waters was the rocky southern coast of Ikaria, where, to this day, that particular species in known locally as the Amerikano.

The most traditional way to cook a lobster is either to broil it or to grill it over coals and serve it with a lemon–olive oil vinaigrette. But lobster with spaghetti has become tremendously popular, especially in the islands in the summer, since lobsters can only be caught from May 1 through the fall.

- One 1½- to 2-lb/680- to 910-g Atlantic lobster, or 2 lb/910 g large spiny lobsters
- ½ cup/120 ml extra-virgin Greek olive oil
- 2 large red onions, finely chopped
- 1 medium fennel bulb, trimmed and finely chopped
- 1 green bell pepper, seeded and finely chopped
- 2 garlic cloves, minced
- 6 to 8 large firm, ripe tomatoes, peeled and coarsely chopped, with their juice and seeds
- Salt and pepper
- Pinch of sugar
- 2 tsp chopped fresh oregano
- 8 oz/225 g spaghetti
- 2 tbsp chopped fresh parsley for garnish

Bring a large pot of water to a boil. Carefully drop in the lobster and simmer for about 4 minutes until its shell turns bright red (or bright orange if using spiny lobster). Remove the lobster with kitchen tongs and transfer to a large bowl to cool.

To remove the meat from the Atlantic species: Twist off the claws and place on a heavy cutting board. Using the flat side of a large chef's knife, crack the claws. Remove the meat and put in a bowl. Remove the tail and, using kitchen shears, cut it open lengthwise. Remove the meat and put in the bowl. Remove and discard the dark intestine. Halve the body section of the lobster. Put the roe, if there is any, and the tomalley in the bowl with the lobster meat.

To remove the meat from the spiny lobster: Cut the underside of the tail with kitchen shears, pull apart, and remove the meat.

Cut the lobster meat into large chunks, about 2 in/5 cm. Set aside, covered. You can do this several hours ahead and store the lobster meat in the refrigerator.

In a large, deep frying pan over medium heat, warm the olive oil. Sauté the onions, fennel, and bell pepper until soft, about 10 minutes. Add the garlic and stir for 1 minute. Add the tomatoes and all their juice. Season with salt and pepper and add the sugar. Add the oregano. Partially cover the pan and simmer the sauce over medium-low heat for about 15 minutes, or until most of the tomato juice is cooked off.

While the sauce is cooking, bring a large pot of well-salted water to a rolling boil and cook the spaghetti until al dente. Drain, reserving about 1 cup/240 ml of the pasta water.

Toss the lobster pieces into the sauce and cook, stirring, for about 3 minutes to blend well and warm the lobster. Add the spaghetti to the frying pan, and toss well, adding a little of the reserved pasta water if necessary to moisten the sauce. Serve hot, garnished with chopped parsley.

SHRIMP PASTITSIO

PASTITSIO ME GARIDES

===== SERVES 8 TO 10 =====

Pastitsio is a classic Greek dish of baked bucatini and aromatic meat sauce, covered in a thick layer of béchamel. Throughout Greece and Cyprus, any baked pasta is often called *pastitsio*. Although the classic version always contains meat sauce, there are numerous variations around Greece. I first tasted this version, made with shrimp, in a small seaside taverna along the northwestern coast of Greece, where a one-eyed species called *gambari* prevails.

BÉCHAMEL

4 egg yolks

⅛ tsp grated nutmeg

¾ cup/170 g unsalted butter

1½ cups/170 g all-purpose flour

4 cups/960 ml milk

Salt and pepper

¼ cup/60 ml plus 1 tbsp extra-virgin Greek olive oil

1 large onion, finely chopped

1 medium fennel bulb, finely chopped

2 garlic cloves, minced

1 tsp paprika

1 cup/240 ml dry white wine

2½ cups/440 g peeled, seeded, and chopped plum tomatoes, with their juice (canned are fine)

2½ lb/1.2 kg medium fresh shrimp, shelled, deveined, and finely chopped

Two 1-in/2.5-cm strips orange peel

2 tbsp tomato paste

Pinch of sugar

11 oz/310 g long tubular pasta, such as bucatini

To make the béchamel: In a medium bowl, whisk together the egg yolks and nutmeg and set aside. In a large pot over medium heat, melt the butter. When the foam begins to subside, stir in flour and cook, stirring, for about 1 minute. Pour in the milk slowly, whisking constantly. Continue whisking until the mixture thickens. Remove from the heat. Pour about ½ cup of the hot béchamel into the eggs, whisking vigorously, and pour the egg mixture into the béchamel, whisking. Season with salt and pepper. Cover with a kitchen towel and set aside.

Preheat the oven to 350°F/175°C/gas 4. Heat the ¼ cup/60 ml oil in a large, wide pot over medium heat, and sauté the onion and fennel until soft, about 10 minutes. Add the garlic and stir for 1 minute. Stir in the paprika. Add the wine, bring to a boil, and add the tomatoes, shrimp, and orange peel. Cover and bring to a boil over medium heat. Simmer for about 20 minutes, until the sauce is thick. Five minutes before removing from the heat, add the tomato paste and sugar. Remove the sauce from the heat, remove the orange peel, and stir in 1 cup of the béchamel.

While the sauce is cooking, bring a large pot of salted water to a rolling boil and add the pasta. Boil until a little firmer than al dente. Remove from the heat, drain in a colander, and return the pasta to the pot. Toss with the remaining 1 tbsp of olive oil.

Assemble the pastitsio. In a lightly oiled 11 x 15-in/28 x 38-cm baking dish, spread out half of the pasta. Spoon half the shrimp sauce on top. Layer the remaining pasta and the remaining shrimp sauce over it and spread the béchamel on top. Bake, uncovered, for about 45 minutes, or until browned and bubbly. Cool slightly and serve.

MYKONOS-STYLE GARLIC SPAGHETTI WITH GROUND RUSKS

SKORDOMAKARONA MYKONOU

This simple, rustic dish from cosmopolitan Mykonos is the Lenten answer to pasta with ground meat. The ground rusks are traditionally sprinkled over the pasta as a replacement for meat in times of fasting.

½ cup/120 ml extra-virgin Greek olive oil

6 garlic cloves, peeled and cut into thin slivers

8 large firm, ripe tomatoes, grated (see Note on page 74)

Salt and pepper

Pinch of sugar, or to taste

1 lb/455 g spaghetti

1 barley rusk, broken up and ground into hard crumbs in a food processor or with a mortar and pestle

1 tbsp finely chopped fresh flat-leaf parsley

½ to 1 cup/60 to 120 g coarsely grated *kefalotyri* cheese or any sharp, hard grating cheese (optional)

Heat ¼ cup plus 2 tbsp/90 ml of the olive oil in a large frying pan over low heat and add the garlic slivers. Cook, stirring with a wooden spoon, until soft, being careful not to burn the garlic. As soon as the garlic softens, add the tomatoes to the frying pan, season with salt and pepper, and add the sugar. Raise the heat to medium, and cook until most of the tomato juices have evaporated, 10 to 12 minutes.

Meanwhile, bring a large pot of salted water to a rolling boil and cook the spaghetti until al dente. Drain and toss with the remaining 2 tbsp olive oil.

Add the spaghetti to the sauce, toss to combine, and cook for 1 minute. Spread out on a large serving platter. Sprinkle with the rusk crumbs, parsley, and cheese, if desired. Serve immediately.

SPAGHETTI AND GROUND MEAT SAUCE, FERRYBOAT STYLE

VAPORISIA MAKARONADA

In Greek ground meat dishes, the size of the grind is important. Coarsely ground meat, for example, is considered better for sauces that simmer for hours, such as the one below. In coarsely ground meat, muscles and nerves have not been completely decimated, and these add flavor to the final sauce.

This recipe is known in Greece as ferryboat style because it is an iconic dish made in the galleys of the boats that take tourists between the islands.

¼ cup/60 ml extra-virgin Greek olive oil

2 large onions, finely chopped

1 garlic clove, minced

1 lb/455 g coarsely ground beef

2 cups/350 g peeled, seeded, and chopped plum tomatoes (canned are fine)

½ cup/120 ml dry red wine

1 cinnamon stick, broken in half

3 allspice berries

2 whole cloves

Pinch of grated nutmeg

2 bay leaves, crumbled

Salt

10 black peppercorns

1 lb/455 g spaghetti, cooked according to the package directions

Heat the olive oil in a large, wide pot over medium heat, and sauté the onions, stirring, until soft and translucent, about 10 minutes. Stir in the garlic, add the ground beef, and cook, stirring, for about 8 minutes, or until the ground beef turns brownish gray. Stir in the tomatoes, raise the heat, and when the tomatoes come to a simmer, pour in the wine. Add the spices and bay leaves, season with salt, and add the peppercorns. Cover the pot, reduce the heat, and simmer the sauce for about 1½ to 2 hours, until thick, adding a little water as needed to keep it moist. Remove the cinnamon stick. Serve the sauce over spaghetti.

CORFU-STYLE AROMATIC PASTA AND CHICKEN

KERKIREIKI PASTITSADA ME KOTOPOULO

SERVES 4 TO 6

Pastitsada, made with thick, tubular spaghetti has a highly aromatic, thick tomato sauce, which may contain rooster, chicken, beef, veal, or seafood (mainly lobster or octopus). It is one of the traditional festive dishes of Corfu. The name probably derives from *pastizzada*, a similar dish enjoyed by the Venetians, who ruled the island from 1401 to 1797. The tomato sauce should be thick enough to coat the mustaches of the hirsute men who enjoy it, or so the locals say. Some island cooks have told me that no fewer than nine spices go into a traditional *pastitsada*: allspice, cinnamon, clove, cumin, nutmeg, paprika, cayenne, salt, and black pepper. When *pastitsada* is made with meat it is sprinkled with cheese before serving, but not when it contains seafood.

½ cup/120 ml extra-virgin Greek olive oil

One 3- to 3½-lb/1.4- to 1.65-kg chicken, cut into stewing pieces (fat trimmed and skin removed, if desired)

3 red onions, coarsely chopped

4 garlic cloves, finely chopped

1½ tsp ground cumin

1 tsp grated nutmeg

1 tsp sweet paprika

½ tsp ground cloves

Cayenne pepper

2 cups/350 g peeled, seeded, and chopped plum tomatoes (canned are fine)

1 cinnamon stick

4 to 6 allspice berries

Salt and pepper

2 tbsp tomato paste diluted with 2 tbsp water

2 to 3 tbsp red wine vinegar

Pinch of sugar (optional)

1 lb/455 g tubular pasta, such as bucatini

Grated *kefalotyri* or any hard yellow cheese

In a large stewing pot, heat the olive oil over medium-high heat, and brown the chicken pieces on all sides in batches. Remove from the pot and drain on paper towels.

Add the onions to the pot, reduce the heat to medium-low, and cook, stirring, until wilted, about 7 minutes. Add the garlic, cumin, nutmeg, paprika, cloves, and cayenne to taste and stir for 1 minute, until the spices become aromatic. Return the chicken to the pot and pour in the tomatoes. Add the cinnamon stick, allspice berries, salt, pepper, and enough water to cover the chicken. Cover the pot and simmer over medium-low heat until the chicken is tender, about 40 minutes. Before removing the chicken from the heat, stir in the diluted tomato paste and add 2 tbsp of the vinegar. Taste the sauce and adjust the seasoning as desired, with a bit more vinegar or with the sugar if it too pungent.

While the chicken is cooking, heat a large pot of salted water for the pasta. Boil the pasta until al dente and drain. Arrrange the pasta on individual plates or on a large serving platter with the chicken and sauce over it. Sprinkle with cheese and serve.

VARIATION: Corfu Lobster Pastitsada—Prepare the *pastitsada* sauce, omitting the chicken. Simmer the sauce for 40 to 50 minutes, or until thick. Add the meat of one 2-lb/910-g cooked lobster (see page 181 for boiling and cleaning techniques), and cook for 5 to 7 minutes, to warm through. Serve over thick tubular pasta, but do not sprinkle with grated cheese.

PASTA WITH YOGURT AND CARAMELIZED ONIONS FROM KASSOS

MAKAROUNES KASSOU

SERVES 4 TO 6

Two islands in the southern Dodecanese, Kassos and Karpathos, have versions of this intoxicating pasta dish. It is traditionally prepared with a fresh homemade pasta about the size of ziti; a local soft, sour cheese called *sitaka*, which is about the consistency of thick Greek yogurt; and onions, which are cooked slowly to bring out their sweetness.

> 4 tbsp/60 ml extra-virgin Greek olive oil
>
> 6 large red onions, coarsely chopped
>
> Salt
>
> 1 lb/455 g tagliatelle or penne, preferably fresh
>
> 5 tbsp butter, preferably sheep's milk
>
> 2 cups/480 ml thick Greek yogurt
>
> ½ to 1 cup/60 to 120 g coarsely grated *kefalotyri* cheese or any sharp, hard grating cheese

Heat the olive oil in a large, heavy nonstick frying pan over medium-high heat and add the onions. Reduce the heat to medium-low and cook, stirring frequently, until the onions are soft and golden brown, 25 to 35 minutes. Remove from the frying pan and set aside.

Bring a large pot of salted water to a boil and cook the pasta. Meanwhile, melt the butter in a small, shallow frying pan over medium heat until it browns, about 7 minutes. Drain the pasta, reserving ½ cup/120 ml of the pasta water. Return the pasta to the pot. Mix in the browned butter and yogurt.

Serve on individual plates or on a serving platter, sprinkled generously with the grated cheese and topped with the caramelized onions and their juices.

ONIONS WITH SHORT-GRAIN PASTA

KREMMYDOMANESTRA

SERVES 6 TO 8

This old dish is from the Ionian islands, where orzo is called *manestra*. It is usually made during the summer, when tomatoes are at their best.

> ½ cup/120 ml extra-virgin Greek olive oil
>
> 6 large onions, cut into thick wedges
>
> Salt and pepper
>
> 3 large firm, ripe tomatoes, grated (see Note on page 74), with their juice
>
> Pinch of sugar
>
> 8 cups/2 l water
>
> 1 lb/455 g orzo

Heat 3 tbsp of the olive oil in a large frying pan over medium heat. Add the onions and sprinkle with salt. Cook, stirring, for a few minutes. Cover, reduce the heat to low, and cook for about 20 minutes or longer, until they turn deep gold. Preheat the oven to 350°F/175°C/gas 4.

Add the tomatoes to the onion mixture. Season with salt and add 2 tsp pepper and the sugar. Raise the heat and bring the tomatoes to a boil. Add the water and adjust the seasoning with additional salt and pepper. Bring to a boil, reduce the heat, and simmer for 15 minutes. Add the orzo to the pot and cook until al dente.

Transfer to a large, lightly oiled baking dish and bake until the tomato sauce has thickened but is not too dense, about 20 minutes. Remove from the oven and toss with the remaining olive oil. Adjust the seasoning and serve.

TRAHANA

Trahana is one of the oldest foods in the eastern Mediterranean, a tiny, pebble-shaped wheat product that varies in form all over Greece. It evolved as an ingenious way to preserve milk. *Trahana* is made with either semolina flour (a softer wheat flour), bulgur, or cracked wheat. Milk, buttermilk, or yogurt is usually mixed into the starch to form a thick mass. When buttermilk or yogurt is used, the end product is known as "sour" *trahana*. When plain milk is used, it is called "sweet" *trahana*. The two are used interchangeably, but sour *trahana* has a more complex, earthy flavor. In Thrace, a Lenten *trahana* is made with flour and vegetable pulp, which has been seasoned with sesame seeds and hot pepper flakes. In Lesvos, an island in the northeastern Aegean, *trahana* is made into larger, cup-shaped pieces called *koupes*.

Some historians believe that *trahana* evolved from the gruel that fed Greek and later Roman foot soldiers as they tried to conquer the world. Apicius, the Roman cookbook author who lived in the first century B.C., mentions something similar to *trahana*, called *tractae*, another kind of dense gruel used to thicken all sorts of foods.

Although few country cooks bother to make *trahana* at home, Greeks still love eating it. As a result, regional artisan producers, mainly women's cooperatives, have stepped in to satisfy the demand. Thanks to them, the tradition is surviving.

Traditional home cooks make *trahana* into porridge and serve it with yogurt or feta. The pebbly grains exude their tart milkiness as they disintegrate in the pot. In Epirus, in northwestern Greece, home cooks prepare sour *trahana* with sausages, lamb, and goat and add it to savory pies. In Crete, cooks add the local *trahana*, called *xinohondros*, to a whole range of vegetable dishes. *Trahana* is combined with tomatoes in a delicious northern Greek meatball soup, with pumpkin in an old soup recipe from the Peloponnese (see page 107), and as a stuffing for squid and for tomatoes (see pages 251 and 190).

Chefs have embraced this ancient product, too. There are modern Greek dishes that incorporate *trahana* in novel ways, for example, by making it into a cream and serving it as a bed for octopus.

MAKING TRAHANA

Trahana is always made at the end of the summer, because there is enough of a breeze and enough heat to dry the morsels quickly, either indoors or outside, and also because the summer is a time, in the agrarian cycle, when there is excess milk.

On a windy afternoon in late August, I watched Maria Kalimouikou, the caretaker at the Theoktisti Monastery on Ikaria, make a version of *trahana* with bulgur wheat. She brought about 2 qt/2 l of goat's milk, not an hour old, to a boil in a deep, wide pot on a small gas burner in the monastery kitchen. Then she added salt and bulgur wheat, measured out with glass dessert plates, about eight of them. She stirred constantly until the mixture became as thick as oatmeal and the surface was dimpled with holes that gurgled and sputtered.

Nearby, in two plastic washbasins, other *trahana* dough in varying stages of readiness waited for her attention. One was very wet, the other about as sticky as fresh pizza dough. "I didn't have time to finish them last night," she explained.

She left the bulgur-and-milk mixture to cool for a few hours before breaking it into pieces about the size of her fist. These she dries in the sun, then breaks into smaller pieces in the course of a day until finally the *trahana* has dried sufficiently to be passed through her giant wood-framed sieve, which looks something like a Chinese bamboo steamer, except that the wire-mesh bottom is strong enough to withstand the force of Maria's hands as she pushes and rubs the dry pellets against it, crumbling them until they are small enough to fall through the holes.

The pebbles change from honey-colored to ash blond as they dry, a process that takes anywhere between one and four days, depending on the humidity, winds, sunlight, and temperature. They are spread out on long tables and covered with netting that's secured to the table with clothespins, to protect the *trahana* from curious insects and potential germs. Once the *trahana* has dried, she bakes it at 122°F/50°C as an extra safety measure. She sells the *trahana* in small bags as a source of income for the monastery.

TOMATOES STUFFED WITH OCTOPUS AND RICE

DOMATES GEMISTES ME HTAPODI KAI RIZI

 SERVES 10

This recipe hails from the coastal town of Mt. Pelion, in central mainland Greece.

1 small octopus, about 8 oz/225 g

1 cup/240 ml dry white wine

1 bay leaf

1 strip orange peel, 1 in/2.5 cm wide and 2 in/5 cm long

10 large firm, ripe tomatoes

Salt and white pepper

Pinch of sugar

RICE FILLING

½ cup/120 extra-virgin Greek olive oil, plus extra for drizzling

2 large red onions, minced

2 garlic cloves, minced

1 cup/200 g long-grain rice such as Greek *nihaki* or basmati, or Carolina, a medium-grain variety

2 cups/480 ml water

1 red bell pepper or 2 long red Florina peppers, roasted (see Note on page 70), peeled, seeded, and finely chopped

3 tbsp chopped fresh oregano

1 tbsp grated orange zest

Salt and pepper

Clean the octopus. Remove its saclike head and discard. Using a sharp paring knife, cut away the beaklike mouth. Put the octopus in a medium pot, and add the wine, bay leaf, and strip of orange peel. Cover and cook over low heat for 45 to 50 minutes, until the octopus is almost done but still a little al dente. (The cooking time will vary slightly, depending on the size and innate tenderness of the octopus.) Drain the octopus, reserving the pan juices, and set aside to cool slightly. When cool enough to handle, chop the octopus into very small pieces.

While the octopus is cooking, using a small, sharp paring knife, cut the tops off the tomatoes and reserve. Cut a tiny bit off the bases so that they can stand upright in a baking pan. Using a small spoon or melon baller, carefully hollow out the tomatoes without tearing the skin. Finely chop the tomato pulp and set aside. Season the insides of the tomatoes with salt and white pepper and a little sugar and turn upside down on a large platter to drain. Preheat the oven to 400°F/200°C/gas 6.

To make the rice filling: Heat the olive oil in a large frying pan over medium-low heat and cook the onion for 8 to 10 minutes, stirring, until soft. Add the garlic and stir. Add the rice and stir for 1 to 2 minutes to coat in the oil. Pour in the water, raise the heat slightly to bring the water to a boil, and cook, stirring, until the water is absorbed. Remove the frying pan from the heat.

Add the octopus to the rice mixture. Stir in the tomato pulp, chopped roasted red pepper, oregano, and grated orange zest. Season with salt and pepper.

Lightly oil a baking dish large enough to hold the tomatoes snugly in one layer. Spoon the filling into each tomato up to the rim and place in the pan. Spoon a little of the octopus pan juices into each tomato. Cover each tomato with its cap. Drizzle with a little olive oil. Cover with aluminum foil and bake for 45 minutes, or until everything is tender. Serve immediately.

TOMATOES STUFFED WITH TRAHANA

DOMATES GEMISTES ME TRAHANA

SERVES 6

This dish was inspired by a traditional Cretan recipe. At Pylos, a restaurant where I sometimes cook in New York, we serve it as an accompaniment for grilled lamb chops. The sourness of the *trahana* and feta coupled with the sweetness of the tomatoes and mint are irresistible.

2 cups/120 g fresh mint leaves, loosely packed

¾ cup/120 g crumbled Greek feta cheese

½ cup/120 ml extra-virgin Greek olive oil

12 medium firm, ripe tomatoes

Salt

1 tsp sugar

1 large red onion, finely chopped

1 small fennel bulb, finely chopped

1 garlic clove, minced

1 cup/170 g sour *trahana*

1 cup/240 ml dry white wine

2 cups/480 ml chicken or vegetable broth

¼ cup/15 g finely chopped fresh dill

¼ cup/15 g finely chopped fresh flat-leaf parsley

Pepper

¼ cup/60 ml water

Combine the mint, feta, and ¼ cup/60 ml of the olive oil in the bowl of a food processor or in a blender and pulse on and off until creamy. Set aside.

Preheat the oven to 350°F/175°C/gas 4. Using a small, sharp paring knife, cut the caps off the tomatoes and reserve. Cut a tiny bit off the bases so that they can stand upright in a baking pan. Using a small spoon or melon baller, carefully scoop out the tomato pulp without tearing through the skins. Put the pulp in a large bowl and set aside. Season the tomatoes inside and out with a little salt and the sugar and place upside down on a large plate to drain.

Heat the remaining ¼ cup/60 ml of olive oil in a large nonstick frying pan over medium heat, and sauté the onion and fennel until soft, about 8 minutes. Add the garlic and stir. Add the *trahana* and stir to coat in the oil. Pour in the wine. As soon as it steams up, pour in the broth. Bring to a boil over medium heat, then lower the heat and simmer the *trahana* until it is al dente and has absorbed all the liquid, about 20 minutes. Remove from the heat. Transfer the *trahana* mixture to the bowl with the tomato pulp. Stir in the dill and parsley and the feta-mint mixture. Season with salt and pepper. The mixture should be fairly loose.

Lightly oil a baking dish large enough to stand all the tomatoes upright in one layer. Spoon the *trahana* filling into the tomatoes, leaving about ½ in/12 mm of space at the top of each one. Place upright in the pan and place the reserved tomato caps back on the tomatoes. Add the water to the pan and bake, uncovered, for 50 to 55 minutes, until the *trahana* is cooked and the tomatoes are tender. Remove from the oven and set aside to cool. Serve either warm or at room temperature.

SAVORY BAKED RICE AND FETA FROM LEFKADA

GALATOPITA ALMYRI

SERVES 4

Although this recipe is called a *pita*, the Greek word for "pie," it's more like a rice casserole. My kids devour this.

- ½ cup/100 g Greek Carolina rice, rinsed
- 2¼ cups/540 ml milk
- ½ tsp salt
- 3 large eggs
- ¼ cup/60 ml extra-virgin Greek olive oil
- 1 cup/150 g crumbled Greek feta cheese

Preheat the oven to 350°F/175°C/gas 4.

Combine the rice in a medium pot with 2 cups/480 ml of the milk and the salt. Cover, bring to a boil, reduce the heat, and simmer for 5 minutes.

Meanwhile, whisk the eggs with an electric mixer at medium speed until foamy. Add the remaining ¼ cup/60 ml milk and the olive oil, and stir to combine. Lightly oil a 9- or 10-in/23- or 25-cm square baking dish.

Let the rice mixture cool slightly, then stir in the feta cheese, followed by the egg mixture. Spread out in the oiled baking pan. Bake, uncovered, for 20 minutes, then cover and bake for another 25 minutes, or until set and golden. Serve hot.

EGGPLANT PILAF FROM MILOS

MELITZANOPILAFO MILOU

SERVES 4 TO 6

This easy island dish is made in the summer, when eggplants and tomatoes are both at their peak.

- ¼ to 1 cup/60 to 240 ml extra-virgin Greek olive oil
- 2 medium red onions, finely chopped
- 2 garlic cloves, minced
- 2 medium eggplants, trimmed and cut into ½-in/12-mm chunks
- ½ cup/100 g long-grain rice such as Greek *nihaki* or basmati, or Carolina, a medium-grain variety
- 2 cups/350 g peeled, seeded, and finely chopped tomatoes
- 2½ cups/600 ml water
- Salt and pepper
- 3 tbsp chopped fresh oregano
- 1 tbsp finely chopped fresh flat-leaf parsley

In a large, wide pot heat ¼ cup/60 ml of the olive oil over medium heat and cook the onions until soft and pale gold, 8 to 10 minutes, stirring frequently. Add the garlic and stir for a few minutes to soften. Add the eggplant chunks and cook until they begin to soften.

Stir in the rice. Pour in the tomatoes and the water. Season with salt and pepper, cover, and simmer until the rice and eggplants are tender, stirring occasionally. About 5 minutes before removing from the heat, add the oregano and parsley. Just before serving, stir in all or part of the remaining ¾ cup/180 ml olive oil, if desired.

SPICY CABBAGE AND RICE FROM KOZANI

LAHANORIZO KAFTERO KOZANIS

SERVES 6

Cabbage and rice slowly cooked together is a popular dish throughout Macedonia and Thrace, where cabbage is put to many uses in the country kitchen. The hot pepper is another telltale sign of northern Greek cooking. Peppers are one of the most traditional crops all over the north, which was once a center for the production of hot peppers. Only Hungary offered any competition.

⅔ cup/160 ml extra-virgin Greek olive oil

1 large red onion, finely chopped

2 celery stalks, finely chopped

1 hot chile pepper, seeded and thinly sliced

1 small cabbage head, shredded

1 cup/200 g long-grain rice such as Greek *nihaki* or basmati, or Carolina, a medium-grain variety

4 medium firm, ripe tomatoes, grated (see Note on page 74), or 2 cups/350 g peeled, seeded, and chopped canned tomatoes

½ cup/120 ml water

Salt and pepper

Paprika for garnish

In a large, heavy, deep sauté pan or a wide pot, heat ⅓ cup/80 ml of the olive oil over medium heat and cook the onion and celery until soft, 8 to 10 minutes. Add the chile pepper and stir for 2 to 3 minutes to soften. Add the cabbage, cover the pot, and cook until wilted. Add the rice and stir to coat in the oil. Pour in the tomatoes and water, and season with salt and pepper. Cover, raise the heat, and bring to a boil. Then reduce the heat and simmer until the rice and cabbage are tender and the rice has absorbed all the liquid, about 15 to 20 minutes.

Pour in the remaining ⅓ cup/80 ml of olive oil and serve, sprinkled with a little paprika. Serve immediately.

DODECANESE BLACK RICE

MAVRO PILAFI APO TA DODEKANISSA

SERVES 4 TO 6

Greek island cooks have long known that cuttlefish ink is one of the most delicious raw ingredients, and a natural partner to rice. Only fresh cuttlefish still have their ink sacs because when stacked and frozen, the sacs break. However, the ink is sometimes sold separately in small packets in specialty gourmet shops.

1 lb/455 g fresh or frozen cuttlefish

½ cup/120 ml extra-virgin Greek olive oil

1 large red onion, minced

1 small garlic clove, minced

1 bay leaf

1 cup/240 ml dry white wine

2 cups/480 ml water

1 cup/200 g long-grain rice such as Greek *nihaki* or basmati, or Carolina, a medium-grain variety

1 envelope squid ink, if needed

Salt and pepper

2 tbsp snipped fresh dill or wild fennel (optional)

If using frozen cuttlefish, defrost completely. It will already be cleaned. If using fresh, you will need to clean it. Remove the tentacles and trim. Using your fingers, scoop out and discard the viscera and cartilage from the inside of the cuttlefish cavities. If the ink sac, located at the head end of the cuttlefish's tubular body, is still intact, remove it carefully and place in a bowl of water.

Heat the olive oil in a wide pot over medium heat, and cook the onion until soft and translucent, 8 to 10 minutes. Add the garlic and stir. Add the cuttlefish and bay leaf and cook, stirring, until the cuttlefish begins to to become opaque, 4 to 6 minutes. Pour in the wine. Bring to a boil, reduce the heat to low, and simmer, covered, for about 30 minutes, or until the cuttlefish are al dente. Add the water. Raise the heat to medium. As soon as the liquid begins to simmer, add the rice, stir gently, and continue cooking for about 15 minutes, until the rice is almost cooked.

In the meantime, smash the ink sacs with a fork and strain through a small, fine-mesh sieve. Add to the rice and stir. Or add the packet of ink to the rice. Season with salt and pepper. Cover and simmer for about 15 minutes, or until the rice is cooked and the cuttlefish is very tender. If desired, stir in the chopped dill. Remove from the heat and cool slightly. Remove the bay leaf and serve.

ZUCCHINI BLOSSOMS STUFFED WITH RICE AND HERBS

KOLOKYTHOLOULOUDA GEMISTA ME RIZI KAI MYRODIKA

SERVES 4 TO 6 AS A MAIN COURSE
OR 8 TO 12 AS A MEZE

Summer gardeners and zucchini growers always pick the flowers in the morning, when they are open like bells. Place one inside the other to keep them open until you are ready to use them. The male flowers, which are attached to thick stalks, are best for stuffing. The female flowers bear the zucchini. If you find baby zucchini with flowers attached, you may also use these.

25 to 30 zucchini blossoms

½ cup/100 g long-grain rice such as Greek *nihaki* or basmati, or Carolina, a medium-grain variety

2 cups/480 ml water

Salt

¾ cup/180 ml extra-virgin Greek olive oil

2 large red onions, minced

2 scallions or spring onions, white and tender green parts, finely chopped

1 small zucchini, grated

2 tbsp finely chopped fresh flat-leaf parsley

½ cup/30 g finely chopped fresh mint

Salt and pepper

2 tbsp strained fresh lemon juice

Gently wash the blossoms in a colander, drain slightly, and place one inside the other to keep open.

Put the rice in a small pot and add ½ cup/120 ml of the water and a little salt. Cover and cook over very low heat until the rice has absorbed all the water. It will be about halfway cooked. Remove and transfer to a mixing bowl.

Heat 2 tbsp of the olive oil in a frying pan over medium heat, and sauté the onions and scallions until wilted, about 8 minutes. Transfer to the bowl with the rice and add the grated zucchini, parsley, and mint. Drizzle in 2 tbsp of the olive oil, season with salt and pepper, and mix thoroughly.

Pour the remaining 1½ cups/360 ml water, or enough to come about 1½ in/4 cm up the sides of a large, wide pot, and fit a large, preferably silicone, steaming basket inside.

Taking one blossom at a time, gently pry it open and fill with 1 tsp of the rice mixture. Fold the petals over a little to close. Place in the steaming basket. Repeat with the remaining blossoms and filling. Cover, bring the water to a simmer, and steam the blossoms for about 12 minutes, or until the rice is very tender and the blossoms are cooked.

Whisk together the remaining ½ cup/120 ml olive oil, the lemon juice, and a little salt. Remove the blossoms from the steamer, place on a platter, and drizzle with the lemon vinaigrette to serve.

CABBAGE LEAVES STUFFED WITH GROUND BEEF, RICE, AND FETA

LAHANODOLMADES ME KYMA, RIZI KAI FETA

SERVES 6 AS A MAIN COURSE

Lahanodolmades, stuffed cabbage leaves, are one of my favorite rustic winter dishes. In this classic version, the feta lends a tart undertone to the meat filling, while the herbs add a refreshing note.

1 cabbage head (about 2 lb/910 g)

Oil for the pot

1 large red onion, finely chopped

8 oz/225 g ground beef

½ cup/100 g long-grain rice such as Greek *nihaki* or basmati, or Carolina, a medium-grain variety

⅔ cup/100 g crumbled Greek feta cheese

½ cup/30 g chopped fresh mint

½ cup/30 g chopped fresh dill

Salt and pepper

3 to 4 cups/720 to 960 ml chicken or vegetable broth

AVGOLEMONO

2 large eggs, lightly beaten

Juice of 2 lemons, strained

Bring a large pot of salted water to a rolling boil. Using a large knife, cut away the base of the cabbage head and quarter the cabbage lengthwise. Blanch the quarters in the boiling water for 3 minutes. Remove with a slotted spoon, transferring immediately to a colander to rinse with cold water, drain, and cool slightly. Remove the cabbage quarters to a cutting board and press the leaves down to soften or slightly break the thick veins. Separate the leaves. Put the leaves that are too small or torn to fill in a separate pile.

Lightly oil a large, wide pot. Cover the bottom with a layer of the small or torn leaves. In a large bowl, combine the onion, ground beef, rice, feta, and herbs. Season with salt and pepper. Place the whole leaves in rows on a work surface, vein-side up. Place a scant 1 tbsp of filling near the bottom of each leaf, at the center, and roll up into a cylinder, folding in the edges as you roll to keep the filling from spilling out. Place the rolls, seam-side down, over the leaves on the bottom of the pot, tucking them in snugly next to one another in one layer.

Pour enough broth into the pot to come about two-thirds of the way up the leaves. Place a heat-proof plate over the cabbage leaves to keep them securely in place. Cover and bring to a boil over medium-high heat. Reduce the heat to low and simmer until the cabbage is tender and the filling is cooked, about 20 minutes.

To make the avgolemono: Whisk the eggs until frothy in a medium bowl. Add the lemon juice and continue whisking. Slowly add one ladleful of the pot juices to the avgolemono, whisking vigorously. Repeat with a second ladleful.

Pour the avgolemono into the pot, tilt to distribute evenly, and serve.

CABBAGE LEAVES STUFFED WITH SHRIMP, WITH GREEK SAFFRON BÉCHAMEL

LAHANODOLMADES ME GARIDES KAI BÉCHAMEL ME KROKO

===== SERVES 6 AS A MAIN COURSE =====

This recipe was inspired by one that a friend and chef, Lefteris Lazarou, has made on occasion at his restaurant Varoulko in Athens. If you don't want to make the saffron béchamel sauce, you can simply drizzle the finished cabbage leaves with a little olive oil.

8 oz/225 g small shrimp, with their shells on

⅔ cup/160 ml extra-virgin Greek olive oil, plus extra for drizzling

1 large red onion, minced

1 large carrot, peeled and minced

2 garlic cloves, minced

1 lb/455 g plum tomatoes, peeled, seeded, and chopped (canned are fine)

2 cups/480 ml fish or vegetable broth or water

1 cabbage head (about 2 lb/910 g)

½ to ⅔ cup/100 to 130 g long-grain rice such as Greek *nihaki* or basmati, or Carolina, a medium-grain variety

Heaping 2 tbsp dried mint, or 3 tbsp chopped fresh mint

Salt and pepper

1 cup/240 ml dry white wine

SAFFRON BÉCHAMEL (OPTIONAL)

1 tbsp extra-virgin Greek olive oil

1 tbsp unsalted butter

2 tbsp all-purpose flour

1 cup/240 ml heavy cream, at room temperature

1 cup/240 ml milk, at room temperature

Pinch of Greek saffron (Krokos Kozanis)

½ tsp ground turmeric

Salt and white pepper

1 tbsp strained fresh lemon juice

Lemon slices or fresh mint leaves, or both, for garnish

Remove the shells from the shrimp and reserve for the sauce. Devein the shrimp with a small paring knife. Rinse the shrimp under cold water and set aside.

Heat ⅓ cup/80 ml of the olive oil in a saucepan over medium heat. Add the onion and carrot and cook, stirring, for about 10 minutes, until soft. Add the garlic and stir a few times to coat in the oil and soften. Pour in the tomatoes and broth or water. Add the reserved shrimp shells. Bring to a boil and then reduce to a simmer. Simmer for 35 to 40 minutes, until the sauce is thick and reduced to about 2 cups/480 ml. Set aside.

Heat the remaining ⅓ cup/80 ml of the olive oil in a large, nonstick frying pan over medium heat, and sauté the shrimp just until pink. Remove from the heat, finely chop, and set aside.

Bring a large pot of salted water to a rolling boil. Using a large knife, cut away the base of the cabbage and quarter the head lengthwise. Blanch the quarters in the boiling water for 3 minutes. Remove with a slotted spoon, transferring immediately to a colander to rinse with cold water, drain, and cool slightly. Remove the cabbage quarters to a cutting board and press the leaves down to soften or slightly break the thick veins. Separate the leaves. Put the leaves that are too small or torn to fill in a separate pile.

Oil the inside of a large, wide pot and cover the bottom with some of the small or torn cabbage leaves. Chop two handfuls of cabbage from the same pile. Add them to the shrimp. Remove the shells from the sauce and add the chopped shrimp and cabbage. Add the rice and mint. Season with salt and pepper.

Lay the cabbage leaves out on a work surface, vein-side up. Place about 1 tbsp of the filling at the bottom of a cabbage leaf, near the center. Roll up the leaf into a cylinder, beginning at the bottom and folding in the edges as you roll to keep the filling from spilling out. Continue filling and rolling the leaves until you've used most of the cabbage leaves up.

Place the rolled leaves seam-side down very snugly next to one another on the bed of torn cabbage. Pour in the white wine and add enough water to come about halfway up the leaves. Drizzle with some olive oil.

Place a heat-proof plate over the cabbage leaves to keep them securely in place. Cover the pot and bring to a boil over medium heat. Reduce the heat and simmer for about 20 minutes, or until the rice is tender.

To make the béchamel: Heat the olive oil and butter in a medium, heavy saucepan. When the butter melts and the foam begins to subside, add the flour and stir with a whisk or wooden spoon for about 5 minutes, until golden brown. Pour in the cream and milk and cook over medium-low heat, whisking constantly, until thick, 7 to 10 minutes. Toward the end, crumble in the saffron, add the turmeric, and season with salt and pepper. Remove from the heat and stir in the lemon juice.

Serve the dolmades with a bit of the béchamel spooned over and around them (if using), and drizzle with a little olive oil, too. Garnish with lemon slices and/or mint.

STUFFED ONIONS

SOUGANIA

SERVES 8 TO 10 AS A SIDE DISH OR MEZE
OR 4 TO 6 AS A MAIN COURSE

Recipes for stuffed onions vary slightly from region to region in Greece. In some places, the onions are hollowed out like tomatoes or bell peppers, filled with rice and herbs, and cooked upright. Elsewhere, especially in the islands, the onions are treated like dolmades: once scored and blanched, their papery layers are pulled apart and rolled around the filling. In this dish the onion layers are separated. It typically calls for an oblong variety of white onion, which tapers at both ends, so that the layers close up naturally around the filling. You can use any large white onion as long as you place the rolled-up layers snugly in the pan to keep the filling from spilling out.

2 lb/910 g large white onions, preferably oblong

¼ cup/60 ml extra-virgin Greek olive oil

2 small red or yellow onions, finely chopped

1 cup/200 g long-grain rice such as Greek *nihaki* or basmati, or Carolina, a medium-grain variety

Scant 1 tsp ground cumin

1 large firm, ripe tomato, grated (see Note on page 74)

½ cup/120 ml dry white wine

½ cup/120 ml water

Salt and pepper

⅔ cup/40 g finely chopped fresh mint

½ cup/30 g finely chopped fresh flat-leaf parsley

Bring a large pot of lightly salted water to a rolling boil. In the meantime, remove the root ends and skins from the large white onions. Using a sharp paring knife, in each onion make one slit along its length, pushing the knife all the way to the core. Drop the onions into the boiling water and blanch for about 3 minutes. Remove with a slotted spoon, transfer to a colander, and rinse under cold water to cool the onions. Gently peel away each layer and set them aside. Chop the tight inner part of each onion and set aside separately.

Heat the olive oil in a large, heavy frying pan over medium heat, and add the chopped raw red or yellow onions. Reduce the heat and cook, stirring, until soft, 10 to 12 minutes. Add the blanched chopped onion cores of the large white onions. Add the rice and stir to coat in the oil. Add the cumin and stir for a few minutes. Stir in the tomatoes, and pour in the wine and water. Season with salt and pepper. Cover and cook the onion-rice mixture until the rice is al dente and has absorbed almost all the liquid, about 5 minutes. Remove from heat and stir in the herbs.

Oil a large, wide pot. Take 1 tbsp of the filling and place it inside an onion "leaf." Roll up along the long side, pressing down the free end to seal the roll. Repeat until the filling and onions are used up. Place the onions side by side very snugly in the pot. Lay a second layer on top if necessary. Add enough water to come about halfway up the contents of the pot. Cut a piece of parchment or wax paper to match the circumference of the pot and place it on top. Weigh it down with a heat-proof plate to keep the onions in place and closed. Cover and cook over medium-low heat until the onions are tender and the filling is cooked, about 30 minutes. Remove from the heat, cool slightly, and serve.

KROKOS KOZANIS (SAFFRON)

The lake region of northern Greece stands out for the fruity rosé and spicy red wines produced in Amyndaion and Goumenissa, and also for its place of honor as one of the world's four major production centers for saffron. Saffron, or Krokos Kozanis as it is known officially in Greece, is the world's most expensive spice. The prefecture of Kozani—with its warm, humid summers; cold, rainy winters; and rich soil—is home to some of the best. Greek saffron is renowned for its deep, crimson color and full, almost intoxicating aroma.

Krokos Kozanis, one of Greece's many products designated with the European Union's Protected Designation of Origin, is grown and harvested by about 1,500 families in the thirty-nine villages and hamlets around the city of Kozani. The harvest takes place in late October and early November, when tiny purple flowers burst out of rain-soaked fields. The temperatures chill bones young and old. Nevertheless, the saffron harvest must go on, and the whole area is busy with it. First the flowers are plucked and gathered up in baskets and crates. Then at home on cold nights, hopefully with a fireplace roaring, women from extended families sit around the table pinching out the flowers' valuable crimson-colored stigmas. Sorting is next, an activity that is also exclusively reserved for nimble female fingers over many months. The trick is to get the real stuff, the high-priced red threads, and to discard the ersatz gold threads. Both are inside the crocus's little bell-like cavity. Getting 1 kilo of saffron means plucking the powdery threads from about 150,000 flowers.

After sorting, the families turn over their saffron to the Saffron Producers Cooperative of Kozani, founded in 1971. All families involved in the cultivation of saffron belong to the co-op, which has the exclusive right to process the spice.

Saffron made its way to the damp, humid villages of Kozani as recently as the seventeenth century, when local merchants carried the crocus bulbs back with them from Austria. Up until a few years ago, saffron was sold almost entirely in bulk to Italy and Spain. In Kozani itself, it was mainly used to flavor local distilled spirits and coffee. Now, though, saffron plays a central role in contemporary Greek cooking. The spice is no longer sold mainly in bulk, but rather beautifully packaged and available both as whole stigmas and in powdered form.

THE CUISINE OF THE IONIAN ISLANDS

The Ionian islands—Corfu, Paxoi, Cephalonia, Zakynthos, Ithaca, Lefkada, and numerous tiny specks of inhabited islands in between—have always been a strategic bridge between the East and the West, attracting the political and economic powers of every historical era. During the Byzantine Empire, these islands, far from Constantinople, were hard to govern. So the Byzantines turned to Venice for help, in exchange for trading privileges. As a result, for most of the next four hundred years, Venice exercised almost total command over these islands. Only Lefkada fell to the Ottoman Turks for two hundred years, before falling again under the dominion of the doge. Venice exited the Ionian islands at the end of the eighteenth century, a power gap filled by the Russians, then Napoleon, and, finally, the English. The islands were united with the Greek state in 1865.

The Russians, French, and even the English all left a few quirks in the culinary mosaic of the Ionian islands, most enduring among them ginger beer and pudding, favorite English treats. But it was the four centuries of Venetian rule over these islands—emerald gems in the bluest, calmest waters of the Mediterranean—that penetrated every aspect of life, from language to customs to food. In the Ionian islands, many dishes have Italian names—*pastitsada, bianco, sofrito, bourdetto* are just a few. Yet, despite the etymological stamp on many culinary specialties, few if any of the grand dishes of Venice itself ever penetrated the cooking here. The anchovies, sage, and rosemary that perfume Venetian cooking are nowhere to be found in the flavor palette of the Ionian islands. But New World fruits and vegetables, many of which arrived in Europe via the Venetians' formidable fleet, made their way to Greece via a first stop in the Ionian islands, among them tomatoes, bell peppers, green beans, corn, potatoes, sweet potatoes, and pumpkin (named "Venetian squash" in the local dialect of Zakynthos).

The one indelible stamp that Venice did leave on the cooking of these islands is less culinary than social. Nowhere else in Greece is the local cuisine divided by class as vividly as it is in the Ionian islands, especially in Corfu. While the nobility feasted on New World turkeys, the poor made due with humble cod, even on the Christmas table. The rich seasoned their foods with imported black pepper—for centuries, one of the world's most valuable commodities. The poor, on the other hand, turned to growing hot chile peppers, usually on rented land, to spice up their meager foods.

Today the cuisine of these islands is a mix of the indigenous and the adopted. Ancient lentils from the highlands of Lefkada, for example, considered the best in Greece, are turned into a local soup flavored with the island's unique rosewater vinegar. But then we encounter a gamut of dishes clearly rooted in the cooking of Italy: local pastitsio with a pastry crust modeled after the *pizza rustico* of the Italians, and sweets with names like *mantolato* (a type of almond-flavored sugar paste)*, mandoles* (candied nuts), and *zabaglione*.

The Venetians left the Greeks in the Ionian islands with a penchant for charcuterie. Specialties like the salami of Lefkada; Corfu's herb-smoked *noumboulo* (pork loin); Zakynthos's smoked pork cutlet, called *pancetta*, and its prosciuttolike *hoiromeri* are now renowned all over Greece and well beyond. A pecorino-like cheese called *korfu* was first produced on Corfu in 1965 and is a local specialty, as are the olive oil–steeped cheeses of Zakynthos and *pretza*, a soft, sharp cheese that is traditional on Cephalonia.

CHAPTER 8

FLATBREADS
AND
SAVORY PIES

I KNOW FROM MY OWN IMMEDIATE EXPERIENCE IN THE FAMILY KITCHEN THAT NO OTHER FOOD BRINGS PEOPLE TOGETHER LIKE A SAVORY PIE—*PITA* IN GREEK. SAVORY PIES ARE THE SOUL OF GREEK COOKING, THE ULTIMATE COUNTRY DISH, REQUIRING A SKILLFUL, AND, I DARE SAY, WOMAN'S HAND.

Traditionally phyllo is rolled thin using a long, slim dowel, which requires dexterous but graceful movements so as not to tear the dough. Good homemade phyllo is the prerequisite for any good, authentic savory pie.

The tradition belongs to every part of Greece, but in some places savory pies bear a local stamp. Macedonia, Thrace, Epirus, and Thessaly—all in northern Greece, where itinerant shepherds roamed until a generation ago—are the spiritual home of Greece's greatest savory pies. The pies evolved from a time when extended clans moved with their flocks from the lowlands to the highlands twice a year. The pies could be made with anything these families had on hand, most notably cheese and freshly foraged greens from the environs of the day's camp. Since the filling was enclosed, it was less perishable in an age before refrigeration. The *pita* was filling, an important thing when feeding a large family. And you could hold a slice in your hand, which made it easy to carry while herding a flock. Even the oven was mobile: nothing more than a copper dome, carried with the rest of the kitchen panoply, and set over a shallow pit sizzling with charcoal or wood.

The variety of Greek savory pies is enormous and is differentiated by shape, size, filling, and phyllo crust (or the lack thereof). Some pies have no phyllo at all. They are made from thick batters mixed with cheese or greens and baked, or they are topped with a cornmeal crust. There are vegetable pies of every sort: zucchini, eggplant, tomatoes, cabbage, leeks, onions, and peppers. Then there are the greens pies, including the classic spinach pie, but also pies filled with dozens of different greens and aromatic herbs. Mushrooms make an earthy filling in regions where they grow wild, especially Macedonia. The pies can be made in large, round baking pans or square or rectangular pans. Or they can be shaped into triangles, crescents, or cylinders. In the Aegean islands, where wood to fuel the oven was historically scarce, most pies are small parcels of stuffed dough fried in olive oil.

Loose fillings need to be enriched with something that will absorb moisture. Greek country cooks add *trahana*, rice, bulgur wheat, semolina flour, and broken bits of pasta to accomplish this.

Then there is the olive oil–butter dilemma. In most of Greece, cooks brush their phyllo with generous amounts of olive oil, which helps make the pastry crisp. In the north at least one kind of phyllo resembles puff pastry and calls for butter, which was the lubrication of choice in cold regions, where the olive tree did not flourish and olive oil was not readily available commercially.

Economical and satisfying, *pitas* are also seasonal and festive. Cinnamon-flavored rice pies without eggs or milk, but rich in nuts, are a Lenten sweet made in Epirus. Meat pies sit proudly on the table at Christmas or New Year's, especially in northern Greece. A fluffy cheese pie is a traditional dish prepared on *Tyrini*, or Cheese Sunday, which precedes the start of the Easter fast. Zucchini pies abound all over Greece, but especially on the islands in the summer, when squash grows rampant. Pumpkin pie is a fall treat and is made in both sweet and savory versions all over the country.

The women who traditionally made pies also made simple flatbreads out of leftover dough and topped it or kneaded it with something savory. These become instant cheese pies or pizzalike dishes, such as the *ladenia* (olive oil flatbreads) on page 211. Generally, they were treats meant for the kids who always gravitated toward the worktable, like my own do, in anticipation of something savory, warm, and too delicious to resist.

KEFALOTYRI PANCAKES

TIGANITI TYROPITA ME KEFALOTYRI

This pan-fried cheese bread, made with sharp *kefalotyri* cheese, makes a lovely lunch or brunch. The cheese is available in well-stocked cheese shops and Greek markets.

4 cups/450 g all-purpose flour, or more as needed

¼ tsp salt

¼ cup/60 ml extra-virgin Greek olive oil

Juice of ½ lemon, strained

1 cup/240 ml water

2 cups/240 g coarsely grated *kefalotyri* cheese

2 tbsp unsalted butter or more extra-virgin Greek olive oil

Combine the flour, salt, olive oil, lemon juice, and water in the bowl of an electric mixer fitted with a dough hook attachment. Mix at medium speed until a dough mass forms and continue kneading at medium speed, adding more flour if necessary, until a smooth, firm dough forms. Remove the bowl from the body of the mixer and cover with plastic wrap. Set aside to rest for 30 minutes.

Divide the dough into 2 equal balls. Roll out the first ball to a circle 10 in/25 cm in diameter. Sprinkle a quarter of the cheese over the surface of the circle, and fold over the edges of the dough at the top and bottom and left and right, covering the cheese and squaring off the circle. Roll out again to a 10-in/25-cm circle and sprinkle with another quarter of the cheese. Repeat the folding procedure a second time, and roll out the dough to a 9-in/23-cm circle. Set the circle aside and repeat the whole procedure with the remaining ball of dough and cheese.

In a 10-in/25-cm round, nonstick frying pan (preferably well-seasoned cast-iron), heat 1 tbsp of the butter over medium-low heat, and place the cheese bread in the frying pan. Cook, covered, until lightly browned on one side, and flip to cook on the other side, about 25 minutes total. Remove the cheese bread from the pan and repeat with the remaining cheese bread. Serve hot, cut into quarters.

ONION, MINT, AND CHEESE CRESCENTS FROM MILOS

KREMMYDOPITARAKIA MILOU

DOUGH

4 cups/450 g all-purpose flour, or more as needed

½ cup/120 ml extra-virgin Greek olive oil, plus more for oiling the bowl

3 tbsp strained fresh lemon juice

1¾ cups/420 ml water

1 tsp salt

FILLING

8 oz/225 g *kefalotyri* cheese, grated

2 tbsp dried mint

2 large red onions, finely chopped

Olive oil for frying

To make the dough: Put the flour in a large mixing bowl and make a well in the center. Add the olive oil, lemon juice, water, and salt. Using a large fork, stir the flour into the liquid until a sticky dough forms. Continue stirring with a wooden spoon to form a dough mass. Turn out onto a floured surface and knead, adding more flour as necessary, to make a smooth, silky, pliant dough. Or you can mix the dough ingredients in an electric mixer outfitted with a dough hook. Transfer to an oiled bowl, cover with plastic wrap, and let rest for 30 minutes.

To make the filling: In a large bowl, combine the grated cheese, mint, and onions.

Divide the dough into 5 equal pieces. With a rolling pin, roll out each piece into a large sheet, about 1/16 in/2 mm thick, sprinkling the dough with flour as you roll. With a 4-in/10-cm round cookie cutter or saucer, cut circles out of the dough. Collect the remains of the cut dough, reroll, and cut more circles. Place 1 tbsp of the filling in the middle of each circle, fold over to make half-circles, and taper the ends to shape crescents. Press the edges together with a fork to seal.

Pour about 1 in/2.5 cm olive oil into a deep frying pan or sauté pan. Heat to about 360°F/180°C. Fry the small pies on both sides until golden, 4 to 5 minutes. Remove with a slotted spoon and drain on paper towels. Let cool slightly and serve.

VARIATION: To make little pancakes called *plakopites*, after resting the dough, divide it into 30 small balls, about 1½ in/4 cm in diameter. Using your thumb, make a deep indentation into each ball and fill it with a heaping 1½ tbsp of the filling. Pinch closed. On a floured surface roll out each ball to a circle 4 to 5 in/10 to 12 cm in diameter. Pan-fry on both sides in a hot, nonstick frying pan lightly brushed with olive oil until golden.

OLIVE OIL FLATBREAD FROM MILOS

LADENIA MILOU

These lovely little open-faced tomato and onion pies, called *ladenia*, are almost like pizza and make for what is arguably the best-known dish on the islands of Milos and Kimolos in the Cyclades. The pies are typically made and sold by local bread bakers. Served with a fresh green salad, they make a great light lunch or buffet dish.

1 package (¼ oz/7 g) active dry yeast (2¼ tsp)

1½ cups/360 ml warm water, or more as needed

1¾ cups/205 g bread flour

1½ cups/170 g all-purpose flour

1½ tsp salt

⅓ cup/80 ml extra-virgin Greek olive oil

2 large onions, cut into thin rings

2 large firm, ripe tomatoes, seeded and chopped

1 tsp pepper

2 tsp dried Greek oregano

Preheat the oven to 325°F/165°C/gas 3.

In a large bowl, dissolve the yeast in the warm water and cover with a kitchen towel. Let stand for 5 minutes, or until the yeast starts to bubble. Combine the two flours and 1 tsp of the salt in a medium bowl. Slowly add the flour to the yeast mixture, mixing with a wooden spoon until a dough mass forms. Add a little more warm water if the mixture is too dense, or add a little more flour if it is too loose. The dough should be malleable, like pizza dough. Knead the dough in the bowl until smooth and pliant and the sides of the bowl come clean. (This can also be done in a mixer with a dough hook on medium speed.) Cover the bowl with plastic wrap and set aside for 1 hour to double in bulk.

Meanwhile, heat the olive oil in a large frying pan over medium heat and cook the onions for about 5 minutes, or until they start to soften. Add the chopped tomatoes, raise the heat to medium-high, and cook until most of the liquid has evaporated. Remove from the heat.

Oil a baking pan, approximately 15 in/38 cm square or a jelly roll pan. Roll out the dough on a lightly floured surface to the size of the pan and place inside. Cover and let the dough rise for 15 minutes.

Spread the tomato-onion mixture evenly over the dough. Sprinkle with the remaining ½ tsp salt, the pepper, and oregano and bake for about 1 hour, or until the dough is crisp and the topping is caramelized. Remove from the oven, cool slightly, and serve.

SERIFOS ZUCCHINI BREAD

KOLOKYTHOPSOMO APO TINSERFO

SERVES 8

Most filled breads in the Greek country kitchen tend to be flatbreads. I discovered this unusual recipe in a small taverna on the island of Serifos, which is in the Cyclades. It is usually made with the island's hard local cheese, which is impossible to find outside of Serifos. I suggest a more accessible Greek *kefalotyri* or any hard sheep's milk cheese.

2 lb/900 g zucchini

½ cup/120 ml plus 1 tbsp extra-virgin Greek olive oil

Salt and pepper

1½ cups/170 g flour

½ tsp baking soda

3 large eggs

1 cup/240 ml milk

½ cup/30 g plain dried bread crumbs

1 lb/455 g feta cheese

10 oz/280 g *kefalotyri* or another hard, yellow sheep's milk cheese, coarsely grated

3 tbsp finely chopped parsley

2 tbsp sesame seeds (optional)

Preheat the oven to 400°F/200°C/gas 6. Wash and trim the zucchini. Cut into ½-in/1.25-cm cubes.

Heat the 1 tbsp olive oil in a nonstick skillet and sauté the zucchini. Season with salt and pepper, lower heat, cover, and cook for 5 to 8 minutes, until the zucchini is soft but firm enough to hold its shape. Remove from the heat.

In a bowl, mix together the flour, baking soda, eggs, milk, the ½ cup/120 ml olive oil, and bread crumbs. Toss in the zucchini, both cheeses, parsley, and a pinch of pepper.

Lightly oil a 9 x 3 x 3-in/22.5 x 7.5 x 7.5-cm loaf pan. Spread the mixture into the pan, patting it evenly with the back of a spoon. Sprinkle with sesame seeds, if desired, and bake at 375°F/190°C/gas 5 for about 50 minutes, or until set and golden. Let cool slightly and serve.

CHEESE PIES FROM CRETE

PARTHENOPITES

============ SERVES 10 TO 12 ============

The name of these lovely baked cheese crescents, from a small village in the mountain plain above Heraklion, the capital of Crete, literally means "virgin pies." The reason for that unusual name is unknown. There are many similar recipes for pan-fried cheese pies all over Crete. Most are made with the island's specialty cheese, *xinomyzithra*, a soft, mild whey cheese that is similar in texture to ricotta but more sour. It is difficult to find, but a combination of feta and *anthotyro* or ricotta will work in this recipe as well.

1 package (¼ oz/7 g) active dry yeast (2¼ tsp)

1½ cups/360 ml warm water

5 cups/635 g all-purpose flour

1 tsp salt

½ cup/120 ml extra-virgin Greek olive oil, plus more for oiling the bowl

FILLING

1 lb/455 g Cretan *xinomyzithra* cheese; or 6 oz/170 g feta, crumbled, plus 12 oz/340 g fresh *anthotyro* or ricotta, drained

1 egg

2 tbsp finely chopped fresh mint

1 egg, lightly beaten

To prepare the dough: Dilute the yeast in ½ cup/120 ml of the warm water and stir to dissolve. Sift together the flour and salt in a large mixing bowl. Make a well in the center and add the yeast, the remaining 1 cup/240 ml of warm water, and the olive oil. Mix with a wooden spoon until a dough mass forms, and then knead on a work surface, adding a little more flour if necessary, until a smooth, pliant dough forms. Put the dough in an oiled bowl, cover with plastic wrap, and let stand in a warm place for 1 hour, until doubled.

To make the filling: Combine the cheeses, egg, and mint in a mixing bowl.

Lightly oil 2 baking sheets. Preheat the oven to 350°F/175°C/gas 4.

Remove the dough from the bowl, divide in half, and gently punch down. Shape into 2 balls. Let the dough rest again, covered, for 10 minutes. On a lightly floured work surface, use a rolling pin to roll out the first dough ball to a circle about 18 in/46 cm in diameter and ⅛ in/3 mm thick. Using a 3-in/7.5-cm round cookie cutter, cut out circles. Place ½ tbsp of filling in the center of each circle of dough and fold over to make a half-circle. Taper the ends to shape each half circle into a crescent. Using the tines of a fork, press the seam decoratively to secure. Repeat with the remaining dough and filling. If you have filling left over, gather up any leftover dough after rolling, shape into a ball, let rest for 15 minutes, roll out again, and fill.

Place crescents on the baking sheets 2 in/5 cm apart, brush with the beaten egg, and bake in the oven until golden brown, 15 to 20 minutes. Let cool slightly and serve.

THE CUISINE OF EPIRUS

Greece is eternal summer in the mind's eye of most tourists. Slow days, sweet as honey, segue into seductive nights, perfumed with jasmine and cooled by the sea. This is the postcard image of Greece, where the hot sun makes you languid and the sea revives you.

Then there is Epirus, where, in mid-August, an icy rain, not the sea, might chill your bones, and a fireplace, not sunshine, can warm them. Unlike the Aegean islands, which bustle with life for half the year, Epirus is tranquil, a land of vast lush mountains, ancient stone bridges, frozen rivers, and isolation. Epirus is a rural place where the mountainous terrain has historically been difficult to farm. So locals turned to shepherding many eons ago, for what Epirus lacks in arable land it more than makes up for in grazing land.

Much of the cuisine in this part of Greece evolved out of the age-old needs of itinerant shepherds, who have been plying the mountains and valleys since time immemorial. Epirus is a land of butter and cheese eaters, where lambs and goats roam free, and the mountains have always provided both shelter and food, much of it wild, from an enormous range of greens, mushrooms, and game.

The cuisine of Epirus has evolved from its location and its history. The region shares many dishes with Macedonia, especially with western Macedonia, but also with the neighboring Balkans. Peppers and cabbage, two Balkan and Macedonian staples, are also staples in Epirus.

The denizens of these mountains had access to meat, especially lamb and goat, but also game birds, wild boar, and roe deer, called *zarkadi*. Some of Greece's most bountiful rivers slice through the Pindus Mountains, and for centuries local waters—rivers as well as lakes—have provided everything from trout to sweetwater crabs to frogs' legs, a specialty of Ioannina.

Specialty foods and products from Epirus include some of the best cheeses in Greece and a wealth of pasta, from egg noodles to the pebbly *trahana* pasta. Many freshwater fish are farmed there today, too.

Epirus is also blessed with a host of other foods, all more or less linked to its cool, alpine clime. Fruits like citrus thrive along the coast, while apples, pears, cherries, peaches, and apricots flourish inland. Epirus nuts, especially almonds and walnuts, are some of the best in the country, thanks to its rainy climate. And the forests provide a bounty of what is arguably the world's most revered natural treat—mushrooms, from chanterelles to morels and more. These provide the basis for a thriving cottage industry.

THIN-BATTER PIE WITH FETA

ALEVROPITA AGINOTI

SERVES 8 TO 10

Epirus, the land in northwestern Greece of countless savory pies, favors more than a few "lazy" pies (as these are sometimes called), which don't require the laborious tasks of making phyllo or chopping greens. They are basically batter pies poured into a pan and baked. This is one of my favorites. It comes from the Zagorohoria, a group of perfectly preserved stone villages about an hour's drive north of the region's largest city, Ioannina.

> 2 cups/225 g all-purpose flour, plus more for flouring the pan
>
> Scant 1 tsp salt
>
> 2 large eggs
>
> 1½ cups/360 ml plus 3 tbsp water
>
> 1 lb/455 g Greek feta cheese, preferably made from sheep's milk, crumbled
>
> ¼ cup/60 ml plus 1 tbsp extra-virgin Greek olive oil

Preheat the oven to 325°F/165°C/gas 3. Brush a 15-in/38-cm round baking pan, 2 in/5 cm deep, with olive oil and sprinkle with a little flour, tapping the sides of the pan so the flour coats the surface evenly.

Combine the 2 cups/225 g flour and the salt in a large bowl and make a well in the center. Add 1 egg to the well and pour in 1½ cups/ 360 ml of the water. Mix with a fork, beginning in the center of the well, gradually working in the flour, to form a batter about as thick as pancake batter. Pour two-thirds of the batter into the prepared pan and tilt the pan so that the batter spreads evenly all over the surface. Sprinkle the crumbled feta evenly over the batter.

Beat the remaining egg and mix it into the batter remaining in the bowl. Add the olive oil and the remaining 3 tbsp water, mix well, and spoon the mixture over the feta. There will not be enough to cover the whole surface—some of the cheese will show through.

Bake until the pie leaves the sides of the pan, about 40 minutes. The *alevropita* should be about ½ in/12 mm thick once baked. Remove from the oven, cool slightly, and serve hot or at room temperature.

SORREL PIE WITH CORNMEAL CRUST

ARADOPITA

SERVES 12

Aradopita comes from the Greek word *arada*, which means "line." The lines are actually the layers of this pie: a layer of cornmeal, then one of filling, and one more of cornmeal. It is made mainly in the Zagorohoria in northwestern Greece.

> 2 lb/910 g sorrel, trimmed, coarsely chopped, washed well, and drained
>
> 2 large leeks, white and tender green parts, chopped, washed well, and drained
>
> 10 scallions, white and tender green parts, chopped
>
> 1 cup/60 g chopped fresh flat-leaf parsley
>
> 1 cup/60 g chopped fresh dill
>
> Salt
>
> 1¾ cups/420 ml extra-virgin Greek olive oil
>
> 2 cups/300 g fine white cornmeal
>
> 1 lb/455 g Greek feta cheese, crumbled
>
> 2½ cups/600 ml milk
>
> 1 to 1½ cups/240 to 360 ml water
>
> 2 large eggs

Combine the sorrel, leeks, scallions, parsley, and dill in a large colander and sprinkle with 1 tbsp salt. Rub and knead the mixture, pressing it with the palm of your hand against the holes of the colander until the greens and other vegetables exude their liquid. Do this for about 15 minutes. Squeeze the excess water out of the vegetables between the palms of your hands and put in a large bowl.

Place an oven rack in the center of the oven and preheat the oven to 375°F/190°C/gas 5.

Drizzle 1 cup/240 ml of the olive oil into the bowl with the greens. Knead the greens with the oil for 10 minutes. Add 1 cup/150 g of the cornmeal and the feta and mix together.

In a medium saucepan over medium heat, bring the milk to just below the boiling point. Add the remaining 1 cup/150 g of cornmeal in a slow, steady stream, whisking all the while so that it doesn't clump. Season with a little salt. Keep stirring until the mixture thickens to the consistency of a heavy batter. Remove from the heat.

Use some olive oil to grease an 18 x 12-in/46 x 30.5-cm baking pan with 2-in/5-cm sides. Spoon half of the cornmeal batter over the bottom of the pan, spreading it out evenly. Spread the vegetable filling evenly over the batter and smooth the surface with a spatula.

Dilute the remaining half of the batter with as much of the water as needed to obtain a thick but pourable batter. Pour this over the top of the filling, spreading it out as evenly as possible. Don't worry if the batter does not cover the entire surface of the greens.

Beat together the eggs and remaining ¾ cup/180 ml olive oil and pour this over the batter. Place on the center rack of the oven and bake until the pie is dense and the cornmeal crust has set and turned golden, about 1 hour. Remove from the oven and cool for about 20 minutes before serving.

IKARIAN ZUCCHINI, CHARD, AND HERB PIE

KOLOKYTHOPITA ME SESKOULO KAI MYRODIKA

===== SERVES 8 =====

Zucchini grows in great abundance in many Greek country gardens in the summer and my island garden on Ikaria is no exception. Zucchini is something of a local specialty on the island: Cooks there make everything from fritters to omelets to salads to pies like this one in countless variations. The tell-tale local seasonings are wild fennel and fresh oregano.

2 lb/910 g zucchini, preferably large

Salt

1 lb/455 g Swiss chard, trimmed, washed, spun dry, and chopped

6 tbsp extra-virgin Greek olive oil, plus extra for brushing the phyllo

3 large onions, finely chopped

6 zucchini blossoms, finely chopped (optional)

1 bunch wild fennel or dill, trimmed and finely chopped

1 bunch fresh mint, trimmed and finely chopped

1 bunch fresh parsley, trimmed and finely chopped

6 fresh oregano sprigs, trimmed and finely chopped

1½ cups/225g crumbled feta

Pepper

1 recipe Homemade Rustic Phyllo Pastry (page 224), at room temperature; or one 1-lb/455-g package commercial phyllo, defrosted overnight in the fridge and brought to room temperature

Shred the zucchini with a hand grater or in the food processor with a grater disc. Transfer to a colander, sprinkle with salt, toss, and let drain for 1 hour. Press down on it occasionally to release its liquid. Squeeze little bits between the palms of your hands to get as much of the moisture out as possible. Transfer to a large mixing bowl.

In a medium frying pan, sauté the chard in 2 tbsp of the olive oil until just wilted. Transfer to the bowl with the zucchini. Add the onions, zucchini blossoms (if using), herbs, and feta. Season with salt and pepper, add the remaining 4 tbsp of olive oil and mix well.

Preheat the oven to 350°F/175°C/gas 4.

If using homemade phyllo, oil a 15-in/38-cm round baking pan. Divide the phyllo into 2 or 4 equal balls. On a lightly floured work surface roll out the first ball to a circle slightly larger than the pan. Place in the pan and brush with oil. Repeat with second ball if you are using a total of 4. If not, spread the filling directly over the bottom circle of dough. Roll out the remaining dough in the same way, oiling each layer. Pinch the excess dough from the top and bottom layers together and roll inward to form a decorative ring. Score the pie in several places with a sharp knife.

If using commercial phyllo, oil a large rectangular pan about 13 x 15 in/ 33 x 38 cm wide and 2 in/5 cm deep. Spread half the phyllo on the bottom of the pan, brushing each layer with olive oil. Spread out the filling on top and cover with remaining phyllo sheets, brushing each one with olive oil. Score the pie into serving-size pieces and sprinkle the top sheet with a little water.

Bake the pie for 50 to 60 minutes, or until the pastry is golden. Cool to room temperature and serve.

CORFU ZUCCHINI PIE WITH TOMATOES, HOT PEPPER, AND RICE

KERKIREIKI KOLOKYTHOPITA ME DOMATES, KAFTERI PIPERIA KAI RIZI

===== SERVES 8 TO 10 =====

Corfu, rife as it is with tourists for half the year, still maintains a few of its old culinary traditions. When tomatoes, bell peppers, and squash reached the island from the New World, they probably arrived via the Venetians, who ruled Corfu from the fifteenth to the nineteenth centuries and, as avid merchants and seamen, traded in many New World crops and Old World spices. Black pepper, expensive and exotic, was confined to the kitchens of the rich. But red pepper could be had by anyone willing to plant the seeds, cultivate the plants, and dry the peppers. This pie, made with various New World ingredients, is a good example of the rustic dishes that evolved with the introduction of new foods to the island.

2 lb/910 g medium zucchini

½ cup/120 ml extra-virgin Greek olive oil

2 large onions, finely chopped

½ cup/120 g short- or medium-grain rice, such as
Greek *glasé* or Valencia

¼ cup/45 g peeled, seeded, and chopped tomatoes,
with their juice; or 1 tsp tomato paste

½ cup/30 g chopped fresh mint

½ tsp cayenne pepper, or more to taste

1 tsp sweet paprika

1 large egg, lightly beaten

1¾ tsp salt

1 tsp pepper

1 recipe Homemade Rustic Phyllo Pastry (page 224),
at room temperature; or one 1-lb/455-g package
commercial phyllo, defrosted overnight in the fridge
and brought to room temperature

Trim the zucchini and grate it coarsely, either with a box grater or a food processor fitted with a grater disc. Heat 2 tbsp of the olive oil in a large, heavy frying pan over medium heat. Add the zucchini (in two batches if necessary) and cook until soft and most of the water exuded from the zucchini has boiled off, about 15 minutes. Transfer to a large bowl.

Wipe the frying pan clean, add 2 tbsp olive oil and cook the onions over medium heat, stirring constantly, until soft and translucent, 8 to 10 minutes. Add the rice and cook for 2 to 3 minutes with the onions.

Transfer the onions and rice to the bowl with the zucchini. Add the tomatoes, mint, cayenne, paprika, and 2 tbsp olive oil and mix together with a fork. Add the egg.

Preheat the oven to 350°F/175°C/gas 4.

If using homemade phyllo, oil a 15-in/38-cm round baking dish, 1 in/2.5 cm deep. Divide the phyllo into 2 equal balls. On a lightly floured work surface roll out the first ball to a circle slightly larger than the pan, at least 18 in/46 cm. Place in the pan and brush it with 1 tbsp olive oil. Spread out the filling evenly in the pan. Repeat with the second ball of dough so it's the same size as the first, and place it over the filling. Cut off the excess dough, leaving 1 in/2.5 cm all around the pan. Pinch the bottom and top phyllo sheets together to seal and form a rim of crust. Brush the top with the remaining 1 tbsp oil. Make three slashes with a sharp paring knife in the top crust.

If using commercial phyllo, oil a 13 x 15-in /33 x 38-cm pan, 2 in/5 cm deep. Spread half the phyllo on the bottom, brushing each sheet with olive oil as you lay it down. Spread out the filling evenly on top and cover with remaining phyllo, brushing each sheet with olive oil.

Gather up the excess phyllo from around the perimeter and fold it inward to form a rim. Sprinkle a little water over the top layer. Slash the top of the pie a few times with a sharp knife.

Bake the pie until the phyllo is golden, 45 to 50 minutes. Remove from the oven, let cool, and serve.

CHEESE AND BÉCHAMEL PIE FROM POGONI

TYROPITA POGONIOU

SERVES 8 TO 12

There are countless cheese pies all over Greece. The simplest call for commercial phyllo and a filling of feta and eggs, sometimes seasoned with a little dried mint and black pepper. The following recipe from Pogoni, in Epirus, is arguably one of the oldest and most complex in the country kitchen. It calls for a phyllo technique that was common among the itinerant shepherd tribes of the north, who traveled with their families and their household goods between the lowlands and highlands twice each year. They always had a makeshift oven, essentially a dome, under which exceptional savory pies would be baked. Sometimes the phyllo would be prebaked, which made it a little easier to assemble a cheese pie on a moment's notice. This is a pie that requires time and patience; it won't work with commercial phyllo.

1½ recipes Homemade Rustic Phyllo Pastry (page 224),
at room temperature

Cornmeal for sprinkling

3 tbsp unsalted butter, preferably made from sheep's
milk, plus ⅔ cup, melted

2 tbsp all-purpose flour or semolina flour

2 cups/480 ml milk

1½ tsp salt

3 large eggs, lightly beaten

12 oz/340 g Greek feta cheese, crumbled

Pinch of ground nutmeg

On a lightly floured work surface, using the palms of your hands, roll out the dough into a long rope about 1 in/2.5 cm thick. Divide into 10 equal pieces. Roll each piece into a ball and set aside for 15 minutes, covered, to rest.

Preheat the oven to 400°F/200°C/gas 6. Invert a 14- or 15-in/35.5 or 38-cm round nonstick baking pan, 2 in/5 cm deep, and place it, upside down, on the bottom of the oven so that it gets very hot, almost like a makeshift griddle. Dust the bottom of a large round tray with cornmeal and have a bowlful of cornmeal handy.

If necessary, dust the work surface with flour again. Take the first ball of dough and flatten it slightly with the palm of your hand. Sprinkle the surface of the dough lightly with flour. Using a rolling pin, roll out the dough to a circle 14 or 15 in/35.5 or 38 cm in diameter. Place on the tray sprinkled with cornmeal and dust the top amply with more. Cover and set aside. Repeat this with 4 more balls of dough, stacking them on top of one another, and generously dusting with cornmeal.

Bring the tray over to the oven and have another empty tray handy. Open the oven, pull out the hot upside-down pan (wear oven mitts for this part), and place a sheet of phyllo over it. Immediately slide it back into the oven and bake just long enough for the phyllo to stiffen and get some color, 3 to 4 minutes. Using kitchen tongs or a two-pronged fork, flip the phyllo sheet over on the other side to bake for another 3 to 4 minutes. Remove the phyllo and set aside on the spare tray. Repeat with the remaining 4 sheets. When done, remove the pan from the oven and set aside to cool. (You will need it again.) Reduce the oven temperature to 375°F/190°C/gas 5.

In a medium pot, melt 2 tbsp of the butter. When the foam subsides add the flour and cook, stirring continuously with a whisk over low heat until the flour browns ever so lightly. Pour in the milk in a slow, steady stream, whisking constantly. Season with ½ tsp of the salt and continue stirring until the sauce thickens to the consistency of a heavy batter, about 10 minutes. Remove from the heat and mix in the eggs, stirring vigorously. Next, stir in the crumbled feta and the nutmeg. Set aside, covered with a kitchen towel, until ready to use.

When the baking pan is cool, rub the inside with the remaining 1 tbsp butter. Sprinkle 1 tsp of the remaining salt over the surface and, with the tips of your fingers, rub the salt into the butter. This is an old cook's trick to keep the pie from sticking to the pan.

On a lightly floured work surface, roll out another ball of dough, this one to a circle about 18 in/46 cm in diameter. Place it in the pan with its edges dangling over the sides. Drizzle 1 tbsp of the melted butter over its surface. Roll out 2 more balls of dough to circles 14 or 15 in/35.5 or 38 cm in diameter, depending on the size of your pan. Place them over the bottom sheet, drizzling each of them with 1 tbsp of the melted butter. Spoon about ½ cup of the filling evenly over the phyllo. (If the filling has thickened to the point of solidity, dilute it slightly with a little milk.) Next, layer the 5 prebaked phyllo sheets on top, one at a time, drizzling each generously with melted butter and spreading ½ cup of the filling over each. Roll out the remaining 2 balls of dough to 14-in/35-cm circles. Layer them over the filling, buttering them generously. Bring the excess phyllo that is dangling over the sides up over the top layer and gather it up

to form a rim. Make a few slits in the pie for the steam to escape and pour any remaining melted butter over the surface of the pie. Bake until golden, about 50 minutes.

Remove the pie from the oven. Using kitchen mitts, place a large, heat-proof plate over the pan and immediately flip the pie onto it. Slide the upside-down pie back into the pan, so that the bottom layer is on top. Let cool slightly and serve.

CHICKEN PIE FROM NAXOS

KOTOPITA NAXOU

===== SERVES 8 =====

Chicken pies prevail in the cuisines of several regions in Greece. They were usually a way to make use of leftover chicken, helping to stretch the little meat literally left on the bone into something substantial enough to feed a family. Many chicken pies call for the same combination of warm spices as the one below.

One 3-lb/1.4-kg chicken

6 cups/1.4 l liters water

3 bay leaves

2 carrots, trimmed, peeled, and left whole

1 celery stalk, cut into chunks

1 onion, peeled and left whole

Salt

8 to 10 peppercorns

2 tbsp extra-virgin Greek olive oil, plus extra for brushing the phyllo

1 leek, washed well, trimmed and chopped

½ cup/100 g long-grain rice

½ tsp ground cinnamon

¼ tsp ground cloves

½ tsp ground cumin

¼ tsp grated nutmeg

½ cup/100 g golden raisins

½ cup/70 g pine nuts

½ cup/75 g blanched almonds

9 oz/255 g *kefalotyri* cheese, grated

9 oz/255 g *graviera* cheese, grated

Pepper

1 recipe Homemade Rustic Phyllo pastry (page 224); or one 1-lb/455-g package commercial phyllo, defrosted overnight in the fridge and brought to room temperature

Put the chicken in a large pot with the water, bay leaves, carrots, celery, and onion. Bring to a boil, reduce the heat, season with salt, and add the peppercorns. Simmer, covered, for about 1½ hours, or until the chicken is falling off the bones. Skim off the scum that rises to the top of the water. Remove the chicken and set aside. Strain the broth and set aside. Discard the bay leaves and vegetables.

When the chicken is cool enough to handle, transfer to a cutting board or bowl, remove and discard the skin, and debone. Shred the chicken by hand into small pieces and set aside.

Heat the 2 tbsp olive oil in a medium frying pan over medium heat, and sauté the leek until soft and translucent, about 8 minutes. Season with a little salt.

Pour 1½ cups/360 ml of the chicken broth into a medium pot, add the rice, and bring to a boil. Reduce the heat to medium and cook the rice until it absorbs all the broth. Transfer the rice to a large bowl and add the shredded chicken, spices, raisins, pine nuts, almonds, and cheeses and season with salt and pepper. Stir in another 1½ cups/360 ml of broth. Mix in the sautéed leeks.

Preheat the oven to 350°F/175°C/gas 4, and lightly oil a 10 x 13-in/ 25 x 33-cm baking pan, 2 in/5 cm deep.

If using homemade phyllo, divide the phyllo into 2 equal balls. On a lightly floured work surface, roll out the first ball to a rectangle slightly larger than the baking pan. Place in the pan and brush with olive oil. Spread the filling evenly over the phyllo. Roll out the second ball in the same manner. Place it on top of the filling and press down slightly. Take the excess phyllo from the bottom crust, which is hanging over the pan, and fold it in, rolling it to form a decorative rim. With a sharp knife, score the pie into serving pieces.

If using commercial phyllo, layer 5 phyllo sheets on the bottom of the pan, brushing each one with olive oil. Spread out the filling evenly over the top and cover with 4 more sheets, brushing each one with olive oil. Press the layers down lightly with the palms of your hands. Trim the edges with a sharp paring knife to neaten them. Score the pie into serving pieces and bake for about 50 minutes, or until golden. Remove, let cool, and serve either warm or at room temperature.

GROUND MEAT AND FETA PIE

MIKRASIATIKI KREATOPITA

SERVES 6 TO 8

Meat pies, both festive and pedestrian, abound in the Greek kitchen. For example, in the north, especially in Epirus, ground meat pies are made on New Year's Day and a coin is inserted for good luck. One of the most famous meat pies calls for a combination of pork, lamb, and beef and hails from Cephalonia. I found this old recipe in the family collection of a friend, whose grandmother was a Greek refugee from Asia Minor, present-day Turkey.

> ¼ cup/60 ml plus 1 tbsp extra-virgin Greek olive oil, plus extra for brushing the phyllo
>
> 1 lb/455 g finely chopped red onions
>
> 1 lb/455 g lean ground beef
>
> ½ cup/100 g long-grain rice
>
> 1½ cups/360 ml water
>
> 11 oz/310 g Greek feta cheese, crumbled
>
> ½ cup/30g finely chopped fresh mint
>
> Salt and pepper
>
> 1 recipe Homemade Rustic Phyllo Pastry (page 224), at room temperature; or one 1-lb/455-g package commercial phyllo, defrosted overnight in the fridge and brought to room temperature

Heat the ¼ cup/60 ml olive oil in a large, deep frying pan or sauté pan over low heat. Cook the onion slowly for 35 to 40 minutes, stirring occasionally, until caramelized and deep gold. Transfer to a small bowl.

Add the remaining 1 tbsp oil to the same pan and add the meat. Cook for 12 to 15 minutes, until browned. Add the rice and water and stir. Cook over medium heat for about 15 minutes, until the rice has absorbed most of the water. Remove from the heat and add the cooked onion, crumbled feta, and mint. Season with salt and pepper.

Preheat the oven to 350°F/175°C/gas 4 and lightly oil a 9-in/23-cm round baking pan.

If using homemade phyllo, divide the phyllo into 2 equal balls. On a lightly floured work surface roll out the first ball to a circle about 12 in/30.5 cm in diameter. Place in the pan and brush with olive oil. Spread out the filling evenly over the phyllo. Roll out the second ball into a 9-in/23-cm circle. Place it on top of the filling and press down slightly. Take the excess phyllo from the bottom crust, which is hanging over the rim of the pan, and fold it in, rolling it decoratively to form a rim. Make several slashes in the top of the pie to let the steam escape. Brush the surface with olive oil.

If using commercial phyllo, use a rectangular pan instead. Lay 6 sheets on the bottom of the pan, brushing each with about 1 tsp olive oil. Leave some phyllo hanging over the edges of the pan. Spread the filling over the phyllo and cover with 4 more sheets, brushing each with olive oil. Trim the edges so that about 2 in/5 cm of phyllo hangs over the edge of the pan. Join the top and bottom phyllo layers around the circumference of the pan, rolling them in toward the pie to form a decorative rim. With a sharp knife, score the pie into serving pieces.

Bake the pie until the filling is set and the phyllo is golden, about 50 to 55 minutes for a pie with homemade phyllo and about 40 to 45 minutes for a pie made with commercial phyllo. Let cool slightly and serve.

HOMEMADE RUSTIC PHYLLO PASTRY

SPITIKO HORIATIKO PHYLLO

MAKES ENOUGH FOR 1 PIE
UP TO 15 IN/38 CM IN DIAMETER

Phyllo means "sheet" or "leaf" in Greek, and it refers to a whole range of pastries in the Greek kitchen. The recipe below is my standard, all-purpose phyllo recipe. It makes a very pliant and easy-to-handle dough that can be rolled out with a rolling pin or dowel or even stretched by hand until it is as thin as you are able or willing to get it. Although experienced home cooks manage to roll out their phyllo to almost gossamer thinness, it is not a requirement. If the dough tears during rolling, don't worry. Just pinch the torn part together and keep going.

> 3 to 3¼ cups/380 to 410 g all-purpose flour
>
> 1 tsp salt
>
> 1 cup/240 ml water
>
> ½ cup/120 ml extra-virgin Greek olive oil
>
> 1 tbsp strained fresh lemon juice, red or white wine vinegar, ouzo, *tsipouro*, or white wine

Put 3 cups of flour in the bowl of an electric mixer outfitted with a dough hook and stir in the salt. Make a well in the center and add the water, olive oil, and lemon juice or acid of choice. Mix with the dough hook at medium speed until a pliant but firm dough takes shape, stopping every few minutes to push the dough down into the bowl if necessary, and to add more flour incrementally if the dough is too sticky. The end result, after 7 to 10 minutes of kneading in the mixer, should be a very smooth, silky, pliant dough. Shape the dough into a ball and place in an oiled bowl. Cover the bowl with plastic wrap and let rest for at least 30 minutes or up to 2 hours. When rolling out the dough for each recipe, you will need additional flour to dust on the work surface.

Note: You may freeze or refrigerate the dough, so long as it is wrapped well in plastic and sealed. Make sure to defrost slowly and to bring to room temperature before using.

CHAPTER 9

GIFTS FROM THE SEA

THE SIMPLICITY WITH WHICH SEAFOOD IS COOKED REFLECTS THE PHILOSOPHY OF THE GREEK KITCHEN: FRESH INGREDIENTS PREPARED WITH MINIMAL INTERVENTION.

A decent-sized piece of fish seared on a grill is an all-time favorite way to enjoy seafood, and is, by the way, almost exclusively the terrain of taverna cooks, as few Greeks grill at home. The frying pan is the receptacle of choice for small fish, from red mullets to smelts, anchovies, and whiting.

In the Aegean islands, where fishing is still the livelihood of many a local, whole fish baked in the oven with seasonal vegetables is about as complicated as the recipes get. Many of these are delicious paeans to what grows locally, coupled with what swims locally. Fish such as snapper, bream, and bass might be baked with zucchini, tomatoes, or potatoes on any of the Aegean islands. In Crete, fish baked whole with okra or leeks is popular, and so are an array of fish and bean stews, especially when made with chickpeas. Wild fennel, which lends most Aegean islands their characteristic perfume, is paired frequently with fish and seafood.

Greek country cooks are avid connoisseurs of shellfish, cephalopods (squid, cuttlefish, and octopus), and other, more unusual, sea creatures. For example, the not-quite-plant, not-quite-animal sea anemone is a specialty of the northern Aegean islands, where it is pan-fried. Sea urchins are plucked off rocks in summer and eaten right there on the beach or cleaned and served in shallow bowls, their coral, soft, almost liquid flesh redolent of the sea's iodine.

In the lake regions of the north, freshwater fish, such as trout and carp, which are typically bland, are married with robust sauces, many of them containing walnuts and garlic. The fish traditions of the Pontian Greeks, who emigrated from the Black Sea, have insinuated themselves into the fish cookery of the north. Like most Asia Minor Greeks, they brought with them a penchant for the sardine, which they bake with leeks or wrap in grape leaves. Fresh anchovies, cooked in omelets or fried, are classic dishes of the Black Sea Greeks, too.

Shellfish—especially shrimp, mussels, and clams from the coves along the eastern and northern coasts of the mainland—are an important part of the cuisine. Indeed, mussels are something of a national dish, either stuffed or prepared with rice or pasta, feta, tomatoes, and wine. Squid and octopus are popular just about everywhere, either grilled or braised. Squid is stuffed with rice, *trahana*, and cheese, or cooked in wine and tomato sauces.

One of the least known Greek regional fish traditions is the custom of preparing sun-dried or salted fish. Anchovies, picarel, and sardines are salted and sun-dried on various Greek islands. Sardines, salted for just a few hours, are a specialty of the Bay of Kalloni in Lesvos. Larger fish are butterflied and hung to dry on clotheslines in the sun. Then they're flaked and added to stews, or grilled as is, dried and salty, as a meze par excellence for island firewater. Octopus is a classic dried seafood, and can still be seen hanging spiderlike from clotheslines under the summer sun.

The following recipes are a sampling of some of my favorite regional fish and seafood dishes.

THE MOST IMPORTANT GREEK FISH

In Greece, the most delicious big fish are considered to be the red snapper, *synagrida* ; the grouper, *rofos*; the sea bream and gilthead bream, *fagri* and *tsipoura*, respectively; a kind of perch, *sfyrida*; and the sea bass, *lavraki*.

Red snapper is *the* trophy fish, a favorite which is grilled or baked, as on page 232. A generation ago, we called a good-looking woman *synagrida*, maybe because the fish has tight, lean, sweet flesh! Recreational fishermen have a different epithet, calling the fish a horse for its powerful resistance when hooked. It can reach a whopping 33 lb/15 kg. It can be aggressive, daring to bite even the moray eel, should one cross its path.

The grouper is another delicious fish that can grow to 100 lb/45 kg. It lives in one place in relatively shallow waters. Grouper can be caught with nets, but is also the most prized catch among spear fishermen. The flesh is sweet and tender, and it's a great fish for the grill or oven. The huge head, which contains a lot of natural gelatin, makes the most delicious soup.

The sea bream, *fagri*, is a relatively small fish, not reaching more than 5 to 8 lb/2.3 to 3.6 kg. Its flesh is firm and white, perfect for grilling whole. Gilthead bream, *tsipoura*, is one of the two most important farmed fish in Greece. Americans and Europeans might know it as Dorade Royale. It, too, has firm, white flesh and is perfect for the grill.

Sfyrida (a kind of perch) also has firm flesh, but its flavor isn't as nuanced as that of the red snapper or grouper. It can grow to be a big fish and is perfect whole on the bone, grilled, or baked. Its head also makes a delicious soup.

Sea bass, *lavraki*, is, like the gilthead bream, the other most important farmed fish. When wild, it lives close to the surface and near the coast, and it is one of the great scavenger fishes of the Mediterranean. You see a lot of them near ports, for example. It's a good fish for the oven or for pan-searing. Of course, Greek cooks consider almost every large- or medium-sized fish fitting for the grill.

HARVESTING SEA SALT

At least once every summer, my family takes a two-hour drive and then a forty-five minute walk along the rocky path near Ikaria's Byzantine castle, down past the ancient church of Agios Yiorgos (St. George), and finally onto the sparkling beach that also bears his name. It is probably the most isolated beach on the island. We come here not only to swim and take in some sun, but also to collect salt from the shallow, natural basins carved into the rocky coast by eons of wind and waves.

I come with low-tech equipment for this ancient task: a big spoon to crack and scrape off the hard, gristly salt and a few strong bags in which to carry it back uphill. It's worth the effort; first, because I love the idea of performing a task in almost the same way that Greeks did two thousand years ago—relying on my own energies to gather one of nature's most elemental seasonings. And second, because natural Greek sea salt, although relatively unknown to connoisseurs who seek Himalayan pink salt, Hawaiian black salt, and other rarities, is really delicious. I love the feel of the crystals and the way they sparkle in the sun like tiny, rough-cut gems.

I went to Greece's foremost salt expert, Christos Milas, head of the Greek Saltworks, to find out more about how salt travels from sea to shaker. The basic method for harvesting Greek sea salt hasn't changed much over the millennia: seawater is collected in a series of shallow basins, called salt pans, and left to evaporate.

In Greece, as Milas explained, the saltworks are built around lagoons where the sea is shallow, the surrounding topography relatively flat, the winds strong and dry in summer, the rainfall almost nonexistent, and the sunshine relentless—all of which affect the speed and efficiency with which the seawater evaporates. In early summer the water is directed via shallow canals made of packed earth into a series of basins shaped like huge parallelograms. At the Greek Saltworks at the Messolongi Lagoon, for example, each salt pan is about 650 feet/200 meters wide and 2,600 feet/800 meters long, covering a total area of 3,000 acres/1,200 hectares.

About 300 acres/120 hectares are devoted to the last of the basins, called a crystallizer, which is different from all the rest. In the crystallizer, the surface has been packed down and smoothed out completely, first to be able to withstand the weight of the machinery used to harvest the salt, but also to make it impermeable when filled with the dense salt water of the last stage, when the water is as viscous as olive oil, according to Milas. One liter of seawater yields about 3 ounces/100 grams of salt. Once crystallized, the salt then needs to be washed, strange as that sounds. But washed it is, with seawater, evaporated to a certain salinity so as not to destroy the crystals.

When salt is harvested manually, it is one of the most arduous, specialized tasks in the world. Salt pans existed as early as the Mycenaean era (1900 to 1100 B.C.). The ancient Athenians got most of their salt from the saltworks at the nearby coastal areas of Rafina, Voula, and Sounio, the latter under the shadow of the temple of Poseidon. The Byzantines went farther afield for salt, all over the Aegean, and also west to the Adriatic and north to the Black Sea.

The production and sale of salt, an essential commodity, has been controlled by the powers that be from time immemorial through modern times. Until 1900, all Greek saltworks fell under the aegis of the state. Today the nine existing saltworks in Greece are private, but in almost each case, the Greek state has a majority share.

Until 1988, harvesting was done manually in most of the saltworks. Nowadays, the harvest is totally mechanized, except for a few places, such as Kythera, an island between the Peloponnese and Crete, and the Mani, which is in the southern Peloponnese, where a handful of artisan salt producers collect the sea's crystal bounty throughout the year and sell it in gourmet shops around Greece.

For all its long history of salt harvesting, Greece is actually an importer of salt because it is cheaper to import. Milas says the country could easily produce 500,000 metric tons a year, but instead production is somewhere between 120,000 and 200,000 metric tons, depending on weather conditions. Milas, taking a cue from artisan producers, has been experimenting with *afrina*, the Greek word for fleur de sel, the fine-grained, purest sea salt collected from the surface of the basins. Several Greek companies sell it.

FISH BAKED WITH OKRA

PSARI ME BAMIES

=== SERVES 4 ===

Whole fish baked with okra is one of my favorite Cretan dishes and one of the most regal in the repertoire of Greek fish cuisine.

One 2½- to 3-lb/1.2- to 1.4-kg sea bream, sea bass, or snapper, cleaned, gutted, and scaled

Juice of 1 lemon, strained

Salt and pepper

1½ lb/680 g fresh small okra

1¼ cups/300 ml red wine vinegar

½ cup/120 ml extra-virgin Greek olive oil

2 medium onions, quartered and thinly sliced

2 garlic cloves, finely chopped

8 to 10 plum tomatoes, peeled, seeded, and coarsely chopped (canned are fine)

½ cup/120 ml dry white wine

1 bunch fresh dill, snipped

Sprinkle the fish inside and out with the lemon juice, salt, and pepper. Cover with plastic wrap and refrigerate for 1 hour.

Trim the okra by removing the tough upper rims and a bit of the stems. Rinse, drain, and marinate in the vinegar in a large nonreactive bowl for 30 minutes.

Preheat the oven to 375°F/190°C/gas 5.

Remove the okra from the vinegar. In a large pot, heat the olive oil over medium heat and cook the onions, stirring, until wilted, 7 to 8 minutes. Add the garlic, then the okra, stirring gently to combine. Pour in the tomatoes and wine, cover the pot, and simmer over medium-low heat until the okra is tender but al dente, 35 to 40 minutes. About 5 minutes before removing from the heat, add the dill.

Spread out half the okra evenly on the bottom of a baking pan large enough to hold the okra and fish. Lay the fish over the okra and spread the remaining okra around and over the fish. Bake, uncovered, until the fish is flaky, about 25 minutes. Serve hot.

FISH WITH LEEKS

PSARI ME PRASSA

=== SERVES 4 TO 6 ===

This is a winter dish that I came across years ago in Crete. It's a good example of Cretan fish and vegetable cookery, and is pretty typical of Aegean island cuisine in general.

One 3-lb/1.4-kg red snapper, sea bream, or sea bass, cleaned, gutted, and scaled

Salt and pepper

Juice of 3 lemons, strained

¾ cup/180 ml extra-virgin Greek olive oil, plus extra for drizzling

2½ lb/1.2 kg leeks, white and tender green parts, washed well and cut into 2-in/5-cm lengths

2 cups/480 ml water

2 large eggs, at room temperature

Put the fish on a platter and sprinkle with salt, pepper, and one-third of the lemon juice. Cover with plastic wrap and refrigerate until ready to use.

Heat ½ cup/120 ml of the olive oil in a large, wide pot and put the leeks in the pot. Sprinkle with a little salt. Cover and steam in the oil over low heat, turning them occasionally, until lightly caramelized, about 25 minutes.

Place the fish over the leeks, add the water, cover, and simmer over low heat until the fish is fork-tender, 20 to 25 minutes.

Separate the egg yolks and whites. Beat the whites vigorously until foamy and nearly stiff. Beat the egg yolks with the remaining two-thirds of the lemon juice and then whisk into the whites. Add a ladleful of the pot juices to the lemon mixture in a slow, steady stream, whisking all the while. Pour the sauce into the pot and tilt the pot to distribute it evenly. Pour in the remaining ¼ cup/60 ml of olive oil and serve.

RED MULLET

Red mullet (*Mullus surmuletus*), with its red skin, delicate flesh, and characteristically earthy (some say muddy) flavor, is a quintessential Mediterranean fish. One of the great twentieth-century Greek chroniclers of fish, Themos Potamianos, in a classic book called *The Deep Is Here* (published in Greek in 1994), notes that the *barbouni*, as the Greeks call red mullet, gets its name from the Greek word *barbarossa* ("red beard"), after the fish's color and its whiskers. The *barbouni* has been one of the most esteemed and sought-after fish in the Aegean from antiquity to the present, though its numbers have dwindled dramatically because of overfishing and pollution. Once a common treat, red mullet is now one of the most expensive fish in Greece.

The classic way to cook red mullet is to dust it with flour and fry it, but in the Aegean islands and beyond, people prepare it in unusual ways. It's the most common fish in the classic dish *savoro*, which preserves leftover fried fish in a sweet and sour sauce made with vinegar, rosemary, garlic, and sometimes raisins, tomatoes, and wine. In the tiny Dodecanese island of Lipsoi, red mullets are filled with ground rusks, garlic, and parsley and then baked. In Lesvos, they are fair game for a local pilaf, and in the Cyclades, they are fried and served with caper sauces. In the coastal areas around lush Mt. Pelion, which straddles the Pagasitikos Gulf, mullet is served in a sauce called *spetsofai*, made with bell peppers and tomatoes (see page 234).

Contemporary chefs have taken another direction with this delicious small fish: They painstakingly remove its many bones, usually with tweezers, and they marinate the fish, ceviche style, in lemon juice, olive oil, and herbs, inspiring contemporary home cooks, even a few in country kitchens, to do the same.

RED MULLETS COOKED WITH PEPPERS AND TOMATOES

BARBOUNI SPETSOFAI

===== SERVES 4 =====

This unusual dish comes from the coastal region of Mt. Pelion, in central Greece. *Spetsofai* typically refers to a meatball and pepper stew. This variation is yet another testimony to the resourcefulness of country cooks, who use what is available in imaginative ways.

Flour for dredging

Salt and pepper

8 red mullets, cleaned and gutted

1 cup/240 ml extra-virgin Greek olive oil

1 large red onion, finely chopped

6 large green bell peppers, seeded and cut into thin strips

3 garlic cloves, crushed

1 cup/240 ml white wine

2 large firm, ripe tomatoes, grated (see Note on page 74)

Pinch of sugar

3 fresh oregano sprigs

2 fresh thyme sprigs

Put the flour on a plate, season with salt and pepper, and dredge the fish lightly in the flour. Heat ⅔ cup/160 ml of the olive oil in a large, preferably nonstick, frying pan over medium-high heat and pan-fry the fish lightly until almost done, turning to cook both sides, about 6 minutes. Remove the fish with a slotted spoon carefully, so it will not break apart. Set aside, covered.

Remove the oil and scrape the frying pan clean with a rubber spatula or wooden spoon. Add the remaining ⅓ cup/80 ml of oil to the same pan and heat over low heat. Add the onion and bell peppers and cook until the vegetables soften, 12 to 15 minutes. Stir in the garlic and cook for a minute or so, until soft. Pour in the wine, raise the heat to medium, and as soon as the alcohol has cooked off (the aroma should be mellow, with no hint of a sharp smell), pour in the grated tomatoes. Season with salt, pepper, and the sugar. Cook, covered, until the sauce is thick. Add the oregano and thyme and simmer for 5 minutes.

Return the mullets to the frying pan and cook in the sauce until warmed through, about 5 minutes. Remove the herbs and serve immediately.

BONITO WITH UNRIPE GRAPES AND POTATOES

TONAKI ME AGOURIDA KAI PATATES

===== SERVES 2 =====

This is an old dish from Lefkada, in the Ionian Sea.

2 lb/910 g bonito, gutted but whole

Salt

3 large boiling potatoes, peeled and coarsely chopped

Pepper

1 large onion, cut into thin wedges

2 cups/200 g unripe green grapes

⅔ cup/160 ml extra-virgin Greek olive oil

In a colander, sprinkle the fish with salt and let stand for 15 minutes.

Spread out the potatoes in the bottom of a large pot. Season with salt and pepper and place the fish on top. Season with more pepper and spread the onion on top of the fish. Pour in enough water to just cover the potatoes.

Add the grapes to the pot and pour in the olive oil. Bring to a boil over medium heat, reduce the heat to low, and simmer, covered, until the potatoes are soft and most of the juices from the grapes have been absorbed by the potatoes and the fish is tender. Remove from the heat and serve.

BONITO

Bonito, *palamida* in Greek, is one of the great oily fish of the Aegean and Mediterranean. It looks like tuna and mackerel and, in fact, is in the same family but is smaller. While it abounds in many places in Greece (mainly along cove-laced coastlines), some of the most interesting country recipes come from Greeks who emigrated from Istanbul, Turkey, in 1922. There are also some fine recipes from Lesvos, where bonito used to be roasted in concave ceramic roofing tiles, and from Lefkada, where it is fished on the eastern side of the island and off another small, neighboring island, Meganisi. There, as Greek author Kostas Palmos recounts in a book about his native island, *Meganisiotika* (in Greek), between April and June, the season for bonito fishing, you can sometimes still hear the echo of fishermen's voices (if they fish the old-fashioned way), shouting and moving along the rocky coast, pulling their nets along the surface of the water with long ropes. At midnight, they go back to the nets with flashlights to pull up the ones that have sunk from the weight of so many bonitos, which swim in large schools.

Three-year-old bonito, weighing between 3 and 12 pounds/1.4 and 5.4 kilos, are used to make one of the great preserved fish specialties of Greece, *lakerda*, which involves brining thick fillets of the fish and then covering them with olive oil. *Lakerda* was the food of the poor in the ancient Greek city of Byzantium, but today it is one of the most select meze. It is a specialty of the Greeks who came as refugees from Asia Minor in 1922; of the islanders on Lesvos, near the waters where bonito thrives; and of the islanders of Naxos, where it is still made at home today. The trick is to preserve the bonito in just enough brine and only for several hours, so that its flesh stays sweet and succulent. It is available in tins at the deli sections of Greek and Middle Eastern grocers across the United States and in Western Europe. If you find some, serve it with thinly sliced raw onion on top.

BONITO WITH YOUNG FAVA BEANS, WILD FENNEL, AND GARLIC

PALAMIDA ME FRESKA KOUKIA, SKORDAKI, KAI AGRIOMARATHO

SERVES 2

The traditional version of this dish, from Lefkada, in the Ionian Sea, calls for tender green stalks of spring garlic.

2 lb/910 g fresh young fava beans, shelled

1 cup/60 g finely chopped wild fennel fronds, or 1 medium fennel bulb, trimmed and finely chopped

2 large garlic cloves, minced; or 4 garlic scapes, trimmed and chopped

2½ to 4½ tbsp extra-virgin Greek olive oil, depending on whether you are cooking wild fennel or a fennel bulb

1 tbsp strained fresh lemon juice

Pinch of sugar

Salt and pepper

One 2-lb/910-g bonito, cleaned and filleted

½ cup/120 ml vegetable or fish broth

Preheat the oven to 350°F/175°C/gas 4 and lightly oil a casserole dish with a lid.

Using a sharp paring knife, remove the "eye" from each bean. Bring a pot of salted water to a rolling boil and blanch the beans for 7 to 8 minutes. Drain the beans. Peel the outer skin off each bean and transfer them to a bowl. Toss with the wild fennel (if using) and the chopped garlic. If using a fennel bulb, cook the chopped fennel in 2 tbsp of the olive oil until soft, about 8 minutes over low heat. Add it to the beans.

Put the beans in the baking dish and toss with 2 tbsp of the olive oil, the lemon juice, and sugar. Season with salt and pepper. Spread out the beans in an even layer. Place the fish over the beans and drizzle with the remaining ½ tbsp of olive oil. Pour in the broth. Bake, covered, for 25 to 30 minutes, until the fish and beans are tender. Serve immediately.

MACKEREL BRAISED WITH GARLIC AND ROSEMARY

PALAMIDA MAGEIREFTI

SERVES 2

The flavors in this fish dish, which hails from Lefkada, are typical of the cooking of the Ionian, where the Venetian influence in the kitchen is still evident. Most Greek cooks typically season fish with oregano, but the rosemary and garlic in the dish below allude to Italian flavors.

2 medium whole mackerels (about 8 oz/225 g each), cleaned and filleted; or 4 mackerel fillets (about 4 oz/115 g each); or 1 lb/455 g bluefish fillets

2 cups/480 ml water

3 tbsp red wine vinegar

Salt and pepper

½ cup/120 ml extra-virgin Greek olive oil

6 garlic cloves, crushed and thinly sliced

1 fresh rosemary sprig

2 bay leaves, broken in half

⅔ cup/160 ml white wine

Juice of ½ to 1 lemon, strained

Rinse the mackerel. Put in a large, shallow bowl, add the water and the vinegar, and let stand for 15 minutes. Remove and rinse. Season with a little salt and pepper and set aside.

Preheat the oven to 350°F/175°C/gas 4. Pour half the olive oil into a baking pan large enough to hold the mackerel fillets snugly in one layer. Sprinkle the garlic evenly over the surface. Place the rosemary sprig and the bay leaves in the center. Place the fish on top and pour the remaining olive oil over the fish. Add the wine. Bake the fish, uncovered, for 25 minutes or until fork-tender. About 5 minutes before removing from the oven, pour in lemon juice to taste. Remove from the oven, remove the bay leaves and rosemary, and serve immediately.

PEPPERY FISH AND LEEK CASSEROLE FROM CORFU

BOURTHETO KERKYRAS

======== SERVES 6 ========

Bourtheto is a legacy of the Venetians, who ruled parts of Greece for several hundred years. The name comes from the Italian *brodeto,* for "broth." In the Ionian islands the dish is something of a local specialty, especially in Corfu, where the most beloved versions are made with bony scorpion fish, fresh cod, or octopus. But regional variations exist in other parts of Greece, too. On Ios, an island in the Cyclades, the fish of choice is a gelatinous *savridi,* which is horse or jack mackerel. The following recipe is a classic Corfu country dish.

> 2 lb/910 g whole white-fleshed fish, such as grouper, scorpion fish, or cod, cleaned and gutted
>
> Salt and pepper
>
> 3 tbsp extra-virgin Greek olive oil
>
> 1 large leek, white and tender green parts, washed well and thinly sliced
>
> 2 garlic cloves, finely chopped
>
> Heaping 1 tbsp sweet paprika
>
> Scant 1 tsp cayenne pepper, or to taste
>
> 1 tbsp tomato paste
>
> 1 cup/240 ml dry red wine
>
> 1 cup/240 ml water

Season the fish with salt and pepper, cover with plastic wrap, and store in the refrigerator until ready to use.

Heat the olive oil in a large, heavy skillet, add the leek and garlic, and sweat over low heat until the leek is very soft, about 20 minutes. Add the paprika and cayenne and stir with a wooden spoon for about 1 minute. Add the tomato paste and stir for another minute. Pour in ½ cup/120 ml of the wine and the water. Bring to a gentle boil, reduce the heat to low, and simmer, covered, until the sauce is thick and dark, about 15 minutes. Season with salt and pepper.

Place the fish over the leeks in the skillet. Add the remaining ½ cup/120 ml wine, cover the skillet, and simmer until the fish is flaky and tender, another 15 minutes or so, depending on the size of the fish. Remove from the heat, let stand for about 5 minutes, and serve.

STRIPED SEA BREAM WITH SCALLIONS

MOURMOURES ME KREMMYDAKIA

======== SERVES 4 ========

Here's a country dish that I witnessed being made by Marianthi Gerovassiliou, mother of Vangelis Gerovassiliou, one of Greece's most talented winemakers. "Fish and sweets should not be covered," she advised. "You never cover fish as it's cooking in a pot so it doesn't smell, well, fishy," according to *kyria* (Mrs.) Marianthi. "Even God would love this dish," she adds. She used an unusual technique when making this dish: she halved the lemons and then chopped them, rind and all, before adding them to the fish.

> ⅔ cup/160 ml extra-virgin Greek olive oil
>
> 5 large scallions, trimmed and cut into ⅓-in/8-mm rounds
>
> 1 small lemon, coarsely chopped or diced
>
> ½ cup/30 g coarsely chopped fresh mint
>
> Salt and pepper
>
> 1½ lb/680 g striped sea bream, cleaned and gutted

Heat the olive oil over medium-low heat in a large, deep frying pan, sauté pan, or wide pot and cook the scallions until soft, about 10 minutes, stirring occasionally. Add half the lemon and the mint. Season with salt and pepper and stir.

Place the fish on top of the scallions and add enough water to come about halfway up the fish. Season again with a little salt and pepper. Cook over medium-low heat, uncovered, until the fish is fork-tender and the sauce is thick, 20 to 25 minutes. Remove from the heat, cool slightly, and serve with remaining lemon.

GILT-HEAD BREAM ROASTED WITH POTATOES AND FETA

TSIPOURA ME PATATES KAI FETA

SERVES 4

Gilt-head bream, *tsipoura* in Greek, is typically roasted or grilled very simply with olive oil, salt, pepper, and herbs. Country cooks typically serve it with potatoes. I took a few liberties with this dish and married the potatoes and fish with a little feta and lemon, adding welcome acidity to the mild flavor of the bream. In Greece most bream is farmed nowadays, and there is a growing industry in organically farmed fish.

6 medium waxy potatoes, peeled and cut into 1 in/2.5-cm rounds

Salt and pepper

½ cup/70 g plus 1 tbsp finely chopped celery stalks and leaves, preferably from wild or Chinese celery

¼ cup/40 g crumbled Greek feta cheese

½ cup/120 ml extra-virgin Greek olive oil

4 whole gilt-head bream (about 12½ oz/355 g each), cleaned, gutted, and scaled, with heads left on

2 small lemons, cut into thin rounds, seeds removed

Preheat the oven to 350°F/175°C/gas 4. Oil a glass baking dish large enough to hold the fish in one layer.

Spread out two-thirds of the potatoes over the bottom of the pan in one layer, overlapping them slightly if necessary. Season with salt and pepper and sprinkle 3 tbsp of the celery and the crumbled feta evenly over the potatoes. Drizzle with 3 tbsp of the olive oil.

Lightly salt and pepper the fish inside and out. Place 1 tbsp of the celery in the cavity of each fish and place the fish over the potatoes in the pan. Cover the fish with the remaining potatoes. Sprinkle 2 tbsp of chopped celery on top and drizzle with ½ tbsp of the olive oil. Place the lemon rounds over the potatoes covering the fish. Each fish should have 4 to 5 rounds of lemon over it. Cover the pan with aluminum foil and bake for 35 minutes, or until fish is fork-tender and the potatoes are soft. Remove from the oven, cool for a few minutes, drizzle with the remaining olive oil, and serve fish topped with lemon and with the potatoes on side.

SARDINES BAKED OVER SUMMER VEGETABLES

SARDELES BRIAM

SERVES 4 TO 6

This is a classic summer dish from Lesvos. Most aficionados of the humble but healthful sardine—filled as it is with omega-3 fatty acids—savor it as the perfect foil for the complex flavors of the island's ouzo. But there are myriad recipes for the fish. This one is all bound up with summer, the sardine's fishing season.

1 lb/455 g zucchini, cut on the bias into large, thin oval slices

Salt

3 large firm, ripe tomatoes, coarsely grated (see page 74)

Pepper

2 tsp sugar

1 cup/60 g finely chopped fresh flat-leaf parsley

1 large red onion, halved and thinly sliced

3 garlic cloves, minced

3 tbsp fresh oregano leaves, or 1 tsp dried

2 lb/910 g sardines, cleaned, scaled, and deboned

½ cup/120 ml extra-virgin Greek olive oil

⅓ cup/80 ml ouzo

Put the zucchini in a colander, toss with a scant 1 tsp salt, and let stand to drain for 1 hour. Pat dry.

In a medium bowl, season the tomatoes with a little salt and pepper and stir in the sugar and the parsley. Set aside.

Preheat the oven to 350°F/175°C/gas 4. Lightly oil a glass or ceramic baking dish.

Place the zucchini slices in one overlapping layer in a 9 x 13-inch/ 22 x 32-cm baking dish. Sprinkle with the onion slices, half the garlic, and half the oregano. Spoon the tomato mixture evenly on top. Cover with the sardines, placing them in one snug layer over the vegetables. Sprinkle with the remaining garlic and oregano and drizzle the olive oil and ouzo over the sardines. Season lightly with more salt and pepper. Bake, covered, until the sardines are fork-tender and the vegetables are cooked, about 45 minutes. Serve immediately.

VARIATION: *Briam*, a classic summer baked vegetable dish, stands up perfectly on its own, without the addition of sardines.

THE BEST SARDINES IN THE WORLD

Sardine season starts in June and ends in October in the Bay of Kalloni, on Lesvos, an island in the northeast Aegean. Dawn is the busiest time along the pier. The sardine boats come in around 6:00 A.M., about fifty to sixty of them. Connoisseurs of the silvery local catch, including taverna owners, fishmongers, and resourceful home cooks, arrive early to get the real thing: day-boat sardines. Anything older is considered second-rate; anything fished just a little farther out to sea, beyond the border of the bay, is considered a downright insult.

Day-boat Kalloni sardines are savored in one of three ways: grilled and flavored with a drizzle of the island's earthy olive oil; seasoned with salt from the Kalloni saltworks, usually right there on the docks or on the boat, and eaten by nightfall; or preserved for the months that follow the fishing season. So entrenched is the sardine culture in Kalloni that experts differentiate by size which sardines are edible that same day and which should be put up to savor all winter long with a shot or two of ouzo, the island's favored drink. The small ones, called *papalines*, which are in season from late May through late July, are salted and savored the same day; plump August sardines and anything fished after that are preserved. The island, in fact, boasts a vibrant canning industry for its prized local catch.

The Kalloni sardine is unique: It is small and plump with white flesh and a complex flavor, which it acquires by feeding on the bounty of plankton in the shallow, rich bay.

Five hundred or so families make a good living from Kalloni sardines. For fishermen, the day starts long before dawn, under the star-filled blackness of an Aegean night. Most are out in the bay by 3:00 A.M., without lights, which would scare away the surface-hugging sardine.

The fishing follows a rigid set of rules to ensure that the catch is as good as possible. No one, for example, brings in sardines too early in the season. "It's an embarrassment to the profession to fish for infants," as a long-time Kalloni fisherman put it bluntly. Early in the season, fishermen lay nets with holes around ⅓ inch/8.5 millimeters in diameter. Sardines swim in large schools and the catch numbers in the thousands each time, but the fishermen never leave the sardines to linger for more than a half hour or so in the submerged nets to prevent them from eating too much plankton at once, which swells them unpleasantly. As the season progresses and the fish grow larger, the nets grow larger, too, with holes about ½ inch/12 millimeters in diameter.

The process of salting the day-boat fish is surprisingly low-tech. Plastic containers, local coarse sea salt, and an eye for handpicking each and every fish are all that's needed. Most fishermen don't gut the fish, but instead place them in layers in plastic containers, salting the layers generously. By evening the fish are ready to consume, and you can buy them right there on the dock. But all over Lesvos and well beyond its shores, you can also find colorful flat cans of salted local sardines—the fatter ones—to be enjoyed long after the sardine season has faded into winter.

ANCHOVIES BAKED WITH OREGANO AND TOMATOES

GAVROS RIGANATOS

============ SERVES 4 ============

Silvery, smooth-skinned anchovies are among the most esteemed, albeit humble, fish in Greece. Ancient chroniclers of Greek gastronomy held a certain disdain for it, most likely because Greek waters teemed so profusely with slithering shoals of the fish that elite gourmands of the time considered it too common to be of any worth. Anchovies were the fish from which the much-touted *garum*, a fermented fish sauce that was the basis of countless ancient dishes, was made. Like sardines, anchovies are rich in omega-3 fatty acids, as well as antioxidants.

Anchovies are excellent fried. Meze lovers savor them raw but brined, as one of the best accompaniments for ouzo and *tsipouro*. The Greeks of the Black Sea have a special affinity for anchovies and make all sorts of unusual dishes with them, including an omelet. In the country kitchen, anchovies are also baked with tomatoes, herbs, olive oil, garlic, and lemon, and they are delicious that way.

2½ lb/1.2 kg fresh anchovies

Salt and white pepper

Juice of 1½ lemons, strained

¼ cup/60 ml dry white wine

⅓ cup/80 ml extra-virgin Greek olive oil

1 large red onion, finely chopped

4 garlic cloves, cut into slivers

1 tbsp dried Greek oregano, or 3 tbsp fresh

3 tbsp capers, rinsed, drained, and chopped

½ cup/30 g finely chopped fresh flat-leaf parsley

8 campari or plum tomatoes, cut into thin rounds

Wash and gut the anchovies and remove and discard their heads. Put them in a large bowl and season with salt and white pepper. Add a third of the lemon juice and the wine and toss to combine. Refrigerate for 15 minutes, and then drain.

Preheat the oven to 375°F/190°C/gas 5.

Arrange the anchovies in one layer in a shallow, lightly oiled 8-inch/20-cm baking dish. Sprinkle the anchovies with the remaining lemon juice, the olive oil, onion, garlic, oregano, capers, and parsley. Cover with the sliced tomatoes. Bake for 15 to 20 minutes, until tender. Remove from the oven and serve hot.

SALT COD WITH CELERY AND CHESTNUTS

PASTOS BAKALIAROS ME KASTANA KAI SELINO

============ SERVES 8 ============

This is a very old recipe from Arcadia, one of the mountainous areas of the Peloponnese, where salt cod made inroads into local kitchens. Chestnuts, which grow there, figure prominently in several local dishes from the region, including this one.

2 lb/910 g salt cod

1 lb/455 g chestnuts in the shell, or 2½ cups shelled chestnuts (see Note)

½ cup/120 ml extra-virgin Greek olive oil

4 celery stalks, trimmed and finely chopped

3 garlic cloves, minced

4 large firm, ripe tomatoes, finely chopped; or 2 cups/350 g chopped canned plum tomatoes, with their juice

Salt and pepper

Rinse the cod to remove the outer layer of salt. Cut into serving-size pieces and put in a bowl filled with water. Let sit, refrigerated, for 12 to 24 hours, changing the water every 4 to 5 hours. Take a tiny bit of cod and taste it for saltiness. Continue soaking if necessary.

If using fresh chestnuts in the shell, score them with a sharp paring knife and put them in a pot with enough water to cover by 2 in/5 cm. Bring to a boil over high heat, reduce the heat, and simmer until the chestnuts are soft, 35 to 40 minutes. Drain the chestnuts, cool, and peel. Boil already shelled fresh chestnuts until soft, 20 to 25 minutes. Either way, cool the chestnuts and cut in half.

Heat the olive oil in a wide, shallow pot over medium heat and sauté the celery until soft, about 5 minutes. Add the garlic and chestnuts and continue cooking for about 5 minutes. Add the tomatoes and season with salt and pepper. Raise the heat, bring the tomatoes to a boil, and reduce the heat to a simmer. Cook, uncovered, for 10 minutes to reduce some of the tomato liquid.

Place the cod over the vegetables. Cover, reduce the heat to medium-low, and cook for 10 to 15 minutes, until the fish is fork-tender. Serve immediately.

NOTE: For shelled chestnuts you can use fresh, sous vide, frozen (defrosted), or canned unsweetened chestnuts. If using sous vide, put the bag in boiling water and cook according to the package directions.

SALT COD AND SWEET POTATO STEW

BAKALIAROS ME GLYKOPATATES

SERVES 8

The regional kitchen is filled with recipes for salt cod cooked with just about everything, including raisins, greens, sweet potatoes, bell peppers, leeks, eggplants, tomatoes, and parsley. In Crete, people eat salt cod with chickpeas, and in the Peloponnese they enjoy it with black-eyed peas. In some places, the desalted fish is shredded and rolled with rice to make dolmades. Islanders also make a very Frankish-sounding dish called *brandatha*, similar at least in name to the classic French dish, brandade, but with a characteristic local twist: a tomato-based vinegary skordalia is added to the cod as it simmers in a pot. This unusual combination of cod and sweet potatoes, which flourish on the island of Naxos, marries the saltiness of the cod with the sweetness of the potatoes beautifully.

2 lb/910 g salt cod

3 cups/720 ml water

Juice of ½ lemon, strained

2 lb/910 g sweet potatoes

¼ cup/60 ml extra-virgin Greek olive oil

2 medium red onions, finely chopped

1 cup/175g finely chopped canned tomatoes

Pepper

2 tbsp finely chopped fresh flat-leaf parsley

Rinse the cod to remove the outer layer of salt. Cut into serving-size pieces and put in a bowl filled with water. Let sit, refrigerated, for 12 to 24 hours, changing the water every 4 to 5 hours. Take a tiny piece of cod and taste it for saltiness. Continue soaking if necessary.

Pour the 3 cups/720 ml water into a bowl and add the lemon juice. When the cod is sufficiently desalted, peel the sweet potatoes. Cut into large chunks and drop into the acidulated water.

Heat the olive oil in a wide, heavy pot over medium heat, and sauté the onions, stirring, until wilted, about 10 minutes. Add the potatoes and sauté until lightly browned. Add the tomatoes, season with pepper, and add enough water to cover the contents of the pot. Cook, covered, for 20 minutes.

Spread the cod pieces on top of the potatoes and sprinkle the parsley over the fish. Cover the pot and simmer for 10 minutes, or until the fish is cooked through and flaky. Serve immediately.

CLASSIC BATTER-FRIED SALT COD

BAKALIAROS SKORDALIA

SERVES 4 TO 6

Batter-fried salt cod is the traditional food Greeks eat on March 25, the Assumption, and on Palm Sunday, when fish is allowed, despite Lent. But in the country kitchen, this once humble, imported fish was enjoyed often. Itinerant merchants used to ply the countryside hawking salt cod and, in the Ionian, stockfish, which is air-dried cod. These were, until a generation ago, the mountain dweller's delicacies. Some of the most interesting recipes for salt cod, in fact, hail from areas that are farthest from the sea. The regions of the Peloponnese and mainland Greece have a special affinity for it.

1½ to 2 lb/680 to 900 g salt cod

BATTER

About 2 cups/225 g all-purpose flour, as needed

Salt and pepper

1 tsp baking powder

⅔ cup/160 ml beer

2 tbsp strained fresh lemon juice

Olive or vegetable oil for frying

Arcadian Walnut Skordalia (page 54) or another skordalia recipe for serving

2 lemons, cut into wedges, for garnish

Rinse the cod to remove the outer layer of salt. Cut the cod into 2-in/5-cm pieces and put in a bowl filled with water. Let sit, refrigerated, for 12 to 24 hours, changing the water every 4 to 5 hours. Take a tiny piece of cod and taste for saltiness. Continue soaking if necessary.

When the cod is ready, prepare the batter: In a medium bowl, stir together 1¼ cups/145 g of the flour, some salt and pepper, and the baking powder. Pour in the beer and whisk until smooth, adding more flour as needed to form a thick batter.

Remove the cod from the water and rinse and drain very well. Sprinkle with the lemon juice.

In a medium pot or a deep-fryer, heat 4 in/10 cm of oil to about 360°F/180°C. Spread a little flour onto a clean plate and dust the cod. Using a slotted spoon, dip the cod into the batter, a few pieces at a time, and let the excess drip off. Submerge the pieces into the hot oil and fry until golden and crisp, turning to cook evenly on all sides. Drain on paper towels. Serve hot with the skordalia and lemon wedges on the side.

SHRIMP SAUTÉED WITH GARLIC, PARSLEY, AND BREAD CRUMBS

GARIDES SOTARISMENES ME SKORDO, MAINTANO KAI FRYGANIA

===== SERVES 6 TO 8 =====

This tangy, easy dish can be served as a main course or meze.

½ cup/120 ml extra-virgin Greek olive oil

6 garlic cloves, crushed

2 lb/910 g large shrimp, shelled and deveined

⅔ cup/40 g finely chopped fresh flat-leaf parsley

1 cup/240 ml dry white wine

Salt and pepper

⅔ cup/35 g coarse dry bread crumbs (see Note on page 57)

Juice of ½ lemon, strained

1 lemon, cut into wedges, for garnish

Heat the olive oil over low heat in a wide pot. Add the garlic and stir for 1 minute. Do not let it brown. Raise the heat to medium and add the shrimp. As soon as they turn pink, add the parsley. Pour in the wine, which will sizzle. Season with salt and pepper and reduce the heat to low. Sprinkle the bread crumbs on top of the shrimp. Simmer, uncovered, over low heat until most of the shrimp juices have been absorbed, about 5 minutes. Drizzle in the lemon juice and remove from the heat. Serve immediately, garnished with lemon wedges.

SHRIMP BAKED WITH FETA

GARIDES ME FETA

===== SERVES 6 =====

Shrimp baked with feta are one of the many taverna classics that can be made at home and served as a meze or main course.

2 lb/910 g large shrimp, with their shells on

12 cups/2.8 l water

1 tbsp red wine vinegar

5 tbsp unsalted butter, cut into small pieces, plus more for greasing the pan

3 large firm, ripe tomatoes, grated (see Note on page 74)

1 scant tsp sugar

Salt and pepper

8 oz/225 g Greek feta cheese, crumbled

3 tbsp chopped fresh flat-leaf parsley

Wash and drain the shrimp. Pour the water and vinegar into a medium pot, bring to a rolling boil, and blanch the shrimp for 1 minute. Remove immediately with a slotted spoon. (Discard the water.) Cool the shrimp slightly and remove their heads and shells, leaving the tails intact.

Melt 2 tbsp of the butter over medium heat in a medium saucepan and add the tomatoes. Add the sugar and season with salt and pepper. Bring to a boil over high heat, reduce the heat to very low, and simmer for 15 minutes.

Preheat the oven to 350°F/175°C/gas 4. Butter a glass baking dish large enough to hold the shrimp in one layer. Place the shrimp in neat rows in the baking dish, fitting them snugly next to one another. Sprinkle half the feta over them. Pour the sauce over the shrimp and sprinkle with the remaining feta. Dot with the remaining 3 tbsp butter and bake for 5 to 7 minutes, or just until the feta begins to melt. Remove, sprinkle with the parsley, and serve.

COUNTRY SHRIMP

Easy to catch and delicious to boot, shrimp have been considered a delicacy in Greece since antiquity. The first-century A.D. chronicler of ancient tastes and foods, Athenaeus, writes about an early Greek recipe for large shrimp grilled inside fig leaves.

Greece is blessed with a fair number of shrimp species, differentiated mainly by their size, color, and whether they are outfitted with antennae or spines. Among the best known are the one-eyed *gambari* of the northern Ionian and the tiny orange-red shrimp from the coves of Symi, Rhodes, Kastelorizo, and other islands in the southeastern Dodecanese. The tiny ones make an irresistible fried treat and go by the name *Symiako*

Garidaki, "small shrimp from Symi." The large one-eyed *gambari* can run as large as 8 in/20 cm long. It has a characteristic yellow, red, or gray-black shell and inhabits the Gulf of Corinth and the waters of the Amvrakikos Gulf, off the northwest coast of Greece. These are generally cooked in the simplest way: in the shell, fried with a little salt, a method that helps retain all the shrimp's delicious juices (and makes it messy to eat).

Most shrimp recipes are the domain of either the meze kitchen (think shrimp saganaki and grilled shrimp) or the restaurant kitchen. Of the few main-course shrimp recipes enjoyed on country tables, the two on the facing page are among my favorites.

SQUID STUFFED WITH SWEET TRAHANA

KALAMARAKIA GEMISTA ME TRAHANA

"Two or 20 is the rule for squid," my friend Lefteris Lazarou, one of Greece's premiere seafood chefs, confides. That would be either 2 minutes of cooking time or at least 20 to ensure the squid's flesh remains tender and doesn't become rubbery. Greeks have a special affinity for squid, one of the sea's smartest cephalopods, and they generally disdain it when frozen. In fact, honorable restaurateurs always alert diners if the squid they are serving has been on ice. Fresh squid is only in season from the end of summer into the fall. Greeks know it by its luminescent, pearly white inner flesh.

In Greek country kitchens, there are all sorts of recipes for squid: stuffed and fried, stuffed and braised, floured and fried, and grilled. I like this one, from the Ionian island of Lefkada, because it includes one of the most traditional Greek grain products, *trahana*. Most Greek stuffed squid recipes call for rice.

6 to 8 fresh squid, about 8 in/20 cm long each

¾ cup/180 ml extra-virgin Greek olive oil

1 large red onion, finely chopped

1 large leek, white and tender green parts, finely chopped

2 garlic cloves, minced

1 cup/170 g sweet *trahana*

1 cup/240 ml dry white wine

2 cups/350 g peeled, chopped, and seeded plum tomatoes (canned are fine), with their juice

Salt and pepper

Heaping 1 tsp dried marjoram

½ tsp dried thyme

½ tsp pink peppercorns

½ cup/30 g chopped fresh flat-leaf parsley

6 to 8 bay leaves

If the squid have not been cleaned, clean them one at a time. Hold a squid in one hand and with the other, pull out the head, tentacles, and viscera. Using your index finger or a long teaspoon, remove and discard the gelatinous viscera inside the squid's cavity, on the bottom. Rinse well inside and out and set aside. Pull out the quill. Cut the head of the squid just below the eye to remove the tentacles. Do not include the eyes, which can be bitter. Rinse the tentacles and set aside. Set aside the cleaned, rinsed bodies. If desired, for purely aesthetic reasons, you can peel off the thin purple membrane on the outside of the squid.

In a large, deep frying pan or sauté pan, heat ½ cup/120 ml of the olive oil over medium heat, and sauté the onion and leek for about 8 minutes, or until soft. Add the garlic and stir. Add the *trahana* and toss to coat in the oil. Cook, stirring, for 3 to 4 minutes. Pour in the wine and as soon as it steams up, add 3 tbsp of the chopped plum tomatoes. Reduce the heat to low, stir, and season with salt and pepper. Continue cooking, stirring occasionally, until the *trahana* is al dente, 5 to 7 minutes. Add the dried herbs, pink peppercorns, and chopped parsley and mix well. Set aside for a few minutes to cool slightly.

Preheat oven to 375°F/190°C/gas 5. Lightly oil a shallow casserole dish large enough to hold the squid in one layer. Using a teaspoon, fill the cavity of a squid with the *trahana* mixture. Press down gently to get the filling as deep into the cavity as possible, but do not overstuff, and leave about ½ in/12 mm of space at the opening. Insert a tentacle into the opening, pushing it in to secure. This will help keep the filling from spilling out. Lay the squid in the oiled pan. Repeat with the remaining squid and stuffing. Season the outside of the squid lightly with salt and pepper. Spoon any remaining stuffing into the casserole dish, fitting it snugly between the squid. Pour over the remaining tomatoes, and the remaining ¼ cup/60 ml olive oil. Insert the bay leaves between the stuffed squid. Cover the dish and bake for about 45 minutes, or until tender. Remove from the oven and cool slightly. Remove the bay leaves.

For each serving, using a serrated knife, cut a squid into 1-in/2.5-cm rings. Arrange decoratively on a plate, and spoon a little pan juice on top.

CUTTLEFISH BRAISED WITH CHARD

SOUPIES ME SESKOULA

================ SERVES 4 TO 6 ================

Cuttlefish with spinach is a classic Greek Lenten dish that, when made well, is a masterpiece of subtle, earthy flavors and the unique, almost musky, taste of cuttlefish. (When made poorly, however, the flavors become muddled.) Spinach isn't the only green paired with cuttlefish; chard is another favorite.

2 lb/910 g fresh or frozen cuttlefish

½ cup/120 ml extra-virgin Greek olive oil, plus more for drizzling

1 red onion, very finely chopped

2 garlic cloves, minced

3 lb/1.4 kg chard, trimmed, washed, spun dry, and coarsely chopped

¼ cup/15 g chopped fresh flat-leaf parsley

½ cup/120 ml dry white wine

Salt and pepper

Juice of 1 lemon, strained

Clean the fresh cuttlefish. Remove the tentacles, trim, and chop. Using your fingers, scoop out and discard the viscera and cartilage from the inside of the cuttlefish cavities. If the ink sac, located at the head end of the cuttelfish's tubular body, is still intact, remove it. Cut the body crosswise into ¾-in/2-cm strips. If using frozen cuttlefish, they will already be cleaned. Just defrost and cut into strips.

Heat the olive oil in a wide, deep pot over medium heat, and cook the onion until soft, about 8 minutes. Add the garlic and cook, stirring, for 1 minute. Toss the cuttlefish into the pot and cook, stirring, until it turns from opaque to bright white. Add the chard and parsley, stirring until the chard cooks down and loses enough of its volume to fit into the pot with about 2 in/5 cm of room to spare at the top. Cover, reduce the heat slightly, and cook until the chard wilts. Remove the cover, raise the heat a little, and pour in the wine. When the wine steams up, season with salt and pepper. Cover the pot, reduce the heat to low, and let the cuttlefish and chard cook in their own juices for about 1 to 1½ hours over low heat until the cuttlefish is very tender. Check occasionally and add water as needed to keep the contents moist.

Remove from the heat, stir in the fresh lemon juice, and drizzle in a little more olive oil. Let cool for 10 to 15 minutes. Serve warm or at room temperature.

NOTE: In the main recipe and the variation you may substitute large squid for the cuttlefish.

VARIATION: This variation is a traditional Lenten dish from the village of Zakros in southeastern Crete. Clean, gut, and wash the cuttlefish as directed. Heat the same quantity of olive oil in a large pot over medium-high heat. Add 10 chopped scallions (green and white parts), season with salt and pepper, reduce the heat to medium-low, and cook until the scallions are translucent, 7 to 8 minutes. Add the cuttlefish and cook, turning frequently, for about 5 minutes. Add ½ cup/30 g chopped dill or fennel fronds, ½ tsp ground fennel seeds, and 1 cup/240 ml white wine. Simmer, covered, for 25 minutes and add 2 lb/910 g fresh fava beans (peeled, trimmed, and shelled), or an equal amount of frozen, defrosted fava beans. Cook, covered, for another 35 to 40 minutes, or until the beans and cuttlefish are very tender. Adjust seasoning with salt and pepper and serve hot, warm or at room temperature.

THE GREEK TOUCH

OCTOPUS

GREEK COUNTRY COOKS "OWN" OCTOPUS. IT IS MORE
CLOSELY ASSOCIATED WITH THE NATIONAL CUISINE THAN
ANY OTHER SEAFOOD. IN GREEK RESTAURANTS IN THE
STATES, OCTOPUS IS ALMOST ALWAYS PRESENTED GRILLED,
BUT THERE ARE DOZENS AND DOZENS OF OTHER WAYS TO
PREPARE IT. OCTOPUS IS THE STAR OF COUNTLESS STEWS,
AND IT PAIRS WELL WITH ALL SORTS OF SEASONAL VEGE-
TABLES, FROM WINTER LEEKS TO SUMMER EGGPLANTS.

In all my years swimming in the Aegean, I've never seen an octopus in the water, but I've come out plenty of times to see a fresh catch being tenderized the old-fashioned way, by some able-bodied spear fisherman beating one against the rocks. Greeks adore this gangly, delicious cephalopod; images of it appear on Greek vases from as early as the Minoan and Mycenaean civilizations (3000–1100 B.C.) as well as from the classical era much later (510–323 B.C.).

The octopus likes its solitude. It spends the winter at great depths and approaches the sea's surface in spring, when it looks for well-concealed crevices and rocks in which to hide all summer long.

Many varieties find their way to Greek dinner plates, but one is especially esteemed—*Octopus vulgaris*, with its double row of suckers running up along each tentacle. *O. macropus* is another popular species, with thinner but longer tentacles. One octopus species with a single row of suckers, *Eledone cirrosa*, isn't savored much in Greece. The musk octopus, *Eledone moschata*, suffers from a similar disdain, its aroma way too strong for the taste of most cooks.

Regardless of the species, octopus does need to be tenderized to taste good, and the two national groups that eat it most—Spaniards actually consume more octopus than Greeks—have different ways of ensuring the right texture. The Greeks beat it a biblical forty times against the rocks that buttress so many Greek beaches, while the Spanish throw a cork into the pot while it simmers. Arguably, the best way to tenderize octopus is also the easiest: just freeze it, which helps break down cell structure, thus making the octopus softer.

OCTOPUS BRAISED IN MAVRODAFNI WINE

HTAPODI KRASATO ME MAVRODAFNI

===== SERVES 4 =====

There are dozens of recipes in the regional Greek kitchen for octopus braised in wine. This one, inspired by one of my favorite dishes at Varoulko, a restaurant in Athens, calls for Mavrodafni, which is a sweet red wine. The wine cooks down and thickens into a rich, complex, almost syrupy sauce. This dish goes perfectly with Lesvos Green Split Pea Purée (page 60), made with yellow split peas. Spread out the purée on a serving platter and top with the octopus pieces and thick sauce.

1 medium octopus (about 3 lb/1.4 kg)

2 cups/480 ml Mavrodafni wine

1 large bay leaf

2 tbsp tomato paste diluted in 2 tbsp water

1 dried chile pepper

½ bulb roasted garlic

2 tbsp extra-virgin Greek olive oil

12 large round boiling onions, about 1 to 1½ in/ 2.5 to 4 cm in diameter, peeled and left whole

Using a sharp knife, cut off the octopus's hood just below the eyes and discard. With a small paring knife, remove its beak and cartilaginous mouthpiece. Rinse under cold water and drain.

Put the octopus in a heavy pot, cover the pot, and cook over extremely low heat for 20 to 25 minutes, until it exudes most of its own liquid and turns deep pink. Cook the octopus in its own juices until about half done, another 20 to 25 minutes.

Remove the octopus with a slotted spoon, reserving the cooking liquid in the pot. Cut the octopus into 8 pieces along its tentacles. Put back in the pot, with its juices. Pour in the wine, and add the bay leaf and diluted tomato paste, stirring gently to combine. Add the chile pepper. Squeeze the soft cloves of roasted garlic into the pot and stir. Cover the pot, bring to a boil over medium heat, and reduce the heat to low. Continue cooking until the octopus is tender and the liquid has reduced and thickened to a thin, syrupy consistency, 25 to 30 minutes.

In a large, heavy frying pan, preferably cast-iron, heat the olive oil over medium heat. Add the onions, cover, and reduce the heat to very low. Cook the onions for 30 to 40 minutes, shaking the frying pan back and forth so the onions caramelize evenly. Check occasionally so as not to burn them. Remove from the heat and set aside.

About 10 minutes before the octopus is done, add the caramelized onions, shaking the pot so that they are well distributed. When the octopus is done, remove the bay leaf and serve immediately.

PELION BRAISED OCTOPUS WITH QUINCE

HTAPODI ME KYDONIA APO TO PELION

===== SERVES 4 =====

I came across this recipe in a small pamphlet on the local cooking of Mt. Pelion, one of the most lush and fecund places in Greece, just outside Volos, in the central part of the country. I have never encountered this unusual combination of octopus and quince anywhere else in Greece. Quince is the Mediterranean's most regal winter fruit, and it turns this otherwise rustic stew into something elegant and exotic.

1 medium octopus (about 3 lb/1.4 kg)

2 tbsp red wine vinegar

½ cup/120 ml plus 2 tbsp extra-virgin Greek olive oil

1 large red onion, minced

1 garlic clove, minced

½ cup/120 ml dry white wine

1½ cups/260 g chopped, peeled, and seeded plum tomatoes (canned are fine)

1 large cinnamon stick

2 bay leaves

4 allspice berries

10 to 12 peppercorns

2 large quinces, cored and sliced (do not peel)

2 tsp tomato paste diluted in 1 tbsp water

Heaping 1 tsp dried mint

Salt and pepper

Using a sharp knife, cut off the octopus's hood just below the eyes and discard. With a small paring knife, remove its beak and cartilaginous mouthpiece. Put the octopus in a bowl and rub vigorously with the vinegar. (This is a trick for tenderizing it.) Rinse thoroughly, drain, and cut into 8 pieces along the tentacles.

Heat the ½ cup/120 ml olive oil in a large, wide pot over medium heat. Combine the octopus, onion, and garlic in the pot and cook over medium heat, stirring constantly, until the onion wilts slightly and the octopus turns bright pink, about 8 minutes. Add the wine. As soon as it steams up, add the tomatoes, cinnamon stick, bay leaves, allspice, and peppercorns. Reduce the heat to low, cover, and cook until the octopus is tender, 45 to 50 minutes.

While the octopus is simmering, heat the remaining 2 tbsp olive oil in a heavy frying pan and sauté the quinces until they turn pale gold.

After about 30 minutes of cooking the octopus, gently add the quince to the pot, using a slotted spoon to remove the slices from the frying pan. Add the diluted tomato paste and stir gently. Add the mint, taste the sauce, and add more salt and pepper if needed. Simmer until the octopus and quince are tender. Remove the cinnamon stick and bay leaves and serve hot.

GRILLED OCTOPUS WITH SHAVED BLACK TRUFFLES

HTAPODI PSITO ME TROUFES

=== SERVES 8 AS A MEZE ===

Panagiotis Koukouvitis is a bon vivant and guiding spirit behind some of the most progressive new food products in northern Greece. He is a great proponent of the highly aromatic truffles that he and two friends cultivate in Macedonia, and suggested combining them with something unmistakably Greek—octopus.

1 large octopus (about 6 lb/2.7 kg)

2 cups/480 ml Rapsani or another dry red Greek wine

3 bay leaves

5 garlic cloves, crushed

1 tsp peppercorns

Salt

2 to 4 tbsp extra-virgin Greek olive oil for brushing the octopus

2 oz/55 g fresh black truffles

Using a sharp knife, cut off the octopus's hood just below the eyes and discard. With a small paring knife, remove its beak and cartilaginous mouthpiece. Rinse under cold water, drain, and put in a heavy pot without any liquid. Cover the pot and cook the octopus over extremely low heat for about 30 minutes, until it exudes most of its own liquid and turns deep pink. Add the wine, bay leaves, garlic, peppercorns, and salt to taste and raise the heat to medium. Bring to a boil, then lower the heat again and simmer the octopus until tender but toothsome, about 1 hour or a little longer, depending on the thickness of the tentacles. Remove from the heat and cool. Cut up the octopus into 8 pieces along its tentacles.

Light a hot fire in the grill or preheat a gas grill to high. Oil the rack. Brush the octopus with 1 or 2 tbsp of olive oil and grill until lightly charred and pleasantly crusty. Remove to a serving platter or 8 individual plates. Drizzle, if desired, with another 1 or 2 tbsp olive oil and shave some truffle over the grilled tentacles. Serve immediately.

OCTOPUS, FENNEL, AND POTATO STEW

HTAPODI ME MARATHO KAI PATATES

=== SERVES 4 AS A MAIN COURSE ===
OR 8 AS A MEZE

Crete is the provenance of this hearty springtime stew, which is enjoyed when feathery fennel grows wild all over the Greek countryside. I substitute fennel bulb and dill since wild fennel is hard to find in the United States.

1 medium octopus (about 3 lb/1.4 kg)

1 cup/240 ml extra-virgin Greek olive oil

2 large red onions, finely chopped

2 fennel bulbs, finely chopped

2 garlic cloves

10 to 12 peppercorns

½ cup/120 ml strained fresh orange juice, or one 2 x 6-in/5 x 15-cm strip orange peel

1 cup/240 ml red wine

1 bunch wild fennel, finely chopped, or 1 cup/60 g chopped fresh dill

5 large boiling potatoes, peeled and either quartered or cut into 2-in/5-cm cubes

Using a sharp knife, cut off the octopus's hood just below the eyes and discard. With a small paring knife, remove its beak and cartilaginous mouthpiece. Cut into 8 pieces along the tentacles.

Heat ½ cup/120 ml of the olive oil in a large, wide pot over medium-low heat and sauté the onions and fennel bulbs for about 5 minutes, stirring occasionally. Add the garlic and cook, stirring, until soft. Put the octopus tentacles in the pot and add the peppercorns, orange juice, and wine. Cover, reduce the heat to low, and cook until the octopus has exuded its own juices and turned deep pink, 35 to 40 minutes, depending on the thickness of the tentacles. Stir in the wild fennel and potatoes. Continue simmering the octopus, covered, for 25 minutes, or until the potatoes are tender and the octopus is cooked. Remove from the heat, pour in the remaining ½ cup/120 ml of the olive oil, cool slightly, and serve.

VARIATION: Octopus with orange and fennel also goes very well with green olives (pictured on the facing page). Replace the potatoes with 1 unpeeled orange, cut into 8 wedges. Substitute ⅓ cup/80 ml ouzo for the wine, and add 16 rinsed pitted green olives about 10 minutes before removing the dish from the heat.

OCTOPUS WITH EGGPLANT FROM EPANOMI

HTAPODI ME MELITZANES APO TIN EPANOMI

SERVES 4 AS A MAIN COURSE
OR 8 AS A MEZE

One glorious fall day last year, we visited the winemaker Vangelis Gerovassiliou in Epanomi, near the city of Thessaloniki. His mother, *kyria* (Mrs.) Marianthi, made this delicious local specialty for us. "Food needs olive oil, " she said matter-of-factly when I remarked on the copious amount of olive oil in the dish. She also explained that she bakes the dish, rather than cooking it on the stove top, to prevent the eggplant from disintegrating. Contrary to my own inclination, she also boils the octopus.

½ cup/120 ml red wine vinegar

1 medium octopus (about 3 lb/1.4 kg)

5 to 8 allspice berries

6 bay leaves

1 cup/240 ml extra-virgin Greek olive oil, plus extra for drizzling

3 long eggplants (about 2 lb/910 g total), trimmed and sliced ¾ in/2 cm thick

4 large firm, ripe tomatoes, seeded and grated (see Note on page 74)

Salt and pepper

Fill a large bowl or basin with warm water, add the vinegar, and soak the octopus for a few minutes. Rinse well. Using a sharp knife, cut off the octopus's hood just below the eyes and discard. With a small paring knife, remove its beak and cartilaginous mouthpiece. Rinse and drain the octopus.

Put the octopus in a large pot with enough water to cover. Add the allspice and 3 of the bay leaves. Bring to a boil, reduce the heat, and simmer for 40 to 50 minutes, until the octopus is somewhat tender but still firm to the touch. Remove from the heat, and remove the octopus from the pot. Reserve ½ cup/120 ml of the cooking liquid and discard the rest. Cool the octopus slightly, and cut into 8 pieces along the tentacles. Set aside. Preheat the oven to 350°F/175°C/gas 4.

While the octopus is simmering, heat the 1 cup/240 ml olive oil over medium heat in a large, heavy frying pan and sauté the eggplants for a few minutes, until al dente. Remove the eggplants from the frying pan with a slotted spoon and set aside. Add the grated tomatoes to the pan and cook over medium heat until most of their liquid has cooked off and the tomatoes are thick. Remove from the heat. Put the eggplant in a large baking pan, add the octopus, tomato, and remaining 3 bay leaves, and toss together. Season with salt and pepper and add the reserved octopus cooking liquid. Drizzle with olive oil and bake, uncovered, for about 25 minutes. Remove the bay leaves and serve.

OCTOPUS COOKED WITH LEEKS AND SUN-DRIED TOMATOES

HTAPODI ME PRASA KAI LIASTES DOMATES

SERVES 4 AS A MAIN COURSE
OR 8 AS A MEZE

This dish is a specialty of the seaside towns along the eastern fringes of Macedonia. Leeks are one of the most typical vegetables of the north, and sun-dried tomatoes are a local specialty, produced in Larissa, Drama, and other parts of northern Greece. The dish is traditionally served over rice, but it's equally good over the local noodles, which are called *hilopites*.

8 sun-dried tomatoes

1 medium-large octopus (about 4½ lb/2 kg)

⅔ cup/160 ml extra-virgin Greek olive oil

½ cup/120 ml dry white wine

2 bay leaves

10 to 12 peppercorns

6 plum tomatoes, peeled, seeded, and chopped (canned are fine)

4 leeks, white and tender green parts, cut into 2-in-/5-cm-long cylinders

Heaping 1 tbsp light brown sugar

3 tbsp Greek balsamic or red wine vinegar

Salt and pepper

Put the sun-dried tomatoes in a bowl and cover with warm water.

Using a sharp knife, cut off the octopus's hood just below the eyes and discard. With a small paring knife, remove its beak and cartilaginous mouthpiece. Cut into 8 pieces along the tentacles. Rinse the octopus well, drain, and put in a large, wide pot. Cover and cook over very low heat until bright pink, and tight and curled up in the pot, about 30 minutes. Add ⅓ cup/80 ml of the olive oil, the wine, bay leaves, and peppercorns. Cook for 15 minutes and add the plum tomatoes.

While the octopus is cooking, heat the remaining ⅓ cup/80 ml of olive oil in a large, wide pot. Add the leeks, reduce the heat to low, and cook until they soften and caramelize lightly, about 15 minutes, turning from time to time. Sprinkle with the brown sugar and add the vinegar. Let the vinegar steam up and reduce slightly, about 10 minutes.

Drain the sun-dried tomatoes, reserving their soaking liquid. Cut in half or quarters. Add to the leeks, together with the tomatoes' soaking liquid. Continue cooking for another 5 to 10 minutes, until the leeks are deeply caramelized and almost syrupy.

Add the leek mixture to the octopus. Continue cooking until the octopus is very tender but firm and not at all stringy. Season with salt and pepper. Remove from the heat and cool slightly. Remove the bay leaves and serve.

CHAPTER 10

COUNTRY CHICKENS
AND
GAME BIRDS

WHEN DINNER IS ANTICIPATED, A CHICKEN COOP IS A FRE-NETIC PLACE. THEY KNOW IT, THOSE BIRDS DO, AND SQUAWK AND RUN AND FLAP THEIR WINGS, FRIGHTENED, LITER-ALLY, FOR THEIR LIVES. I'VE SEEN SUCH A SCENE ONCE AT THE HOME OF A FAMILY FRIEND ON IKARIA, WHOSE MERE PRESENCE A FEW FEET AWAY FROM THE COOP WREAKED HAVOC, SHATTERING THE SERENITY OF THE CHICKENS.

Mitsos entered the chicken coop, swooped one up by the neck, secured it under his formidable arm, and carried it off to its place of ultimate surrender. A few hours later, we were enjoying its succulent, dark flesh under a cover of lemons, garlic, and oregano, the trinity of classic Greek flavors. It was a Sunday and we had been invited for a long, leisurely lunch. In the country, chicken is a special treat.

Chicken is an old food in Greece. The bird traveled west to Greece from India, via Persia, sometime before the sixth century B.C., which scholars have learned from the chickens depicted on prehistoric vases, especially on pieces found in Rhodes and Sparta. One ancient Greek name for the chicken was *alektoron*, *lektron* being one's bed, and *alektron* the creature (actually the male) that causes one to leave it abruptly. Only the Sybarites, Greeks who lived in southern Italy, had the where-withal to ban the bird from urban settings, lest they lose their beauty sleep.

There are dozens of recipes for chicken, and in the country, the recipe of choice is determined by the size of the bird, its sex, and its age. Chickens are fried, roasted, stuffed, braised, stewed, grilled, boiled, poached, and picked apart to add to soups and pies. Most Greek chickens nowadays are either Cobbs or Redbros. Before cooking, most of the birds weigh in at around 4 to 5 pounds/1.8 to 2.3 kilos. Old hens have the most flavor, and so are reserved for soup and sold as such in markets around the country, including in downtown Athens. There are a few recipes for small game hens, which are called *frangokotes*, "French hens." These are mainly found in areas where there was a large Catholic population, especially in the Ionian islands.

Roosters are the celebrated bird of the Greek country kitchen, even higher in stature than the turkey, a relative newcomer that has usurped the rooster's traditional place on the holiday table. Just one cock occupies a coop, so sacrificing it for dinner needs a justifiable excuse, such as the Christmas or New Year's table or to honor an esteeemed guest. There are two basic ways to cook a rooster: *krasato*, which means "with wine," a method that helps tenderize the rooster's tawny, tough, but tasty flesh; and with noodles, a dish that is made in many versions all over the country.

SPICED EPIRUS CHICKEN WITH PEPPERS

KOTOPOULO ME PIPERIES APO TIN IPIRO

This hearty dish from Epirus calls for butter, rather than olive oil, which was scarce in the northernmost reaches of Greece. All the warm Greek spices—allspice, cloves, cinnamon, and hot pepper—make this a perfect fall dish, when bell peppers are at their peak and the weather just starts to turn chilly.

One 2½- to 3-lb/1.2- to 1.4-kg chicken, cut into serving pieces

Salt and pepper

¼ cup/30 g all-purpose flour

4 tbsp unsalted butter, preferably sheep's milk

3 large onions, halved and sliced

3 garlic cloves, minced

4 large green bell peppers, cut into ½-in/12-mm-thick rings

¼ tsp ground allspice

½ tsp ground cloves

½ tsp ground cinnamon

1 to 2 small dried hot peppers

1½ cups/260 g peeled, seeded, and chopped tomatoes (canned are fine)

If desired, remove and discard the chicken's skin. Season the meat with salt and pepper. Put the flour in a shallow dish and dredge the meat lightly in the flour. Melt 2 tbsp of the butter in a large, wide pot or Dutch oven over medium-high heat. Sear the chicken pieces, in batches if necessary, until lightly browned on all sides, 7 to 8 minutes. Remove from the pot with a slotted spoon and set aside.

Melt 1 tbsp of the butter (or more if needed) in the pot and cook the onions, garlic, and bell peppers over medium heat, stirring, until wilted, 7 to 8 minutes. Return the chicken to the pot. Season with salt and pepper, stir in the allspice, cloves, cinnamon, and hot peppers, and pour in the tomatoes. Add enough water to barely cover the chicken. Cover the pot, bring to a boil, and reduce the heat to low. Simmer slowly until the chicken is very tender and the sauce is thick, about 50 minutes to 1 hour. Just before removing from the heat, swirl in the remaining 1 tbsp butter. Serve hot.

CHICKEN WITH NOODLES AND WALNUTS

KOTOPOULO ME HILOPITES KAI KARYDIA

I love this rustic, homey version of chicken with noodles. It comes from the central part of Macedonia, where walnuts are a common addition to many savory foods and sauces.

One 4- to 4½-lb/1.8- to 2-kg chicken, cut into serving pieces and skin removed

Salt and pepper

2 tbsp extra-virgin Greek olive oil

1 tbsp unsalted butter

2 large onions, coarsely chopped

4 large ripe tomatoes, peeled, seeded, and coarsely chopped; or 1½ cups/260 g chopped canned tomatoes

Pinch of sugar

3 tbsp chopped fresh mint

1¼ cups/200 g small, square Greek egg noodles (*hilopites*) or another small pasta

½ cup/60 g finely chopped walnuts

Season the chicken pieces with salt and pepper. In a large, wide pot, heat the olive oil and butter together over high heat and brown the chicken on all sides until golden, in batches if necessary, 7 to 8 minutes. Remove with a slotted spoon and set aside. Reduce the heat to medium, add the onions to the pot, and season with salt and pepper. Cook, stirring, until wilted and translucent, 8 to 10 minutes.

Return the chicken to the pot and pour in the tomatoes and sugar. Add enough water to barely cover the chicken. Cover the pot and bring to a boil over medium heat. Reduce the heat and simmer until the chicken is very tender, about 1 hour.

Preheat the oven to 275°F/135°C/gas 1. Add the mint about 10 minutes before the chicken is cooked. Remove the chicken with a slotted spoon and set aside, covered, in the warm oven.

Add 1 cup/240 ml or more of water to the liquid in the pot, so there is enough to cook the noodles in, and bring to a boil. Add the noodles, reduce the heat, and simmer until tender. Serve the noodles, which will be soupy, in a deep platter with the chicken on top, sprinkled with the walnuts.

MARINATED CHICKEN BREASTS STUFFED WITH FIGS AND OLIVES

KOTOPOULO STITHOS GEMISTO ME SYKA KAI ELIES

===== SERVES 6 =====

Figs and olives, quintessential Greek foods, pair deliciously in this rustic yet sophisticated stuffed chicken breast recipe.

6 boneless, skinless chicken breast halves (about 2¼ lbs/1 kg total)

2 cups/480 ml Metaxa or another Greek brandy

1 cup/240 ml strained fresh orange juice

4 garlic cloves, crushed

6 fresh thyme sprigs

20 peppercorns

⅔ cup/150 g chestnuts in the shell, or 14 oz/400 g sous vide chestnuts

2 oz/55 g raisin-walnut bread

3 tbsp unsalted butter, plus 1 tbsp, melted

1 large onion, finely chopped

¼ cup/50 g coarsely chopped green olives

6 dried figs, finely chopped

⅓ cup/20 g finely chopped fresh flat-leaf parsley

Salt and pepper

¾ cup/180 ml chicken broth

2 tbsp extra-virgin Greek olive oil

Put the chicken breasts in a nonreactive bowl. Whisk together 1 cup/240 ml of the brandy, ½ cup/120 ml of the orange juice, 2 garlic cloves, 3 thyme sprigs, and 10 peppercorns and pour this over the chicken. Marinate for 6 hours or overnight, covered and refrigerated. Return to room temperature before cooking.

If using fresh chestnuts, score them with a sharp paring knife and place in a pot with enough water to cover by 2 in/5 cm. Bring to a boil over high heat, reduce the heat, and simmer until the chestnuts are soft, 35 to 40 minutes. Drain the chestnuts, let cool, and peel. If using sous vide chestnuts, put the bag in boiling water and cook according to the package directions. Either way, cool the chestnuts and coarsely chop.

Preheat the oven to 325°F/165°C/gas 3. Cut the bread into ½-in/12-mm cubes. Spread out on a dry baking sheet and bake until the cubes are hard and dry, about 15 minutes. Remove from the oven and cool. Raise the oven temperature to 400°F/200°C/gas 6.

Heat 1 tbsp of the butter in a nonstick frying pan over medium heat and sauté the onion until soft and translucent, about 8 minutes.

Transfer the croutons to a mixing bowl. Add the onion, chestnuts, olives, figs, and parsley, season with salt and pepper, and toss well. Drizzle in the 1 tbsp melted butter and the chicken broth to dampen the mixture. Set aside.

Remove the chicken breasts from the marinade and discard the marinade. Pat the breasts dry. Using a sharp knife, make a pocket-like incision in each breast, cutting horizontally through its side without puncturing the other side. Divide the stuffing into four equal parts. Stuff each breast with a portion of the filling. Press closed and secure, if desired, with a few toothpicks.

In a medium bowl, whisk together the remaining 1 cup/240 ml brandy, ½ cup/120 ml orange juice, 2 garlic cloves, 3 thyme sprigs, and 10 peppercorns and set aside. In a large, deep ovenproof frying pan or shallow, wide ovenproof pot, preferably nonstick, heat the remaining 2 tbsp butter and olive oil. Sauté the chicken breasts, turning once, and cook until browned on both sides. Pour in the brandy mixture, and put the pan in the oven. Bake for 16 to 18 minutes, until the chicken is cooked through. Remove from the oven and let the chicken rest slightly before serving. Serve with the pan juices.

ROOSTER STUFFED WITH BREAD

KOKORAS PATIDO

===== SERVES 6 =====

Patido (or patoudo) is the name of a stuffed meat dish, typically the Easter lamb or goat, traditionally made on some of the Cyclades islands. This unusual variation comes from the tiny island of Antiparos. A large roasting chicken can be substituted for the rooster.

¾ cup/180 ml extra-virgin Greek olive oil, plus extra for rubbing on the bird

1 chicken liver, finely chopped

2 large red onions, finely chopped

3 garlic cloves, crushed

2 cups/480 ml dry red wine

2 cups/60 g coarsely chopped stale country bread

1½ cups/90 g finely chopped fresh flat-leaf parsley

⅔ cup/65 g dark raisins

Salt and pepper

1 large egg, lightly beaten

1 rooster or large roasting chicken (about 5 lb/2.3 kg)

2 lb/910 g baking potatoes, peeled and halved

Preheat the oven to 400°F/200°C/gas 6.

Heat ¼ cup/60 ml of the olive oil in a large, deep frying pan or sauté pan over medium heat and sauté the liver until browned on both sides. Remove from the pan. Lower the heat to medium-low, add the onions, and cook until soft and lightly colored, about 12 minutes. Stir in the garlic, return the liver to the pot, stir, and pour in 1 cup/240 ml of the wine. Cook until the wine is reduced by half. Transfer the mixture to a large bowl. Add the bread, parsley, raisins, salt and pepper to taste, and egg and stir to combine well.

Spoon the stuffing into the cavities of the rooster from both ends. Using kitchen string, truss the rooster. Rub the outside of the bird with olive oil and season generously with salt and pepper. Place in a large roasting pan.

In a large bowl, toss the potatoes with salt, pepper, and the remaining ½ cup/120 ml olive oil. Place them around the rooster in the pan. Put in the oven and bake for 15 minutes. Pour in the remaining 1 cup/240 ml wine. Continue to roast for about 1½ hours, or until the rooster is cooked through and the potatoes are very tender, basting the rooster every 15 minutes with the pan juices. Remove from the oven, cool slightly, and serve.

LEMONY STUFFED ROASTED CORNISH GAME HEN

FRANGOKOTA LEMONATI GEMISTI

===== SERVES 4 =====

Lemony roasted chicken is many a Greek grandma's specialty and a Sunday classic. This is my interpretation of the dish, slightly gentrified thanks to the small game hens.

MARINADE

½ cup/120 ml extra-virgin Greek olive oil

½ cup/120 ml strained fresh lemon juice

⅓ cup/80 ml dry white wine

4 garlic cloves, minced

½ cup/30 g chopped fresh oregano

Salt

Scant 1 tsp pepper

2 Cornish game hens

STUFFING

6 sun-dried tomatoes

3 tbsp extra-virgin Greek olive oil

1 medium onion, finely chopped

1 large garlic clove, minced

⅔ cup/100 g crumbled Greek feta cheese

½ cup/70 g green olives, pitted and chopped

Pepper

To make the marinade: In a large, nonreactive bowl, whisk together the olive oil, lemon juice, wine, and garlic until smooth and emulsified. Mix in the oregano, season with salt, and add the pepper.

Put the hens in the marinade, cover, and refrigerate for at least 2 hours or up to 8. Remove the hens from the refrigerator and bring to room temperature in the marinade. Preheat the oven to 375°F/190°C/gas 5.

To make the stuffing: Soak the sun-dried tomatoes in warm water for 30 minutes, or until soft. Drain and finely chop. Heat the olive oil in a medium frying pan over medium heat, add the onion, and cook until translucent and soft, about 10 minutes. Add the garlic and stir for 1 or 2 minutes, until soft. Remove from the heat. Transfer the onion-garlic mixture to a medium bowl and add the sun-dried tomatoes, feta, and olives. Season with pepper.

Remove the hens from the marinade, reserving the marinade. Pat the birds dry and fill their cavities with the stuffing. Truss the legs to keep the stuffing from spilling out. Place the birds in a lightly oiled roasting pan and pour the reserved marinade over the birds. Roast for 1 hour, brushing and basting the birds with the marinade every 10 to 12 minutes. The birds are done when a meat thermometer inserted in the thickest part of the thigh, without touching the bone, registers an internal temperature of 165°F/74°C. Cool slightly and serve.

OUZO-GLAZED DUCK BREAST

PAPIA GLASARISMENI ME OUZO

SERVES 2

No fewer than twenty species of wild duck soar over the Greek countryside. Wild ducks congregate in many of the protected nature preserves that dot Greece: in the Evros delta, in Vistonida, Lake Kerkyni, the delta of the Axios River, in the lakes of Ioannina and Karla, in the marshlands along the western coast of Greece, and in Kalloni, on Lesvos, among others. Restaurant demand has encouraged the growth of a cottage industry for farm-raised species, and several Greek companies, mainly in Chios, now raise ducks.

Most Greek duck recipes, including this one, derive from the rich, wintry cooking of northern Greece. There duck is braised or roasted with wine and spirits; with other local specialties, such as dried fruit and nuts; and also with honey, olives, and oranges. In a small country restaurant outside Thessaloniki, I came across a version of this dish and took copious notes.

Two 6-oz/170-g duck breasts

Salt and pepper

1 small red onion, minced

2 garlic cloves, minced

½ cup/120 ml ouzo

⅔ cup/160 ml strained fresh orange juice

2 tsp Greek honey

2 tsp chopped fresh thyme

Preheat the oven to 375°F/190°C/gas 5. With a small, sharp knife, score the fatty side of the duck breasts in a crisscross pattern and season generously with salt and pepper. Heat a dry ovenproof, non-stick frying pan over medium heat. Place the duck breasts in the frying pan, fatty-side down. Sear until the skin is brown. Remove the duck breasts from the pan and set aside. Pour off all but 2 tbsp duck fat.

In the same pan sauté the onion until soft, about 8 minutes. Stir in the garlic and cook, stirring, for a minute or so, to soften. Remove the pan from the heat and carefully add the ouzo, and then the orange juice. Return the pan to the heat and season the liquid with salt and pepper. Bring to a simmer and cook until reduced by about a third. Add the honey and stir to blend.

Place the duck breasts in the frying pan, skin-side up, and spoon the liquid over them. Place in the oven and bake, uncovered, for about 6 minutes, until the meat is medium-rare and the liquid is thick and almost syrupy. Remove from the heat and serve sprinkled with chopped thyme.

HONEY-GLAZED DUCK BREAST WITH QUINCE

PAPIA ME KYDONIA KAI MELI

SERVES 2

Some cooks like to combine quince and game meat in northern Greece, where I first came across this recipe.

GLAZE

2 tbsp Greek thyme honey

1 tbsp Greek raisin or balsamic vinegar

¼ cup/60 ml strained fresh orange juice

2 thyme sprigs

1½ tsp unsalted butter

1 tbsp extra-virgin Greek olive oil

1 medium onion, halved and thinly sliced

Salt

Two 6-oz/170-g duck breasts

Pepper

½ large quince, cored and sliced ⅛-in/3-mm thick

½ tsp sugar

Pinch of fresh thyme leaves

To make the glaze: Whisk all the liquid ingredients together. Add the thyme sprigs, and set aside until ready to use.

Melt the butter with the olive oil in a nonstick frying pan over low heat. Add the onion slices and season with salt. Cook for 25 to 30 minutes, until caramelized, turning frequently to keep from burning.

Preheat the oven to 400°F/200°C/gas 6. With a small, sharp knife, score the fatty side of the duck breasts in a crisscross pattern and season generously with salt and pepper. Heat a dry ovenproof, non-stick frying pan over medium heat. Place the duck breasts in the frying pan, fatty-side down. Sear until the skin is browned. Remove the duck breasts from the pan and set aside. Pour off all but 2 tbsp of the fat that is left in the frying pan.

Add the quince to the pan, season with salt, and add the sugar. Cook until lightly browned, and then add the caramelized onions to the pan. Season with pepper and add the thyme leaves. Place the duck, fatty-side up, on top and brush with the glaze. Put the pan in the oven and bake, uncovered, for 6 minutes for medium-rare.

To serve, divide the quince-onion mixture evenly between 2 plates, spooning it in the middle of each. Place the duck breasts over the mixture and drizzle with the pan juices. Serve hot.

QUAIL

Many years ago I drove down to the tip of the Mani, in the southern Peloponnese, to a small port called Porto Kagio, which roughly translates as Port Quail. I was in search of a long-lost tradition. It wasn't the time of year when quail migrate, so the birds were nowhere to be seen. I was told that the glory days for hunting quail had long since passed, and their disappearance was tied to the advent of DDT and other pesticides in the region around 1960. Porto Kagio once teemed with so many quail on their stopover between continents that locals could catch them with nets. A formidable little business sprang up around salting and brining the quail. The preserved delicacy was shipped off to Italy, among other places, until the wild birds became endangered and their capture illegal.

Despite the disappearance of wild quail, this ancient delicacy still captures the imagination of country cooks, especially, but not exclusively, in the Peloponnese. Farmed quail is widely available in Greece, and hunters still prize quail when it is in season in the early fall. Greek country cooks savor quail in many different ways: salted or stuffed into bread, a specialty of the Mani; grilled and skewered; braised with raisins and spinach, or with tomatoes, both specialties of the Asia Minor Greeks; wrapped in bacon and grape leaves, a specialty of northern Greece (see page 272); cooked with eggplant, and even stuffed into oversized eggplants; and flambéed with brandy and parsley, which was once a popular taverna dish in Volos.

QUAIL BAKED IN
GRAPE LEAVES

ORTYKIA SE AMBELOFYLA

=== SERVES 4 ===

This dramatic, rustic dish, which is prepared all over central and northern Greece, is one of my favorite Greek country recipes. The secret is in the quality and flavor of the bacon that is wrapped around the otherwise lean quail. After a chance meeting with one of the owners of the Fotiades Boar Farm, in Pieria, northern Greece, I tried making the dish with smoked boar bacon. It added a rich flavor dimension that perfectly complemented the tartness of the grape leaves and the mild flavor of the quail. You can find wild boar bacon in the United States through purveyors of exotic meats, such as D'Artagnan.

8 quail

16 large fresh or brined grape leaves

Salt and pepper

1 tbsp ground fennel seeds

2 tsp dried thyme

2 garlic cloves, crushed

8 slices wild boar bacon, smoked bacon, or pancetta, halved lengthwise to make 16 strips

½ cup/120 ml extra-virgin Greek olive oil

2 tbsp unsalted butter

½ cup/120 ml white wine

2 cups/480 ml chicken broth

Juice of 2 lemons, strained

Wash the quail and pat dry. Set aside.

Bring a medium pot of water to a rolling boil. If using brined grape leaves, remove from the brine, rinse, and drain. Blanch the grape leaves, fresh or brined, in the boiling water for 1 minute. Remove, rinse them briefly under cold running water, and drain in a colander.

Season the quail with salt, pepper, the fennel seeds, thyme, and garlic. Wrap each one in a thin strip of bacon and then in a grape leaf. Wrap another thin piece of bacon around the grape leaf and secure with a toothpick.

Heat the olive oil and butter over medium heat in a wide, shallow pot big enough to hold the quail in one layer. Sear the quail lightly, turning once. Pour in the wine, let it steam up, and then add the chicken broth. Bring to a boil, reduce the heat, and simmer, covered, for 1 hour, or until the quail are tender. About 10 minutes before the quail are done, add the lemon juice. Serve as soon as you take them off the heat.

QUAIL WITH GREEN OR
KALAMATA OLIVES

ORTYKIA ME ELIES KALAMON APO TIN LAKONIA

=== SERVES 6 ===

The Peloponnese is still the heart of Greek quail cookery. Here the small bird is coupled with the region's most famous agricultural product—Kalamata olives.

12 quail

Salt and pepper

Flour for dredging

½ cup/120 ml extra-virgin Greek olive oil

1 large red onion, finely chopped

2 garlic cloves, minced

½ cup/120 ml dry white wine

1 cup/175 g chopped canned plum tomatoes

1½ cups/360 ml chicken broth or water

18 green or Kalamata olives in olive oil, drained, pitted, and halved lengthwise

4 fresh oregano sprigs, trimmed and chopped

Rinse the quail and pat dry. Season lightly with salt and pepper. Put some flour on a large plate or sheet of wax paper and dredge the quail lightly in the flour, shaking off the excess.

Heat the olive oil in a large, wide pot over medium-high heat. Add the quail and sear in the hot oil, turning to brown on all sides. Add the onion and cook, stirring together with the quail, until slightly wilted, 3 to 4 minutes. Stir in the garlic.

Pour in the white wine. As soon as it steams up, add the tomatoes and chicken broth. Season with salt and pepper, and bring the mixture to a simmer. Reduce the heat, cover, and cook for about 1 hour, or until the quail are tender. About 15 minutes before the quail are done, add the olives and oregano. Remove from the heat and serve hot.

CHAPTER 11

LAMB, GOAT, AND RABBIT

LAMB AND GOAT MEAT HAVE BEEN SOURCES OF PROTEIN IN GREECE SINCE THE FIRST SHEPHERDS ROAMED THE COUNTRYSIDE SEVERAL MILLENNIA AGO. TODAY THEY ARE ENJOYED ON THE GREEK COUNTRY TABLE IN SPRING AND SUMMER. LAMB OR GOAT IS ESSENTIAL FOR GREEK EASTER, ROASTED WHOLE ON THE MAINLAND, AND STUFFED AND ROASTED IN THE OVEN ON THE AEGEAN ISLANDS.

But the countless recipes for both lamb and goat attest to the fact that neither is limited to the Easter feast. These include roasted leg of lamb (or goat), lamb baked in parchment paper, and lamb or goat slowly braised with vegetables, beans, and greens in a variety of sauces—tomato, wine, and avgolemono. (As for grilled lamb or goat, Greeks eat them in restaurants, and rarely barbecue at home.)

Connoisseurs of lamb in the Greek country-side can discern the age of an animal by its flavor, and those in the know say that the best *kontosouvli* (short skewers of grilled lamb) is made with milk-fed lamb and goat. Year-old animals are good for one-pot braises, while older animals are meant for ground meat dishes. There are even old recipes for *mounoukia*, eunuch lambs.

Goat meat is part of the traditional cookery of the Aegean islands. Goat meat—especially in times of dearth—was salted and preserved, to be added in small quantities to winter bean soups and other dishes. In Ikaria, where my family is from and where we spend at least three months a year, free-range goat is the local specialty, something for Sunday lunches and communal feasts alike. Greek goat meat, especially from animals that graze near sea-sprayed fields, is delicious, a fact that surely has to do with diet as much as with the species of goat. In spring and summer, the Greek countryside is bursting with aromatic herbs and plants, and these are fodder for free-ranging animals.

Young, milk-fed goats are an Easter treat, while older animals, from six to eighteen months, for example, are savored in countless recipes year-round. Old goats—*gida* in Greek—are boiled for soup. Some parts of Greece are known for their goat meat. Naxos's goats, for example, are said to be extremely tasty, and some butchers in Athens carry only Naxos goat meat. The wild goats of Ikaria, called *rasko*, are a unique breed that has learned to survive in extreme conditions on the island's precipitous cliffs. Just to give a sense of the place of goats in Greek island culture, Ikaria, home to 8,000 permanent residents, is home to more than 30,000 goats. Agricultural subsidies provide herders with a large per-capita stipend, a practice that surely has encouraged animal husbandry to the point that in some places, such as Ikaria, the animals actually pose an environmental threat, devouring precious greenery on the arid land.

RABBITS ON THE COUNTRY TABLE

Rabbits, wild and farmed, are Greeks' favorite exotic meat. Every region has its rabbit specialty. *Stifado*, a slow-braising techinique that takes its name from the small whole onions included in the dish, is a favorite everywhere, with slight regional variations from place to place. Cretan country cooks, for whom the rabbit is something of a national dish, like to stuff its cavity with soft cheese. In the Peloponnese and in Santorini, rabbit is cooked in a garlicky sauce, though the sauce is not the same in both regions. Because rabbit is lean, the best way to cook it is in a pot with plenty of liquid, usually wine and tomatoes. Many cooks insist on marinating it overnight before cooking it.

In the recipes that follow, I have tried to give a sampling of the variety of Greek dishes for lamb, goat, and rabbit, while choosing recipes with ingredients that are accessible for most cooks. No stuffed lamb's spleen follows, just plenty of one-pot dishes, slow braises, and a few delicious roasts.

PELION-STYLE MEAT LOAF BAKED IN GRAPE LEAVES

ROLO ME AMBELOFYLLA

=============== SERVES 8 ===============

Meat loaf, *rolo* in Greek, used to be a weekly dish on many household menus, but it has fallen into obscurity, mainly because women no longer have the time to prepare it. My husband's grandmother, the first country cook I have observed and learned from, used to invite us twice a month for *rolo*.

She had a very definite opinion about everything and anything that pertained to food, and her meat loaf was an all-day undertaking. I learned about the minutiae of home economy from her, too. Once she finished baking her *rolo*, as if mistrustful of modern tools such as electric ovens, she would remove it from the oven, slice it, sauté each thick piece in olive oil, tie it back together, and continue baking it until the whole thing miraculously remolded into one dense, luscious loaf. The string never went to waste but was instead washed, hung out to dry, and reused on the next meat loaf, a week or so later.

Other country cooks deal with the issue of keeping the loaf from disintegrating in a different way. Some meat loaf recipes, such as one from the Greeks of Constantinople, calls for wrapping it in phyllo. My favorite is this old dish from Mt. Pelion, which calls for wrapping the loaf in grape leaves.

2 oz/55 g fresh or brined grape leaves

¼ cup/60 ml extra-virgin Greek olive oil

1 carrot, peeled and minced

1 medium red onion, minced

1 red bell pepper, seeded and minced

2 garlic cloves, minced

1 medium zucchini, trimmed and minced

4½ oz/130 g stale country bread, crusts removed

9 oz/255 g ground beef

9 oz/255 g ground lamb

1 scant tsp dried oregano

2 large firm, ripe tomatoes, grated (see Note on page 74)

1 medium egg, lightly beaten

Salt and pepper

Preheat the oven to 350°F/175°C/gas 4. Lightly oil a baking pan big enough to hold a meat loaf that is about 6 x 13 in/15 x 33 cm.

Bring a large pot of unsalted water to a rolling boil. If using brined grape leaves, remove from the brine and rinse and drain in a colander. Blanch either fresh or brined grape leaves for 3 to 4 minutes, until softened. Drain in a colander, rinsing under cold running water immediately.

In a large sauté pan or deep frying pan, heat the olive oil over medium heat and cook the carrot, onion, bell pepper, and garlic until soft, about 8 minutes. Add the zucchini and stir for about 5 minutes more, until soft. Remove from the heat and cool slightly.

Dampen the bread under cold running water, squeeze out all the water, and crumble into a large mixing bowl. Add both meats, the cooked vegetables, oregano, tomatoes, and egg and combine. Season with salt and pepper. Place on a clean work surface and shape into a loaf.

Layer enough grape leaves, vein-side up, to cover the bottom of the oiled baking pan. Place the meat loaf on top, and wrap the bottom half of the meat loaf with the grape leaves. Spread as many grape leaves as needed over the meat loaf to cover the top and sides, pressing them together over and around the meat so that they adhere. Bake for 1 hour, or until the meat is cooked through and the grape leaves are tender. Remove from the oven and cool slightly. Use a serrated or other sharp knife to slice the meat loaf into serving-size portions.

CLAY-BAKED GARLICKY LAMB WITH GREEN PEPPERS

SKORDATO ARNI ME PIPERIES

SERVES 4 TO 6

This is an old dish from the northern Greek town of Kozani. Traditionally it is baked overnight in a low oven. I've modified the baking time for modern kitchens.

- 2 lb/910 g boneless leg of lamb or shoulder, cut into 2-in/5-cm chunks
- Salt and pepper
- 1 tsp grated nutmeg
- ⅔ cup/160 ml extra-virgin Greek olive oil
- 2 lb/910 g long green peppers, such as cubanelles, seeded and cut into 1-in/ 2.5-cm strips
- 2 garlic cloves, minced
- 1 large firm, ripe tomato, grated (see Note on page 74)
- 2 cups/480 ml dry white wine

Season the lamb with salt, pepper, and the nutmeg and set aside, covered, until ready to use.

Preheat the oven to 400°F/200°C/gas 6. Drizzle about 1 tbsp olive oil in the bottom of a clay baking or another casserole dish with a lid that is large enough to hold the lamb. Spread out the green peppers on the bottom of the dish. Season very lightly with salt. Put the lamb pieces on top and sprinkle with the garlic. Pour in the grated tomato, the remaining olive oil, and wine.

Bake for 30 minutes, uncovered, and then lower the heat to 350°F/175°C/gas 4. Cover and continue to bake for another 1½ to 2 hours, until the meat is very tender and the vegetables are almost caramelized inside the dish. Remove from the oven, cool for a few minutes, and serve.

LAMB BAKED IN YOGURT FROM FLORINA

YIAOURTOTAPSI FLORINIS

SERVES 4 TO 6

In northern Greece all sorts of meats—from chicken to savory meatballs to lamb and goat—are cooked in sauces based on the local delicious, thick, strained sheep's milk yogurt. This dish comes from the traditional cooking of the Vlachs, at one time an itinerant shepherd tribe, and is sometimes called *vlachiko*.

- 2 tbsp extra-virgin Greek olive oil
- 1 tbsp unsalted butter
- 1 lb/455 g boneless leg of lamb or goat, cut into 2-in/5-cm chunks
- 4 scallions, trimmed and finely chopped
- 2 garlic cloves, minced
- ½ cup basmati or another long-grain rice
- ½ cup/120 ml dry white wine
- 1 cup/240 ml water
- Salt and pepper
- 2 large eggs
- 2 cups/480 ml thick Greek yogurt
- 3 tbsp all-purpose flour
- 2 tbsp finely chopped fresh mint
- 3 tbsp grated *kefalotyri* cheese (optional)

Preheat the oven to 350°F/175°C/gas 4.

Heat the olive oil and butter in a large, wide pan over medium-high heat and brown the lamb pieces, turning to color them evenly. Add the scallions and cook, stirring, until soft. Stir in the garlic and cook for a few minutes to soften. Add the rice and pour in the wine and water. Cover, bring to boil, and reduce to a simmer. As soon as the rice has absorbed most of the liquid, season the contents of the pot with salt and pepper and remove from the heat.

Whisk the eggs in a medium bowl until foamy. In a separate bowl, whisk together the yogurt and flour. Whisk the eggs into the yogurt mixture and stir in the chopped mint. Season lightly with a little salt.

Spread out the lamb mixture in a casserole dish with a lid or divide evenly between individual ramekins, about 3 in/7.5 cm deep. Spread the yogurt mixture evenly over the meat. Bake, uncovered, for 45 minutes, until the yogurt is set and lightly browned on top. Cover and cook for another 45 minutes, or until the lamb is tender. If using ramekins, check after 25 minutes. Ten minutes before removing from the oven, sprinkle, if desired, with grated *kefalotyri* cheese. Serve immediately.

LAMB IN PAPER WITH SAGE, WINE, AND GARLIC

ARNI EXOHIKO ME FASKOMILO, KRASI KAI SKORDO

===== SERVES 4 =====

Lamb wrapped in parchment paper is a mainland specialty. This dish comes from the area around Mt. Pelion, in central Greece.

> 4 lamb shanks, trimmed, ¾ to 1 lb/375 to 440 g each
>
> 10 garlic cloves
>
> 6 fresh or dried sage leaves
>
> 1 tbsp red wine vinegar
>
> 2 tbsp strained fresh lemon juice
>
> 3 tbsp dry white wine
>
> 3 tbsp extra-virgin Greek olive oil
>
> Salt and pepper

Rinse the lamb and pat dry. Finely chop the garlic cloves and sage together. In a large nonreactive bowl, whisk together the vinegar, lemon juice, wine, and olive oil. Add the sage, garlic, and lamb and toss. Let stand, covered, for 1 hour or refrigerate for up to 12.

Preheat the oven to 350°F/175°C/gas 4. Cut 4 pieces of parchment paper large enough to wrap 4 equal portions of lamb. Remove the lamb to a large, clean bowl and season generously with salt and pepper. Put a portion on each piece of parchment. Drizzle a little of the marinade over the lamb. Fold the long sides of the parchment over the lamb and then bring the remaining two ends together, rolling the edges to close the parcel. Secure with kitchen string and place on a lightly oiled baking pan. Sprinkle a little water over the parcels. Add about an inch of water to the pan. Bake the parcels for 1 hour and 45 minutes, or until the lamb is tender. During cooking, sprinkle more water in the pan and over the lamb parcels, to keep the meat moist.

Remove from the oven and transfer parcels to a platter. Snip open the paper and serve.

HALKIDIKI-STYLE EASTER LAMB, BAKED OVER HERBED RICE

PSIMA

===== SERVES 8 TO 10 =====

Lamb or goat baked over vegetables is an Easter specialty in various parts of Macedonia. In Pella and Goumenissa, for example, one dish calls for baking the meat in an egg crust over a bed of scallions. This recipe, called *psima* in local parlance, is also baked over a hearty layer of vegetables and rice, and is made even more flavorful with the addition of raisins, a traditional product in Halkidiki.

> Salt
>
> 1 lb/455 g lamb's liver (optional), trimmed of membranes
>
> 4½ lb/2 kg lamb shoulder, bone in, trimmed of fat and cut into stewing-size pieces
>
> Pepper
>
> ¼ cup/60 ml extra-virgin Greek olive oil
>
> ½ cup/115 g unsalted butter
>
> 2 lb/910 g spring onions or scallions, white and tender green parts, cut into 2-in/5-cm pieces
>
> 1 cup/200 g short-grain rice
>
> 1 cup/200 g golden sultana raisins
>
> 1 cup/60 g chopped fresh dill
>
> ½ cup/30 g chopped fresh mint
>
> 3½ cups/840 ml water

Preheat the oven to 375°F/190°C/gas 5 and lightly oil a large baking pan.

If using the liver, bring a large pot of salted water to a rolling boil and blanch for 5 to 8 minutes, until lightly browned. Remove and finely chop.

Season the meat with salt and pepper. Heat the olive oil in a large pot over high heat and sear the meat, turning to brown the meat on all sides. Remove from the pot.

Using the same pot, melt the butter and sauté the spring onions, rice, raisins, and herbs. Season with salt and pepper. Add the chopped liver to the rice mixture.

Spread out the rice mixture over the bottom of the pan and place the meat on top. Pour in the water and cover the pan with aluminum foil. Bake for 1½ to 2 hours, adding more water to the rice mixture if necessary. Remove from the oven, let cool slightly, and serve.

BRAISED LAMB SHANK AND CHICKPEAS IN TOMATO SAUCE

ARNI KOTSI ME REVITHIA

===== SERVES 6 =====

This country dish is inspired by some of the classic meat and chickpea combinations from both northern Greece and the northern Aegean islands.

1½ cups/300 g dried chickpeas, picked over, rinsed, soaked overnight in water to cover, and drained

6 fresh or dried bay leaves

1 large onion, peeled, plus 1 large onion, finely chopped

6 lamb shanks (1½ lb/680 g each)

Salt and pepper

½ cup/120 ml extra-virgin Greek olive oil

2 celery stalks, finely chopped

1 carrot, peeled and halved crosswise

6 allspice berries

1 cinnamon stick

One 3-in/7.5-cm dried chile pepper (optional)

4 fresh thyme sprigs

1½ cups/360 ml white wine

2½ cups/260 g chopped canned plum tomatoes

3 to 5 cups/720 to 1.2 l water or chicken broth for cooking the meat

½ cup/30 g finely chopped fresh flat-leaf parsley

Put the chickpeas in a large pot with enough water to cover by 2 in/5 cm. Add 2 bay leaves and the whole onion. Bring to a boil over medium-high heat, reduce the heat to low, and simmer for 1 hour, or until about halfway cooked. Remove from the heat, remove the bay leaves and onion, and drain.

While the chickpeas are cooking, season the shanks with salt and pepper. In a Dutch oven or another heavy pot, heat the olive oil over medium-high heat and sear the lamb shanks until browned on all sides. Set aside.

Put the chopped onion and celery in the same pot, reduce the heat to medium, and cook until softened, about 8 minutes. Return the lamb shanks to the pot and add the carrot, the 4 remaining bay leaves, the allspice, cinnamon stick, chile pepper (if using), thyme, and wine. Bring to a boil. As soon as the wine has steamed up, add the tomatoes and enough of the water so the liquid comes about halfway up the contents of the pot. Season with salt and pepper and bring to a simmer. Cover and simmer over low heat for 1 hour, until about halfway cooked.

Add the chickpeas to the pot. Raise the heat slightly to return the contents of the pot to a boil. Cover, reduce the heat, and continue cooking until the meat and chickpeas are very tender, about another 2 to 2½ hours. Stir in the parsley, and remove from the heat. Remove the carrot, chile pepper, and bay leaves. Cool slightly and serve.

VARIATION: You can also make this dish with pork shanks. Cook them for about 1½ hours before adding the chickpeas.

BRAISED LAMB SHANKS WITH QUINCE

KYDONATO

===== SERVES 4 =====

Kydonato—from *kydoni*, the Greek word for "quince"—is a popular Sunday dish in northern Greece, typically made with either lamb or beef, which stews with the quince. Lamb shoulder or other stewing cuts are the norm, but this recipe calls for lamb shank, which results in a much more elegant, even dramatic, presentation.

3 tbsp chopped fresh thyme

3 tbsp chopped fresh rosemary

2 tbsp chopped fresh sage

3 tbsp chopped fresh mint

4 lamb shanks (1½ lb/680 g each)

Salt and pepper

Flour for dusting

½ cup/120 ml extra-virgin Greek olive oil

2 large onions, finely chopped

4 garlic cloves, minced

2 cups/480 ml dry red Greek wine

2 cups/350 g peeled, seeded, and chopped plum tomatoes (canned are fine), or grated fresh tomatoes (see Note on page 74)

2 bay leaves

2 cinnamon sticks

8 whole cloves

1 lemon, halved

4 quinces

2 tbsp unsalted butter

1 to 2 tsp sugar

Fresh parsley or thyme sprigs for garnish

In a mortar with a pestle, crush the thyme, rosemary, sage, and mint together to form a paste. Season the lamb shanks generously with salt and pepper and dust lightly with flour.

In a Dutch oven or another large, heavy pot, heat the olive oil over medium-high heat. Sear the shanks until browned on all sides. Add the onions, lower the heat to medium, and cook until the onions are soft, about 8 minutes. Stir in the garlic. Pour in 1½ cups/360 ml of the wine. As soon as it steams up, add the tomatoes, bay leaves, 1 cinnamon stick, and the pounded herb mixture. Add 6 cloves and pour in enough water to come about two-thirds of the way up the meat. Cover and bring to a simmer over high heat. Reduce the heat to low and simmer the lamb for about 1½ to 2 hours, or until very tender.

Meanwhile, squeeze the lemon into a bowl of cold water. Cut the quince lengthwise into quarters and remove the seeds and core. Slice each quarter lengthwise and put in the acidulated water to keep from oxidizing.

Heat the butter in a large, nonstick frying pan. Add the quince, the remaining 1 cinnamon stick, and the remaining 2 cloves. Sauté over high heat until the slices begin to brown. Pour in the remaining ½ cup/120 ml of wine, season with salt and pepper, and add the sugar to taste. Reduce the heat, cover, and cook until the quince is tender and almost syrupy, 12 to 15 minutes. A few minutes before removing from the heat, spoon 3 to 4 tbsp of the lamb's pot juices over the quince and shake the pan to distribute evenly. Remove the bay leaves.

For each serving, put one lamb shank in the center of a large plate. Spread some quince slices and their pan juices evenly around the shank. Spoon some of the sauce from the lamb over the shank, garnish with parsley, and serve.

BRAISED GOAT OR LAMB WITH QUINCE AND PETIMEZI

SOFEGADA LEFKADITIKI

SERVES 4 TO 6

Sofegada is one of the most interesting dishes in the Greek country kitchen. In Crete, a dish by the same name is a slow-cooked, one-pot vegetable stew. This version, from Lefkada, is a slowly cooked goat (or lamb) stew with an unusual array of fruits and vegetables and decidedly sweet notes, thanks to the grape must syrup. The word *sofegada* may come from the Italian *soffocare*, "to suffocate," or from *soffriggere*, which means "to cook slowly." The Venetians were in Lefkada for 113 years. They left their imprint on the local cooking.

Flour for dredging

Salt and pepper

2 lb/910 g boneless goat or lamb meat, cut into 2-in/5-cm chunks

½ cup/120 ml plus 2 tbsp extra-virgin Greek olive oil

1 medium onion, finely chopped

2 bay leaves

1½ lb/675 g small stewing onions, peeled and left whole

1 large quince, cored and seeded, cut into 8 slices lengthwise, skin left on

2 tbsp grape must syrup (*petimezi*)

2 to 3 tbsp red wine vinegar

2 tbsp finely chopped fresh flat-leaf parsley for garnish

Put some flour on a plate, season lightly with salt and pepper, and dust the meat, shaking off the excess. In a large stew pot or Dutch oven, heat the ½ cup/120 ml olive oil over high heat and add the meat, turning to brown on all sides. Reduce the heat to medium and add the chopped onion. Cook, stirring, until soft, about 8 minutes. Add the bay leaves and enough water to come about halfway up the contents of the pot. Cover, raise the heat, and bring the liquid to a boil. Reduce the heat and simmer the goat for about 1 hour, or until almost tender.

In a large, heavy frying pan, heat the remaining 2 tbsp olive oil over medium heat and cook the stewing onions until they are deep golden brown, shaking the frying pan back and forth every few minutes so that the onions brown all over, 15 to 20 minutes. Remove the onions from the frying pan with a slotted spoon and add to the meat.

Add the quince slices to the same frying pan and brown lightly over medium heat. Remove and gently place in the pot with the meat and onions. Add the grape must syrup and vinegar. Gently shake the pot back and forth so that the grape must syrup and vinegar are evenly distributed. Cover and continue simmering for another 30 minutes, or until the sauce is thick. Adjust the seasoning, remove from the heat, and cool slightly. Remove the bay leaves, sprinkle with parsley, and serve.

THE FOODS OF GREEK EASTER

Come Monday or Tuesday of Holy Week, the week before Easter, the whole country is in a frenzy, exiting the cities by car, boat, and plane and heading into the countryside, straight to the ancestral village. Easter is one of my favorite times of year in Greece. There is a palpable sense of anticipation. The country is a blanket of wild flowers and greens, bursting with color. The first whiff of summer lifts most people out of their winter doldrums. A sense of mystery, even for nonbelievers, pervades the countryside.

We almost always spend Easter in Ikaria, where the rhythms of this, the most sacrosanct of holidays, follow tradition to a tee. Thursday and Saturday of Holy Week are the busiest days for country cooks. On Thursday, women bake and dye eggs. The day begins very early, so that there is time to knead and let the breads rise before shuffling off with a stack of baking trays to the village baker, where the wood-burning oven makes the plaited *tsourekia* (Easter breads) taste better.

Our local bread bakery is a small place, fifty or sixty years old, with charcoal-colored walls. The sweet smell of years of fermenting yeast has soaked through every nook and cranny. The baker, Dimitra, is ruddy from a life spent standing and stooping next to the oven door, and jolly, like a figure in a Franz Hals painting, her lively personality attracting a constant stream of people, who stop in to buy their daily loaf and chat awhile. Dimitra has an elephant's memory, knowing exactly which tray belongs to whom. When the baking is done, women and kids go back to the kitchen to spend a couple of hours dyeing eggs, often the old-fashioned way, by steeping them in water filled with onion skins, which produces a brownish red color.

Good Friday is a day of solemnity on the Greek calendar, devoted to decorating the epitaph, a wooden structure that is carried in a symbolic funerary procession, with spring's most luxurious flowers. The food is Spartan: custom dictates plain lentil soup and no olive oil.

Then on Saturday the spirit of the week changes, and impending festivities loom large in people's minds. Soups to break the fast at midnight simmer, filled with all the insides of the lamb or goat destined to be the centerpiece of the Easter feast.

When it comes to the Easter feast, the range of foods is huge, even within the same region. Lamb or goat are always part of the table, as are pillowy, braided, glazed sweet breads; Easter cookies; springtime vegetable dishes; eggs; and seasonal cheese specialties, both sweet and savory.

Lamb on a spit is probably what most people think of when they think of the main course at the Easter table, but the *souvla* or *ovelia,* as it's called here, is really a mainland tradition, foreign to most islanders. On the islands, goat is eaten more often than lamb, and it is usually stuffed and roasted. One thing that every Greek Easter table shares, though, is a range of offal dishes, born of the sense of home economy that's part of every cook's mind-set.

The crisp caramelized skin of a goat or lamb roasted on a spit is a delicious thing, but I've been honed on island recipes for herb-stuffed milk-fed goats. Goats are the island meat mainly because they flourish in the craggy, rocky, precipitous terrain of most Aegean islands. Sheep don't climb as easily and need to graze more.

Goats are stuffed with different things in different places. On some islands, rice and herbs such as dill and fennel go into the stuffed goat or lamb. Pine nuts, raisins, cinnamon, and almonds are also popular. In some places, the stuffing also contains cheese. In Andros, the paschal lamb or goat is stuffed with local fresh cheese, eggs, lettuce or wild greens, spring onions, dill, fennel, and mint. In tiny Irakleia, goats are stuffed with bulgur wheat, butter, cheese, and walnuts. A combination of viscera, liver, cheeses, and herbs make up the filling for *batoudo,* Naxos's Easter meat specialty. In the Dodecanese, the fillings include raisins, pine nuts, red wine, cumin, cloves, tomatoes, and rice.

Nothing is wasted on the Easter table, and Greeks have long savored plenty of offal as part of the traditional feast. The best-known offal dish is the *kokoretsi,* a kind of large sausage usually roasted on a spit but sometimes in the oven. There are countless recipes for sautéed liver and for various skewered offal dishes. One of the most delicious is a dish called *souflitses,* lettuce leaves stuffed with various innards and cooked in tomato sauce. It is a specialty of central Greece.

GOAT BRAISED WITH WILD FENNEL

KATSIKAKI ME MARATHO

In the spring, goat and wild fennel are a natural duet of flavors all over Greece.

Flour for dredging

Salt and pepper

2 lb/910 g goat shoulder or leg, bone in, cut into serving-size pieces

⅓ cup/80 ml extra-virgin Greek olive oil

6 scallions or spring onions, trimmed and finely chopped

6 fresh garlic cloves, peeled, and scapes (optional) minced

⅔ cup/160 ml dry white wine

Pinch of sugar

2 cups/120 g chopped wild fennel; or 2 medium fennel bulbs, finely chopped

1 bunch dill, finely chopped

Juice of 1½ lemons, strained

Put some flour on a plate, season with salt and pepper, and dredge the meat in the flour, shaking off any excess. Heat the olive oil in a large pot over medium heat and sear the meat, turning to brown on all sides. Remove the meat to a plate.

Put the scallions, garlic, and the garlic scapes (if using) in the same pot. Cook over medium heat, stirring for a few minutes, until soft. Return the meat to the pot. Pour in the wine, and as soon as it steams up, add enough water to cover the meat. Season with salt and pepper and add the sugar. Cover and bring to a boil over medium heat. Reduce the heat to low and simmer for 1 hour and 40 minutes, or until the meat is so tender it falls off the bone. Check the level of the liquid every so often and add water as needed.

About halfway through the cooking time, add the fennel and dill to the pot. Pour in the lemon juice, stir, and resume cooking until the meat is done. Remove from the heat, cool slightly, and serve.

RABBIT SALMI WITH GROUND WALNUTS AND RED WINE

KOUNELI SALMI ME KARYDIA KAI KRASI APO TIN KOZANI

The Greek word *salmi* derives from the French *salmifondis*, which means "condiment made of boiled meat." *Salmi* is a term applied almost exclusively to game. There is wild boar *salmi*, pheasant and partridge *salmi*, and this more accessible rabbit *salmi*, from the environs of Kozani, in Macedonia. Red wine, tomatoes, and various spices seem to be the common threads in most *salmi* recipes, although I've seen a few that also call for walnuts as this one does.

1 large rabbit (about 4 lb/1.8 kg)

1 cup/240 ml plus 3 tbsp red wine vinegar

Flour for dredging

Salt and pepper

⅔ cup/160 ml extra-virgin Greek olive oil

2 cups/480 ml dry red wine

4 garlic cloves, peeled and crushed with the side of a knife

8 allspice berries

4 bay leaves

¾ cup/90 g walnuts, toasted and ground in a food processor

Wash the rabbit and cut into serving pieces. Put in a large non-reactive bowl. Pour in the 1 cup/240 ml vinegar and enough water to cover the rabbit. Cover and refrigerate for at least 8 hours or overnight. Remove, drain, and pat the rabbit pieces dry.

Put some flour on a large plate or on a sheet of wax paper and season with salt and pepper. Dredge the rabbit pieces, shaking off any excess. Heat the olive oil in a large, heavy, wide pot or Dutch oven over medium-high heat. Sear the dredged rabbit pieces in the hot oil, in batches, turning until browned on all sides. Pour in the wine, reduce the heat to medium, and as soon as the wine steams up, add the remaining 3 tbsp vinegar. Add the garlic, allspice berries, and bay leaves and cover the pot. Reduce the heat and simmer the rabbit until tender, about 1 hour and 20 minutes. Just before removing from the heat, stir ½ cup/60 g of the toasted, ground walnuts into the rabbit. Remove the bay leaves. Serve on a platter, sprinkled with remaining ¼ cup/30 g ground walnuts.

RABBIT STUFFED WITH FETA, RICE, AND HERBS

KOUNELI GEMISTO ME FETA, RIZI, KAI MYRODIKA

===== SERVES 4 TO 6 =====

Cheese and rabbit are considered natural partners in the Greek country kitchen. In Santorini, in the Cyclades islands, for example, one of the great rustic dishes is rabbit *tyravgoulo*, cooked in a cheese and egg sauce. On Crete the local sour cheese, *xinomyzithra*, is stuffed into the rabbit's cavity. This version from Arcadia, in the Peloponnese, includes feta, which is made locally.

1 cup/200 g Greek Carolina rice or another medium-grain rice

1 cup/240 ml water

Salt

1 large rabbit (about 4 lb/1.8 kg)

½ cup/120 ml extra-virgin Greek olive oil

2 medium onions, finely chopped

2 garlic cloves, minced

1½ tbsp finely chopped fresh flat-leaf parsley

1½ tbsp finely chopped fresh dill

1 tbsp chopped fresh basil

1 tbsp chopped fresh mint

7 oz/200 g Greek feta cheese, crumbled

2 large eggs, beaten

Pepper

2 lb/910 g ripe tomatoes, puréed in a food processor, or 2½ cups/440 g canned tomatoes, chopped

4 fresh bay leaves

2 carrots, peeled and left whole

10 peppercorns

2 allspice berries

1 tbsp Greek thyme or pine honey

1 tbsp balsamic or Greek raisin vinegar

Combine the rice, water, and a little salt in a medium saucepan. Cover and bring to a boil over medium heat. Reduce the heat and simmer until the rice absorbs all the water, about 10 minutes. Remove from the heat.

Wash the rabbit. Remove the liver, rinse well in a colander, and finely chop. Remove and discard any other viscera that might still be inside the rabbit's cavity.

Heat ¼ cup/60 ml of the olive oil in a large, deep frying pan or sauté pan over medium heat, and sauté the liver until lightly browned. Season with salt. Add the onions and cook, stirring, until soft, about 8 minutes. Stir in the garlic and cook for 1 minute. Remove the contents of the frying pan and transfer to a mixing bowl. Let cool for a few minutes.

Add the cooked rice, herbs, feta, and eggs to the mixing bowl and toss with the sautéed liver mixture. Season with pepper.

Spoon the rice mixture into the cavity of the rabbit and, using several sturdy toothpicks or a thick needle and thread, secure or sew closed. Tie the rabbit's legs together.

In a wide pot large enough to hold the rabbit, such as a Dutch oven, heat the remaining ¼ cup/60 ml olive oil over medium-high heat. Season the rabbit with salt and pepper and place carefully in the hot oil. Sear, turning carefully, until lightly browned on both sides.

Pour in the tomatoes and enough water to come about halfway up the rabbit. Add the bay leaves, whole carrots, peppercorns, and all-spice berries. Season lightly with salt and pepper. Cover and bring to a boil over medium heat. Reduce the heat and braise the rabbit over low heat until tender, about 1 hour and 20 minutes. Stir in the honey and balsamic vinegar about 10 minutes before removing from the heat. When the rabbit is done, remove the bay leaves, cool slightly, and transfer to a platter. Remove the thread or toothpicks and cut the rabbit into serving pieces. Spoon out a little of the filling for each portion, and spoon the sauce over the meat and rice.

VARIATION: This rustic dish becomes more elegant if the rabbit and rice are cooked separately. Cook the rabbit as described, searing it in ¼ cup/60 ml olive oil and simmering it in the tomato sauce, herbs, and spices. To make a separate rice pilaf, in a wide saucepan, cook the onion and garlic in ¼ cup/60 ml olive oil until soft. Stir in the chopped liver and cook until lightly browned. Add the rice, stir to coat in the oil, and add 2 cups/480 ml water and a little salt. Cover, reduce the heat to low, and simmer the rice until done. Five minutes before removing from the heat, add the parsley, dill, basil, mint, and feta. Omit the eggs.

RABBIT STEWED WITH SWEET AND TART PRUNES

KOUNELI STIFADO ME DAMASKINA

========= SERVES 4 TO 6 =========

Several years ago, while I was in the lovely town of Nymphaio, a preserve of Vlach culture and wild bears, I met the president of the local women's food cooperative, who gave me this recipe. She informed me that unlike the tomato-based rabbit stews cooked in most of the rest of Greece, rabbit stew in Nymphaio was almost always cooked "white," without tomatoes, that is—despite the fact that the rabbit is cooked in the region's famed red wine, Xinomavro. This dish includes prunes and sour cherry plums, which are relished by local cooks in all sorts of meat stews.

> 1 large rabbit (about 4 lb/1.8 kg), cut into serving-size pieces
>
> 2½ cups/600 ml dry red wine, preferably Xinomavro from Naoussa
>
> 6 garlic cloves, peeled and crushed with the side of a knife
>
> ¼ cup/120 ml extra-virgin Greek olive oil
>
> 2 lb/910 g small stewing onions, peeled and left whole; or 5 medium onions, cut into chunks
>
> Salt
>
> 2 bay leaves
>
> 8 pitted prunes
>
> 8 dried sour cherry plums (see Note)
>
> 3 to 4 tbsp red wine vinegar
>
> Pepper

Put the rabbit in a nonreactive bowl and pour in 1 cup/240 ml of the wine and 3 of the crushed garlic cloves. Marinate, covered and refrigerated, overnight.

Remove the rabbit from the marinade and pat dry with paper towels. Heat ¼ cup/60 ml of the olive oil in a large stewing pot or Dutch oven over high heat. Brown the rabbit on all sides. Remove with a slotted spoon and set aside.

Add the onions to the pot, cover, and steam in the oil over medium heat until golden, about 15 minutes. Return the rabbit to the pot, season with salt, and add the remaining 3 crushed garlic cloves, the remaining 1½ cups/360 ml of wine, and the bay leaves.

Cover, bring to a boil over medium-high heat, reduce the heat, and simmer until the rabbit is very tender, about 1½ hours. Add water during cooking, if necessary, to keep the stew moist. Twenty minutes before removing the rabbit from the heat, add the prunes and dried cherry plums. Ten minutes later, add the vinegar and adjust the seasoning with pepper and additional salt to taste. Remove from the heat, let stand for 10 minutes, and serve. This is lovely with wide noodles.

NOTE: If dried cherry plums are unavailable, increase the number of the prunes to 12.

CHAPTER 12

PORK
AND
BEEF

UNTIL THE 1960S, MEAT WAS A RARE TREAT FOR MOST GREEKS. TODAY, HOWEVER, THEY CLAIM THE DUBIOUS HONOR OF BEING THE LARGEST CONSUMERS OF RED MEAT IN THE EUROPEAN UNION. IN FACT, MOST GREEK FAMILIES CONSIDER A MEAL INCOMPLETE IF MEAT IS NOT INCLUDED.

One of the most revealing aspects of Greek meat cookery is how it follows the seasons. Meats braised with leeks or legumes—for example, chickpeas and white beans—are winter dishes. In springtime, meats braised with greens are classic dishes. Late summer and fall bring a bevy of dishes like veal or beef braised with red bell peppers. Country cooks often keep large gardens and a few animals, which means there are always chores to do. So they prefer dishes that can basically cook themselves in a big pot over several hours.

In the Odyssey, Homer praises the swineherd, responsible for the health and safety of thousands of animals. Pigs have remained immensely important in the country kitchen, providing meat for almost a third of the year, between the ritual pig slaughters of December and January to the beginning of Lent. (These slaughters still take place, especially in the

Aegean islands.) No part of the animal is wasted: Trotters and heads become headcheese, *pykti* in Greek, a classic Christmas and New Year's dish. The fat is rendered and was, until a generation ago, poor man's butter. In Ikaria, where my family is from, people over the age of fifty recall with nostalgia the *glina*—rendered fat—that their mothers and grandmothers used to spread on bread and sprinkle with sugar as an after-school snack. Intestines are used to make sausages, which are smoked or air-dried. Chops hang over fireplaces or in special outdoor areas to be smoked over aromatic wood. The tender belly, either smoked or grilled, is treasured throughout Greece. In some Aegean islands, pork chops are preserved in lard and cooked with tomatoes and eggs, a rare treat one might still find in Tzia and other Cyclades islands.

Small bits are also preserved in lard or olive oil, depending on the region. This is called *siglino*, and is a unique specialty of the Peloponnese. In the last decade, Greek gourmet shops have been carrying commercialized versions of it. The rind becomes chitlins, while the loin or thigh is sometimes encrusted in a layer of spices, flattened, and air-dried to make a specialty called *louza*, which is a local treat in some of the Cyclades. And, finally, stewing cuts are cooked up in countless dishes, with egg and lemon, leeks, cabbage, greens, fresh and dried beans, tomatoes, olives, wine, and nuts and dried fruits.

Beef has a more exalted status than pork. It has always been esteemed, probably because of its relative scarcity in Greece, a country with little grazing land. And its significance is not lost on historians and linguists, as the cow provided the inspiration for the first letter of the alphabet. *Alpha—alef* in ancient Phoenician and Semitic languages—is shaped like a bovine head, demonstrating early man's reverence for the animal as a primal source of wealth. Even today, the wholehearted embrace of beef among people who, until a generation ago, almost never savored a steak, speaks volumes for how the traditional Greek diet has changed as people became more affluent.

Beef consumption grew by leaps and bounds in Greece after 1960, when the country was just starting to pull itself together after the terrible famines and starvation during and after World War II and the bloody Greek civil war between 1946 and 1949. Suddenly beef became a symbol of social mobility, and a way to dispel painful memories of the years when the diet, especially in cities, was extraordinarily meager. The beef industry got a push, too, in the 1960s, when the Agricultural Bank of Greece began providing development loans.

Meat cookery in Greece is both a paean to simple, robust preparations; seasonal ingredients; and economy. Indeed, many beef stews are really vegetable stews with a bit of meat added as a way to help stretch expensive protein, so that every member of the family gets a little. It's a practice that took generations of country cooks to perfect, but then was lost as Greeks embraced their carnivorous pleasures with alacrity. Now, as all the ailments related to a meat-heavy diet tax the country, cooks are starting to return to the practices that gave the Greek diet its healthy reputation. They're cooking with smaller quantities of meat and embracing vegetables and beans.

SMYRNA-STYLE SMALL MEAT "SAUSAGES"

SOUTZOUKAKIA SMYRNEIKA

=========== SERVES 4 ===========

Soutzoukakia came to Greece via the Greek refugees from Asia Minor in 1922. These delectable little ground beef cylinders are flavored with cumin and cooked in a rich, thick tomato sauce. Rice and bulgur make great side dishes for *soutzoukakia*. In northern Greece, the *soutzoukakia* are sometimes grilled rather than cooked in sauce.

SAUCE

2 tbsp extra-virgin Greek olive oil

½ small red onion, finely chopped

1 garlic clove, minced

¼ cup/60 ml dry red wine

3 cups/525 g canned plum tomatoes, with their juice

Salt and pepper

1 tsp sugar

½ tsp red pepper flakes

1 tsp unsalted butter

SOUTZOUKAKIA

1½ lb/680 g ground beef

⅓ cup/40 g coarsely chopped white onion

1 large garlic clove, minced

¼ tsp ground allspice

¼ tsp ground nutmeg

1½ tsp paprika

Pinch of cinnamon

2½ tsp ground cumin

Salt and pepper

1 egg

2 tbsp dry white wine

¼ to ½ cup/25 to 50 g dry bread crumbs

2 tbsp extra-virgin Greek olive oil

Flour for dredging

Olive oil for frying

To make the sauce: Heat the olive oil in a medium saucepan over medium heat and sauté the onion until soft. Add the garlic and stir. Add the wine. Squeeze the tomatoes by hand into the pot and pour in their juice. Bring to a boil over medium heat. Season with salt and pepper and add the sugar. Reduce the heat to low and simmer, uncovered, until slightly thickened, about 10 minutes. Stir in the red pepper flakes and butter, and set the sauce aside until ready to use.

To make the soutzoukakia: In a large mixing bowl, combine the ground beef, onion, garlic, and spices, and season with salt and pepper. Mix with your hands to blend. Add the egg and wine and knead well to combine. Add the bread crumbs judiciously (you want just enough to give body to the mixture so that the *soutzoukakia* hold their shape when formed). Mix in the olive oil. Cover and refrigerate the mixture for 30 minutes to 1 hour to firm up.

Take a golf ball–size piece of meat and shape in the palms of your hand into an elongated sausage about 2½ in/6 cm long and 1 in/2.5 cm thick.

Put some flour on a plate and dredge the *soutzoukakia*. Heat about ½ in/12 mm of olive oil in a heavy frying pan. Brown the *soutzoukakia* in batches. As soon as they are browned on one side, shake the pan back and forth over the heat so that the *soutzoukakia* roll back and forth a little to brown on all sides.

Place the *soutzoukakia* side by side in one layer in a wide pot and pour in the sauce. Cover and simmer until the *soutzoukakia* are tender and moist and cooked through, about 30 minutes. Alternatively, you can preheat the oven to 350°F/175°C/gas 4, put the *soutzoukakia* in a lightly oiled baking pan in one layer, and pour in the sauce. Bake, covered, for about 40 minutes. Serve hot.

MEATBALLS BRAISED WITH GREEN PEPPERS

KEFTEDES SPETSOFAI

===== SERVES 8 TO 12 =====

I don't know if there is any dish as common as Greek meatballs—*keftedes*—with such an illustrious history.

The word *kefte* derives from the Turkish *köfte*, which in turn derives from the Persian *kofta*, both of which likely come from the ancient Greek *koptos*, which means "finely chopped" or "pounded." *Kefte* thus relates directly to the ground or chopped meat that is the first and absolutely most necessary component in making this simple dish. The classic Greek meatball is made of ground meat, stale bread that has been dampened and wrung out, mint, salt, pepper, and an egg, which binds the whole thing together. It is typically fried. But variations on the theme abound, including meatballs cooked in avgolemono or in sauces with prunes and tomatoes. In some recipes, wine or milk or tomato pulp are kneaded into the mix. Then there is the whole category of *keftedes* called *pseudokeftedes*, which are made with vegetables, greens, and pulses, but not meat. These are really fritters and you will find them on pages 72 to 79.

Greek meat keftedes require finely ground meat because they cook in a short time. Greek butchers actually ask their customers if they prefer their meat put through the grinder once (appropriate for dishes such as meat loaf, see page 279) or twice. The fat content of ground meat, whether it's lamb, beef, or pork, should be somewhere around 20 percent to ensure a juicy finished dish. These *keftedes* may be served alone or over rice or pasta.

MEATBALLS

8 oz/225 g stale country bread, crusts removed

1 lb/455 g minced beef

1 lb/455 g minced pork

2 large red onions, finely chopped

2 green bell peppers, finely chopped

1 cup/60 g chopped fresh flat-leaf parsley

1 cup/60 g chopped fresh mint

3 tbsp extra-virgin Greek olive oil

2 large eggs, lightly beaten

Salt and pepper

3 to 6 tbsp soda water or seltzer

SAUCE

½ cup/120 ml extra-virgin Greek olive oil

10 green bell peppers, each cut lengthwise into 4 strips

2 garlic cloves, minced

3 cups/525 g peeled, seeded, and chopped plum tomatoes (canned are fine)

½ cup/120 ml water

1 tbsp tomato paste

Salt and pepper

2 tsp chopped fresh oregano, or more to taste

Olive oil for frying

To make the meatballs: Dampen the bread under cold running water and wring it dry in the palms of your hands. Crumble into a large mixing bowl. Add the ground meats, onions, bell peppers, parsley, mint, Greek olive oil, and eggs. Season with salt and pepper. Add as much of the soda water as possible without making the mixture too loose. Cover with plastic wrap and refrigerate for 1 hour.

To make the sauce: Heat the ½ cup/120 ml olive oil over medium heat in a large, wide pot and sauté the bell peppers until soft, about 12 minutes. Add the garlic, stir to soften for a minute or two, and add the tomatoes. Add the water and tomato paste and season with salt and pepper. Cover and simmer the sauce until thickened, about 30 minutes. Add the oregano and remove from the heat.

Take 1 tbsp at a time of the ground meat mixture and shape into small balls, about 1½ in/4 cm in diameter. Heat 2 in/5 cm of olive oil in a large, heavy frying pan and fry the meatballs in batches, turning to brown lightly on all sides. Do not cook through, since they will cook in the sauce. Remove and set aside on paper towels to drain.

Put the meatballs in the sauce and bring to a simmer over medium heat. Reduce the heat to low, cover, and cook the meatballs in the sauce for 20 to 25 minutes, until cooked through and tender. Serve immediately.

COUNTRY HOG SLAUGHTERS

Christmas belongs to the humble pig. Or, rather, the humble pig belongs to our dinner table on that day and on many others following it, right up through Lent. Innocent lambs and not-so-innocent goats capture our imaginations just before Easter and right up through the end of summer. But from November through March, pork provides a delicious roster of traditional foods.

From December 6, the feast day of Saint Nicholas, to late January, when Saint Anthony is celebrated, the *hoirosfagia*—festive hog slaughters—take place in agrarian communities. Many families raise a hog or two and slaughter it in midwinter. They often have a kind of work party around that activity, and invite friends and neighbors over to enjoy the feast. In most places there is a specific order to the preparations, and it takes about three days to complete all the work. Those who do all the dirty work usually have first dibs on the best parts of the pig, and everyone has his own idea about which parts are best. The liver is a delicacy, pan-fried and

consumed with liters of fresh wine. The neck is another much-esteemed cut, full of tasty meat that is perfect in slow braises.

The pork slaughter has its gender divide, with the men doing all the heavy work and the women handling the smaller cured preparations, such as sausage making. And sausage making is one of the most laborious tasks after the slaughter. The sausages follow a regional palette: In the Peloponnese, orange is the main flavor of pork sausages. Fennel is the favorite sausage seasoning in the Cyclades, while the spicy cuisine of Macedonia produces sausages spiked with cumin and hot pepper.

Whole roasted suckling pig is probably the king of the Christmas table. It is usually seasoned simply with lemon and oregano, but there are also recipes from northern Greece for suckling pig stuffed with chestnuts, pine nuts, cheese, onions, and spices. And there are many traditional Christmas dishes based on the innards of the humble pig.

YIOUVARLAKIA WITH CUMIN AND ORANGE, COOKED IN TOMATO SAUCE

YIOUVARLAKIA ME KYMINO KAI PORTOKALI

===== SERVES 6 TO 8 =====

Yiouvarlakia are uniquely Greek. They are related to meatballs in the sense that they contain ground meat, onions, and herbs. But they are also quite different because they contain rice, which makes these little balls filling and more complete nutritionally. Another difference is that *yiouvarlakia* are not fried like typical meatballs. They're simmered in either an avgolemono or tomato sauce, which is why the dish falls somewhere between a soup and a hearty main course. I've tasted one creative version, made with fish, prepared by Chrysanthos Karamolengos, one of the best known chefs in Athens. Kids love *yiouvarlakia*, too.

YIOUVARLAKIA

1 lb/455 g ground beef

½ cup/100 g medium-grain rice

1 medium yellow onion, minced or grated

1 garlic clove, minced

½ cup/30 g finely chopped fresh flat-leaf parsley

1 small egg, lightly beaten

Salt and pepper

SAUCE

12 large firm, ripe plum or campari tomatoes

2 tbsp extra-virgin Greek olive oil

½ large white onion, finely chopped

1 celery stalk, finely chopped

1 garlic clove, minced

Salt

3 cups/720 ml chicken broth

1 bay leaf

1 cinnamon stick

1 scant tsp cumin

Two 1-in/2.5-cm strips orange peel

Pepper

Pinch of sugar

3 to 4 fresh thyme sprigs

To make the *yiouvarlakia*: Combine the meat, rice, onion, garlic, parsley, and egg in a mixing bowl. Season with salt and pepper and knead until well blended. Shape the mixture into 1- to 1½-in/2.5- to 4-cm balls. Set aside.

To make the sauce: Chop the tomatoes. Transfer to the bowl of a food processor and purée. Heat the olive oil in a large, wide pot and sauté the onion and celery until soft, about 8 minutes. Add the garlic and stir for 1 or 2 minutes. Season with a little salt. Add the puréed tomatoes, chicken broth, bay leaf, cinnamon stick, cumin, and orange peel, and season with a little more salt and some pepper. Add a little sugar to adjust the acidity of the tomatoes. Bring to a boil over medium heat, reduce the heat to low, and simmer for 10 minutes.

Add the *yiouvarlakia* to the sauce. Return to a boil over medium heat and reduce again to a simmer. Add the thyme sprigs. Continue simmering until the meat and rice are cooked and the sauce is thickened, 30 to 35 minutes. Remove from the heat and cool slightly. Remove the cinnamon stick, peel, and bay leaf and serve.

VARIATION: Classic *Yiouvarlakia* with Avgolemono: Omit the tomato sauce. Cook the *yiouvarlakia* in 6 cups/1.4 l of chicken broth for the same amount of time. Then, whisk 1 large egg in a nonreactive bowl until very foamy. Add the strained juice of 1 large lemon and continue whisking. Take a ladleful of the hot broth and very slowly drizzle it into the egg-lemon mixture, whisking vigorously all the while. Repeat with a second ladleful of broth. Pour the mixture back into the pot, turn off the heat immediately, and tilt the pan back and forth to distribute the sauce evenly. If you wish, you can also add a pinch of saffron to the broth before you add the egg-lemon mixture to the pot.

PORK LOIN STUFFED WITH PISTACHIOS AND GRAVIERA

GEMISTO PSARONEFRI

===== SERVES 6 TO 8 =====

This is a contemporary country recipe from Naxos, in the Cyclades. It is lovely and makes a great Sunday or festive main course.

1 lb/455 g pork tenderloin, trimmed and butterflied (see Note)

Salt and pepper

4 garlic cloves, minced

11 oz/310 g *graviera* cheese, cut into ½-in/12-mm cubes

1 cup/150 g pistachios, lightly toasted and coarsely chopped

Grated zest from 2 lemons; plus 2 lemons, cut into wedges, for serving

½ cup/120 ml extra-virgin Greek olive oil

2 cups/480 ml dry white wine

Preheat the oven to 375°F/190°C/gas 5. Spread the butterflied pork on a work surface and season both sides generously with salt and pepper. Sprinkle the garlic, cheese, about ⅔ cup/100 g of the pistachios, and lemon zest over the meat. Starting from the end closest to you, roll up the meat to form a tight cylinder, tucking any filling that falls out back inside. Using kitchen string or toothpicks, secure the roll so that it stays closed.

Over medium-high heat, heat the olive oil in an ovenproof frying pan large enough to hold the meat. Sear the pork loin, turning it to brown on all sides. Reduce the heat to medium and pour in the wine. As soon as the wine steams up, remove the pan from the heat, cover with aluminum foil, and transfer to the oven. Roast the pork for about 45 minutes, or until tender, basting with the pan juices every few minutes.

Remove the pork from the oven, cool slightly, and slice into rounds. Sprinkle the remaining pistachios on top of the pork and serve with the lemon wedges, or squeeze the lemon wedges over the sliced pork.

NOTE: You can ask your butcher to butterfly the pork. To do it yourself, put the tenderloin on a cutting board and cut it lengthwise, leaving about 1 in/2.5 cm still attached. Open it like a book. Use a mallet and pound the tenderloin slightly to flatten it out.

BRAISED PORK WITH CELERY AND EGG-LEMON SAUCE

HOIRINO ME SELINO AVGOLEMONO

SERVES 6

Pork braised with celery is one of the great classics of the Greek kitchen. Although it is found all over Greece, in the Peloponnese it's a local favorite savored in winter, during the olive harvest.

4 lb/1.8 kg celery

¾ cup/180 ml extra-virgin Greek olive oil

4 lb/1.8 kg pork shoulder, cut into 2½-in/6-cm pieces

2 large red onions, finely chopped

Salt and pepper

1 cup/240 ml dry white wine

AVGOLEMONO

2 large eggs

½ cup/120 ml strained fresh lemon juice

Cut the celery into 3-in/7.5-cm pieces. Heat the olive oil in a large, wide pot over medium heat and add the pork. Stir until browned on all sides. Reduce the heat to low and add the onions and celery. Cook, stirring, until wilted, about 10 minutes. Season lightly with salt and pepper. Pour in the wine. As soon as it steams up, pour in enough water to barely cover the meat. Cover the pot, raise the heat, and bring to a boil. Reduce heat to low and simmer for about 1½ to 2 hours, or until the celery and pork are both very tender.

To make the avgolemono: Whisk the eggs and lemon juice together in a medium bowl. Add a ladleful of the pot juices to the egg mixture, whisking all the while. Repeat with another ladleful.

Remove the pot from the heat and pour in the egg-lemon mixture. Tilt the pan so that it is well distributed. Serve immediately.

MEAT PRESERVED

The ancient art of preserving meat is something Greek country cooks still do, and the wide variety of regional charcuterie is proof. Specialty sausages with unique seasonings, unusual cured salamis, and spice-crusted pork loins are just some of the regional offerings. Some areas are especially esteemed for their charcuterie, among them Lefkada, where a thick, savory salami is a Protected Designation of Origin product; Corfu, home to the *noumboulo*, a smoked pork tenderloin; and Lake Kerkyni, in Macedonia, where buffaloes roam and provide the meat for one rare preserved meat called *kavourmas*. The Cyclades, where country cooks are schooled better than most other Greeks in the preservation of the humble pig, has a wide range of cured meat products that are still an important part of the local diet and food culture. Newer producers, especially those in Karpenissi, Pieria, and other parts of northern Greece, have been making excellent untraditional preserved meats, among them an award-winning prosciutto and a range of products from wild boars, including liver pâté.

One of my favorite preserved pork specialties is spiced, air-dried *louza*, which means "loin," the cut from which it is made. *Louza* is produced by butchers and home cooks in Syros, Tinos, Andros, Mykonos, and Kea,

all in the Cyclades, with slight variations from place to place. A smaller version of *louza*, called *bouboulo,* is made in Mykonos. Many of the most interesting and obscure preserved pork specialties are truly the domain of country cooks, unavailable commercially and made less and less frequently. Many of these come from the Cyclades. From tiny Anafi, for example, comes *sopsaro*, salted, spiced pork preserved in vinegar and then hung to dry indoors. Anafi cooks make use of the shoulder, too, in a specialty called *lagaro*, which is cured in salt for forty days and then air-dried. Santorini has a preserved pork loin called *apokti*, which is soaked in vinegar, rubbed with sweet spices, and left to dry, fanned by the island's formidable winds.

Last but not least is the most commercially available preserved pork, which hails from the Peloponnese: *siglino*, a specialty of the Mani, which now can be found in airtight packages at supermarkets all over Greece. *Siglino* is made with bite-size chunks of boneless pork preserved in lard or in olive oil and flavored with orange zest, a regional favorite. *Siglino* is cooked in omelets and is also beloved by modern cooks, who put slivers of it into salads and soups.

PORK TENDERLOINS WITH CHESTNUTS, HAZELNUTS, AND DRIED FIGS

PSARONEFRI ME XIROUS KARPOUS

SERVES 4

The combination of pork with nuts and dried fruit is a favorite in the Greek country kitchen. This dish goes well with Mashed Potatoes with Feta and Greek Yogurt (page 123) and a glass of northern Greek red wine.

1 lb/455 g chestnuts, in the shell

3 lb/1.4 kg pork tenderloins

1 tbsp extra-virgin Greek olive oil, plus extra for rubbing the pork

Salt and pepper

2 large onions, coarsely chopped

1½ cups/360 ml dry red wine

1½ cups/260 g chopped canned plum tomatoes

2 bay leaves

⅔ cup hazelnuts, toasted

8 to 10 dried figs, trimmed and halved

If using fresh chestnuts, score them with a sharp paring knife and put them in a pot with enough water to cover by 2 in/5 cm. Bring to a boil over high heat, reduce the heat, and simmer until the chestnuts are soft, 35 to 40 minutes. Drain the chestnuts, let cool, and peel. If using sous vide chestnuts, put the bag in boiling water and cook according to the package directions. Preheat the oven to 350°F/175°C/gas 4).

Rub the pork tenderloins with olive oil and season with salt and pepper. Heat the 1 tbsp olive oil in a large, deep, nonstick frying pan or sauté pan over medium-high heat and brown the pork. Add the onions and stir for 2 to 3 minutes, just until slightly wilted. Raise the heat and pour in the wine. As soon as it steams up, add the tomatoes, bay leaves, and half the chestnuts. Cover and simmer for 10 minutes.

Transfer the meat and all the pot juices to a medium baking dish. Cover with aluminum foil and bake the pork until tender, about 30 minutes. About halfway through baking, add the remaining chestnuts, the hazelnuts, and figs. Remove from the oven when the meat is tender, let cool slightly, and serve.

NORTHERN GREEK BRAISED PORK AND LEEKS

HOIRINO ME PRASA

SERVES 4 TO 6

This dish is made all over northern Greece, but it is associated most with Naoussa. In this town in central Macedonia, local cooks swear the best cut is pork collar, which they cook with tomatoes. It is one of the all-time classics and a favorite on the Sunday and festive table.

½ cup/120 ml extra-virgin Greek olive oil

3 lb/1.4 kg pork, preferably shoulder or collar, bone in, cut into stewing-size pieces

Salt and pepper

1½ lb/680 g leeks, washed well, trimmed, and coarsely chopped

1 cup/240 ml blanc de noir Xinomavro wine, or another dry white northern Greek wine

1 cup/175 g chopped canned plum tomatoes, with their juice

AVGOLEMONO

3 large egg yolks

Juice of 2 lemons, strained

Heat the olive oil in a large, wide pot over high heat and brown the meat. Season with salt and pepper. Add the leeks and cook, stirring, until soft. Pour in the wine. As soon as it steams up, add the tomatoes. Add enough water to cover the contents of the pot by about two-thirds. Cover, raise the heat to high, and bring to a boil. Reduce the heat and simmer the stew until the meat is very tender, about 2 hours.

To make the avgolemono: In a medium nonreactive bowl, whisk together the egg yolks and half the lemon juice until smooth and thick. Take one ladleful of the pot juices, being careful not to take up any solids, and very slowly drizzle the liquid into the egg mixture, whisking vigorously. Repeat with a second ladleful of juices.

Remove the meat from the heat and pour in the avgolemono. Tilt the pot back and forth to distribute the avgolemono evenly. Adjust the seasoning with additional salt, pepper, or lemon juice, and serve.

BEEF STEW WITH GREEN OLIVES

KAPAMAS ME PRASINES ELIES

──────── SERVES 4 ────────

Kapamas is one of the most enigmatic Greek dishes, mainly because the word is used to define dozens of completely different recipes. *Kapamas* comes from the Turkish word *kapamal* or *kapatmak*, which means "to cover." It generally refers to some kind of stewed meat, usually in tomato sauce, cooked in a covered pot over very low heat. There are dozens of such stews. Some contain beef, others chicken, lamb, lamb's trotters, or even octopus. At least one version, an old dish made by the Greeks from the Black Sea, calls for no meat at all but is rather a slow-cooked concoction of onions, cabbage, tomatoes, and bulgur.

This recipe is a really simple dish. Allspice, bay leaf, oregano, and orange make up the subtle flavors in the tomato sauce, while green olives lend a pleasant sharpness. Slow-cooking these flavors with the meat makes it all delicious. Serve this dish with Mashed Potatoes with Feta and Greek Yogurt (page 123), Greek noodles, or, as my husband's grandmother would have it, with silver-dollar-sized potatoes fried in Greek olive oil (see page 123).

½ cup/120 ml extra-virgin Greek olive oil

2 lb/910 g stewing beef, preferably from the shoulder, cut into chunks

Salt and pepper

2 large red onions, finely chopped

2 large garlic cloves, minced

1½ cups/360 ml dry white wine

2 large firm, ripe tomatoes, grated (see Note on page 74); or 2 cups/350 g chopped canned plum tomatoes, with their juice

2 small carrots, peeled and left whole

4 stalks Chinese celery with leaves, or 1 large stalk regular celery, trimmed at the root end and halved

3 bay leaves

5 allspice berries

Two 3 x 1-in/7.5 x 2.5-cm strips of orange peel

16 pitted Greek green olives, rinsed and drained

2 tbsp fresh oregano, chopped

Heat the olive oil in a large, wide pot over medium-high heat and brown the meat on all sides. Season with salt and pepper. Add the onions, reduce the heat to medium, and cook, stirring, for 8 minutes, or until the onions are soft. Add the garlic and stir once or twice.

Pour in the wine. As soon as it steams up, add the tomatoes. Bring to a simmer. Pour in enough water to cover the meat and add the carrots, celery, bay leaves, allspice berries, and orange peel to the pot.

Reduce the heat, cover, and simmer for 1 ½ to 2 hours, until the meat is extremely tender. About 15 minutes before removing from the heat, add the olives to the pot. Remove the bay leaves, sprinkle with oregano, cool slightly, and serve.

KOZANI BEEF STEW WITH GRAPE MUST SYRUP AND PRUNES

KOZANITIKOS KAPAMAS ME DAMASKINA KAI PETIMEZI

──────── SERVES 4 TO 6 ────────

This is a winter dish from Kozani, in central Macedonia. The stew has a delicious sweet-sour undertone. Serve it with mashed potatoes, plain rice, or noodles.

2 large onions, grated on the coarse holes of a box grater

½ cup/120 ml extra-virgin Greek olive oil

2 lb/910 g boneless beef shoulder, cut into 2½-in/6-cm pieces

Salt and pepper

1 large carrot, trimmed and halved crosswise

2 celery stalks, trimmed and halved crosswise

2 bay leaves

12 peppercorns

4 allspice berries

Scant 1 tbsp sweet paprika

12 to 15 pitted prunes

⅓ cup/80 ml grape must syrup (*petimezi*)

Chopped fresh flat-leaf parsley for garnish

Put the grated onion in a large, wide pot with enough water to cover by ⅛ in/3 mm. Bring to a simmer over medium heat and cook until almost all the water evaporates. When the onions are practically dry, add the olive oil. Raise the heat to medium and add the meat. Cook, stirring, until lightly browned. Season with salt and pepper.

Add enough water to come three-quarters of the way up the meat. Add the carrot, celery, bay leaves, peppercorns, allspice, and sweet paprika. Cover, raise the heat to high, and bring to a boil. Reduce the heat and simmer for about 1 hour and 15 minutes, or until the meat is about three-quarters cooked. Add the prunes and drizzle in the grape must syrup. Tilt the pan back and forth to distribute the grape must syrup evenly. Cover and simmer for another 20 minutes or so, until the sauce is thick and the meat is very tender. Remove the carrot, celery, and bay leaves, and stir in the fresh parsley. Serve immediately.

VEAL STEWED WITH ROASTED RED PEPPERS

MOSCHARI STIFADO ME PSITES KOKKINES PIPERIES

SERVES 4 TO 6

This festive dish is reserved for Sundays and holidays in the central and western parts of Macedonia, where the red pepper reigns supreme. Ideally, it should be made with the local Florina pepper, a long, fleshy red pepper that inundates the markets in late summer and fall.

Flour for dredging

Salt

2 lb/910 g veal or beef shoulder, trimmed and cut into large stewing-size pieces

½ cup/120 ml extra-virgin Greek olive oil

3 medium red onions, halved and sliced

1 tsp coarsely crushed peppercorns

2 medium firm, ripe tomatoes, grated (see Note on page 74)

16 fresh Florina peppers or 10 to 12 medium red bell peppers, roasted, peeled, seeded (see Note on page 70), and cut into 1-in-/2.5-cm-wide strips

2 bay leaves

1 cup/60 g chopped fresh mint

2 to 3 tbsp red wine vinegar

Put some flour on a plate, season with salt, and dredge the meat lightly, tapping off any excess. Heat the olive oil in a large stewing pot or Dutch oven over high heat. Add the meat, in batches if necessary, and brown on all sides. Remove with a slotted spoon and set aside. Scrape any burnt flour out of the pot.

Add the onions to the pot, lower the heat to medium, and cook, stirring, until soft, about 8 minutes. Place the meat over the onions, then season with salt and half the crushed peppercorns. Spread the tomatoes and Florina peppers over the meat, covering it completely. Season with more salt and the remaining peppercorns. Add the bay leaves to the pot. Cover, reduce the heat to very low, and simmer until the meat is very tender, about 2 hours. (Add water, white wine, or stock to the dish, if necessary during cooking, to keep it from burning. The end result, however, should be a thick, not watery stew.) About 10 minutes before removing from the heat, stir in the mint and vinegar to taste. Remove the bay leaves and serve warm.

THE RED WINES OF GREECE

Greece has always been a wine-producing land. Two of the most unique aspects of the Greek vineyard are the wealth of indigenous grape varietals and the array of excellent red wines produced by this mountainous, temperate country.

The wine-making industry of today's Greece is highly progressive, and is inhabited by some of the most creative, globally minded Greeks. This force has helped reshape the Greek vineyard and re-brand the retsina-tinged image that characterized Greek wines for so long.

There are hundreds of local grape varietals, many that have existed in Greece, even by the same name, since antiquity. Some of the noblest are red varietals. The two most important native Greek red grape varietals are Xinomavro and Agiorgitiko. Xinomavro is a northern grape grown mostly in Naoussa in Macedonia, but is also vinified in other areas of Greece. This grape produces beautiful wines filled with untamed tannins that age wonderfully, bear a resemblance to the Italian Nebbiolo, and offer aficionados of the worldly, familiar Pinot Noir a unique, delicious alternative.

Xinomavro wines tend to be complex. They are filled with a range of flavors and aromas, from wild berries to sun-dried tomatoes, olives, and spices. One of the most intriguing expressions of this grape is the rosé produced in Amyndeon, a vineyard at the highest altitude in Greece, located north of the lake region, in Macedonia. Xinomavro is delicious with Greek lamb dishes, but also with game and classics like moussaka and other tomato and eggplant dishes. It pairs well with most of Greece's hard yellow cheeses, and can stand up to spicy, non-Greek cuisines with ease.

Xinomavro also thrives on the southeastern slopes of Mount Olympus, in Rapsani. Other reds also thrive there, including less-known varieties such as Krassato and Stavroto. Wines made from these grapes are redolent of ripe berries and packed with tannins, and are some of the rising stars of the Greek vineyard.

No mention of Greece's red wines would be complete without a nod to the "Blood of Hercules," as locals once called the deep red wines produced from the Agiorgitiko (St. George) grape. Agiorgitiko wines come from Nemea in the Peloponnese, an area of soft, rolling hills just two hours southeast of Athens by car.

The Agiorgitiko wines of Nemea are aromatic and velvety and range from very drinkable young wines to full-bodied vintages that age extremely well. Agiorgitiko generally has soft tannins, great body, and lively flavors full of ripe fruit. Greeks sometimes drink this red wine slightly chilled. It pairs well with fish and seafood, especially octopus and red mullet, and goes beautifully with grilled meats.

While Greek wine makers have rediscovered and experimented with their country's indigenous grapes, both red and white, producing some of the most unique single varietal wines on the planet, they have also experimented fearlessly by marrying Greek varietals with international selections to produce some of the world's most luscious blends.

Among the reds, arguably the most delicious blends are the wines that marry the Xinomavro grape with Syrah and Merlot, which tame and balance the Greek varietal's aggressive tannins, making for a very drinkable wine.

Many Greek reds, both single varietals vinified from indigenous Greek grapes, and blends of Greek and international grapes, have garnered the world's top wine prizes and are more and more available in restaurants and wine shops across the United States and Europe.

CHAPTER 13

FRUITS OF THE HARVEST

EACH YEAR IN EARLY SEPTEMBER, WE HEAD BACK TO ATHENS AFTER A BLESSED THREE-MONTH HIATUS IN IKARIA. BEFORE WE LEAVE, I CROSS THE GRAVEL PATH INTO MY NEIGHBOR TITIKA'S GARDEN TO SAY *"KALO HEIMONA"* ("HAVE A GOOD WINTER"), THE CUSTOM-ARY WAY TO SAY GOOD-BYE AT THE END OF SUMMER.

I usually find her butterflying figs and laying them out to dry on the gray stone slabs that cover the wood-burning oven, which protrudes from the side of her house. This is an end-of-summer ritual in the Greek country kitchen. In a day or two, when the figs are sufficiently dried, she will transfer them to a sheet and dry them further. Then she'll bake them and, finally, store them in muslin bags, sand-wiched together with bay leaves or oregano.

Watching her reminds me of how little some things have changed in the Greek countryside over the millennia. Drying figs and sun-drying apples, pears, and grapes (for raisins) are all occupations that country cooks, at least in the deep country villages of my ancestral island of Ikaria, have been doing forever. In prehistoric Greece, apples, pears,

and figs were all dried so they could be stored over long periods. Figs were, and still are, highly regarded because of their high nutritional value.

Today the array of preserved fruits goes well beyond raisins and dried figs. Marmalades, jams, fruit pastes—especially those with apricots and quinces—are all things that Greek country cooks make, albeit in dwindling numbers.

Of all the ways to preserve a season's bounty, however, none captures the spirit of the Greek country kitchen better than the fruit, nut, and, yes, vegetable preserves that Greeks charmingly call spoon sweets. These are the quintessential seasonal preserves put up in sugar syrup or, in some regions, grape must syrup (*petimezi*). An impressively wide variety of raw ingredients may be preserved, from the arcane to the mundane: lemon blossoms, watermelon rind, citron or bergamot rind, baby eggplant, and unripe pistachios and walnuts still soft in their shells are among the most unusual of these sweets. Oranges, lemons, sour cherries, sweet cherries, and apples are among the most common.

When it comes to Greek hospitality, spoon sweets are the confection of choice, offered to guests in one's home and unfailingly offered to visitors at monasteries. In fact, spoon sweets are often a source of income for monasteries and some are famous for their products. The Taxiarchon Monastery in the northern Peloponnese, for example, sells its rose petal spoon sweet and jam in select shops around Greece; the Chrysopigi Monastery in Hania is famous for what is arguably the most unusual Greek spoon sweet ever—potatoes put up in syrup, flavored with a little vanilla. At monasteries and in people's homes, the ritual for serving them is the same: The sweet is placed on a spoon, which is placed on a small glass or crystal plate and brought to the guest with a tall glass of cold water. They are called spoon sweets because the portion is typically not more than a heaping teaspoon.

Until a generation ago, every young woman knew how to make the full range of spoon sweets, which she learned from years of watching and helping her mother, aunts, and other female relatives make them. Country cooks and plenty of urban cooks still make the *glyka tou koutaliou*, as they're known in Greek. But for the most part, women today are too busy balancing work and family to have the time required to, say, remove the pits from 10 lb/4.5 kg of sour cherries with the eye of a needle, one of the traditional requirements for making *vyssino*, the famed Sour Cherry Spoon Sweet of Greece (page 319).

Seeing a need and a demand, small artisan producers, many of which are regional women's cooperatives, have assumed the role of keeper of the flame of tradition. Shops all around Greece sell the products of these artisans, as they do the spoon sweets prepared by a few giant Greek food companies. (The products of the latter are all too often bastardized with corn syrup, food coloring, and fruits that aren't necessarily grown in Greece but are inexpensive.)

A SHORT HISTORY OF SPOON SWEETS

Ancient Greek and Byzantine literature is filled with references to fruits preserved in honey or grape must syrup (*petimezi*)—the world's oldest sweeteners. To this day, eggplant and pumpkin rounds are still put up in grape must syrup, especially in wine-producing regions like Naoussa. The first spoon sweets as we know them, in sugar syrup, appeared in the haute Byzantine kitchen and slowly became more widespread as sugar, brought to Greek shores by Arab traders in the fourteenth century, became more readily available and economically accessible. The use of sugar later spread with the Ottoman Empire, as did so many foods. Spoon sweets are enjoyed all over the Balkans and in Turkey today.

In the sweet kitchen, spoon sweets follow the seasons: quince and apples in the fall; bitter oranges, orange rind, lemons or lemon rind, bergamot, citrons, and grapefruits in winter; strawberries, apricots, and green, unripe figs in spring; watermelon rind, plums, sweet cherries, sour cherries, and grapes in summer. Nuts are invariably preserved when immature, their shells still soft and downy. Flowers, mainly rose petals and lemon blossoms, are two of the rarest, most delicious spoon sweets.

SOUR CHERRY SPOON SWEET

GLYKO VYSSINO

MAKES ENOUGH TO FILL SIX
1-PT/480-ML JARS

Sour cherry spoon sweet is arguably the most popular of all Greek spoon sweets, even though the sour cherries that it is made with are not cultivated commercially in great quantities these days. (Cheaper foreign varieties have inundated the market.) Two regions are known for their sour cherries: Florina, in Macedonia, and Arcadia, in the Peloponnese. There are dozens of local varieties of sour cherries grown mainly for personal consumption.

2½ lb/1.2 kg sour cherries

2½ lb/1.2 kg sugar

2 cups/480 ml water

2 tbsp strained fresh lemon juice

Wash the cherries and remove their stems. Using the loop side of a hairpin, a sewing needle, or a cherry pitter, push out their pits, being careful not to squash the cherries. Reserve the pits to make liqueur (see page 320).

Spread out about a fifth of the cherries in a large pot and cover with a fifth of the sugar. Repeat, alternating between cherries and sugar until both are used up. Add the water. Cover and refrigerate for at least 8 and up to 12 hours.

Heat the sour cherry–sugar mixture over medium heat. As soon as the mixture comes to a boil, add the lemon juice. Reduce the heat to low and simmer the sour cherries and sugar for 30 to 35 minutes, skimming the foam off the surface, until the syrup is thick enough to coat the back of a spoon. Remove the pot from the heat, and let the mixture cool.

Ladle the cherries and their syrup into clean, heat-proof jars, filling each to about ½ in/12 mm from the top. Loosely screw the lid on each jar. Place in a clean pot with enough water to come about two-thirds of the way up the height of the jars. Cover and bring to a boil. Reduce the heat and simmer for 5 minutes. Using kitchen tongs, carefully remove each jar, and, using a kitchen towel, screw its lid on tightly. Immediately flip upside down. Let stand until cool. Store, well-sealed, in a cool, dark place for up to 2 months.

SWEET CHERRY SPOON SWEET

GLYKO KERASI

MAKES ENOUGH TO FILL FOUR
1-PT/480-ML JARS

May and June are the months for cherries in Greece. They flourish in the north, especially in Macedonia, where one variety, taut-skinned, ruby-red, crunchy Vodenon of Rodohori, boasts a Protected Designation of Origin status. Other great Greek cherries come from the Macedonian villages that lie between the towns of Edessa and Naoussa, as well as farther south in Agia, near Larissa.

The following recipe is my variation on the classic Sour Cherry Spoon Sweet, *vyssino*. It has less sugar, more lemon juice, and some spices.

3 lb/1.4 kg sweet cherries

2 lb/910 g sugar

1 cup/240 ml water

3 to 4 rose geranium leaves or fresh basil leaves

6 to 8 peppercorns

4 allspice berries

¼ cup/60 ml strained fresh lemon juice

Wash the cherries and remove their stems. Using the loop side of a hairpin, a sewing needle, or a cherry pitter, push out their pits, being careful not to squash the cherries. Reserve the pits to make liqueur (see page 320).

Put a quarter of the cherries in a large pot and cover with a quarter of the sugar. Repeat, alternating between cherries and sugar, until both are used up. Add the water. Let the cherries stand in the sugar for at least 8 hours, or until the sugar is almost entirely dissolved.

Add the geranium leaves, peppercorns, and allspice to the mixture and bring to a simmer over medium-low heat, but no hotter because the water will foam up and spill over the pot if the heat is too high. Simmer for 10 minutes, skimming the foam off the surface. Let the cherries stand in the syrup for 24 hours, unrefrigerated. Return to a simmer over medium-low heat and simmer for another 10 minutes, skimming the surface as needed. About 5 minutes before removing from the heat, pour in the lemon juice.

Ladle the cherries and their syrup into clean, heat-proof jars, filling each to about ½ in/12 mm from the top. Loosely screw the lid on each jar. Place in a clean pot with enough water to come about two-thirds of the way up the height of the jars. Cover and bring to a boil. Reduce the heat and simmer for 5 minutes. Using kitchen tongs, carefully remove each jar, and, using a kitchen towel, screw its lid on tightly. Immediately flip upside down. Let stand until cool. Store, well-sealed, in a cool, dark place for up to 2 months.

HOMEMADE COUNTRY LIQUEURS

My mother-in-law collects many things, among them the pits of fresh apricots, sour cherries, and plums. These, each in its time, she steeps in big, juglike bottles filled with *tsipouro* (a local firewater) or vodka. Into the mix goes some sugar, about 2 cups/400 g per 2 cups/480 ml of alcohol. She places the jugs in the sun, usually on her roof in Athens or in the garden in Ikaria, and forgets about them for about two months. The pits impart the full flavor of the fruit as they macerate all summer under the hot sun. When the first chill of winter slips through the window, homemade liqueur is her antidote.

These lovely, colorful liqueurs are made by country cooks all over Greece. In addition to my mother-in-law's choices, blackberries are a favorite, for those who have the patience to collect them from the thorny bramble.

THE GREEK ORANGE GROVE

After many years of living in Greece, I, an oak- and elm-loving New Yorker, am still in awe of the fact that bitter oranges grow on almost every street in Athens. Why bitter? Because they grow from seed, which makes them easy to plant. Sweet orange trees need to be grafted, and that would be too much to handle for city gardeners.

We once lived in a neighborhood in the foothills of Mt. Hymettus (don't imagine some bucolic oasis on the outskirts of Athens, but rather a bland area of apartment blocks and narrow sidewalks), where a surprisingly spry, apron- and kerchief-clad Greek *yiayia* (grandmother) across the way spent hours every winter day collecting bitter oranges from the neighborhood trees. To me this was the epitome of the Mediterranean, and still is exotic to my American eyes.

Greece, with its dry, sunny clime, is so ideal for the production of citrus fruits that they flourish even on polluted city streets. Citrus fruits are a major crop, and about 70 percent of the country's citrus cultivation is devoted to oranges, most of which are of the sweet, not bitter, kind. These grow mainly in Crete, the Peloponnese (especially the Argolid), and Aitoloakarnania, which is up the northwestern coast of the mainland.

Winter is citrus season, but oranges grow and are harvested for about nine months out of the year. Navels are harvested all winter, from the beginning to the end of the season. Juice oranges, with their thin skins, come next, arriving at markets throughout Greece just in time for head-cold season, in December, and lasting well through March. Actually, these make up an important part of the orange crop. Greece produces juice and sends it to Europe, where it is processed. Valencias come into the markets around March and last all summer, through September. Late navels and Lane Lates, another variety, last from March through June.

All this rather arcane information on the Greek orange calendar might seem a little too detailed for readers outside of Greece. The point is that this fruit plays an important role in the kitchen, and is in demand all year long, savored fresh, but also used in sweets, either by itself as a preserve or to lend flavor to countless cakes, festive breads, cookies, biscuits, phyllo and nut desserts, and cream desserts. And it appears in savory dishes, too, from octopus to rabbit. Oranges flavor many of Greece's cured sausages, especially those made in the Peloponnese, where orange groves flourish below snowcapped peaks. I've seen goats munching on the fallen fruit on many a road trip through the region.

ORANGE SPOON SWEET

GLYKO PORTOKALI

MAKES ENOUGH TO FILL FOUR
1-PINT/480-ML JARS

Orange Spoon Sweet is usually made like all other citrus sweets, by paring away the peel in thick pieces, blanching it, sewing it into curls then stringing them, and, finally, cooking the strung peel in sugar syrup. This recipe, which came from the kitchen of my good neighbor Titika in Ikaria, calls for something totally different. Essentially the fruit is peeled, the peel discarded, and the oranges preserved whole. It is delicious with one of Greece's many soft cheeses or with *manouri*, a buttery pressed whey cheese.

2 lb/910 g oranges with thick rinds, washed

2 lb/910 g sugar

2 cups/480 ml water

Wash the oranges and pat dry. Grate the oranges down to the white pith and reserve the grated zest for another use. You may also use a vegetable peeler to do this.

Put the peeled, whole oranges in a large pot filled with water and bring to a boil over medium-high heat. Reduce the heat and simmer for 15 minutes. Drain the oranges and put them on lint-free kitchen towels. Let stand for 8 hours or overnight. Cut each orange into wedges.

In a large pot, bring the sugar and the 2 cups/480 ml of water to a boil, reduce the heat, and simmer for 10 minutes. Add the oranges. Partially cover the pot and simmer the oranges in the syrup for about 50 minutes, or until the syrup is thick. Remove from the heat and let stand to cool completely. Transfer to 4 clean 1-pt/480-ml heat-proof jars. Screw the lids loosely on the jars and place upright in a pot large enough to hold them snugly. Add enough water to come two-thirds of the way up the height of the jars. Cover the pot, and bring to a boil. Reduce the heat and simmer for 5 minutes. Remove the jars carefully with kitchen tongs and, using a kitchen towel, tighten the lid on each jar. Flip upside down and let stand until cool. Store, well-sealed, in a cool, dark place for up to 2 months.

APRICOT SPOON SWEET

GLYKO VERIKOKO

MAKES ENOUGH TO FILL SIX
1-PT/480-ML JARS

Spoon sweets made with soft fruit such as apricots and strawberries generally require an initial first step of soaking the fruit in a wood-ash or slaked-lime solution to help firm it up and maintain its shape and texture when cooked. I decided to bypass that step to make this recipe more approachable. I've also added two things that a traditional cook may not be accustomed to: a real vanilla bean and a few fresh basil leaves, which pair perfectly with the tartness of the apricots. The end result may not be as toothsome as, say, an apricot spoon sweet in which the fruit has first been firmed in lime, but it is delicious in its own right and makes for a perfect springtime offering.

2 lb/910 g firm, slightly underripe apricots

Juice of 3 lemons, strained

2 lbs/910 g sugar

2⅔ cups/630 ml water

3 large fresh basil leaves

1 vanilla bean, halved lengthwise

Wash the apricots and pat dry. With a sharp paring knife, split the apricots in half lengthwise, and carefully remove the pits, using a dull knife or your fingernail. Put the apricot halves in a non-reactive bowl and pour the lemon juice over them. Let stand for 2 hours.

Bring the sugar and water to a boil in a pot over medium-high heat, reduce the heat, and simmer the syrup until thick and viscous, about 10 minutes. Remove from the heat and let cool.

In the meantime, drain the apricots and pat dry. Add them to the cooled, thickened syrup. Put the basil leaves and vanilla bean in the syrup, too. Bring back to a simmer and cook for 2 minutes. Remove from the heat and let stand for 8 hours or overnight. If the apricots have exuded water and made the syrup thinner, return to a boil and simmer for another 3 minutes or so at medium-high heat. Let cool.

Put the apricot sweet into 6 clean 1-pt/480-ml heat-proof jars. Screw the lids on loosely and place upright in a pot large enough to hold them snugly. Add enough water to come two-thirds of the way up the height of the jars. Cover the pot and bring to a boil. Lower the heat and simmer for 5 minutes. Remove the jars carefully with kitchen tongs and, using a kitchen towel, tighten the lids. Flip upside down and let stand until cool. Store, well-sealed, in a cool, dark place for up to 2 months.

APRICOTS AND PEACHES

Apricots are one of the harbingers of summer on the Greek country table, filling the markets with their many shades of yellow and peachy orange. The army of Alexander the Great may have brought them to Greece in the fourth century B.C. from the East. (Apricots are thought to have originated in China.) Greece's climate is supremely conducive to their cultivation, and there are many regional varieties.

The varieties provide the point of differentiation, seized upon by hawkers at every farmers' market in June and July, which is apricot season. "*Bebecou*" (*be-BE-koo*), they shout (it's the name of a common Greek variety) in loud, staccato voices, drawing out the middle syllable, while trying to draw in customers.

Most of Greece's apricots come from Halkidiki, in the north, and the Peloponnese. One of the most renowned, but a rare find, is the old, *petite kais* variety of Ikaria, which grows only in a handful of gardens nowadays. It was once was the most sought-after belle of the apricot season.

Apricots have many uses beyond their place in the fruit bowl. Dried, they make for a popular snack. And dried apricots also go into rice stuffings for turkeys, chickens, and game. The kernel of the apricot is fodder for the liqueur cabinet in Greek country homes (see page 320).

With fresh apricots, Greeks make jams and marmalades, the former a classic filling in a pastry called *pasta flora*. Fresh apricots are also sometimes pitted and stuffed with aromatic ground meat.

The temperate, sunny summers, plentiful autumn rains, and cool winters in these parts make the climate perfect for peaches. So it's no surprise that at least one, the Naoussa peach, with its bright-red skin, enjoys Protected Designation of Origin status. More than twenty varieties are cultivated there, the pink and white blossoms fluttering in the springtime breeze before the first harvest begins in June. It ends when summer does, toward the end of September.

Peaches come in many forms—yellow-fleshed, white-fleshed, clingstone, and freestone. But it is the freestone, whose halves separate from one another easily, that is the star of the local canning industry, which is formidable in the north. Greek peaches are canned at peak freshness by state-of-the-art processors.

QUINCE JAM

MARMELADA KYDONI

MAKES ENOUGH TO FILL THREE
1-CUP/240-ML JARS

Quince might have been the golden apple that Paris gave to Aphrodite, an act that led to the fall of Troy but secured this ancient fruit's place as a symbol of love almost to this day. Until not long ago, for example, newlywed couples in some parts of Greece ate a slice of quince before consummating their marriage to ensure they'd each wake up with sweet morning breath. It had a place in the marriage ceremony of the ancients, and country cooks continue to preserve it whole and fresh, by hanging it by its stems in the dark, cool house cellar. Quince, with its high pectin content, is also easily transformed into more conventional preserves, spoon sweets, and marmalades, which are among the most esteemed in the Greek sweet kitchen.

2 large quinces (about 1½ lb/680 g total)

About 2 cups/400 g sugar

2 rose geranium leaves

2 tbsp strained fresh lemon juice

Peel, core, and seed the quinces, cut into wedges, and put in a medium saucepan. Pour in just enough water to cover the quinces. Bring to a boil, reduce the heat to low, and simmer for about 25 minutes, until the quinces are so soft they are almost a purée. Drain the fruit, reserving the liquid. Measure out 3½ cups/840 ml of the liquid. For every 1 cup/240 ml of this liquid, you will need ½ cup/100 g of sugar. Set aside the liquid. Purée the quince pulp in a food processor or blender.

Return the puréed quince, its juice, and the sugar to the saucepan. Bring to a boil and add the rose geranium leaves. Reduce the heat and simmer, partially covered, for 45 to 55 minutes, until the jam is set. It will coat the back of a spoon and be thick. Add the lemon juice about 5 minutes before removing the jam from the heat. Let cool in the pot.

Spoon the jam into 3 clean 1-cup/240-ml heat-proof jars. Screw the lids very loosely on the jars. Put the jars in a small pot deep enough to hold them. Fill two-thirds of the way with water. Cover the pot, bring to a boil, reduce the heat, and simmer the jam for 5 minutes. Remove carefully with kitchen tongs and, with a kitchen towel, screw the lids very tightly onto the jars. Flip upside down and let the marmalade cool. Store in a cool, dark place.

TITIKA'S IKARIAN FRESH FIG AND PEACH JAM

MARMELADA ME SYKA KAI RODAKINA TIS TITIKAS APO TIN IKARIA

MAKES ENOUGH TO FILL FOUR
1-PINT/480-ML JARS

Titika, my neighbor in Ikaria, taught me how to make this end-of-summer treat. Her recipe is the classic one, which is to cook equal parts of fruit pulp and sugar. Figs are so innately sweet that too much sugar makes the jam unbearably cloying. I reduced the amount of sugar by about a third.

8 cups/1.4 kg coarsely chopped fresh ripe black or green figs

3 ripe, aromatic peaches, peel left on, chopped

2 cups/480 ml water

4 cups/800 g sugar, plus extra as needed

3 to 4 rose geranium leaves

⅓ cup/80 ml strained fresh lemon juice

Put the figs and peaches in a medium pot and add the water. Cover and bring to a boil over medium heat. Reduce the heat and simmer for 10 to 15 minutes, until the fruit is soft.

Transfer the contents of the pot to the bowl of a food processor and pulse to coarsely chop or, if a smooth jam is desired, purée. Pour the fruit mixture into a measuring cup. You should have approximately 6 cups/1.4 l of pulp.

Return the puréed fruit to the pot and cover with the sugar. Cover the pot and let the fruit sit and macerate the sugar for 6 to 8 hours. (You can do this in the morning and continue making the jam in the early evening, or prepare the fruit in the evening and finish the jam in the morning.)

Bring the fruit and sugar mixture to a boil over high heat, gently stirring so that the sugar is evenly distributed, which will make it easier to dissolve. Boil for 10 minutes, covered, reduce the heat to very low, and uncover the pot. Add the rose geranium leaves and simmer the jam for 25 to 30 minutes, stirring occasionally. It is ready when large bubbles break on the surface. Stir in the lemon juice and remove from the heat.

Let the jam cool in the pot. Spoon it into four clean 1-pt/480-ml heat-proof jars. Screw the lids loosely on the jar lids. Place the jars in a pot large enough to hold the jars upright and fill two-thirds of the way up the jars. Cover the pot and bring to a boil over medium-high heat. Reduce to a simmer and continue simmering for 5 minutes. Carefully remove each jar with kitchen tongs and, with a kitchen towel, tighten the lids and turn the jars upside down. Let cool and keep in a cool, dark place. The jam will keep indefinitely.

A MILLION FIG TREES

A million wild fig trees provide Greek country cooks with one of nature's most beguiling fruits. It provides the sweetest possible end to the long Greek summer, but it also keeps country cooks busy at the end of August and into early September drying this delicious, nutritious fruit, and making jams and marmalades with it. Fig spoon sweets are a Greek classic, too, but these are made in June, with a particular variety of small, firm, green, unripe fig.

Figs are one of the earliest Greek gourmet foods. Athletes ate a careful diet that included energy-boosting figs. In classical Attica, local figs were so valued, their consumption was reserved exclusively for citizens. Demand for them grew, and so did a lively illicit trade, rife with informants, known as sycophants—those who exposed the figs (from the Greek word for fig, *syko*, and *phenomai*, "to show"). Eventually, the fig trade was legalized and the fruit became an important cash crop. It still is today, bringing in an annual agricultural revenue of about twelve million euros.

In ancient times, Attica figs were especially prized, but so were those from Rhodes, Megara, Laconia, Kimolos, Chalkis, Chios, and the Asia Minor coast. There are dozens of regional Greek fig varieties, including white, black, purple, red, and green, but only about eight commercially important ones. The most famous dried figs are the figs of Kalamata, in the Peloponnese, and Taxiarches and Kymi, in Evia, the second-largest Greek island. Today, figs are processed in much the same way Greeks have been preserving them for eons: hand-picked and sun-dried for anywhere between three and twelve days, depending on the temperature and humidity. Country cooks who process their own figs usually split them open first then dry them further in the oven, to kill any bugs or eggs. As of this writing, commercial processors still use a methyl bromide solution, but are slowly phasing this out, as it damages the ozone layer. Once dipped in the solution, the figs are thoroughly rinsed and dried again sous vide. The commercially processed reddish-brown Kalamata figs are dried whole, not split, and come strung along reeds in tight garlands. The thin-skinned blond figs of Kymi and Taxiarches, which enjoy a Protected Designation of Origin status, are usually packed in small boxes.

Country cooks season their dried figs with the local herb of preference, which could be dried oregano, savory, bay leaves, sage, basil, or myrtle. Most home-processed figs are split (butterflied) and flattened, then pressed like a sandwich between herbs. Sometimes almonds are stuffed or sandwiched into these fig confections, too. These treats are usually stored in muslin bags.

There are many variations on these little dried fig treats. In Corfu, a traditional delicious confection is the local *sykomaida*: chopped figs kneaded with black pepper and ouzo and wrapped in chestnut leaves to dry. You can find them at farmers' markets on the island in October. In Chios, *mastiha* seasons dried, dark, plump local figs, which are wrapped in grape or chestnut leaves. In the Aegean islands another specialty is *pastelaries*, for which the figs are pressed with sesame seeds, walnuts, or cinnamon, among other things.

Country cooks in Crete serve dried figs dipped in grape must syrup or in whey. In Kalamata, one of the most delicious things I've ever tasted is a snack of dried figs poached in salt water and then roasted under embers—a snack to munch on during the nights of the olive harvest, when whole families gather and sit around the living room, a fire roaring, slitting open the year's fresh raw olives with a razor to prepare them for desalting.

POACHED AND ROASTED
KALAMATA FIGS

PSITA SYKA TIS KALAMATA

SERVES 12

This is a snack that home cooks in the Kalamata region make during the olive harvest. The pepper is my addition, borrowed from the custom in Corfu, an Ionian island, where figs are seasoned with pepper and ouzo.

8 cups/2 l water

3 tbsp salt

2 lb/910 g dried Greek figs, preferably dark Kalamata figs

2 tsp dried oregano

½ tsp pepper

Preheat the oven to 350°F/175°C/gas 4. Pour the water into a large pot and add the salt. Bring to a rolling boil. Add the figs and blanch for 5 minutes, or until plump and softened. Remove from the heat and drain.

Put the hot figs on a large sheet of wax or parchment paper. Sprinkle with the oregano and pepper. Wrap in the wax paper and then in aluminum foil to form a tightly closed parcel. Bake the figs for 20 minutes. Serve warm.

RAISINS IN THE SUN

Tiny black currants once were all the rage among sultans, Venetian aristocrats, and northern Europeans, who were introduced to currants after the Frankish conquest of the Peloponnese in the thirteenth century. The diminutive fruit brought down the whole Greek national economy and fostered a commercial war during the first decades of the fledgling modern Greek republic.

Currant production supported thousands of small farmers and revived the life and spirit of the Greek countryside in the early part of the nineteenth century, after the Greek War of Independence. Unlike other Greek cash crops, such as tobacco and cotton, currants were almost exclusively exported and provided one of the most important sources of income for the young republic. In the 1880s, however, foreign competition, mainly from the United States and Australia, brought the price down, and the Greek economy collapsed.

The tiny black currant, as well as the blond sultana raisin, named for Sultaniye in Iran, from whence they both come, were first imported in the ninetenth century. Today they are still among Greece's most important agricultural products. In fact, Greece produces 90 percent of the world's currants. There are two kinds: the dark, sweet, soft Corinthian variety and the Vostitsa, a smaller, dark, sweet raisin that is cultivated only in Aigio, in the northern Peloponnese.

These days not that many country cooks go to the bother of sun-drying their own grapes, a process that takes care and time and requires that the fruit be soaked in a wood ash and water solution, the preparation of which a younger generation of Greek cooks knows little about. Nevertheless, currants and raisins are the stuff of everyday snacks and festive meals, used with equal ease in savory and sweet dishes. They are munched as a snack; served with nuts as an accompaniment to liqueur and wine; tucked into breads, cookies, cakes, rusks, and biscuits; folded into puddings; tossed into both sweet and savory pie fillings; and added to the rice pilafs and rice-stuffed vegetables of the Asia Minor Greeks; and to rice stuffings for chicken, turkey, and the paschal lamb or goat. In the cuisine of the Peloponnese, raisins are a constant, even used to embellish dishes with salt cod and vegetables or add sweetness to *savoro*, a dish of small fried fish in sweet-and-sour sauce.

Raisins also sweeten *kolyva*, an ancient, ritualistic dish of boiled whole-wheat berries, fruit, and cinnamon that is offered at Orthodox Greek funerals, memorial services, and on All Souls' Day. It harks back to the ancient, pagan fruit and grain offerings made to the gods of the underworld when a person died.

CHAPTER 14

THE GREEK
SWEET TOOTH

WHILE SWEETS HAVE ALWAYS BEEN PART OF THE GREEK KITCHEN, DESSERT IS A RELATIVELY NEW DEVELOPMENT. THE MOST TYPICAL ENDING TO A MEAL IN THE COUNTRY IS A PLATE OF FRESHLY CUT SEASONAL FRUIT.

Most Greek sweets—syrupy phyllo pastries, cakes, nut-stuffed sweets, and puddings—are traditionally served either for an occasion (special cookies for Christmas, New Year's, and Easter, and cakes to mark a saint's day, for example) or at the end of the afternoon, with a cup of Greek coffee and a cold glass of water. Cakes and cookies are also morning food, and there is a whole range of hard, sweet biscuits called *voutimata*, literally "dunking cookies," to be dipped into one's morning brew.

But Greeks do, indeed, have a sweet tooth. In addition to the above-mentioned treats, there is a whole bevy of cream-based pastries from Greece's Francophile past. Things like almond cream tortes, charlottes, mille-feuilles, and more entered Greek cuisine at the turn of the nineteenth century thanks largely to the arrival of what would become one of the best-selling Greek cookbooks of all time, the cooking bible of Nikos Tselementes, whose name, in fact, became synonymous with the generic word for

cookbook. To this day, to write or read a Tselemente is to write or read a cookbook. A century ago, especially in the upper-class homes of Asia Minor and Egyptian Greeks, many of whom were literate in French and aristocratic enough to have cooks in their employ, the techniques of French and northern European pastry were sometimes used in the home kitchen. Today such pastries are by and large bought at patisseries.

Greek country sweets tend to be fairly healthful, filled with nuts and dried fruits and sweetened with honey or *petimezi*, grape must syrup. I don't attempt to cover the full range in this chapter, and I have egregiously omitted classics like baklava and other well-known confections for which recipes abound in many other cookbooks. Instead, I wanted to offer up a dessert tray of my own country favorites, which include some unusual nut-filled confections, phyllo pastries, regional cakes, and homey milk-based or sweet cheese pies.

OLIVE OIL IN THE GREEK SWEETS KITCHEN

Greek country cooks rely on olive oil for a surprising number of confections. Many evolved out of the need to create something sweet during periods of fasting, when dairy foods are forbidden. Olive oil actually helps make cake batters smooth because it acts as an emulsifier, and its antioxidant qualities work to preserve cakes and cookies, giving them a longer shelf life. Confections made with olive oil actually require less overall fat, about 25 percent less, than those made with butter, and therefore have fewer calories. And they have no saturated fat. Olive oil also helps distribute the aromatics of spices and herbs, so that the end result is fuller flavored. Greek cooks and bakers even use olive oil to brush the layers of phyllo pastry for desserts like baklava.

GREEK DESSERT WINES

Greece is a country with a long and illustrious wine-making history, and sweet wines have been a part of this tradition since at least the days of the ancient symposia. The most famous Greek dessert wines are the sweet Muscats of Samos and Lemnos, both islands in the northern Aegean, and the dark, full-bodied Mavrodafni wines from Patras, in the Peloponnese, and from Cephalonia, in the Ionian Sea. In addition, Santorini has long had a traditional elixir called Vinsanto, a delicious, almost chocolaty wine made with the sun-dried local Assyrtiko grape.

The Muscats of Samos are enjoyed either young or oak-aged. The latter are complex, luscious, aristocratic wines. I will never forget the chocolate aftertaste of a thirty-year-old, amber-colored Samos Muscat, which a friend found at auction in London. It was as long lasting on the palate as the best chocolate. The Muscats of Lemnos are more traditional and delicate.

Mavrodafni, which we knew as communion wine as kids, literally means "black laurel." It is a dark, intense wine heavy with fruit and fragrant with sweet spices and herbs. It is not a particulary tannic wine, and therefore silky on the palate and easy to drink. Most Mavrodafni comes to market early, but the aged wine is worth seeking out because the oak barreling transforms this sweet red into a very complex, spicy, almost mysterious pour.

In the last few years dessert wines have captured the imagination of Greek winemakers, and more will be coming to market. In the meantime, if you chance upon a bottle of Santorini Vinsanto, Samos Muscat, or Mavrodafni, sip with pleasure. These are still some of the most affordable aristocratic wines around.

ALMOND SHORTBREAD COOKIES

KOURAMBIEDES

========= MAKES ABOUT 48 COOKIES =========

Kourambiedes are the most traditional Christmas confections, something that is never absent in the Greek holiday home. The secret to getting the melt-in-your-mouth texture just right is to whip the butter for a good 20 minutes.

- 10 oz/300 g blanched almonds
- 2 cups/450 g unsalted butter, at room temperature
- 2 egg yolks
- 3 to 5 cups/300 to 500 g sifted confectioners' sugar
- ½ tsp baking powder
- 1 tbsp whisky or brandy
- 2 to 2½ cups/250 to 310 g sifted all-purpose flour

Preheat the oven to 350°F/175°C/gas 4. In a nonstick frying pan over low heat, lightly toast the almonds. Remove and set aside to cool. Coarsely chop the almonds.

In the bowl of an electric mixer, using the paddle attachment, beat the butter at medium-high speed for 10 minutes, until light and fluffy. Add the egg yolks, ¼ cup/20 g of confectioners' sugar, and the baking powder to the butter and continue beating at medium-high speed for another 5 minutes. Add the almonds and liquor and beat for another 5 to 7 minutes.

Remove the bowl from the mixer. Add 1½ cups/185 g of the sifted flour to the butter mixture, combine with a wooden spoon, then knead by hand in the bowl. In ¼-cup/20-g increments, add enough of the remaining flour, kneading as you go, for a total of about 8 minutes more, or until a smooth, silky, soft dough forms.

Take walnut-size pieces of dough, one at a time, and shape either into an oblong, crescent, or round. Place on an ungreased, nonstick baking sheet about 1½ in/3 cm apart. Bake for 10 to 12 minutes or until the cookies are lightly golden. Be careful not to overbake or to let the *kourambiedes* darken. Repeat with remaining dough.

Remove the baking sheet from the oven, let the *kourambiedes* cool slightly, then transfer to a wire baking rack to cool. Place the rack inside a pan and generously sift the remaining confectioners' sugar over the batch of *kourambiedes*. You can place each *kourambie* in a cookie wrapper. Store in tins in a cool, dry place for up to 1 week.

NUT-AND-HONEY COOKIES FLAVORED WITH MASTIC

MELOMAKARONA ME MASTIHA

========= MAKES ABOUT 125 COOKIES =========

Melomakarona are classic Christmas and New Year's cookies. There are many regional variations. Typically the cookie is flavored with orange and spiced with the two most popular warm winter spices, cinnamon and cloves. Many versions also call for stuffing the center with ground walnuts. In some regions *melomakarona* are fried, but in most places the cookies are baked. They are most often made with olive oil, not butter. This version, with *mastiha* (mastic), is from the island of Chios, *mastiha*'s home.

- 1½ tsp *mastiha* (mastic) crystals
- 1 cup/200 g plus 1 tsp sugar
- 3 cups/720 ml extra-virgin Greek olive oil
- 1 tbsp baking soda
- ½ cup/120 ml fresh strained orange juice
- 1 cup/240 ml water
- 11 cups/1.2 kg all-purpose flour

SYRUP
- 2 cups/480 ml Greek honey
- 1 cup/200 g sugar
- 1 cup/240 ml water
- 1 cinnamon stick
- Strained fresh juice and 1 strip of peel from 1 large lemon

- Ground cinnamon for sprinkling
- 1½ to 2 cups/170 to 230 g finely ground walnuts

Preheat the oven to 350°F/175°C/gas 4 and lightly oil several baking sheets.

Pound the *mastiha* and the 1 tsp sugar together in a small mortar with a pestle until the mixture is a fine powder. In the bowl of an electric mixer outfitted with a whisk, beat the olive oil with the 1 cup/100 g sugar at medium-high speed until creamy. Dilute the baking soda in the orange juice. Add the *mastiha*, orange juice mixture, and water to the olive oil–sugar mixture and whisk for 30 seconds. Replace the whisk attachment with the paddle attachment and add the flour, 1 cup/115 g at a time, until a soft, malleable dough takes shape. Cover with plastic wrap and let rest for 30 minutes.

Shape the dough into oblong mounds, about 2 in/5 cm long and 1 in/ 2.5 cm thick. Using the tines of a fork, prick the tops lightly to form a decorative pattern. Place on the oiled baking sheets, mounded-side up, about 2 in/5 cm apart. Bake for about 20 minutes, or until lightly browned. Remove from the oven, cool slightly in the pan, and transfer to racks to cool completely.

To make the syrup: Combine all the ingredients in a medium sauce-pan and bring to a boil. Reduce the heat and simmer for 5 minutes.

Soak the *melomakarona* in batches in the hot syrup for 5 to 10 min-utes and place on a platter. Sprinkle with the cinnamon and ground walnuts and serve.

LENTEN NUT-FILLED HALF-MOONS FROM NAXOS

SKALTSOUNIA NISTISIMA APO TIN NAXO

=== MAKES 32 PASTRIES ===

Skaltsounia are almost always a Lenten confection and are found on many of the Aegean islands. Nuts, dried fruits, almond paste, and sometimes marmalade are the fillings of choice. The size of the pastries varies from place to place. In Ikaria, for example, *skaltsounia* can be as large as a woman's hand; elsewhere they are bite-size. *Skaltsounia* are typically dusted with either confectioners' or granulated sugar. This recipe is from Naxos.

DOUGH

4 cups/450 g all-purpose flour, plus more as needed

½ tsp salt

½ tsp baking soda

½ cup/120 ml strained fresh orange juice

½ cup/120 ml extra-virgin Greek olive oil

2 tbsp Greek *tsipouro* or ouzo

½ cup/120 ml water

FILLING

⅓ cup/40 g sesame seeds

⅓ cup/30 g finely ground rusks

1⅓ cups/150 g coarsely chopped walnuts

Heaping 1 tsp ground cinnamon

¼ cup plus 1 tbsp/75 ml Greek honey

2 tbsp water

Confectioners' sugar for sprinkling

To make the dough: Combine the flour and salt in the bowl of an electric mixer outfitted with a dough hook. In a small bowl, dilute the baking soda in the orange juice. Add the juice, olive oil, *tsipouro*, and water to the flour mixture and knead with the dough hook at medium speed until a smooth, firm dough forms. Push the dough down during kneading and add more flour if necessary so that the dough is smooth and not sticky. Transfer to an oiled bowl, cover with plastic wrap, and let rest for 30 minutes.

To make the filling: In a dry nonstick frying pan over low heat, toast the sesame until lightly browned. Transfer to a mortar and grind with the pestle until coarse and mealy. Transfer the sesame seeds to a mixing bowl, and add the ground rusks, walnuts, and cinnamon. Warm the honey with the water in a small saucepan and add to the sesame and nut mixture. Toss to dampen the mix-ture throughout.

Preheat the oven to 350°F/175°C/gas 4. Cover the surface of 2 large baking sheets with parchment paper. Divide the dough into 3 balls. Lightly flour a work surface and roll out the first ball to a circle about 13 in/33 cm in diameter. Take a cookie cutter about 4 in/10 cm in diameter and cut circles out of the dough. Fill each circle with a heaping 1 tbsp of the filling. Fold closed to make a half circle. Dampen the edges lightly with a little water and press closed with the tips of your fingers or the tines of a fork. Gather up the unused dough, shape into a ball, and reroll. Repeat with the remaining dough and filling.

Place the pastries on the baking sheets about 1 in/2.5 cm apart and bake for 8 to 10 minutes, until golden. Remove from the oven, cool slightly, and sprinkle generously with confectioners' sugar. Cool completely and store in a large tin or airtight box in a cool, dry place for up to 1 week.

KYRIA TOULA'S ISLI

ISLI TIS KYRIAS TOULAS

========= MAKES ABOUT 30 PASTRIES =========

One Christmas my office assistant brought these to us as a gift. Her mother, who is an excellent traditional cook and baker, had made them. My son, age seven at the time, finished the tin, downing these delicious pastries with glasses of cold milk. Isli is basically a variation on the *melomakarona* (see page 337), but it is shaped into triangles rather than mounds, and the texture is slightly softer and more crumbly than *melomakarona*.

DOUGH

4½ cups/510 g all-purpose flour

1 tbsp baking powder

1½ cups/285 g vegetable shortening, at room temperature

¼ cup/50 g sugar

1 tbsp brandy

½ cup/120 ml strained fresh orange juice

Grated zest of 1 small orange

FILLING

1¾ cups/200 g ground walnuts

1½ tbsp sugar

Scant 1 tsp ground cinnamon

⅛ tsp ground cloves

SYRUP

2½ cups/500 g sugar

2½ cups/600 ml water

1½ tbsp corn syrup

Juice of 1 lemon, strained

To make the dough: Sift the flour and baking powder together and set aside. Line 2 large baking sheets with parchment paper. Preheat the oven to 350°F/175°C/gas 4.

In the bowl of an electric mixer, beat the shortening at high speed for 3 minutes, until fluffy. Add the sugar and beat for another 4 minutes. Lower the speed and pour in the brandy and orange juice gradually, beating all the while. Add the orange zest. Gradually add just enough of the flour–baking powder mixture to form a soft dough. There might be a 2 or 3 tbsp left over.

To make the filling: Combine the ingredients in a separate bowl.

Shape the dough into walnut-size balls. Press each ball in the palm of your hand, flattening it to form a circle. Place a scant 1½ tsp of filling in the middle. Fold in on 3 sides toward the center to shape a rounded triangle. Using a small kitchen tong or your fingers, pinch the dough tightly to secure closed. Repeat with the remaining dough and filling.

Place the pastries, seam-side down, on the prepared baking sheets about 2 in/10 cm apart and bake for about 25 minutes, until pale gold. Remove from the oven, cool for a few minutes in the pans, and transfer to wire racks.

To make the syrup: In a medium saucepan, combine all the ingredients. Bring to a boil over medium heat, reduce the heat to low, and simmer for 5 minutes.

When the *isli* are cool enough to handle, take a wooden skewer and make 4 to 6 holes on the bottom of each one. Put the *isli,* several pieces at a time, into the hot syrup and let steep for 2 to 3 minutes. Remove with a slotted spoon, and place in pastry wrappers or on a platter or tin. Cool completely and store in a cool, dry place for up to 1 week.

GREEK COUNTRY ALMOND CONFECTIONS

A hole-in-the-wall bakery opened a few years ago in central Athens that sells sweets from the tiny Dodecanese island of Leros. I remember going on the recommendation of a colleague and sending her a text message about how I had found heaven in the first bite of an almond confection. It turns out that two brothers own the shop, and their mother, Niki Kartofaki, sends them these homemade confections, among other things, several times a week from her small workshop on the island.

The almond is an important nut in the Greek country kitchen, and in the Aegean and beyond many people have almond trees in their gardens. (Almonds are cultivated commercially in Thessaly and Macedonia.) We have almond trees, too, on Ikaria. Three very old trees don't provide much edible fruit anymore, but I can't bring myself to cut them down. In the spring when they are in bloom, they are the most lovely sight.

Although we associate almonds with baklava, almond cakes, and countless biscuits and cookies, the confection that best captures their beguiling taste is the *amygdaloto* (see page 343), a simple sweet made with ground almonds, sugar, and an array of flavoring agents, from liqueurs to rose and orange blossom waters. Sometimes a home baker adds a pinch of bitter almonds, but these are forbidden in the United States because they contain poisonous hydrocyanic acid, which is neutralized when heated but can be deadly when bitter almonds are eaten raw. (Bitter almonds are sold legally in Europe.)

The best *amygdaloto* can be found on the Aegean islands. They can be made with blanched ground almonds or almond paste, are usually round or pear-shaped, and are always covered with confectioners' sugar.

ALMOND CONFECTIONS FROM LEROS

AMYGDALOTO LEROU

===== MAKES ABOUT 100 CONFECTIONS =====

The recipe below can be enclosed in pastry dough, in which case it goes by the name *poungi*, or "purse." In Leros, a pinch of bitter almond is mixed in with the blanched almonds, but bitter almonds cannot be sold in the United States.

SYRUP

2½ cups/500 g granulated sugar

2 cups/480 ml water

ALMOND CONFECTIONS

8 cups/960 g blanched almonds

8 cups/900 g dry bread crumbs

½ cup/120 ml rosewater

2 to 3 cups/200 to 300 g confectioners' sugar, as needed

To make the syrup: Put the sugar and water in a medium saucepan and bring to a simmer. Cook, stirring, over low heat for 20 to 30 minutes, until the sugar dissolves and you have a medium-thick syrup.

To make the almond confections: Finely grind the almonds in a food processor and transfer to a large bowl. If the bread crumbs are coarse, pulse in the food processor to grind more finely. Add the bread crumbs to the almonds. Slowly drizzle in the hot syrup, stirring with a wooden spoon as you pour. When the mixture is cool enough to handle, shape into 1-in/2.5-cm balls.

Dip your fingers into the rosewater and then sprinkle the rosewater over the confections. Place the confections on a deep tray and sift the confectioners' sugar over them to coat generously. Serve or store in tins in a cool, dry place for up to 1 week.

SPICED NUT AND COCONUT ROLLS FROM KASTELORIZO

STRAVA KASTELORIZOU

===== MAKES ABOUT 48 COCONUT ROLLS =====

Tiny Kastelorizo, all the way east in the southern Aegean, is one of the most physically difficult places to live, a barren, rocky speck of an island. But its small port, with its beautifully preserved buildings, is magical. Right before World War II, eighteen thousand people inhabited the island. Now barely two hundred souls live there year-round.

Strava, which means "crooked," is one of the island's specialties. It belongs to the surprisingly large array of fried baklava dishes that abound in Greece.

FILLING

1 cup/115 g coarsely ground walnuts

½ cup/60 g shredded coconut

Scant 1 tsp ground cinnamon

½ tsp grated nutmeg

½ tsp ground cloves

¼ cup/50 g sugar

1 batch Homemade Rustic Phyllo Pastry (page 224)

Olive oil for brushing the pastry

Canola or another oil for frying

3 to 4 cups/720 to 960 ml Greek honey, plus more as needed

3 to 4 rose geranium leaves

To make the filling: In a medium bowl combine the walnuts, coconut, cinnamon, nutmeg, cloves, and sugar. Mix thoroughly.

Divide the phyllo dough into 6 equal balls and set aside on a clean, floured work surface, covered with a cloth. Let rest for another 15 minutes. Have a pan lined with parchment or wax paper nearby.

Roll out the first piece of dough to a rectangular sheet, about 12 x 15 in/30.5 x 38 cm, with the long side facing you. Brush with a little olive oil. Sprinkle about 4½ tbsp of the filling along the bottom of the sheet, about ½ in/12 mm from the edge. Fold in the sides and roll up the pastry to form a fairly tight cylinder. Transfer the cylinder to a cutting board and cut into 1-in-/2.5-cm-thick rounds. Repeat with remaining pastry and filling. Keep the rounds covered with a kitchen towel.

In a large, wide, heavy pot, heat 3 in/7.5 cm of oil. It should not reach the smoking point, which for canola oil is 225°F/110°C. The oil needs to be hot, but not so hot that the pastry rounds become crisp on the outside while their interior remains raw.

Using a slotted spoon, gently slide as many pastry rounds as will fit in one layer into the hot oil. Fry over medium heat, turning to cook on all sides, until cooked through. Drain on paper towels, and let the fried rounds cool to room temperature.

In a small saucepan, warm the honey and geranium leaves. Put the fried pastries, as many as will fit in one layer, in the honey and steep for 2 to 3 minutes. Remove with a slotted spoon and place directly on a platter or in cupcake wrappers. Repeat, replenishing the honey if necessary, until all the pastries have been dipped. Store in a closed container in a cool, dry place.

PUMPKIN- AND WALNUT–FILLED PHYLLO COILS

SARAGLI ME KOLOKYTHA KAI KARYDIA

======== SERVES 8 TO 10 ========

Saragli are among the most delicious of Greece's syrup-drenched pastries—coiled confections that are usually filled with nuts and almost always flavored with cinnamon and clove. The word for this sweet comes from the Turkish *sarayli*, which means "palatial." There is no one standard recipe for them, but rather many regional variations. They may be filled with walnuts, which is the most common version; or with sesame seeds; or, as in the case of this recipe, a combination of pumpkin, walnuts, and raisins. In Thrace there are three types of *saragli*. One of them, called *orto*—the local word for "upright"—is made with very thin phyllo sheets, which are filled with nuts and spices, cut into cylinders, and baked upright.

2½ cups/190 g packed grated pumpkin

¼ cup/50 g sugar

½ cup/60 g ground walnuts

¼ cup/50 g golden sultana raisins

Scant ½ tsp ground cinnamon

13 sheets thin commercial phyllo pastry, defrosted overnight in the refrigerator and brought to room temperature

½ cup/120 ml extra-virgin Greek olive oil

SYRUP

1 cup/240 ml water

½ cup/100 g sugar

1 cinnamon stick

1½ tsp strained fresh lemon juice

One 1-in/2.5-cm strip orange peel

Put the grated pumpkin in a colander, put a plate on top, and weigh it down with some cans or another weight. Let the pumpkin drain for 1 hour. Transfer to a mixing bowl and toss with the sugar, walnuts, raisins, and cinnamon.

Lightly oil a 12-in/30.5-cm round baking pan. Preheat the oven to 325°F/165°C/gas 3. On a clean, dry work surface, place the stack of phyllo vertically in front of you. Keep covered with a dry cloth and a slightly damp cloth over that.

Take the first sheet, brush with olive oil, and spread 2 tbsp of the filling across the bottom. Fold the bottom edge of the phyllo over the filling. Take a 12-in-/30.5-cm-long knitting needle or ⅛-in-/3-mm-thick dowel and place it on the folded dough. Roll up the pastry into a cylinder and then bunch together along the knitting needle or dowel, shirring it like a curtain. Pull out the knitting needle, and place the pastry along the sides of the pan. Continue with the remaining phyllo and filling, placing the bunched-up cylinders next to one another, and working from the sides toward the center, like a coil. Brush the top with the remaining olive oil. Bake for about 1 hour and 30 minutes, or until golden and crisp.

To make the syrup: Bring the water and sugar to a boil in a saucepan. Add the cinnamon stick, lemon juice, and orange peel. Reduce the heat and simmer for 7 to 8 minutes. Remove the cinnamon stick and peel from the syrup.

When the *saragli* are ready, remove from the oven and pour the hot syrup over them, tilting the pan so that it spreads evenly. Let stand at room temperature until all the syrup has been absorbed and the pastries have cooled.

WALNUTS IN GREECE

Walnuts were a gift to ancient Greece from Persia. The word for "walnut" in Greek, *karydi*, comes from the ancient Greek word for "head," *karyon*, and is a reference to the nut's uncanny resemblance to the human brain. Walnuts have been a symbol of fertility since antiquity. When combined with honey they are considered an effective aphrodisiac!

Greece is one of the world's major walnut growers and one of the greatest consumers of walnuts. The nuts thrive in the country's mountainous regions. The best come from Mt. Pelion in Thessaly; Kalavrita and Tripoli, in the Peloponnese; and Florina, Kastoria, and Pieria, in Macedonia. There are three kinds of Greek walnuts, distinguished by their texture: light, semihard, and hard.

Walnuts are one of the most versatile nuts; Greeks use them with equal ease in both the sweet and savory kitchen, in addition to munching on them for a snack, with or without a drink. Ground walnuts are sprinkled over countless Greek cookies, biscuits, and dough fritters and are the main ingredient in the filling for baklava, *kataifi*, and other phyllo pastries. They also form the base of one of the best cakes made by country cooks in winter: *karydopita*, which is a syrupy confection.

In northern Greece, cooks use walnuts to enhance the garlic spread skordalia (see page 54), and the eggplant spread *melitzanosalata* (see page 53). At least one local sauce calls for ground walnuts as a thickener. Greek country cooks like the meaty flavor of ground walnuts and use them to replace meat in several Lenten dishes, among them an unusual ground-walnut patty (see page 76) and a savory pie with walnuts, tomatoes, and onions.

SWEET GREENS PIE FROM NAXOS

SEFOUKLOTI NAXOU

==== SERVES 8 ====

Most country cooks, and more than a few urban ones, have a strong aversion to combining sweet and savory flavors in the same dish. But *sefoukloti* is one of Naxos's most traditional recipes. It hails from the island's mountain villages, which maintain their culinary heritage well.

The name *sefoukloti* comes from the word for chard, *sefouklo*, in the local dialect. The dish is traditionally one of those "quick" snacks or meals made with leftover bread dough on the day the woman of the house lit the wood-burning oven to make the family's bread. She would take the leftover bread dough and spread out a thick layer of it on the bottom of a pan, pulling up the sides. Then she would fill the shell of dough with a combination of chard, fennel, poppy leaves, and other springtime greens. Now, in an age when baking bread at home has all but disappeared from the household routine, *sefoukloti* has morphed into a more accessible pie, made either with homemade or commercial phyllo. This version is sprinkled with honey or grape must syrup and baked, but some versions are not sweet at all, and sometimes they're fried, whether sweet or savory.

DOUGH

5 cups/575 g all-purpose flour

Scant 1 tsp salt

1 cup/240 ml strained fresh orange juice

1 cup/240 ml extra-virgin Greek olive oil

FILLING

½ cup/120 ml extra-virgin Greek olive oil

2 scallions, trimmed and finely chopped

1 lb/455 g chard, trimmed, washed, spun dry, and finely chopped

½ cup/100 g Greek Carolina or another medium-grain rice

Salt

1 tsp ground cinnamon

1 cup/240 ml water

¾ cup/50 g chopped fennel fronds

¾ cup/45 g chopped fresh dill

¾ cup/45 g chopped fresh chervil

Olive oil for brushing the pastry

1 tsp sugar

1½ tsp sesame seeds

Greek honey or grape must syrup (*petimezi*) for drizzling

To make the dough: In a large mixing bowl, stir the flour and salt together and make a well in the center. Pour the orange juice and olive oil into the middle, stir with a fork, and use the fork to stir the flour into the liquid until a dough mass forms. Shape into 2 balls and set aside, covered with plastic wrap, to rest for 30 minutes.

To make the filling: Heat the olive oil in a large, wide pot over medium-high heat, and sauté the scallions and chard, stirring, for 3 to 4 minutes, until wilted. Add the rice, salt, cinnamon, and water, and stir to combine. Bring to a boil, cover the pot, reduce the heat to low, and cook for about 15 minutes, or until there is no liquid left in the pot and the rice is almost cooked. Remove from the heat and stir in the fennel, dill, and chervil. Set aside until cool.

Preheat the oven to 350°F/175°C/gas 4. Lightly oil a 14 x 10 x 2-in/ 35.5 x 25 x 5-cm baking pan. On a lightly floured surface, roll out the first dough ball to a sheet slightly larger than the area of the pan, and transfer it to the pan. Spread the filling evenly over the bottom of the pastry. Roll out the second sheet to fit on top, without much excess dough. Take the overhanging dough from the bottom sheet and roll it in to form a thick rim around the edges of the pie.

Brush the top lightly with olive oil and sprinkle with sugar and sesame seeds. Score with a small, sharp knife into serving pieces. Bake for about 40 minutes, or until the pastry is lightly browned and crisp. Remove and cool slightly. To serve, cut into pieces and drizzle them with honey or *petimezi*.

NAXOS ALMOND CAKE

AMYGDALOPITA NAXOU

========= SERVES 10 TO 12 =========

Country cooks often have a repertoire of nut-based cakes. This syrup-soaked confection hails from Naxos.

SYRUP

1 cup/200 g sugar

1 cup/240 ml water

2 tbsp strained fresh lemon juice

1 strip lemon peel

ALMOND CAKE

7 large eggs

1½ cups/300 g sugar

½ tbsp baking soda

¼ cup/60 ml *tsipouro* or Italian grappa

¼ cup/60 ml brandy

2 cups/300 g ground blanched almonds

2½ oz/70 g barley rusks

Preheat the oven to 350°F/180°C/gas 4. Lightly oil an 11-in/28-cm round springform pan.

To make the syrup: Bring the sugar and water to a boil in a medium saucepan over medium heat. Add the lemon juice and peel and simmer the syrup for 5 minutes. Remove from the heat and set aside to cool.

To make the cake: In the bowl of an electric mixer outfitted with a whisk, beat the eggs and sugar at medium-high speed until very thick and creamy, about 10 minutes. Dilute the baking soda in the *tsipouro* or grappa. Lower the speed and add to the egg mixture. Pour in the brandy, and whisk the batter for 1 minute at medium speed.

Combine the ground almonds and rusks in a mixing bowl. Fold into the batter gradually, until well combined. The mixture will be smooth.

Pour the batter into the springform pan, spreading it out evenly with a spatula. (It will come three-quarters of the way up the pan.) Bake for about 45 minutes, or until springy and a thin knife inserted into the center comes out clean. Remove the cake from the oven and set the pan on a large round plate or tray. Pour the cold syrup over the hot cake. Let the cake sit for at least 2 hours to absorb the syrup completely. Remove from the springform pan and serve.

PORTRAIT OF A BEEKEEPER

Liza pulls up to our house at seven in the morning, driving her beat-up Toyota pickup, the vehicle of choice on Ikaria for most people whose daily routine takes them into the fields and forests. Liza has come to take me to see her beehives. "I want you to hear the bees when they graze," she says. "You will be moved. Have you ever smelled the forest early in the morning?" Indeed, I had, many times, when I was a teenager. Even the dusty dirt roads leading into Ikaria's pine forests smell of honey.

Liza stumbled into this ancient profession by chance one night as she sat chatting with Yiorgos Stenos, probably the most experienced beekeeper on Ikaria and certainly the most colorful merchant. He holds court in an ancient, red-framed general store in the heart of the village square in Christos. Liza noticed a small, mysterious little container about the size of a matchbox on Yiorgos' merchandise-strewn desk. She asked what it was, and when she learned the answer—the receptacle for transferring queen bees from one hive to another—she was, she likes to say, "stung" by a fascination with the art of beekeeping. Yiorgos became her mentor. More than a decade later she is one of the best beekeepers on the island. Greece is a producer of excellent honey. Ikaria's specialties are a delicious pine honey and a rare, buttery heather honey.

August is harvesttime for Ikarian pine honey. We set off for Pezi, a mountain plateau about 7 kilometers/ 4 miles from Christos. In the deep of this particular pine forest, she had placed her thirty or so hives, painted sky blue, to form a loose circle on a small patch of forest. Every beekeeper paints his hives a particular color to distinguish them from other hives, since several different beekeepers usually place their hives in the same area so that their bees can graze on whatever is flowering. The opening of each one faces southeast, so it will be warmed by the heat of the August sun and safe from the meltemia winds, northerly currents that sweep through the Aegean each summer.

The humming is everywhere. We had geared up in the white masks and space suits that beekeepers wear for protection, and had carefully tucked our pants inside thick socks. Only our hands were exposed. "You just need to stay calm around the bees and they won't bother with you." Liza instructs. Before approaching the hives, she fills a special canister with pine needles and sets its contents on fire. The smoke billows out in a thick fog, which she directs at the hives, to anaesthetize but also evacuate the bees.

She approaches the first hive, smokes the bees out, and opens its cap. "When you open a hive, you have to pay attention to the sound. By listening carefully, you can understand if there is a mother in there or not. When there is, the sounds are harmonious; but when the queen is missing, the humming is sharp and acrid. You can understand from the sounds if the hive is diseased or not. Beekeeping is all about paying attention," she explains.

Each hive is shaped like a box and inside are removable frames upon which bees construct their honeycomb. From Liza, I learned that every hive houses anywhere between 10,000 and 70,000 bees. The frames are covered with honeycombs, which are filled with viscous, delicious honey. These she removes, shakes free of bees, and replaces with empty frames.

Liza, who calls her brand Meliza, as a play on words (*melisa* is the Greek word for "bee"), explains calmly that each hive is a whole universe, a geometric architectural masterpiece built with astonishing precision. "You never remove all the honey, only the residuals from the sides. They reproduce in the center and they produce honey along the perimeter."

Once she's shaken out most of the honey-filled frames within the hive, the honeybees start to return. They line up like soldiers reporting for duty and enter through a tiny hole in the front. "They can smell their queen," she says, explaining that the queen remains inside.

During the day's harvest, Liza manages to clean the mature, sealed honeycomb from about thirty frames. She takes these back to her workshop and places the honeycomb in a centrifuge. By spinning the honeycomb, she frees the honey, which comes streaming out from a spout at the bottom. In the meantime, she gives me some of the honeycomb to chew on. It's delicious, like a chewing gum that literally oozes fresh honey into my mouth.

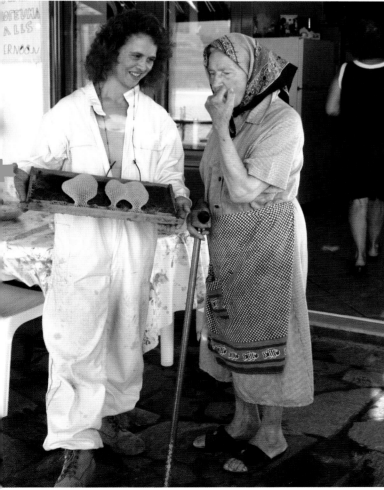

TOULA'S NEW YEAR'S CAKE

VASSILOPITA — KEIK

=========== SERVES 10 TO 12 ===========

New Year's in Greece is always celebrated with *vassilopita*, which means St. Basil's pie, a slightly confusing name, since *vassilopita* may be either a bread, savory meat pie, or cake, depending on the region. St. Basil is commemorated on New Year's Day, hence the name despite the variations. The cake always has a coin, and in rural areas sometimes a piece of hay, baked into it for good luck, which is bestowed upon the person who gets the lucky piece. The most common *vassilopitas* are the ones that resemble a brioche—puffy, egg-and-milk-laden breads flavored with orange or lemon zest and *mastiha* (mastic) or *mahlepi*, the aromatic kernel of a type of cherry. It is usually decorated with numbers indicating the new year and the words *chronia polla*, which literally means "many years," or *kaly chronia* ("happy new year") sculpted in dough, blocked out with blanched almonds, or stenciled with confectioners' sugar. This recipe for a *vassilopita* cake is from one of the best home bakers I know, Toula Foukou, who lives in Athens but hails from Naxos and carries on the island's traditional, seasonal baking in her apartment in an Athens suburb.

½ tsp *mastiha* (mastic) crystals

2 cups/400 g plus a pinch of sugar

5 large eggs, separated

½ tsp strained fresh lemon juice

1 cup/225 g unsalted butter, at room temperature

¾ cup/180 ml milk

2 tbsp brandy

Grated zest and strained juice of 1 large orange

1½ cups/150 g ground blanched almonds

2 oz/55 g couverture chocolate, finely chopped, or dark chocolate chips

4½ cups/500 g self-rising flour

1 tsp baking powder

Confectioners' sugar for sprinkling

Chocolate sprinkles or slivered almonds for decorating (optional)

Preheat the oven to 350°F/175°C/gas 4. Cut out a round piece of wax paper or parchment paper to line the bottom of a 12-in/30.5-cm round springform or conventional baking pan. Butter the surface of the paper and the walls of the pan. With a pestle, pound the mastic with the pinch sugar in a mortar. Set aside.

In the bowl of an electric mixer outfitted with a whisk, whisk the egg whites at medium speed until foamy. Add ½ cup/100 g of the sugar and the lemon juice, increase the speed to medium-high, and whisk the whites until they form a stiff meringue. Remove from the mixer bowl and set aside.

Clean the mixer bowl, attach the paddle, and beat together the butter and remaining 1½ cups/300 g sugar at medium-high speed until light and fluffy, 5 to 7 minutes. Add the egg yolks, one at a time, beating after each addition. Remove the bowl from the mixer stand and whisk in the milk, brandy, and orange juice. With a wooden spoon stir in the the orange zest, almonds, pounded mastic, and chocolate.

Sift together the flour and baking powder. Using a rubber spatula, fold the meringue and flour into the liquid mixture, a little at a time, alternating between them and stirring after each addition.

Pour the batter into the prepared baking pan. Wrap a small coin in aluminum foil and drop it into the batter, submerging it slightly with your finger. Bake the cake for 1 hour, or until a thin knife inserted into the center of the cake comes out clean. Remove the cake from the oven, cool in the pan for a few minutes, and invert onto a wire rack to cool.

Turn the cake right-side up and sift confectioners' sugar over the surface. If desired, write the number of the new year with chocolate sprinkles.

FANOUROPITA

Baking to commemorate saints is a Greek Orthodox tradition. "Christmas bread for Jesus, pancakes for Epiphany, cheese pies on Easter, and bread rings for St. Peter," goes an old saying from the Peloponnese. New Year's, the feast day of St. Basil, is celebrated with *vassilopita*, St. Basil's pie (or bread). On January 21, the feast day of St. Anthony, who is thought of as a healer, women on Crete used to bake anthropomorphic breads shaped into various body parts, as an offering for a sick loved one. St. George, whose feast day always falls after Easter and marks the great springtime migration of itinerant shepherds from the lowlands to the mountains, is celebrated in many parts of Greece with a meal that includes custard pie. The list goes on, but one stands out above all others: *fanouropita*, a raisin-spice cake made to celebrate the feast day of St. Fanourios, the saint to whom one prays for help in finding lost objects, or stolen or lost animals, or, less concretely, for help in finding the path to take in order to achieve a goal. Fanourios is from the Greek word *fanerono*, which means "to make known."

St. Fanourios's feast day is at the end of the summer, on August 27. I went to a service in a very small church in Lampsahades, a tiny village in my ancestral home, the island of Ikaria. There were about thirty people in the tiny church and about twenty cakes, which they had brought earlier and laid out on the table in front of the altar. The priest had blessed the cakes before the liturgy. The church glowed with an autumnal quality, golden beeswax candles providing the only light. The dark, amber hues of the raisin-studded St. Fanourios cakes belonged more to the fall than to the orgy of color that marks the late summer table. After church, the priest and deacon cut each cake into wedges and passed them out instead of *artos*, holy bread, to the congregation. Greek country cooks, whether they are churchgoers or not, almost always prepare this cake on the saint's feast day.

TOULA'S ST. FANOURIOS CAKE

FANOUROPITA TIS TOULAS

SERVES 8 TO 10

The Greek Orthodox say that *fanouropita* has to be made with either seven or nine ingredients. The numbers are symbolic of many things in the religious tradition. Seven is a symbol of perfection, for example, and nine stands for finality. There are many regional versions of this cake, but they all seem to contain olive oil. *Fanouropita* is usually spiced with cinnamon and cloves. Other classic flavorings include orange and lemon zest, mastic, raisins, *petimezi* (grape must syrup), walnuts, and brandy. Sometimes the cake is more like a sweet bread, made with yeast or starter, and perhaps garnished with sesame seeds or powdered sugar.

⅔ cup /110 g golden raisins

2 tbsp brandy

¾ cup/180 ml olive oil

1 cup/200 g sugar

Grated zest and strained juice of 1 large orange

¾ cup/180 ml water

4¼ cups /510 g self-rising flour

1 tsp ground cinnamon

½ tsp ground cloves

1 cup/115 g coarsely chopped walnuts

Preheat the oven to 350°F/175°C/gas 4. Lightly oil a 12-in/30.5-cm round baking pan, 3 in/7.5 cm deep. Soak the raisins in the brandy for 15 minutes.

In the bowl of an electric mixer outfitted with a whisk, whisk the olive oil and sugar together at medium-high speed until creamy. Lower the speed and add the orange zest and juice and water, and whisk to combine. Stir together the flour and spices in a large bowl. Add this to the liquid, 1 cup/240 ml at a time, stirring with a wooden spoon or whisking lightly at low speed after each addition. Stir in the nuts and brandy-soaked raisins, together with their soaking liquid.

Pour the batter into the prepared baking pan. Bake for 45 to 50 minutes, or until a thin knife inserted in the center of the cake comes out clean. Remove the cake from the oven, cool in the pan for 5 minutes, and invert onto a rack. Cool, then serve.

PAN-FRIED SEMOLINA CAKE FROM ZAKYNTHOS

FYTOURA

SERVES 10 TO 12

This simple cake from the Ionian island of Zakynthos is made much the same way as pan-fried polenta, but with sugar sprinkled over it. It is standard street fare at the religious festivals on the island, called *panigyria*, especially for the feast of a local saint, Aghia Mavra, on April 29. The cake tastes a lot like French toast and is a great breakfast treat or afternoon snack.

5 cups/1.2 l milk

2 strips lemon peel

⅓ cup/65 g sugar

1 tsp vanilla extract

1 cup/125 g fine semolina flour

2 tbsp vegetable oil

2 large eggs

Finely ground bread crumbs for dredging

Ground cinnamon for sprinkling

Confectioners' sugar for sprinkling

Preheat the oven to 375°F/190°C/gas 5. Lightly oil a large square or rectangular baking dish. In a large pot over low heat, bring the milk, lemon peel, ⅓ cup/65 g sugar, and vanilla to a simmer. Add the semolina very slowly in a thin stream, stirring constantly with a large wooden spoon. Cook, stirring constantly, until the mixture is very thick and begins to pull away from the sides of the pot, 5 to 8 minutes. Remove from the heat.

Spread out the semolina mixture in the baking dish. It should be about 1 in/2.5 cm thick. Bake until the cake sets, about 25 minutes. Remove from the oven, cool on a rack, and cut into diamond-shaped or rectangular pieces.

When the cake is completely cool, heat the vegetable oil in a large, nonstick frying pan over medium-high heat. Beat the eggs lightly in a shallow bowl. Put the bread crumbs on a plate. Dip each piece of semolina cake into the egg, and then into the bread crumbs. Fry until the crust is golden, flipping to turn and brown on the other side. Remove from the frying pan and repeat as needed until all the pieces have been fried. While the cakes are still hot, sprinkle generously with confectioners' sugar and cinnamon before serving.

BUTTERY POLENTA
WITH SPOON SWEETS

POLENTA ME GLYKA TOU KOUTALIOU

A few years ago, at a food festival in Naoussa, in Macedonia, a very earthy rendition of this dish was served as part of the buffet. It is a dessert that is decidedly rustic and hearty, but when presented elegantly it could easily be a sweet ending to a formal dinner.

4 cups/960 ml water

½ tsp salt

1 cup/150 g finely ground yellow cornmeal

½ cup/100 g sugar

1 tsp finely grated orange or lemon zest

½ cup/120 g unsalted butter, melted

1½ cups/360 ml Orange Spoon Sweet (page 323), Quince Jam (page 325), or another spoon sweet of your choice

Fresh mint leaves for garnish

Bring the water and salt to a rolling boil in a medium saucepan. Immediately stir in the cornmeal in a slow, steady stream, whisking constantly. Reduce the heat to medium-low and add the sugar, orange zest, and ¼ cup/60g of the butter. Cook, stirring constantly, until the sugar dissolves and the mixture starts to come away from the sides of the pan, about 40 minutes. Remove from the heat and cool completely.

Dip 2 tablespoons into the remaining ¼ cup/60g melted butter and scoop out a heaping spoonful of the cornmeal, shaping it with the spoons. Place 3 such mounds on each dessert plate or spoon them all onto a platter.

Top the polenta mounds with the spoon sweets. Drizzle some of the syrup from the spoon sweet on top. Garnish with fresh mint leaves and serve immediately.

HALVA WITH HONEY

HALVAS ME MELI

Stove-top semolina halvas, such as this recipe, are pretty standard fare, known to all Greek home cooks as one-two-three (one part semolina, two parts sugar, three parts water). This is my favorite version. It comes from Crete, where honey is used in combination with sugar.

SYRUP

2 cups/400 g sugar

1 cup/240 ml Greek honey

3½ cups/840 ml water

1 cinnamon stick

1 strip of orange peel

HALVA

1 cup/240 ml extra-virgin Greek olive oil

2 cups/350 g coarse semolina flour

1 cup/120 g blanched almonds, lightly toasted

½ cup/100 g golden sultana or dark seedless raisins

Scant 1 tsp ground cinnamon

Ground cinnamon for garnish

Lightly oil an 8-in/20-cm ring mold.

To make the syrup: Combine the sugar, honey, and water in a saucepan and bring to a simmer over low heat, stirring occasionally until the sugar and honey have dissolved. Add the cinnamon stick and orange peel and simmer together for about 8 minutes, to make a loose syrup. Remove from the heat and set aside.

To make the halva: Heat the olive oil in a large, wide pot over medium heat, and add the semolina. Cook, stirring, until the semolina begins to brown lightly, as if you were making a roux. Add the almonds, raisins, and cinnamon and stir to blend well.

Remove the cinnamon and orange peel from the syrup with a slotted spoon. Carefully pour the syrup into the pot in a slow, steady stream, stirring all the while so that the semolina absorbs it all. Reduce the heat to medium-low and cook, stirring constantly, for 20 to 25 minutes, or until the mixture turns a medium golden color and pulls away from the sides of the pot. Remove from the heat, transfer to the ring mold, and cool for several hours.

Invert the ring mold onto a serving platter and carefully tap the top to loosen the halva. Remove the mold. Sprinkle the halva with cinnamon and serve.

HALVA

In Greece there are two basic types of halva: the bricks of tahini-based halva and the homespun versions that are essentially flour pastes sweetened with sugar syrup. While the homespun stuff is hearty, rustic fare, the brick variety requires years of skill to perfect. The sesame-paste halva arrived in Greece in 1922 with a family from Asia Minor whose name has since become synonymous with the sweet: Haitoglou. They christened the product Makedonikos, after Macedonia, which is how Greeks know it today.

In the Athens area, arguably the most famous halva maker is Kosmidis, another Greek family with roots in Asia Minor. Their workshop is not exactly state of the art the way I imagined it, but rather a hot, sticky, noisy place from which the company's famous halva is produced and shipped all over greater Attica and beyond.

Makedonikos halvas start with tahini and sugar or sugar syrup, which the master craftsman cooks to a paste in a huge copper vat. After that, he kneads the mixture by hand until it starts to cool. Just before it cools completely, he adds extras like almonds, hazelnuts, cocoa, chocolate, or dried fruit. Fresh halva is deliciously fibrous from the strands of warm sugar paste.

Homemade versions of halva are basically simple sweets made with some sort of flour base, such as coarse semolina or rice flour. Flour-based halva, sweetened with either grape must syrup or honey, dates to at least the Byzantine era.

There are plenty of regional variations of Greek halva. The most obscure are cheese-based halvas—almost like primitive fondues—found in some parts of northern Greece as well as on several Aegean islands. The grain-based halvas of Thessaly, Greece's grain belt, are also fascinating. In one version, called *sousamohalva*, wheat starch is mixed with chickpeas, tahini, and sugar. There is also the smooth, glistening halva, *sapoune*, otherwise known as *Farsalon* (from Farsala, in Thessaly), which is made with rice four and has a characteristic burnt-sugar crust. There is the hard, white *kommat halvas*, very similar to nougat, which is studded with walnuts, and is found in bakeries in Salonika.

YIOULA'S DOUGH FRITTERS DRIZZLED WITH HONEY

YIOULA'S LOUKOUMADES

========= MAKES ABOUT 12 =========

Loukoumades are essentially Greek doughnuts, with or without a hole. Two women, both on the island of Ikaria, taught me how to make these irresistible dough fritters. Yioula, a good friend, is one of them. *Loukoumades* are always drizzled with honey, sprinkled with cinnamon, and, of course, served warm.

These fried puffs are the dessert of choice on the name day of St. Andreas (Andrew), which falls on November 30. Fried, dough-based sweets are a traditional celebratory food. In fact, according to tradition, if one doesn't fry something, anything, on this day, the frying pan will end up with holes in it. Most people with an Andrew in the family make *loukoumades*.

The secret, according to Yioula, whose *loukoumades* are the best I have ever tasted, is not to let the yeasty batter sit for too short or too long a time. The former will make for a puff that is too dense, and the latter will make *loukoumades* that have fermented too much and smell slightly alcoholic.

HONEY SYRUP

1 cup/240 ml Greek pine or thyme honey

1 cup/240 ml water

2 cups/400 g sugar

DOUGH FRITTERS

1 package (¼ oz/7 g) active dry yeast

3 cups/720 ml warm water

1 cup/240 ml warm milk

2 pinches of salt

2 large eggs, well beaten

Flour as needed

Canola, corn, or sunflower oil for frying

Ground cinnamon for sprinkling

To make the syrup: Combine the honey, water, and sugar in a large saucepan. Bring to a boil over medium heat, reduce the heat, and simmer for 10 to 12 minutes, until thick. Set aside.

To make the fritters: In a large bowl, preferably ceramic, dilute the yeast in 1 cup of the warm water. Stir and set aside until it begins to bubble up. Add the remaining water and milk and stir. Add the salt and eggs and begin adding the flour, stirring with a wooden spoon, until a thick, sticky, yeasty batter forms. Cover the bowl with a kitchen towel. Put the bowl in a warm, draft-free place and let the dough rise until more than double in bulk, loose and almost foamy in texture. This will take about 1 hour. Stir it down and mix well.

Heat 3 in/7.5 cm of oil in a large, deep pot until almost smoking. Use two tablespoons to scoop up some dough and carefully drop it into the oil. Repeat to fry several *loukoumades* at a time, without crowding the pan. Fry for a few seconds until golden, remove with a slotted spoon, and drain on paper towels. Continue cooking the fritters in this way, allowing the oil to heat up between batches, until all the batter is used up. Replenish the oil if necessary.

Using a slotted spoon, dip the *loukoumades* into the syrup, place on a platter, and sprinkle with cinnamon. Serve hot.

MASTIHA—GREECE'S MOST SEDUCTIVE SPICE

Mastiha (mastic) is crystallized tree resin from a scrubby tree, *Pistachia lentiscus*, and is one of the most beguiling substances in the world. Greeks have always revered *mastiha* for its dual personality—as a spice, but also as a salve for ailments of the stomach (such as ulcers) and mouth. It is a natural chewing gum and the root of our own word "masticate" derives from this tasty ancient resin.

Mastiha comes from one and only one place: Chios, an island in the northeastern Aegean where the mastic tree has been a source of tremendous wealth for many centuries. It is cultivated in twenty-four "mastic" towns, which are architectural jewels on the southern side of the island. I, like most Greek home cooks, have been using *mastiha* in my home kitchen for years, mostly in breads and cookies, its most traditional uses. I've discovered, by experimenting, that *mastiha* pairs beautifully with a wide range of foods, including white, milk, and dark chocolate; sweet and savory citrus dishes; tomato and white wine sauces; and even fish. *Kaimaki* ice cream, an Anatolian and Greek classic, is flavored with mastic, which also lends it a unique, chewy texture. *Mastiha* is, to me, the ultimate Mediterranean spice, able to insinuate itself harmoniously into so many different dishes. But despite its versatility, *mastiha* must be used with care because if you use too much, it leaves a bitter aftertaste.

The process of gathering *mastiha* is a sight to behold and one worth traveling for. Each June, workers prepare the ground beneath the trees, clearing it for the harvest and spreading a fine layer of pulverized marble, as powdery as dust, under the trees to help keep the mastic free of debris as it falls to the ground. Extracting the sap takes time and skill. During June and July, trained workers slit the trees in several places, making it easy for the viscous sap to drip out and fall onto the prepared ground below. The "tears" drop and harden immediately into crystals of various sizes. When the harvest actually begins in August and September, the *mastiha* crystals are separated by size.

The *mastiha* tree is low-lying and craggy, with a canopy of small, dark green leaves that spreads out like an umbrella. An average tree yields a piddling amount of *mastiha*, somewhere between 5 and 7 ounces/140 to 200 grams a year, and it takes about five years for a young tree to start producing any resin at all.

HOW TO USE MASTIHA

In the United States, *mastiha* is available at Greek and Middle Eastern markets and also at the Mastiha-shop in New York City. It is mainly sold in crystal form, although it is also sold as a powder, an oil, and an infused water. The crystals come in several sizes. The small ones are best for cooking and baking, because they do not stick together when pounded with sugar or salt. The medium-size crystals are sold both as a spice and as a natural gum. They are big enough to chew on without having them stick to one's teeth, yet small enough to be pounded into granules like ground glass and used in baking and cooking. The large crystals, which are referred to as *pita* ("pie"), are often used in the drinks industry, especially in the production of distilled alcoholic beverages. These, with their large surface area, impart the most flavor and are softest and stickiest.

The crystals need to be pounded with a little sugar for sweets or salt for savory dishes in a mortar with a pestle (they will stick to the blades of an electric spice grinder). The best guide for determining how much to use is usually your own palate. Best to start with less than to use too much and risk overpowering a dish, or, worse, making it bitter.

CHEESE-AND-MASTIC PASTRIES FROM LESVOS

YIOUZLEMEDES APO TIN LESVO

===== MAKES ABOUT 30 PASTRIES =====

In Roumeli, in the center of Greece's mainland, *yiouzlemedes* are savory cheese-filled pastries. In Lesvos, on the other hand, the pastries are sweet and deliciously excessive. They are stuffed with cheese and mastic and sometimes sprinkled with still more cheese and ground mastic.

SYRUP

1½ cups/360 ml water

1½ cups/300 g sugar

2 tsp strained fresh lemon juice

PASTRY

2 to 2½ cups/225 to 280 g all-purpose flour, as needed

½ tsp salt

½ cup/120 ml water, plus extra as needed

2 tbsp extra-virgin Greek olive oil

FILLING

1 large egg, lightly beaten

1 cup/225 g crumbled fresh *myzithra* cheese

½ tsp ground cinnamon

¼ tsp *mastiha* (mastic) crystals

¼ tsp sugar

Olive oil or another vegetable oil for frying

½ cup/115 g finely crumbled fresh *myzithra* or *anthotyro* cheese

Ground cinnamon

To make the syrup: Combine the water and sugar in a medium saucepan and heat over medium heat. As soon as the syrup begins to boil, reduce the heat to medium-low, add the lemon juice, and simmer for 10 minutes. Remove from the heat, set aside, and let cool.

To make the pastry: In a medium bowl, combine 2 cups/225 g of the flour and the salt. Make a well in the center of the flour and pour the water and olive oil into the well. Little by little mix the flour into the liquid. Knead by hand, either in the bowl or on a floured work surface, until a stiff, smooth dough forms. This will take about 10 minutes. Add a little more flour or water if necessary during kneading if the dough seems either too loose and sticky or too stiff. The pastry may also be made in the bowl of an electric mixer outfitted with a dough hook.

To make the filling: Combine the egg and cheese in a small bowl and mix in the cinnamon. In a mortar with a pestle, pound the mastic with the sugar. Stir into the filling.

Divide the pastry dough into 2 balls. Lightly flour a work surface. Pat down the first ball and roll it out with a lightly floured rolling pin to a circle about 20 in/50 cm in diameter. Using a glass or round cookie cutter about 3 in/7.5 cm in diameter, cut circles out of the dough. Place 1 tsp of the filling on each circle, then fold over to form a half-moon. Pat down the edges with your fingertips or more decoratively with a fork to seal. Collect the remaining dough, knead it, and roll it out again. Continue cutting out circles and filling them until the dough and filling are used up.

Heat about 2 in/5 cm of oil in a large, heavy frying pan over medium-high heat. When the oil is very hot, fry the *yiouzlemedes,* a few at a time, in the hot oil, turning once, until golden on both sides. Remove with a slotted spoon and let drain on paper towels. Place on a large serving platter and drizzle generously with the sugar syrup. Dot with the crumbled cheese and sprinkle with cinnamon. Serve immediately.

PHYLLO PASTRY WITH CREAM

BOUGATSA

===== SERVES 8 =====

Bougatsa is a thin phyllo pastry that is usually sweet, but sometimes savory. Although it is made all over Greece, the best comes from four places: Thessaloniki and Serres, in Macedonia, and Heraklion and Chania, in Crete. To a northern Greek, *bougatsa* is almost synonymous with "pie," sweet or savory. Macedonian *bougatsa* is filled with cream, cheese, potatoes, ground meat, or spinach. Serres is famous among *bougatsa* connoisseurs for the especially thin, crisp phyllo that envelops the filling. There has even been an attempt in recent years to certify the town's *bougatsa* as a Protected Designation of Origin product. In Crete, *bougatsa* is filled with either pastry cream, like this recipe, or with the deliciously sour Cretan soft cheese, *xinomyzithra*. Both versions are dusted with confectioners' sugar and cinnamon.

The word *bougatsa* comes from the Turkish *boğaça*, a transliteration of the Italian *focaccia*, which itself comes from the Latin *focācius*, a bread baked in embers. It arrived in Greece from Constantinople with the wave of a million or so displaced refugees in the early part of the twentieth century. By 1917, the federation of *bougatsa* makers had already been established in Thessaloniki, and within two years it counted fifty-one members. After 1922, with the massive wave of Asia Minor Greeks reaching Greek shores, this delicious pastry made its way across the country.

PASTRY CREAM

2 tbsp unsalted butter

1 cup/125 g fine semolina flour

6 cups/1.4 l milk

½ cup/100 g sugar

1 tsp vanilla extract

3 eggs, lightly beaten

1 lb/455 g commercial phyllo, defrosted overnight in the refrigerator and brought to room temperature

½ cup/115 g unsalted butter, melted

3 tbsp sugar

½ tsp cinnamon

To make the pastry cream: Melt the butter over medium heat in a wide pot. As soon as it melts and the bubbles have subsided, add the semolina. Cook, whisking constantly, until lightly browned, about 7 minutes. Pour in the milk in a slow, steady stream, whisking all the while. Add the sugar and vanilla and continue cooking, stirring all the while, until the sugar dissolves. Remove from the heat and whisk in the eggs vigorously. Set aside.

Lightly butter a 14 x 9-in/35.5 x 23-cm baking pan. Preheat the oven to 350°F/175°C/gas 4. Spread 5 sheets of phyllo on the bottom of the pan, one at a time, brushing each one with melted butter. Using a spatula, spread the pastry cream evenly over the phyllo. Top with 4 more phyllo sheets, brushing each one with butter.

With a sharp knife, score the phyllo into 8 serving pieces, and sprinkle the sugar and cinnamon over the surface. Bake for about 40 minutes, or until the filling is set and the phyllo is crisp and lightly browned. Check on the *bougatsa* while it's baking. If the surface is browning too quickly, cover it loosely with aluminum foil. Remove from the oven, cool, and serve.

MASTIHA-FLAVORED YOGURT CHEESECAKE

TZIZKEIK ME MASTIHA

Sweet cheese pastries flavored with *mastiha* are common all over the Aegean, especially in spring and around Easter. We used to make this cake at Villa Thanassi, a small country restaurant I ran with my husband for a few summers in a small village on the island of Ikaria.

1¾ cups/140 g crumbled speculaas cookies (also called Dutch windmill cookies) or other cinnamon-flavored cookies

3 tbsp unsalted butter, melted

1 tsp *mastiha* (mastic) crystals

1 cup/200 g plus 1 tsp sugar

6 large egg whites

4 oz/110 g fresh Greek *anthotyro* or ricotta cheese, very well drained

12 oz/340 g cream cheese

2 tsp vanilla extract

Pinch of salt

3 cups/720 ml thick Greek yogurt

Greek honey, Orange Spoon Sweet (page 323), or another Greek spoon sweet for serving (optional)

Preheat the oven to 375°F/190°C/gas 5.

Mix together the cookie crumbs and melted butter in a bowl. Press into the bottom and up the sides of a 9-in/23-cm springform pan. Place in the refrigerator until ready to use. With a mortar and pestle, grind the mastic crystals with the 1 tsp sugar.

In the bowl of an electric mixer outfitted with a whisk, whisk together the egg whites, *anthotyro*, cream cheese, remaining 1 cup/200 g sugar, vanilla, ground *mastiha*, and salt. Add the yogurt and mix to combine. Pour the mixture into the prepared pan and bake for 35 to 45 minutes, or until set. The filling will still be a little wobbly in the center.

Remove the cheesecake from the oven and let stand at room temperature for 1 hour. If desired, spread the top with the spoon sweet. Refrigerate until the cheesecake has set completely then remove from the pan and serve. Alternatively, cut the plain chilled cheesecake into wedges and drizzle each one generously with honey.

GRAVIERA TART WITH RAISINS

TARTA ME GRAVIERA KAI STAFIDES

This recipe was inspired by one of my favorite creations from the stellar Greek pastry chef Stelios Parliaros.

DOUGH

2½ cups/280 g all-purpose flour

½ tsp salt

1 tsp sugar

1 cup/225 g cold unsalted butter, cut into pieces

¼ to ½ cup/60 to 120 ml cold water

FILLING

2 medium eggs

½ cup/100 g sugar

½ cup /200 g grated *graviera* cheese

¾ cup/200 ml heavy cream

½ cup/100 g golden sultana raisins

½ tsp ground cinnamon

¼ tsp pepper

Preheat the oven to 350°F/175 °C/gas 4.

To make the dough: Combine the flour, salt, and sugar in a large bowl. Add the cold butter and rub the mixture quickly between your fingers until you have small granules. Add the ¼ cup/60 ml water, and mix and knead well until a dough mass is formed, adding more water as needed. Cover with plastic wrap and let the dough rest in the refrigerator for 1 hour.

Using a rolling pin, roll out the dough on a floured work surface into a thin circle, slightly bigger than the surface of a 9-in/22-cm round tart pan. Transfer the dough to the pan. Cover with aluminum foil and spread pie weights or dried beans on top. Bake for 15 minutes, or until pale gold. Remove from the oven, and remove the weights and the foil from the tart shell. Leave the oven on.

To make the filling: With an electric mixer, beat the eggs, sugar, and cheese together in a large bowl until creamy. Add the cream, raisins, cinnamon, and pepper and mix until well blended.

Pour the filling over the prebaked tart shell, return to the oven, and bake for another 35 to 40 minutes. Remove from the oven, let cool slightly, and serve.

GREEK CHEESE

In the last few years, cheeses have begun to acquire protected status based on the strength of their traditional methods of production and their ties to a particular place. This system, which may be familiar to Americans because for decades it has also been applied to European wines, is called the Protected Designation of Origin (PDO). Twenty Greek cheeses have acquired this status, ensuring that no other EU country can produce the same cheese by the same name.

Since there are too many Greek cheeses to list here in detail, I have concentrated on those with a PDO and on a few unique Greek island cheeses that are my personal favorites. There are online sources for Greek artisan cheeses. Some of them, especially the most well known of these cheeses, are widely available in American supermarkets, specialty cheese shops, and Greek and Middle Eastern food stores.

SOFT PDO CHEESES

Greece's soft, fermented cheeses are refreshingly sour, spreadable, and fine-grained. They have a very long history in Greece, dating, by some accounts, to Neolithic times. The majority of these cheeses are produced from goat's and sheep's milk. Some are made with cow's milk.

Soft cheeses are usually produced in the summer, just after the lactation period for goats and ewes ends. That's when the milk is rich in solids and the weather is warm enough to expedite their natural fermentation. In other words, the milk is left to sour on its own and then ferment over a period of days or weeks. Some of these cheeses acquire either a pinkish or bluish hue, depending on the strain of bacteria that blooms. To a great extent, though, their flavors reflect the natural *terroir* of each region where they are produced. They are delicious with fresh summer vegetables, especially garden tomatoes, and spread over bread or *paximadia*. The following cheeses fall into the PDO category:

ANEVATO (*a-neh-vah-TOH*) is a goat's milk cheese produced in the towns of Grevena and Kozani, in western Macedonia. The cheese has a pinkish hue and is exceedingly sharp, in both flavor and aroma. It is a spreadable table cheese, sometimes eaten with fruit, and it's also used in savory pies. To make *anevato*, the milk is heated slightly, cooled, and left to sour and acquire the desired acidity. Then the milk is reheated, coagulated with rennet, drained, and salted. It's aged for at least two months.

GALOTYRI (*gah-loh-TEE-ree*), a very old, traditional shepherd's cheese, is similar in flavor and texture to *anevato*, and is made exclusively in Epirus and Thessaly, the traditional shepherds' strongholds of northwestern and central Greece, respectively. *Galotyri* literally means "milk cheese." It is a soft, creamy, pungent, spreadable cheese with a grainy, curdlike texture. The curds are incorporated into a very thick and creamy mass, which is why the cheese is served with a spoon. *Galotyri* is made in late summer. After the milk is heated, it is left to sour and thicken on its own for three months, encouraged by the season's high temperatures.

KATIKI DOMOKOU (*kah-TEE-kee doh-moh-KOO*), from Domoko, in central Greece, is smoother and more finely grained than similar cheeses, and it has a mildly sour taste. The milk is heated, cooled, and left to rest over several days while it sours and thickens naturally. It is then drained in cheesecloth until it reaches a moisture content of around 60 percent, at which point it is ready for consumption.

KOPANISTI (*koh-pah-nee-STEE*) is produced mainly in the Cyclades islands of Mykonos, Tinos, and Syros. It is grainier, saltier, more peppery, and more complex than the soft, naturally fermented cheeses of the Greek mainland. Cyclades *kopanisti* can be either yellow-white, pinkish, or even slightly blue. The cheese is usually made with unpasteurized sheep's, cow's, or goat's milk (or a combination thereof). It is left to dry in the sun, forming a mold on the outside, which is kneaded into the cheese. *Kopanisti* has a "dirty sock" or Roquefort-like aroma and a very piquant taste. It is eaten as a table cheese, and goes exceptionally well with strong Greek alcoholic beverages, such as ouzo. Unfortunately, *kopanisti* is difficult to obtain outside of Greece.

PYCHTOGALO HANION (*pee-TOH-gah-loh hah-NEE-on*) translates literally as "thick milk from Hania," the region in western Crete where it is exclusively produced from sheep's milk or a combination of sheep's and goat's milk. Unlike other soft, fermented cheeses, *pychtogalo* is not aged. The milk is heated slightly, coagulated with natural rennet (culled from the intestines of milk-fed lambs and goats), and left to sour. Then it's drained and salted and ready to eat, all within a few days. The cheese has a sour taste and a smooth texture that resembles yogurt, and a distinctive milky, lactic aroma. It is spread on bread for a snack and is also included in savory pies made with greens and meat.

XINOMYZITHRA (*zee-noh-mee-ZEE-thra*) is a whey cheese from Crete that is quite sour and sharp, but low in butterfat. It is produced from either sheep's or goat's whey. The whey is enriched with whole milk, then heated until curds blossom on the surface. These are collected, strained, salted, and kneaded. Then the curds are strained again, this time for about a week in cheesecloth. Next the mass, which has turned acidic and sharp, is pressed into small barrels or clay jugs to ripen and sharpen even more. *Xinomyzithra* has a rather dry and grainy texture and a lovely peppery taste. It's used in some of Crete's many savory pies and its honey-drizzled cheese pies.

FETA AND OTHER PDO BRINE CHEESES

FETA, which means "wedge" or "slice," is the national cheese of Greece. In fact, 70 percent of the cheese consumed in Greece is feta. From the mid-nineteenth century until the early 1960s, feta was aged in barrels. However, because of commercial shipping considerations, most of the cheese is now aged in tins, which fit more easily into the hulls of ships and into large shipping containers.

Feta finally won the coveted PDO status in 2002 and legally may be produced only in central mainland Greece and in Lesvos, Macedonia, the Peloponnese, Thessaly, and Thrace. By law, feta must be made from sheep's milk or a combination of sheep's and goat's milk (up to 30 percent goat's milk is legally allowed). The cheese can only be made with the milk of local animals in one of the designated regions.

Feta can be hard or soft, creamy or crisp, depending on the cheese maker's preference and style, the time of year the cheese is produced, and whether the animals have fed on clover, wild grasses, or grains. Some feta is mild in flavor, while others are sharp and peppery or sour. There are some obvious regional variations: Feta from the Peloponnese tends to be harder, drier, and saltier than cheese made in Thessaly. Feta from Macedonia tends to be creamy and mild. Regardless of texture and tang, good Greek feta should always be solid, with a glistening surface and a complex flavor that suggests both fresh milk and the cultures that helped create the cheese.

BATSOS (BAHT-sos), named for the thatched mountain hut in which itinerant Vlach shepherds used to produce the cheese, is a low-fat, hard or semihard, rindless cheese produced from unpasteurized sheep's milk or a combination of sheep's and goat's milk. It's aged in brine for at least six months. Although salty and dry, the cheese is transformed in the skillet, which is how it is usually eaten, pan-fried in a little olive oil or butter.

KALATHAKI LIMNOU (kah-lah-THAH-kee LEE-mnoo), a goat's milk cheese from the northern Aegean island of Limnos, resembles feta in flavor but not in shape: It is formed in baskets (*kalathi* in Greek, hence its name) and comes in 2-pound/1-kilo heads. Kalathi Limnou tends to have a more pronounced sourness than feta.

SFELA (SFEH-luh), from Kalamata and its environs, is a dense, salty, block-shaped brined cheese. Its compact texture is a result of reheating the curds after they have been cut. *Sfela* is excellent on the grill.

TELEMES (teh-leh-MESS) is a soft, white, brine-aged cheese similar to feta. But unlike feta, *telemes* is always aged in tins. Although by law it can be made with cow's milk, it is usually made with a combination of cow's, sheep's, and goat's milk. *Telemes* is produced in Thrace, Macedonia, Epirus, Thessaly, central Greece, and the Peloponnese.

PDO YELLOW CHEESES

GRAVIERA (grah-vee-AYR-uh) refers to a large group of natural-rind hard cheeses. *Graviera* was first produced at the beginning of the nineteenth century, when Nikos Zigouris, the head cheese maker at the royal estate in the Peloponnesse, was faced with a surplus of sheep's milk. Nikos experimented with the milk, and the result was a cheese in the style of Swiss Gruyère, from which *graviera* gets its name.

Graviera is produced in many regions of Greece, but only three regional *gravieras* have a PDO: those of Agrafa (on the western mainland), Crete, and Naxos. Agrafa *graviera* is the hardest and driest of the three PDO cheeses. It is pale yellow, with small, irregular holes and a mild, nutty, buttery flavor. It is made from unpasteurized sheep's milk or a combination of sheep's and goat's milk.

Cretan *graviera* is made almost exclusively with sheep's milk. The best is produced in the spring, when the flora is thick and rich. Traditionally this cheese was aged in mountain caves, a custom that still survives among some local cheese makers. Cretan *graviera* has a dense, natural rind and few holes. It is usually sweet and mellow, with a faint aftertaste of almonds, although aged Cretan graviera can be very sharp and peppery. The cheese goes exceptionally well with the island's famed thyme honey, with which it is often paired.

The *graviera* from Naxos (as well as the non-PDO *graviera* of Tinos) is produced with cow's milk, from a breed of cows brought to Greece by Venetian overlords in the sixteenth century. The cows eventually evolved into a thin, local species especially suited to the islands' rough terrains. This *graviera* has a pronounced yellow color and peppery flavor. Naxos *graviera* is delicious with winter fruits such as apples and pears.

KASSERI (kah-SEH-ree) was first produced by shepherds in the Pindus Mountains at the beginning of the nineteenth century. It belongs to the family of kneaded cheeses, like mozzarella. Traditional kasseri is made by working the warmed, malleable curd to just the right consistency before forming the cheese into 20-pound/9-kilo heads. Its texture is distinct—semihard and pliable. There is no rind on kasseri.

PDO kasseri is produced in Xanthi (a city in Thrace), Macedonia, Thessaly, and on the island of Lesvos. The best kasseri is from 100 percent sheep's milk, although goat's milk and up to 10 percent cow's milk may also be added. A good kasseri is complex and buttery, with mellow, faintly sweet flavors. It's a great table cheese, especially well suited for full-bodied white wines. It is used in savory pies and on Greek pizza dishes. Because of its pliant texture, it melts very well.

KEFALOGRAVIERA (keh-fah-loh-grah-vee-AYR-ah), made in western Macedonia, Epirus, and Aitoloakarnania, on the western coast of mainland Greece, is a hard, salty, intensely flavored cheese. It is made with a mixture of cow's milk and sheep's milk, at about a 60-to-40 ratio; or exclusively with sheep's milk; or with a combination of sheep's and goat's milk (the goat's milk can't exceed more than 20 percent of the total). It is one of the newest Greek cheeses, first produced in Dodoni, in Epirus, in 1967. As the name suggests, it is a kind of hybrid between *kefalotyri* (see following) and *graviera*.

Kefalograviera is used mainly as a grating cheese and table cheese, and is delicious with strong Greek spirits and full-bodied red wines. It is also excellent in gratins and savory pies.

KEFALOTYRI (keh-fah-loh-TEE-ree) is one of the oldest cheeses in Greece and the most traditional hard cheese. Its name comes from *kefali*, the Greek word for "head," and *tyri*, which means "cheese." *Kefalotyri* is produced all over Greece in more or less the same way, usually from sheep's milk or from a combination of sheep's and goat's milk. Once the milk has been heated and set with rennet, the curds are cut into pieces about the size of rice grains, heated, stirred, left to cool, then drained and pressed into wheel-shaped molds. These are turned and pressed until most of the moisture is forced out. The cheese is then salted in brine for two days, removed from the brine and rubbed with dry salt, almost daily for about two or three weeks before being left to mature for several months. During the last phase of the ripening process, it is washed with brine to keep mold from forming on its rind. *Kefalotyri* is usually quite salty and hard. It is used mainly as a grating cheese, but it is excellent pan-fried to make saganaki (see page 89).

LADOTYRI MYTILINIS (lah-thoh-TEE-ree me-tee-LEE-neess) means "oil cheese from Mytilene," because it is preserved in olive oil after aging. *Ladotyri* is essentially a kind of *kefalotyri* that is stored in olive oil. It is made usually with sheep's milk, and sometimes with a combination of sheep's and goat's milk.

Once the curds have been formed, cut, heated, and rested, they are collected and pressed into 2-pound/1-kilo reed molds, which give the cheese its characteristic shape and uneven, textured exterior. After it has set, the cheese is then removed from the mold, salted, and air-dried for two to three months. After this initial ripening and maturation period, during which time the cheese loses about 40 percent of its moisture content, it is ready to be submerged in olive oil. The longer it remains steeped in olive oil, the sharper it becomes. It is excellent as a table cheese, or grating cheese, or for making saganaki (see page 89).

METSOVONE (mehts-oh-VOH-neh) is a kneaded cheese, like kasseri. Produced in the northwestern town of Metsovo, it is made from either raw or pasteurized cow's milk, or a combination of cow's milk and up to 20 percent raw or pasteurized sheep's and/or goat's milk. Whey from the previous day's cheese making is added to the milk, and makes up about 2 percent of the mixture. Once there is a cheese mass, it is submerged in boiling water and stretched until it becomes pliable and shiny. Then it is kneaded and pressed into its large sausage-shaped molds. These are salted in brine, left to ripen for about five months, and smoked. *Metsovone*, with its full, rich flavor, is an excellent table cheese as well as a wonderful grilling cheese.

OTHER PDO CHEESES

FORMAELLA (for-mah-EH-lah) is more formally called *Formaella Parnassou*, after Mt. Parnassos, in central mainland Greece, where it is made. It is an ivory-colored, mild—some might say bland—semihard grating and grilling cheese. It is distinguished more for its cylindrical shape and ridged exterior than for its flavor. *Formaella* is produced mainly from raw sheep's milk, although small amounts of goat's milk are sometimes added. It is one of the handful of Greek cheeses that taste better cooked.

MANOURI (mah-NOO-ree) is a buttery, alabaster-white mild cheese. It's essentially a whey cheese and resembles the Italian ricotta salata. *Manouri* is usually made with sheep's milk whey, to which whole sheep's milk is added. It is made mainly on the Greek mainland in Thessaly and central and western Macedonia. *Manouri* has a low moisture content and a high fat content. It is eaten young, but can also be air-dried and aged so that it becomes an excellent grating cheese. *Manouri* is characterized by a milky, creamy taste. It is round on the palate, rich, and lightly salted. It makes for an excellent dessert cheese, served with honey, spoon sweets, or poached seasonal fruit. But it is also a delicious table cheese.

THREE CLASSIC GREEK WHEY CHEESES

ANTHOTYRO (an-THOH-tee-roh) is produced with sheep's milk or goat's milk whey, or a combination of the two. *Anthotyro* means "blossom cheese," a reference to the way the curds rise to the top when heated before they are separated and strained. When eaten fresh, the cheese is very mild with a soft, moist texture, not unlike Italian ricotta. It is also dried and used as a grating cheese. Crete and Lesvos are particularly well known for their *anthotyro*, and both islands produce both a fresh and an aged, dry version, which usually has a gray-blue moldy rind and a peppery flavor.

MYZITHRA (mee-ZEE-thrah), like *anthotyro*, is sold in both a fresh and a dried version. Some of the best comes from Crete, but it is produced almost everywhere in Greece from either sheep's or cow's milk whey, to which whole milk is sometimes added. Fresh *myzithra* has the lowest fat content of all Greek cheeses. It is a favorite breakfast cheese and is characterized by its chalk-white color, sweetness, and a distinct aroma of cooked milk. Fresh *myzithra* is excellent with honey, fruit, and nuts. It can also be salted and hung to dry in cheesecloth, so that it obtains the shape of a ball. Hard, aged *myzithra* is the most traditional grating cheese in Greece.

BOOKS CONSULTED

Country cooks have notebooks filled with recipes written out by hand in practiced, almost calligraphic penmanship. These are the recipes passed down from one generation of women to the next. They are treasure troves that keep traditional cuisine alive.

Every Greek home cook of a certain age also has a few old classics on her shelf, including at least one volume by the most famous of all Greek cookbook authors, Nikos Tselemendes, a professional chef who lived in the early part of the twentieth century. Tselemendes is credited with teaching several generations of home cooks the basics of French and continental cuisine. Techniques for making the béchamel sauce that tops pastitsio and moussaka, for example, were spelled out by Tselemendes in meticulous detail, which home cooks followed religiously. Other important cookbook authors and home economists who helped shape the national cuisine in the twentieth century were Chryssa Paradisi, the Fannie Farmer of her day; Sofia Skoura; and Vefa Alexiadou, who was the first cook to go on television in Greece and is still admired by many home cooks.

There wasn't much of a cookbook industry in Greece until the last two decades or so. Since then, many books filled with traditional recipes by home cooks and restaurant chefs have been published. In addition, dozens more books have been written by natives of a particular region or specialists in a particular subject, such as cheese, mushrooms, herbs, greens, or olive oil.

The most well-worn series of Greek cookbooks on my shelf are a five-volume collection of regional recipes that was published in Greek by publisher Fytrakis in 1987. These are a collection of recipes sent in by home cooks all over the country. Although the recipes were unedited and untested, the collection remains a rich source of information on regional Greek cooking. Another favorite collection is a five-volume set by Effie Grigoriadou on the cuisines of northern Greece and of the Greeks from Asia Minor who settled there. Soula Bozi, who emigrated from Istanbul in the early 1960s, is an authority on the cuisines of Greeks from Smyrna (present-day Ismir, Turkey) and Constantinople (Istanbul). Evi Voutsina has published excellent books on the cooking of her native Lefkada (an island in the Ionian), as well as a great four-volume collection of country recipes peppered with literary references and accounts of her interviews with traditional cooks. The series is called *Gefsi Elliniki (Greek Flavor)*.

Books on island cuisine number in the dozens. The husband-and-wife team Nikos and Maria Psillakis have written arguably the best books on Cretan cuisine, having crisscrossed the island and recorded old recipes from country cooks all over Crete. These have been collected in one large volume, called, in English, *Cretan Traditional Cuisine*. The Psillakises also wrote a fascinating encyclopedic tome on the breads and bread customs of Greece.

Among my favorite books on the cooking of the islands is a small volume, *Paradosiakes Gefseis tou Aigaiou (Traditional Flavors of the Aegean)*, by a Greek academic, Lila Karapostoli, who recorded the main local products and most representative dishes from almost all the islands in the Aegean. I also love the heavily researched labor of love by the late grande dame of Corfu, Ninetta Laskari, whose book *Kerkyra (Corfu)*, lays out the illustrious culinary history of this island in a rich tapestry of prose and recipes.

Finally, one of my favorite volumes is a new one highlighting the unique, traditional dishes of a cuisine I will probably never see or taste firsthand: the cooking of Mount Athos. The book, titled *Y Mageiriki tou Agiou Orous (The Cooking of the Holy Mountain)*, was written by a local monk and is richly illustrated with photographs. It is a treasure house of meatless dishes and ritual foods that have sustained monks on Mount Athos for more than a thousand years.

My personal library of Greek recipe books contains hundreds of volumes. When I see a Greek cookbook, I manage to get a copy, one way or another. Missing, though, are the cookbooks produced by Greek-American church groups. These provide a rich view of the way Greek cuisine has developed over the years, thanks to the additions and improvisations of hundreds of thousands of Greek Americans. Such a collection of cookbooks does exist; it was donated to New York University several years ago by tireless cookbook collector and friend to many, Dahlia Carmel.

INDEX